E G L I

CHANGE AND
PERSISTENCE
IN THAI SOCIETY

Bennington-Cornell research group in the Mien Yao village of Phalé, Maechan District, Chiengrai Province, North Thailand, 1964. Lauriston Sharp, *upper left*; *others, clockwise*: William Wohnus, American student, Williams College; Pien Fu-Hin (Lao San Ching), Mien Yao guide and interpreter, Maechan; Lucien M. Hanks, Bennington College and Cornell Thailand Project; Charoen Pinit, Thai medical aid and interpreter, Chiengsaen.

CHANGE AND PERSISTENCE IN THAI SOCIETY

Essays in Honor of Lauriston Sharp

Edited by G. WILLIAM SKINNER
and A. THOMAS KIRSCH

CORNELL UNIVERSITY PRESS

ITHACA AND LONDON

First published 1975 by Cornell University Press.
Published in the United Kingdom by Cornell University Press Ltd.,
2-4 Brook Street, London W1Y 1AA.

International Standard Book Number 0-8014-0860-1
Library of Congress Catalog Card Number 74-25374
Printed in the United States of America

Contents

6   Contents

Maps and Figures

MAPS

FIGURES

Introduction

G. WILLIAM SKINNER *and*
A. THOMAS KIRSCH

In the course of a long and fruitful career in teaching and research at Cornell University, Lauriston Sharp has influenced a diverse group of students and colleagues. A number of us, along with some of his friends and professional associates, have joined together on the occasion of his retirement from Cornell to present him with this book, the second of two in his honor.* Our aim is both to mark his contributions to anthropology and Asian studies and to indicate the degree of our indebtedness to him for his guidance and example over the years. It is our hope that these books will be found useful by many readers who share his interests in the several fields in which he has worked.

The diversity of the contributions to these two volumes is readily apparent; they tell us a great deal about the man and his intellectual concerns. Above all, he has taught us that man's behavior is comprehensible in human terms, and that our understanding of the constructions of the world made by men of other times and places must always be informed by an essential humanism. He has further urged the view that such understanding can be put to practical use.

The generation of scholars to which Sharp belongs has made important theoretical, methodological, and substantive contributions to anthropology, often on the basis of a wide spectrum

---

* The first volume is *Social Organization and the Applications of Anthropology*, edited by Robert J. Smith. A part of the Introduction is common to both volumes.

of field experiences not likely to be matched by future generations. As an active researcher, Sharp has known the American
Indians of the Plains and Southwest, the Berbers of North
Africa, the Australian aborigines, and for over twenty-five years
he has had sustained contact with the peoples of Southeast Asia,
particularly in Thailand. A number of his scientific papers,
notably "Steel Axes for Stone Age Australians," "People without Politics," and "Cultural Continuities and Discontinuities
in Southeast Asia," have been so frequently reprinted as to have
attained the status of anthropological classics.

Sharp's teaching and research have been informed by two
broad intellectual concerns. One has been to view the peoples
of the non-Western world always in the larger cultural context
of the region or area in which they are found. The second has
been to explicate the interplay of the cultural forces of modernization as they have impinged on indigenous cultures. These
two concerns are clearly evident in his years of service at
Cornell, where he played the paramount role in establishing
a department of anthropology which for much of its existence
has been geared to the application of anthropological knowledge, and in setting up both the university's Southeast Asia
Program and its Center for International Studies.

Lauriston Sharp was born on March 24, 1907, in Madison,
Wisconsin. His father, Frank Chapman Sharp, was professor of
philosophy at the University of Wisconsin. As a philosopher, the
elder Sharp had reacted strongly against the extreme cultural
relativism expressed by William Graham Sumner in his influential book *Folkways*. In challenging Sumner's contention that
"the mores make all things right," he used, among other materials, the scattered reports on the Australian aborigines, who
were later to be studied at first hand by his son.

Sharp attended primary and secondary schools in Madison
and entered the University of Wisconsin in 1925. While still a
senior in high school he had met Clyde Kluckhohn, already
then a student at the university. With John King Fairbank and

other friends, Sharp and Kluckhohn formed a "Sanskrit letter" society which met weekly for intellectual discussion; their aim was to provide a counterweight to the conventional "Greek letter" fraternities and their more social concerns. The friendships formed and the interests developed in these undergraduate years were to persist throughout his career. In the summers of 1927 and 1928, Kluckhohn, J. J. Hanks, and Sharp undertook a reconnaissance of the Kaiparowitz Plateau in Arizona and Utah. On these two trips he first came into contact with the contemporary Indians of the region and saw the archeological remains left by earlier peoples. Although majoring in philosophy at the time, Sharp had grown increasingly disenchanted with the subject, which he felt had become divorced from concern with the concrete experiences of real people and with the impact of cultural factors in shaping their lives. Anthropology appealed to him as a discipline within which he could pursue these interests, bringing together data and abstractions.

In 1929–30, having taken his B.A. in philosophy, Sharp served as a Freshman Dean at the University of Wisconsin. This was the second year of Ralph Linton's tenure at Wisconsin, and Sharp attended his lectures. In 1930 he joined an expedition to North Africa sponsored by the Logan Museum of Beloit College, in which Sol Tax and John P. Gillin also participated. This sustained field experience with the Berbers crystallized his preference for ethnography and ethnology over archeology and physical anthropology. It had the further effect of convincing him of the absolute necessity for the cultural anthropologist to be thoroughly grounded in the history and language of the people with whom he works. He also acquired a perspective on culture which has led him always to emphasize the study of areas and regions rather than the more conventional concentration on a single group or society.

Two areas of the world were then still largely *terra incognita* to anthropologists—Latin America and Southeast Asia. The latter seemed to Sharp to hold the greater potential for future research, and he sought advice on how to achieve his goal of carrying on field investigations there. Robert H. Lowie suggested that he enroll in the University of Vienna, where Robert Heine-Geldern, one of the leading students of Southeast Asian culture of the time, was a *Privat Docent*. Ralph Linton advised him to enter the doctoral program at Harvard. Sharp followed both suggestions. He went directly from North Africa to the University of Vienna, where he was awarded the Certificate in Anthropology in 1931. He entered the Harvard doctoral program in anthropology in the fall of 1931, studying under Alfred E. Tozzer, Earnest A. Hooton, and Roland B. Dixon, and taking courses with the sociologist Talcott Parsons and the Sanskritist W. E. Clark. In the summer of 1932 he and Sol Tax were together again, this time on the Fox Indian project in Iowa. Sharp received the M.A. in anthropology at Harvard on the basis of this research.

The mid-1930's were not an easy time for securing financial support for overseas research in anthropology. Funds were so scarce that when W. Lloyd Warner's recommendation of Sharp to A. R. Radcliffe-Brown, who was then at the University of Chicago, produced an opportunity for research in Australia, Sharp set aside his plans for Southeast Asia and accepted it. Under the auspices of the Australian National Research Council, he was with the aborigines of Cape York Peninsula in North Queensland from 1933 to 1935. The bulk of his time was spent with the Yir Yoront. It is ironic that a career so heavily focused on the study of complex societies should have been initiated with research in a hunting and gathering society. Nevertheless, as is probably the case with most anthropologists, Sharp was profoundly impressed by his first lengthy field experience, and the Yir Yoront played a formative role in the development of his continuing interest in problems of social organization and role theory.

Before returning to Harvard to serve as a teaching assistant in the Department of Anthropology, he was able to make brief visits to New Guinea, China, and Southeast Asia. He received the Ph.D. in anthropology from Harvard in 1937; his dissertation was entitled "The Social Anthropology of a Totemic System in North Queensland, Australia."

In 1936 Sharp began his long association with Cornell University. There was no department of anthropology or of sociology at that time, and his intial appointment was as instructor of anthropology in the Department of Economics. A distinguished member of that department, the demographer Walter F. Willcox, had long hoped for an expansion of social and international studies at Cornell, and on his retirement in the late 1920's he brought to the university another demographer, Julian L. Woodward, with similar broad interests. It was Woodward who gained the approval of President Livingston Farrand, himself trained under Franz Boas and for a time professor of anthropology at Columbia, for the addition of anthropology to the Cornell curriculum. In 1939, with the blessing of President Edmund Ezra Day, the social psychologist Leonard S. Cottrell together with Woodward and Sharp set up the combined Department of Sociology and Anthropology. Although President Day was eager to see a development of the social sciences with the establishment of a full-fledged graduate program, the members of the new department were inclined to move more slowly. Sharp in particular felt that there were already enough well-established anthropology departments with the resources to produce an adequate number of professional anthropologists. He argued that for Cornell to establish a minimally acceptable program would require too great a drain on scarce resources and that the result would in any event be redundant. Although the impact of World War II would lead him to change his mind, at the time Sharp was urging that Cornell concentrate on undergraduate education in the social sciences. The only anthropologist to receive an advanced degree at Cornell before the war was David M. Schneider, whose 1941 master's thesis in social psychology was entitled "Aboriginal Dreams." It was not until 1951 that the first Cornell Ph.D. in anthropology was awarded to Charles S. Brant for his research on the Kiowa Apache.

With the entry of the United States into World War II, it became painfully clear that there was a severe shortage of people trained in both the social sciences and area studies. The federal government set up a number of crash programs at American universities designed to train language and area personnel quickly. Academics, businessmen, and missionaries with firsthand knowledge of Asia and the Pacific were in great demand, and like most with such special competence, Sharp was sought out. He had been chairman of the Department of Sociology and Anthropology from 1942 to 1945, and in 1945–46, while on leave from the university, he served as assistant chief of the Division of Southeast Asian Affairs in the Department of State. There he worked closely with Cora DuBois, Rupert Emerson, Raymond Kennedy, Kenneth P. Landon, and Abbot Low Moffat. In 1947–48 he conducted his first field research in Thailand.

Upon his return to Cornell, Sharp set about organizing a program of instruction and research in applied anthropology centering on the problems of change and modernization among tribal and peasant societies. Leonard S. Cottrell, then dean of the College of Arts and Sciences, helped in the development of the joint department, to which Sharp invited Morris Edward Opler, Allan R. Holmberg, and John Adair. Under a grant from the Carnegie Corporation, coordinated studies in North India, Thailand, Peru, and the Navaho Reservation were initiated. Alexander H. Leighton's work in social psychiatry in the Canadian Maritimes was closely associated with these studies, and Leighton himself was involved in the Navaho project. Graduate training and field research proceeded under what become known as the Cornell University Studies in Culture and Applied Science. The program involved personnel from the other social sciences and from many technical fields, particularly agricultural economics, plant science, nutrition, rural sociology, and education. In 1947, with the Carnegie support mentioned above, Sharp had established the Cornell-Thailand Project, which has served as the primary focus of his research ever since. Bāng Chan, a village in the Central Plain, was chosen for intensive long-term study in 1948. A number of Cornell students and other colleagues, both Thai and American, have participated with Sharp in the study of this community as it has changed from an isolated "rice village" to an adjunct of the ever-expanding Bangkok metropolis. In collaboration with Lucien M. Hanks, Sharp is currently completing a social history of Bāng Chan based on more than twenty-five years of periodic study. In recent years his research interests have shifted to northern Thailand and particularly to problems in the relationship between upland minority peoples and contemporary Thai society.

The aim of the Cornell-Thailand Project has been not simply the study of a rice village. Still operating on his assumption that such research must be set in a larger historical, regional, and national context, Sharp encouraged the study of other villages in the Central Plain area and in the south, north, and northeast regions. Nor has the project been limited to the village level; under Sharp's direction it sponsored studies of the Chinese community in Thailand, of Thai national economics and politics and Thai linguistics, of Thai society in the eighteenth and early nineteenth centuries, and of nineteenth-century national educational reform. The bibliography of works engendered by the Cornell-Thailand Project now includes more than 450 items, including some fifty doctoral dissertations. In all of this activity Sharp encouraged Thai scholars to participate and young Thai to be trained who could provide their own perspective on their society. He recruited Thai students to come to Cornell for advanced training in many scholarly fields—in agricultural economics, comparative education, nutrition, economics, government, and rural sociology, as well as anthropology.

Many of these Cornell-trained Thai scholars have assumed prominent positions in Thai educational institutions and are pursuing their own teaching and research. In recognition of his contributions to the study of Thai culture a group of Sharp's students have established a Lauriston Sharp Essay Prize, awarded annually since 1967, as well as a Lauriston Sharp Scholarship Fund aimed at promoting social science research in Thailand.

Although Thailand came to dominate his own research interests, Sharp encouraged his students at Cornell to carry out similar broadly conceived studies in other areas of the world. These studies include work on marriage and family patterns in Taiwan, the social organization of North American Indian tribes, economics and social structure of Burmese communities, social stratification in North India, and community organization in Japan and Peru.

While pursuing his own active field research, Sharp also chaired the Department of Sociology and Anthropology from 1949 to 1956. Despite a full regimen of teaching and research, not to mention his administrative responsibilities, he nonetheless found the time to establish with Rockefeller support Cornell's Southeast Asia Program, of which he was director from 1950 to 1960. In 1960–61 he chaired the faculty committee whose report led to the establishment of the Center for International Studies. Both the Center and the Program are flourishing, and Sharp leaves an independent Department of Anthropology four times as large as the original group which he had assembled in the joint department.

Lauriston Sharp is the author of *Tribes and Totemism in Northeast Australia* (1939) and co-author of *Siamese Rice Village* (1953), *Handbook on Thailand* (1956), *A Report on the Tribal Peoples in Chiengrai* (1964), *Ethnographic Notes on Northern Thailand* (1965), a series of comparative studies on cultural change (1966–67), and *The Dream Life of a Primitive People* (1969). He is the author of reports, articles, and reviews on the cultures and political problems of Southeast Asia and the western Pacific for professional journals, government agencies, and the American Institute of Pacific Relations. He has held visiting appointments at Sydney University, Yale University, Haverford College, the University of California (Berkeley), the University of London, the Army War College, and, as Fulbright Research Professor, Kasetsart University in Bangkok. He has been awarded Ford Foundation, Guggenheim, and National Endowment for the Humanities fellowships. He is a life member of the Siam Society, one of the founders of the Society for Applied Anthropology, and has served on the governing boards of the American Anthropological Association, the Asia Society, the Pacific Science Board of the National Research Council, and as director and past president of the Association for Asian Studies. He is a Fellow of the Royal Anthropological Institute and corresponding member of the Australian Institute for Aboriginal Studies. He has been a consultant for the Department of State and has served on various committees of the Agency for International Development, American Council of Learned Societies, Institute of Pacific Relations, International Congress of Orientalists, International Union of Anthropological and Ethnological Sciences, National Research Council, National Science Foundation, Pacific Science Board, Social Science Research Council, and UNESCO. At present he holds the position of Goldwin Smith Professor of Anthropology and Asian Studies Emeritus.

Reflecting the main focus of Sharp's research interests since the 1940's, the papers in this volume treat various aspects of society and culture among the T'ai peoples of mainland Southeast Asia. They include studies of national elites as well as peasant villagers. They variously treat localities, regions, and the total society. They range from reconstructions of Thai social structure in earlier centuries to analyses that project present trends into the future. They reflect not only traditional anthropological concerns—kinship, religion, cognition, community organization—but also stratification, ethnicity, occupational differentiation, and the structure of government. Each paper has something to say about an analytical problem of disciplinary significance. At the same time, each contributes to our understanding of change and persistence in Thai society, in particular the intriguing pattern whereby certain deep structures perdure even as organizational forms are transformed. In combination, these papers demonstrate the rich diversity of themes and perspectives inherent in the area approach as espoused by Sharp.

In an attempt to draw some general principles from information gathered in their recent studies of epigraphic and chronicular sources, A. B. Griswold and Prasert na Nagara discuss the nature of kingship and social organization in the Thai state of Sukhodaya (Sukhōthai) from the late thirteenth to the early fifteenth century. Kingship in Sukhodaya was paternalistic in character, based on personal loyalty to a sovereign who protected his people, promoted their welfare, and settled disputes in accordance with his sense of justice. Sukhodaya's neighbor to the south, the kingdom of Ayudhyā (Ayutthayā), founded in 1351, was more influenced by Khmer and Mòn models, though the founder himself was a Thai. In contrast to Sukhodaya, Ayudhyā had a fixed body of civil law, a large and expanding bureaucracy, and other institutions that encouraged stability at the expense of personal liberty. Ayudhyā eventually incorporated Sukhodaya into a centralized kingdom; but the Sukhodayan pattern never completely succumbed, and its mark can still be seen in Thai society today.

One can, in fact, identify something of a dialectic in Thailand between bureaucratized formal hierarchy and personalized informal clientship, between royal initiative directed to the reaffirmation and reinvigoration of bureaucratic forms and royal initiative designed to break free of their stultifying effects and strike out in new directions. An aspect of this dialectic is treated in the paper by Akin Rabibhadana, in which we see in the first Čhakkrī reign the re-establishment of Ayutthayan institutions to contain and restrain patronage, the development of nonofficial patronage in the third reign, and in the fourth reign royal initiatives reminiscent of Sukhodayan flexibility and paternalism. Emphasizing the traditional importance of manpower control, Akin sees Thai society in the Early Bangkok period as a vast hierarchy of patron-client, nobleman-commoner, and big man–little man relations, with the king at the pinnacle. Akin analyzes the reciprocal rights and responsibilities of these hierarchical relationships as institutionalized in the various forms of Thai social organization. As Thai society began its course of modernization, the control of resources other than manpower became increasingly important, leading to the proliferation of informal clientship and the development of nonofficial hierarchies, which undermined the formal institutions and paved the way for contemporary patterns of Thai social organization.

A glimpse of the succeeding turn of the dialectic is given in David K. Wyatt's paper, in which we see King Chulalongkorn use Sukhodayan means to provide the basis for bureaucratic reorganization and reform. Wyatt's concern is education, and he sketches out the often faltering efforts of the Thai monarchy in the late nineteenth and early twentieth centuries to establish a national system of education consonant with the needs of a modern society. Premodern education, primarily religious, had been centered in Buddhist temples and dominated by monkish ambitions. Aided by a number of unusually talented kinsmen and followers, Chulalongkorn sought to establish a system of education that would create a pool of skilled talent to staff the rapidly expanding national administration. In tracing these efforts Wyatt spells out the complex motives of the king and the differential response of varied strata of Thai society to the possibilities held out by the modern school system.

Proceeding in a more ethnographic vein, Michael Moerman describes the distinctive pattern of trade found in North Thailand in the "old days," from the 1880's to the 1930's. Whereas trade in the Central Plain was highly localized, involving barter and non-Thai middlemen, Moerman finds that Thai peasant trade in the North was entrepreneurially motivated and involved the cash sale of basic goods transported over long distances without the intervention of non-Thai middlemen. In noting this contrast between peasant trade in the Central Plain and the North, Moerman questions a widely held stereotype that Thai peasant trade was nonrational, conservative, and status-oriented.

In a sense, Moerman's conclusions challenge the validity for Thai society as a whole of the generalizations that form the starting point of the paper by A. Thomas Kirsch, who affirms that in Thailand men have traditionally specialized in religious and political-bureaucratic roles, while women have predominated in economic activities. He relates this pattern to Buddhist beliefs and values that are both manifested by and internalized in the performance of Buddhist rituals. This differentiation is seen to have been reinforced by Thai policies that encouraged non-Thai, particularly Chinese, to take on economic roles when the Thai economy expanded through linkage with international markets in the late nineteenth century. Chinese control of the economy posed no threat to the Thai because Chinese men tended to become quickly assimilated to Thai cultural status through marriage with Thai women. When the increased migration of Chinese women threatened this pattern of assimilation, Chinese economic strength came to be seen as a threat to Thai autonomy, and official policy was changed to encourage greater Thai participation in the economy.

Drawing on his many years of close association with the Cornell Thailand Project, Lucien M. Hanks returns to a problem that has engaged him for some time: how to capture in an integrated formulation the fluidity and complexity of the Thai social order. He points up the relatively undifferentiated and unspecialized quality of Thai society, which he contrasts with social life in the West, and conceives the Thai social order in terms of reordering and recombining certain basic social arrangements which he calls the "entourage" and the "circle." An entourage consists of a patron together with his various clients, while a circle is the hierarchical extension of an entourage to include one or more additional entourages subordinate to it. Hanks applies these notions to the operation of the Thai state, which he sees as waxing and waning collections of entourages and circles with overlapping and sometimes conflicting functions and interests.

Jasper Ingersoll addresses problems that follow directly from Hanks's formulation. How does the individualism that underlies the dynamics of entourage formation and dissolution mesh with the community identification that marks urban and rural life in Thailand? In what sense is it compatible with the apparent absence in Thailand of a pervasive concern, so apparent in the West, with the individual and his unique identity? Ingersoll sees the formation of individual and group identity as a universal human process that occurs in diverse cultural forms, and he argues that in Thailand Theravada Buddhism is the most salient factor in such identity formation. Drawing on his study of a village in the Central Plain as well as his experience in other parts of Thailand, Ingersoll views Buddhist merit-making as simultaneously individual and communal, deeply personal yet widely shared. He concludes that the Buddhist doctrine of karma and the elaborate merit-making activities of Thai villagers provide them with a comprehensive moral explanation of who they are in relation to time and to others, and are thus a major component in the formation of personal and group identity.

In his essay on the cult of tutelary village spirits, Georges Condominas illuminates a Lao variant of a general T'ai cultural phenomenon. He characterizes the spirit beliefs that underlie the cult, specifies the duties of those in charge of venerating the village spirit, and describes the major rituals. Condominas sees the spiritual world of the Lao villagers as focused on two poles, Buddhism and the *phīban* cult. The former manifests one of the major cultural discontinuities in the history of Southeast Asia, while the latter represents one of the major continuities. He concludes that in rural Laos these two contrasting religious orientations form a complementary whole: Buddhism relates the villager to a culturally constituted universal order, while the cult of the village spirit unites him with the local natural order in which his everyday life is lived.

In describing the structure and functioning of kin groups in a Thai-Lao village in Northeast Thailand, Charles F. Keyes contributes to the theoretical discussion of social organization. He views the village itself as a kinship unit, traces the developmental cycle of domestic groups, and examines descent groups based on the individual. He concludes that patterns of marriage, of postmarital residence, and of inheritance of rights to agricultural land shape the formation of the extended domestic groups found in Thai-Lao villages at least as much as the principles of descent which have been emphasized in the classical literature.

Steven Piker is concerned with various social dislocations affecting Thai villagers as the result of the modernization of Thai society that began in the late nineteenth century. The traditional pattern of Thai peasant life was grounded in kinship, the domestic cycle of the family, and patterns of kindred formation and cooperation. Maintenance of this traditional peasant pattern depended on the ready availability of agricultural lands and/or on the possibility of finding a reliable patron outside the village. Linking the Thai economy to international markets led to the commercialization of rice agriculture, to population pressures on agricultural land, and eventually to the emergence of a group of landless villagers who must subsist as agricultural wage laborers and thus cannot maintain the traditional patterns of village life. Piker considers Thailand to be entering a "post-peasant" era, and he speculates about some of the changes in socialization patterns that may prove necessary to prepare a new generation of Thai villagers for this changed social situation.

Herbert P. Phillips describes some of the main features of Thai intellectual culture. He focuses on a number of leading novelists, poets, social commentators, folklorists, religious leaders, and other intellectuals whose writings are widely read. These men tend to specialize in reflections on traditional cultural material in relation to the contemporary scene. In no sense are they heretics, dissenters, or marginal men; for the most part they neither challenge traditional culture nor provide new intellectual orientations. Phillips concludes that these men are, if anything, more Thai than intellectual; more literati than intelligentsia. Their chief function has been to adapt new and alien ideas and highlight their relevance to traditional Thai values and modes of thought and to the problems Thailand faces.

It is fitting that the contributions to this volume include two by historians, that two of those written by anthropologists treat institutions of the past, and that almost all of the contributors are explicit about the ineluctable fact of historical change—fitting because Sharp was among the first to decry the ahistoricity that once characterized American anthropology. He came to view the heurism of the "ethnographic present" less as a convenient fiction than as blinders limiting the anthropologist's sense of problem, and he has always been fascinated by the relation between sociocultural process as observed by the ethnographer and the macroprocesses that are the concern of social historians.

The composition of this collection is appropriate in another sense. Five of the contributions are grounded in the ethnographic study of a particular locality, and in each case ethnography serves the pursuit of generic issues and problems of significance to the entire society. Two papers, drawing on more dispersed data, treat aspects of social organization in Thai society as a whole. Four treat national or societywide institutions. This emphasis and this mix accurately reflect Sharp's own insistence that ethnography serve ethnological ends, that village-centered studies be complemented by macroanalyses, that in fact the worm's-eye view and the bird's-eye view together do not suffice to achieve in the study of complex societies the holism that anthropologists take to lie at the heart of their disciplinary distinctiveness. In his efforts to see Thailand whole, to organize research so that the study of Thai villages and institutions and of the various ethnic groups and regional cultures in Thailand proceeds always in context, with proper attention to complex interrelationships and interactions—in this endeavor Sharp has not only set Thai studies on a firm foundation but also contributed handsomely to the comparative study of agrarian civilizations and their transformation.

The editors are grateful to Richard O'Connor for assistance with bibliographic research, to Scribner Messenger for help in transcribing Thai names and terms, to Jill Leland for drafting the maps, and to A. B. Griswold for financial assistance in preparing the artwork.

Note on Transcription

In this volume we have standardized the transcription of Thai terms in accordance with the following system, which is but a slight modification of that recommended by the Library of Congress Orientalia Processing Committee.

Voiced stops (initial position only)	b, d
Voiceless, unaspirated stops	p, t, čh, k
Voiceless, aspirated stops	ph, th, ch, kh
Voiceless spirants	f, s, h
Voiced nasals	m, n, ng
Lateral	l
Trill	r
Front unrounded vowels	i, e, ae
Central unrounded vowels	ue, oe, a
Back rounded vowels	u, o, ọ
Voiced semivowels: initial position	y; w
final position	i; o (after e, ae, and a), w (after i)

The glottal stop is not transcribed except between vowels, where it is represented by a hyphen to indicate syllable division. Long vowels are indicated by a macron.

Place names in modern Thailand and Laos, Bangkok and Vientiane excepted, are standardized in accordance with the above phonemic transcription. However, in the contribution by A. B. Griswold and Prasert ṇa Nagara, which is based primarily on epigraphic sources, place names as well as other terms are given an orthographic transliteration (see p. 84 below).

The dialectical distinctions of particular localities are not recognized, except for the transcription of Lao terms in Georges Condominas's contribution, where, in accordance with the standard in

Laos, the phonemes *ch*, *h*, and initial *w* are transcribed *s*, *r*, and *v* respectively, and the phoneme *nh* [ñ] also occurs.

Personal names are generally transcribed phonemically, as above, except for persons best known under another spelling (e.g., Prince Damrong and King Chulalongkorn). The term T'ai is used throughout for the inclusive family of languages to which Thai and Lao belong and for the collectivity of ethnic groups whose native languages belong to that family.

CHANGE AND
PERSISTENCE
IN THAI SOCIETY

1. On Kingship and Society at Sukhodaya

A. B. GRISWOLD *and*
PRASERT ṆA NAGARA

Two kingdoms, Sukhodaya and Ayudhyā, confronted each other in Siam in the second half of the fourteenth century. They had much in common: both were founded by T'ai lords in territories previously controlled by the Khmer, who had introduced their own Indianizing civilization there; and both adopted a good deal of their predecessors' culture. But Sukhodaya, founded some time before 1250 in a place that had been a distant outpost of the Khmer empire, remained conspicuously T'ai in its behavior in spite of many cultural borrowings from the Khmer; whereas at Ayudhyā, founded in 1351 in regions where Khmer and Mòn institutions had long been solidly implanted, the T'ai heritage was weakened.[1]

In this paper we shall be concerned chiefly with Sukhodaya, and secondarily with Ayudhyā, whose similarities and contrasts with Sukhodaya will help to illuminate the Sukhodayan social organization and behavior.

In both systems Theravāda Buddhism was an important factor; but as the main features of that religion are well known, we shall discuss it only briefly, giving more attention to other factors which, for the period we are concerned with, have been studied much less. The evidence is sketchy, but there is more of it than might be expected. The Sukhodayan inscriptions are

---

[1] For the system of transliteration used in this paper, see note preceding glossary. For the localities mentioned, see Maps 1 and 2.

our best source of information; and though the formal purpose of most of them was to record donations to religion, the rulers often used the occasion to say a lot of other things too, so that if we read them carefully we can learn a surprising amount on miscellaneous topics.[2] For Ayudhyā we are better served by the Annals and the old laws. For both systems, though the picture is still fragmentary, we can make some sort of sense out of it by putting the material we have gathered into its historical context, and also into the context of other varieties of social organization which preceded and influenced them. The Ayudhyan system, which was increasingly centralized, with a fixed code of laws, made for a more settled society but tended to become formal and stereotyped. The Sukhodayan, based on personal loyalty to a lord and the pledged loyalty of all the lords to the king, was less standardized and allowed more scope for freedom; it achieved spectacular results when the king was a man of strong character but ran into trouble when he was not. The Ayudhyan system triumphed; but the Sukhodayan never entirely succumbed, and it has left its mark on Siamese behavior today.

The T'ai were relative newcomers to Southeast Asia. They had long been settled in what is now South China, in the provinces of Kwangtung, Kwangsi, and Kweichow, where many of their descendants still live. Before the Christian Era some groups of T'ai began spreading westward into Tongking, and later into Laos.[3] Some remained there; others, around the eleventh century or earlier, began moving westward and south-

[2] The text and translation of the most important Sukhodayan inscriptions will be found, together with introductions and notes, in our series "Epigraphic and Historical Studies" published in the *Journal of the Siam Society* (Griswold and Prasert 1968, 1969a, 1969b, 1970, 1971b, 1971c, 1971d, 1972, 1973a, 1973b, 1974a, 1974b, 1974c). See also Coedès (1924).

[3] See Mote (1964, 1966), who refutes the theory invented in the nineteenth century by European Sinologists that the T'ai of Siam originated in the kingdom of Nan-chao in Yün-nan. See also Luce (1959).

westward into Siam, bringing with them their ancient traditions, their tribal organization, and their animist religion. The Yvan, settling in the north of Siam, and the Kāv in the Upper Nān Valley, carved out small independent principalities for themselves at the expense of the peoples who were there before them. Another group of T'ai, called "Syām" by their neighbors, settled in the Nān and Yom valleys in the present provinces of Uttaratittha and Sukhodaya, and then pushed westward to the Ping.

In the reign of Sūryavarman II of Cambodia (1113–c.1150), and again in the reign of Jayavarman VII (1181–c.1219?), Sukhodaya was part of the Khmer empire. Already many T'ai people lived there, ruled by their own T'ai lords as vassals and subvassals of the Khmer suzerain. It seems likely the T'ai far outnumbered the Khmer in the region.

Sūryavarman II, among the bas-reliefs at Angkor Wat depicting the procession of his vassals, has left us a portrait of a contingent of "Syām" soldiery (Figure 1). The T'ai chieftain, armed with bow and arrow, rides a splendidly caparisoned elephant, while his sturdy soldiers, armed with halberds, walk along beside him. In contrast to the vassals from Cambodia and Lavo, who are seen in the other reliefs marching in orderly ranks, the T'ai soldiers walk as they please, turning to talk with one another from time to time. Evidently they were very different from the Khmer. The Khmer sculptor observed them with curiosity, emphasizing the things about their appearance and behavior that struck him as bizarre.

The Syām at first lived in small, tightly knit communities. As their power and wealth increased, the word *möaṅ*, which originally designated such a community, came also to mean a city, a province, a principality, and finally a kingdom. They depended for their livelihood on rice farming, fruit growing, fishing, raising horses and cattle, catching and training elephants, hunting wild game, gathering forest products, and practicing a wide variety of crafts and small commerce. Though

Figure 1. The Syām vassals of Sūryavarman II. Bas-relief in the gallery of Angkor Wat.

they had adopted Theravāda Buddhism, they did not abandon their own ancestral spirits; and the *genii loci*, who had been venerated as owners of the soil before the T'ai arrived, continued to receive honor. As we shall see, there is epigraphic proof of this as late as 1393.

Presumably the T'ai Syām had been converted to the Theravāda by their Mòn neighbors, around the twelfth century. From the seventh to the tenth century the Mòns had constituted the ruling classes of the Indianizing kingdom of Dvāravatī in

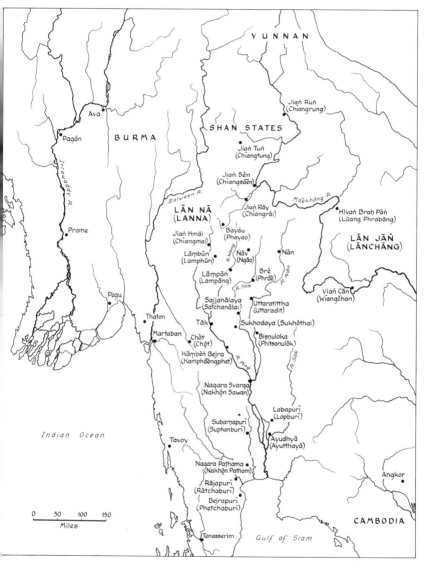

Map 1. Siam and adjacent regions in the fourteenth century.

central Siam, where the Theravāda was the predominant religion, though other forms of Buddhism had a minority following, and the Brahmanical cults lent their luster to royalty. Mòn antiquities have been found in the greatest quantity in the provinces of Nagara Paṭhama, Labapurī, and Subarṇapurī, and to a lesser extent farther east. The Khmer had been gradually encroaching on the eastern Mòns for hundreds of years; and finally, around the year 1000, the kingdom of Dvāravatī disintegrated, much of it falling into Khmer hands. But the little Mòn kingdom of Haripuñjaya at Lāṃbūn in northern Siam retained its independence until 1292. In central Siam a large part of the population remained Mòn for centuries.

Lavo, as Labapurī was then called, became the chief stronghold of the Khmer in central Siam in the eleventh century. Even before it was absorbed by the Khmer empire, the Mòn aristocracy at Lavo had been moving into the cultural orbit of Cambodia; and as the Khmer population increased, the Khmerizing tendency became stronger. Lavo intermittently regained its independence; but during much of the period up to the mid-thirteenth century it was held by the Khmer, together with the routes leading to their possessions to the west and northwest.

In contrast to social conditions in Dvāravatī, about which almost nothing is known, we have quite a lot of information about those in Cambodia, especially at the Khmer capital, Angkor. In Angkorian Cambodia the Brahmanical religions predominated, lending their science and their magic to all official activities, and impregnating the social organization; the two schools of Buddhism, Theravāda and Mahāyāna, generally played a lesser role, though the Mahāyāna enjoyed royal favor in the reign of Jayavarman VII, and finally, around the fifteenth century, the Theravāda triumphed. For the greater part of the Angkorian period, however, the Brahmanical religions had no serious rival. A modified version of the Indian caste system prevailed, with Brahmans and Kṣatriyas forming an aristocracy which was separated by an abyss from the people.

The king was worshiped as a god; he was a withdrawn and mysterious personage who seldom showed himself to his subjects; and when he proceeded through the capital they had to prostrate themselves and remain with forehead to the ground until he passed by. He was so far above ordinary people that they could not even speak of him directly, but only of "the dust under his sacred feet." A large and highly centralized bureaucracy, in which the highest posts were held by princes, ran the business of government, maintained order, upheld property rights, collected heavy taxes, and administered a burdensome corvée. The Chinese writer Chou Ta-kuan, who accompanied the Mongol envoy to the Court of Angkor in 1296, says there were a great many slaves, most of them "wild men from the hills," who were treated with contempt and often beaten; and if one of them tried to run away an iron collar would be fitted to his neck, or gyves to his arms and legs.[4]

Chou Ta-kuan tells us something about the administration of justice in Cambodia. The punishments were mostly fines, but for serious crimes the culprit's nose or toes might be cut off, or he might be buried alive. When a thief was caught in the act, he could be imprisoned and tortured. In case of doubt a suspect might be tried by ordeal, forced to plunge his hand into boiling oil, and judged guilty if it hurt him (Chou Ta-kuan 1967).

According to Chou Ta-kuan, all disputes, however trifling, were taken to the king for decision. It is hard to believe this could have been literally true; it probably means that the sovereign decided all perplexing cases, even those in which the cause of dispute was of little importance. As the late Professor Robert Lingat tells us, there was no fixed body of civil law; the king decided each case on its own merits, using the Hindu Dharmaśāstra as a general guide (Lingat 1950b; 1951). Indian traditional belief held that the universe is governed by an immutable natural law, the Dharma, which was miraculously revealed to the sage Manu; Manu in turn revealed it to other

[4] See Coedès (1962:88f., 138f.); Briggs (1951:244–250 et passim); Chou Ta-kuan (1967:23–31 et passim).

sages, who then made it known to mankind through abridged versions called Dharmaśāstra, treatises on the Dharma. Because the Dharma is immutable and all-embracing, it was not the duty of an Indian or Khmer king to legislate in the modern sense, i.e. to establish laws of a general and permanent character; it was his duty to understand the Dharma by studying the Dharmaśāstra, to interpret it, and to apply it to the specific cases that came before him. In Cambodia as in India, as Lingat (1950b:12) aptly remarks, Manu was the sole legislator.

The Kingdom of Sukhodaya: First Two Reigns

At an uncertain date before 1250, Sukhodaya became an independent kingdom under a T'ai monarch. It may have been soon after the death of Jayavarman VII, which occurred c. 1219 (Coedès 1947a:83f.); alternatively, and in our opinion more probably, it could have been soon after the death of his successor, Indravarman II, in 1243. The story of the campaign for Sukhodayan independence is told in a long retrospective passage in a Sukhodayan inscription composed in the 1340's (Griswold and Prasert 1972:75–87 inclusive of nn. 15–18, 92–112 inclusive of nn. 32–46; Coedès 1924:49f.).

The region was ruled by a T'ai nobleman named Phā Möaṅ, a vassal of Cambodia. He had received his regalia, together with the title Kamrateṅ Añ (king or viceroy) from the Khmer suzerain, who also gave him a Khmer princess in marriage. His capital was at Möaṅ Rāt, which seems to have been near Uttaratittha (see Map 2). He possessed a hundred thousand elephants, we are told; his country was girt about with areca palms, and countless cities paid him homage. Among them were Sukhodaya and Sajjanālaya, as well as Chòt, which lay far away in the mountains on the border of Burma.

Phā Möaṅ had a *sahāya*, a T'ai lord named Pāṅ Klāṅ Hāv, the ruler of a small fief apparently somewhere between Möaṅ Rāt and Sajjanālaya.[5] The word *sahāya* could mean friend,

---

[5] For the reading of the name Pāṅ Klāṅ Hāv, see Griswold and Prasert (1972:80).

ally, or follower; as his fief was part of Phā Möaṅ's domain, he must have been his vassal.

Both of them mobilized their troops; but Pāṅ Klaṅ Hāv, who seems to have been younger and more active, did most of the fighting. First he captured Sajjanālaya, then he routed the Khmer garrison at Sukhodaya. He presented Sukhodaya to Phā Möaṅ, but Phā Möaṅ gave it back to him. Then Phā Möaṅ gave him his own title and regalia, together with the name Śrī Indrāditya, and conferred the *abhiṣeka* (consecration) on him as ruler of the newly independent kingdom.

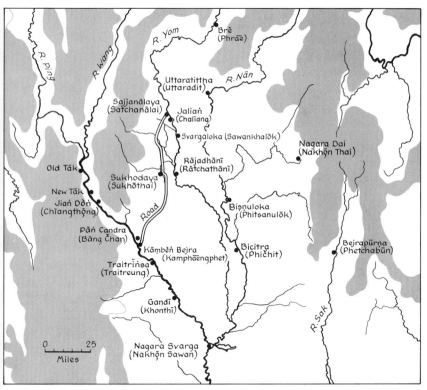

Map 2. The kingdom of Sukhodaya in 1400. The road shown connecting Sukhodaya with Kāṃbèṅ Bejra and with Sajjanālaya represents the remains of the Braḥ Rvaṅ (Phrarūang) highway, which was in use in the fourteenth century.

The transaction was not so strange as it sounds. When a vassal swore allegiance, the oath was an act of magic in which he called down all sorts of supernatural sanctions on himself in case he should ever prove false; but in the nature of things the oath would expire with the death of the person to whom he had sworn it.[6] Presumably while Phā Möan had sworn allegiance to the Khmer king, Pān Klāṅ Hāv had sworn fealty only to Phā Möaṅ. The inscription hints that Phā Möaṅ was not very eager to revolt. Though the death of his suzerain had released him from his oath, he doubtless had feelings of affection for Cambodia, he was married to a Khmer princess, and he owed his high position to Khmer favor. Apparently Pāṅ Klāṅ Hāv put steady pressure on him, and though he treated him with the greatest deference at all times, Phā Möaṅ must have seen the futility of trying to resist the pressure after the Khmer garrison had been routed. The transfer of the Khmer title and regalia was evidently designed to legitimize an accomplished fact and to ensure friendly relations.

The transfer sounds as if Śrī Indrāditya, as Pāṅ Klāṅ Hāv was henceforth known, received Phā Möaṅ's entire domain and became his overlord, reversing the previous relationship. But apparently he got little more than the provinces of Sukhodaya and Sajjanālaya, plus a short stretch of the Ping Valley; Chòt fell into the hands of a rival lord; and Phā Möaṅ probably kept much of his domain for himself.

Śrī Indrāditya, whose eldest son died in childhood, was succeeded by his second son, Pān Möaṅ. When the latter died, the throne went to the third son, Rāma Gāṃhèṅ.

Sukhodaya in the Reign of Rāma Gāṃhèṇ

We do not know the date of Rāma Gāṃhèṅ's accession; our best guess is 1279; and it seems certain that he died in 1298 (Griswold and Prasert 1971d:214 and n. 99; 1972:21 and n. 2).

---

[6] The few surviving texts of such oaths say nothing about an obligation to his successors. For example, see Coedès (1913:11–17).

The kingdom he inherited was small, extending less than sixty miles in any direction from the capital. He expanded it greatly; and before he died it was bigger than France is today. We have little exact information about the means by which he did so; but we can infer quite a lot from the inscription he composed in 1292, as well as from the two epilogues, the first of which seems to have been added a few years later, and the second to have been added by a different hand after his death.[7]

The first epilogue gives a list of the T'ai peoples who were his vassals at the time of writing. All those named were located either between Sukhodaya and Laos or else in Laos itself, which suggests that his ancestors had come from there and that he still had bonds of affection with the peoples along the way. It also suggests that the main concentration of T'ai in his kingdom was in that direction.

The second epilogue gives a long list of places he "subdued." Though he certainly conquered a number of them by force of arms, the term should be understood as including those that submitted to him voluntarily; a good many rulers, observing his prowess as a warrior, may have called him in to dislodge an enemy and then made an act of vassalage to gain his permanent protection; and others, even though not facing any immediate danger, might think themselves safer under his suzerainty.[8]

The list gives the key places radially, first to the east, then to the south, west, and north, placing them in each of the four directions in the order of increasing distance from the capital. To the east, the first place named is Sralvaṅ (between Sukhodaya and Biṣṇuloka); to the south, Gandī; to the west, Chòt; to the north, Brè (see Maps 1 and 2). As these are the nearest places whose submission he received in the four directions, we assume that they were just beyond the frontiers of the kingdom he in-

---

[7] For the text and translation of his inscription, together with introduction and notes, see Griswold and Prasert (1971d).

[8] See Griswold and Prasert (1971d). For further comments on the probable dates and means by which Rāma Gāṃhèṅ gained control of the places listed, see Griswold and Prasert (1972:26–47).

herited, which therefore must have been bounded, on the east, by the River Nān from Uttaratittha to a point somewhere upstream from Biṣṇuloka; on the south, by a line from that point to Traitriṅsa; on the west, by the Ping from Old Tāk down to Traitriṅsa; and on the north by a line a little above Sajjanālaya and Uttaratittha. Our impression that Old Tāk was part of his inheritance is reinforced by the first part of his inscription, which tells us that during his father's lifetime he went to Tāk to fight off an attack by the Lord of Chòt and succeeded in putting him to flight.

Rāma Gāṃhèṅ's first conquests after his accession were necessarily near home. It would be in keeping with his character to begin by attacking his old enemy, the Lord of Chòt, who posed a constant threat to the Ping Valley. The conquest of Chòt in its mountain fastnesses must have been a difficult undertaking, requiring bravery and skill, and his victory there could hardly fail to make a deep impression on his neighbors.

As a result he may have very quickly received the voluntary submission of the towns on the Ping below Traitriṅsa, including Nagara Svarga (called Braḥ Pāṅ at that time) at the junction of the Ping and the Nān, which would leave the towns on the lower Nān with little choice but to capitulate. Nagara Svarga was of vital importance to Rāma Gāṃhèṅ, for it was the key to the riverine communications between the two halves of his kingdom, and all heavy freight traveled by boat or raft.

Perhaps it was fairly early in his career that he built the Braḥ Rvaṅ Highway, linking the capital with Sajjanālaya to the north and with the cities on the Ping to the southwest (see Map 2). It was an all-weather road: where necessary it was raised above the flood level on an embankment, with ditches running along either side for drainage and for navigation by small boats. It would be a useful supplement to the riverine system for trade, especially in goods that were valuable without being bulky; but the main purpose was surely military; and his ability to move his troops quickly from one to another of his chief cities was very likely a big factor in his successes.

The extension of Rāma Gāṃheṅ's power to Lower Burma was due mainly to the machinations of a man named Makado, who had entered his service when young, risen to be governor of the palace, and eloped with his daughter. Taking advantage of a Mòn revolt against Pagán, Makado seized the throne of Martaban in 1281, and later made himself master of Rāmaññadesa, the Mòn country of Lower Burma. At his request Rāma Gāṃheṅ then gave him the investiture as ruler of Rāmaññadesa under Sukhodayan suzerainty, with the title Prince Fā-Rua; he is known to Burmese history as Waréru (Griswold and Prasert 1972:39ff.).

We do not know how or when the provinces of Subarṇapurī, Nagara Paṭhama, Rājapurī, and Bejrapurī fell into Rāma Gāṃheṅ's hands. It may have been soon after 1292. These provinces were old Dvāravatī territory, and later a part of them belonged to a principality known to the Chinese as Chen-li-fu (Griswold and Prasert 1972:29f., nn. 15–16; Wolters 1960: 1–21).

The chronicles tell stories of certain images of the Buddha that were the palladia of principalities, acting as magical protectors of their security and guardians of their prosperity. Usually, when a ruler was conquered by another, he was not dethroned, but required to take the oath of vassalage. At the same time he would have to surrender his palladium and send it to the conqueror's capital, where it would receive the honors due an image of the Buddha, though held as a kind of hostage for the vassal's good behavior.[9] A colossal stone statue of Dvāravatī style, dating from around the seventh century, was discovered many years ago at the Mahādhātu at Sukhodaya.[10] It seems likely that this statue, made in the kingdom of Dvāravatī, was long preserved as the palladium of one of

---

[9] For further information see Griswold (1957:26f.; 1963a:81–84, 90–91, 96–101; 1963b:215f., 225f.). The practice may be connected with one that centered at the Bayon at Angkor; see Coedès (1947b:142ff.). For similar palladia in China, see Soper (1959:passim), and the review of that book by Griswold (1964:121ff.).

[10] The statue is illustrated in Dupont (1959:figs. 367–368).

Dvāravatī's successor states such as Chen-li-fu or Subarṇapurī, and that it was sent to Sukhodaya when the ruler submitted to Sukhodaya.

The greater part of the Malay Peninsula may have submitted to Rāma Gāṃheṅ around 1294 (Coedès 1964:373); but some of the Peninsular states had submitted earlier. Some time before 1292 he had received a learned monk from Nagara Śrī Dharmarāja, whom he made Saṅgharāja and for whom he built a monastery west of the city (Griswold and Prasert 1971d:212). A large stone statue of the Buddha, of Śrīvijayan style and dating from around the eighth century, was found several years ago in the ruins of that monastery. It may have been the palladium of Nagara Śrī Dharmarāja, brought to Sukhodaya by the learned monk in acknowledgment of the city's submission (Griswold 1967:7 and fig. 6).

By the end of the thirteenth century all of Siam was under Rāma Gāṃheṅ's control except the northern provinces, part of the northeast, and the kingdom of Lavo; also tributary to him were the Malay Peninsula, Lower Burma, and a large part of Laos. In northern Siam, the kingdom of Lān Nā, with its capital at Jiaṅ Hmäi, was ruled by Rāma Gāṃheṅ's ally Māṅ Rāy. While Rāma Gāṃheṅ's rule included the upper Sak Valley and extended eastward along the Mè Khoṅ as far as Viaṅ Căn, much of the northeastern provinces probably remained within the political orbit of Cambodia. The kingdom of Lavo, with its capital at Labapurī, had re-established its independence; its ruler, though we do not know who he was, must have been friendly; otherwise Rāma Gāṃheṅ would not have been able to attack Cambodia, which he did around 1295, dealing the country a crippling blow (Chou Ta-kuan 1967:40, 48; Coedès 1962:126).

We have suggested that many of his vassals had come to him of their own accord. He illustrates the point in his inscription, where he says, speaking of himself in the third person: "If anyone riding an elephant comes to see him to put his own country under his protection, he helps him, treats him generously, and takes care of him." He adds that he is always willing to give a deposed ruler asylum: "If [such a ruler] comes to him with no elephants, no horses, no young men or women of rank, no silver or gold, he gives him some, and helps him until he can establish a state of his own" (Griswold and Prasert 1971d:207–208 and nn. 43–46).

The Jian Hmäi Chronicle records an example. After Ñī Pā, the Mòn ruler of Haripuñjaya, lost his city to Rāma Gaṃhèn's ally Măn Rāy, he fled south to Biṣṇuloka, asked its ruler for protection, and lived there until his death.[11] The ruler of Biṣṇuloka, who was of course a vassal of Rāma Gaṃhèn, was acting in accord with the sovereign's policy. There would be no reason for Măn Rāy to object, as he could count on his ally to see that the refugee made no trouble.

While the formal purpose of Rāma Gaṃhèn's inscription is to commemorate the inauguration of his throne in a sugar palm grove in the precinct of the Royal Palace in 1292, it also gives us much information about Rāma Gaṃhèn himself. In the early part of the text he speaks in the first person; and after telling us how he defeated the Lord of Chòt, he says: "In my father's lifetime I served my father and I served my mother. When I caught any game or fish I brought them to my father. When I picked any acid or sweet fruits that were delicious and good to eat, I brought them to my father." What a contrast to the pomp of Cambodian Court life this picture of rustic simplicity gives us! In the remainder of the inscription he refers to himself in the third person, as "Bò Khun Rāma Gaṃhèn, the ruler of Möan Sajjanālaya-Sukhodaya"—a modest enough title, far removed from the extravagant styles of Angkorian monarchs with their claims to divine honors. The expression seems to imply that he ruled the two principal

[11] See Notton (1932:41–44, 61–70). Coedès (1925:ii), whose dates are likely to be right, places the fall of Haripuñjaya in 1292.

provinces directly; while the title *bò khun* 'father lord' (i.e., king) suggests that he ruled the rest of the kingdom through vassal lords over whom he presided like a strict but affectionate father (Griswold and Prasert 1971d:205ff. and n. 20).

The second epilogue to the inscription, probably added after his death, says: "Bò Khun Rāma Gāṃheṅ was sovereign over all the T'ai. He was the teacher who taught all the T'ai to understand merit and the Dharma rightly. Among men who live in the lands of the T'ai, there is no one to equal him in knowledge and wisdom, in bravery and courage, in strength and energy. He was able to subdue a throng of enemies who possessed broad kingdoms and many elephants" (Griswold and Prasert 1971d:218).

The Dharma that he taught them, which is coupled with "merit" (*puñ* = *puñña*), was not the Dharma of the Hindu Dharmaśāstras, but the Theravāda doctrine as a whole. In his own text he writes at length about the flourishing condition of Buddhism in his land, while his only reference to a non-Buddhist cult is to an ancient animistic one: he says the divine spirit who lives on the Braḥ Khbuṅ Hill near the capital "is more powerful than any other spirit in this kingdom," and he adds: "Whatever lord may rule this kingdom of Sukhodaya, if he makes obeisance to him properly, with the right offerings, this kingdom will endure; but if obeisance is not made properly or the offerings are not right, the spirit of the hill will no longer protect it and the kingdom will be lost" (Griswold and Prasert 1971d:214 and n. 95).

Despite his silence regarding the Hindu cults, it seems probable that—like most Southeast Asian monarchs, whether Hindu or Buddhist by faith—he had a body of Brahmans attached to his Court, to advise on technical matters, to regulate the calendar and cast horoscopes, to organize royal ceremonies, and so on. The Theravāda takes no cognizance of these things; they are not in conflict with it, they are simply irrelevant to it. He probably had the help of Brahman *paṇḍitas* when he invented the Siamese alphabet; and at least one Brahmanical image, a bronze statue of Viṣṇu, is thought to date from his reign (Griswold 1967:12f. and fig. 11).

But there is no evidence that he took any interest in the Brahmanical doctrines, or that he thought of himself as a god. He was not in the least a withdrawn or mysterious personage. He installed his throne in the sugar palm grove, he says, "for everyone to see," and of course to see him when he sat on it. Several other passages show that he was easily accessible to his subjects.

His method of ruling was paternalistic and personal, based not on rigid formulas but on his own sense of right and wrong. He does not say a word about the Dharmaśāstra. As for his administration of justice, he tells us he has hung a bell at the palace gate, and adds: "If any commoner in the land has a grievance which sickens his belly and gripes his heart, and which he wants to make known to his ruler and lord, it is easy: he goes and strikes the bell which the King has hung there; King Rāma Gāṃheṅ, the ruler of the kingdom, hears the call; he goes and questions the man, examines the case, and decides it justly for him" (Griswold and Prasert 1971d:208). Surely not many countries the size of his were ruled by sovereigns who invited the humblest citizen to ring for them whenever justice miscarried.

Sukhodayan society was dominated by the aristocracy no less than Cambodian society, but the aristocracy lived in a much less rarefied atmosphere and in closer contact with the people. Order was maintained by personal authority. The capital was small enough for the king to know many of the people by sight; the feudal lords would know their people intimately and count on their unswerving loyalty; and often the loyalty they in turn pledged the king would be reinforced by bonds of friendship and intermarriage. One gets the impression that the network of vassals and subvassals was complex and the official bureaucracy small.

The king prided himself on the prosperity of his land, on the large degree of liberty he granted his subjects, and on their freedom from unjust taxes and arbitrary confiscations. "There is fish in the water and rice in the fields," he says. "The lord of the realm does not levy toll on his subjects for traveling the roads; they lead their cattle to trade or ride their horses to sell; whoever wants to trade in elephants, does so; whoever wants to trade in horses, does so; whoever wants to trade in silver or gold, does so. When any commoner or man of rank dies, his estate—his elephants, wives, children, granaries, rice, retainers, and groves of areca and betel—is left in its entirety to his heirs" (Griswold and Prasert 1971d:205–207).

In other words there were no road tolls; trade in the goods listed, and perhaps a lot more, was not taxed; and there were no death duties on certain kinds of property, though others, such as rice fields, are not mentioned. Rāma Gāṃhèṅ is evidently drawing a contrast between himself and the majority of Southeast Asian monarchs of his time, implying that—in accordance with the Indian practice recommended in the *Śukranīti*—they reserved the most lucrative forms of trade for royal monopolies, taxed the rest heavily, and seized all or part of a decedent's wealth.[12] "When he sees someone's rice he does not covet it," he adds, "when he sees someone's wealth he does not get angry"—implying that other monarchs confiscate whatever takes their fancy, and leave their people at a subsistence level.

A little further on he says: "Areca groves and betel groves are planted all over this country, coconut groves and jackfruit groves are planted in abundance in this country, mango groves and tamarind groves are planted in abundance in this country. Anyone who plants them gets them for himself and keeps them" (Griswold and Prasert 1971d:208).

Of course the king was the absolute owner of all the land in

---

[12] See Griswold and Prasert (1971d:206, n. 25); Donald Brown (1953:71); Walker (1968, vol. 2:487).

the home provinces, if not the whole kingdom, except for such lands as had been permanently alienated by being given to the monkhood. It seems to have been the general custom in Southeast Asia for a king to make allotments of land, or the usufruct of land, to persons who served him in responsible posts, or whom he wished to favor; but such allotments would return to him at his pleasure, and normally they would come to an end with the person's death. As a matter of policy, however, Rāma Gāṃhèṅ seems to be granting more generous terms: in order to encourage fruit growing, he allots land to anyone he thinks will exploit it usefully for that purpose; and he gives the person's heirs the right to inherit it. If this were not unusual, he would hardly have bothered to mention it: apparently in most other kingdoms, if a few great families managed to retain landed property for generations, that of the smallholder was liable to be swallowed up by powerful neighbors or by the Crown.

How did Rāma Gāṃhèṅ finance the business of government? In time of war, his treasury would be swollen by the booty of captured cities, and in time of peace by the tribute of vassal princes; the exemptions he speaks of did not necessarily apply outside the home provinces. The Crown, moreover, owned limitless primeval forests which were rich in teak and other timbers, scented wood such as sandalwood and lignaloes, valuable gums and resins, wild beeswax, birds of bright plumage, deer to provide meat and leather, and rhinoceros whose horns were prized for their virtue as aphrodisiacs; most precious of all were the elephants, which served as the vehicles of princes in war and peace, performed all sorts of work requiring intelligence, precision, and strength, and furnished ivory.

Sukhodaya was not tied to a money economy. There was no coinage; cowries were used as a medium of exchange, especially for small payments; larger ones could be made in silver or gold, measured by weight; and much business was done by barter. It is doubtful if anyone was paid a regular salary; persons in high posts were supposed to live on the income of the land allotments; and many who served the Crown and the vassal lords in humbler capacities would be content with a daily ration of rice, a few clothes, and an occasional gift. A great number of artisans must have been permanently in the service of the royal and noble households: carpenters, masons, boat builders, blacksmiths, armorers, jewelers, and the makers of all sorts of artifacts that archaeology sometimes brings to light, not to mention weavers and makers of other things that have disappeared. Probably most of the craftsmen's production was intended for the use of the owner and his household, or to equip his soldiers, but some of it may have been sold for profit. The potteries near Sajjanālaya had long been producing dark-brown glazed wares, which were sold not only in the home provinces and the vassal states, but also in Cambodia and to some extent overseas.[13]

It is often said that there was no slavery at Sukhodaya, but there is plenty of evidence to the contrary. "When he captures enemy warriors," says Rāma Gāṃhèṅ of himself, "he does not kill them or beat them" (Griswold and Prasert 1971d:208). Of course he does not mean that he set them free; if he did not kill them, it was because he intended to keep them as slaves; if he did not beat them, it was because he thought slaves were more useful when they were well treated. The status of slaves, though we know nothing about it for certain, may not have been radically different from that of ordinary citizens who were in a lord's permanent service without expecting any wages other than food and clothing.

Sukhodaya from 1298 to 1347

Upon his death in 1298, Rāma Gāṃhèṅ was succeeded by his son Lödaiya, who was a very fervent Buddhist.[14] He was also a patron of the Hindu cults, and the Brahmanical tradition

---

[13] For these potteries, see Spinks (1965:ch. 4); Griswold (1967:13).

[14] That Lödaiya was Rāma Gāṃhèṅ's immediate successor is not perfectly certain. It is possible, though in our opinion unlikely, that another reign intervened between the two. See Griswold and Prasert (1972:21, n. 3).

at Sukhodaya seems to have been strengthened during his reign by influences from South India.[15] We know very little about the political events of his reign. Either from incompetence or from bad luck, or most likely from a combination of the two, he lost nearly all his vassals. Subarṇapurī probably broke away not long after his accession; with Subarṇapurī gone, Sukhodaya could have no hope of holding Rājapurī, Bejrapurī, or the Malay Peninsula. Rāmaññadesa broke away in the 1320's or soon after. Sukhodaya's possessions in Laos, and between Laos and Sajjanālaya, reverted to the rule of local princelings about the same time; the alliance with Lān Nā was a thing of the past. By the end of Lödaiya's reign, even the cities on the Ping were lost. Little was left except the provinces of Sukhodaya and Sajjanālaya; and the kingdom was on the verge of collapse (Griswold and Prasert 1972:27–47).

The only known inscription surviving from his reign was apparently composed around 1345 (Griswold and Prasert 1972:75–134). It contains the retrospective passage telling how Sukhodaya gained its independence from the Khmer; the rest is largely devoted to the meritorious deeds of a Mahāthera from Sukhodaya, who spent ten years in Ceylon, where he restored the Mahāthūpa at Anurādhapura and a number of other religious buildings; it describes the reconstruction of the Mahādhātu at Sukhodaya, which was the spiritual and magical center of the kingdom; and it recounts the miracles performed by two relics of the Buddha brought from Ceylon by the Mahāthera (Griswold and Prasert 1972:75–134).

Apart from two passages referring briefly to slaves, it gives us no information about social matters. The first says the Mahāthera assigned "several families" to look after a monastery. The second gives us a glimpse of a market where slaves were offered for sale: the Mahāthera "went through the market

---

[15] See Filliozat (1965:241ff.). For the Brahmanical images attributed to Lödaiya's reign see Griswold (1967:27f.).

buying up all living creatures and setting them free, such as human beings, goats, pigs, dogs, ducks, chickens, geese, birds, fish, deer, and all sorts of creatures of goodly body and handsome form" (Griswold and Prasert 1972:119–120).

On one phase of the economy we can get some information from archaeology. Shortly before his death, Rāma Gāṃhèṅ had brought in a group of Chinese potters skilled in making painted stonewares, and settled them at Sukhodaya. Another group, who probably arrived after his death, were set to work at the Sajjanālaya kilns making celadons and painted wares. Very likely, as suggested by Dr. C. Nelson Spinks (1965: chs. 3, 5–9), both groups were imported in order to take advantage of the demand for glazed ceramics in export markets as far away as Indonesia and the Philippines. Production at both places was enormous in the fourteenth century, and the profits must have been a welcome addition to Lödaiya's shrunken treasury.

Lödaiya's son Ḷīdaiya, the heir apparent to the throne, was appointed *uparāja* at Sajjanālaya in 1340, where he composed a famous treatise on Buddhist cosmology, the *Traibhūmikathā*, in 1345.[16] He was still at Sajjanālaya when he received word that his father had died and the throne had been seized by a man named Ṅua Nāṃ Thaṃ. As soon as he could muster his troops he marched on the capital, took the city in a brisk battle, and removed the usurper (Griswold and Prasert 1973a:71–78).

Mahādharmarājā I of Sukhodaya and Rāmādhipati of Ayudhyā

In May, 1347, immediately after the victory, Ḷīdaiya mounted the throne, assuming the title Mahādharmarājādhi-rāja. We shall call him Mahādharmarājā I for short.

In order to rebuild his kingdom he undertook to make the little that remained of it into a showplace of prosperity and good government; and he issued a standing invitation to the lost vassals to return to the Crown. Though success came slowly,

---

[16] See Coedès and Archaimbault (1973); also Coedès (1957).

and though it seems to have taken him nearly ten years to recover some quite nearby places, he finally regained all the territory from the Ping Valley on the west to the Sak on the east, and from Uttaratittha on the north to Nagara Svarga on the south. But Lower Burma and Loas were permanently lost; and he could have no hope of recovering any of the states south of Nagara Svarga, for they had fallen into the possession of a far more powerful ruler than himself.

This ruler was Rāmādhipati, who founded the kingdom of Ayudhyā in 1351 by consolidating two rich inheritances, one bequeathed to him by his father and the other by his father-in-law.

By piecing together some scattered evidence we can reconstruct the probable history of Rāmādhipati's origin. He was born in 1315 at Traitriṅsa, a little principality on the Ping that had long been tributary to Sukhodaya, and probably still was. His father was a man of obscure origin, while his mother was the daughter of the T'ai ruler of Traitriṅsa, who was very likely related to Sukhodayan royalty. In 1319, Rāmādhipati's father, having made himself king of Lavo in circumstances of which we know nothing, moved to Labapurī, which he renamed Debanagara.[17]

Around 1331, Rāmādhipati married the King of Subarṇapurī's daughter. We do not know the origin of the Subarṇapurī family; it is possible that they were Mòns who had reigned for many generations, becoming partly Khmerized during the period of Khmer ascendancy, and submitting reluctantly to Rāma Gāṃhèṅ at the height of his power when he was too strong for them to resist. If so, we can easily see why they broke

---

[17] Griswold and Prasert (1972:32–33). In an earlier draft of the present article we suggested that Debanagara was Ayodhyā rather than Labapurī; but as we no longer consider the suggestion tenable we have now eliminated it (see Griswold and Prasert 1972:37, n. 35). The name Debanagara (i.e., Devanagara 'city of the gods') is a conventional term for the capital of a kingdom. Kruṅ Deb, an epithet now commonly used for Bangkok, has the same meaning.

away from Sukhodaya and re-established their independence after Rāma Gāṃheṅ's death. Probably, indeed, they were trib- utary to Sukhodaya for only a very short time, perhaps not much over ten years.

The location of their capital at the time of Rāmādhipati's marriage is not known; it must have been near the present towns of Subarṇapurī and Ū Dòṅ, but not on the exact site of either of them. Wherever it was, Rāmādhipati settled there and helped his father-in-law expand his kingdom until it included Rājapurī, Bejrapurī, Tavoy, Tenasserim, and a good deal of the Malay Peninsula. Upon the king's death a few years later, Rāmādhipati inherited his domain and became known as Cau Ū Dòṅ, 'ruler of Ū Dòṅ'. The name Ū Dòṅ, 'source of gold', is in effect a synonym of Subarṇapurī, 'city of gold'; and the reason why Rāmādhipati's father-in-law left the kingdom to Rāmādhipati rather than to one of his own sons seems to have been a rule of inheritance which prevailed, under certain cir- cumstances, among Mòn and Khmer royalty (Griswold and Prasert 1972:34–35). There may have been other reasons as well: perhaps the king's sons were the children of minor wives, whereas his daughter was the child of his chief consort, a lady of high rank; perhaps he chose Rāmādhipati as his son-in-law because he observed his unusual ability and decided to desig- nate him as his successor (Griswold and Prasert 1972:34 and n. 29). Though the King of Subarṇapurī passed over his own sons, at least one of them remained a power to be reckoned with. This was a prince called Paramarājā, who was the elder brother of Rāmādhipati's queen.

Rāmādhipati was almost certainly a T'ai by birth, as his father and mother were both Traitriṅsa people. Upon his father's death in 1344/5, he inherited the kingdom of Lavo-Debanagara in accordance with the usual T'ai succession, which ran from father to son. Rāmādhipati then took up his residence at Labapurī. His patrimony must have been approx- imately the same territory as the kingdom of Lavo in Rāma

Gaṃhèṅ's time, which of course included the old city of Ayodhyā, some thirty miles south of Labapurī. Rāmādhipati chose a site at or near Ayodhyā, because of its strategic and economic advantages, to build a new capital for the kingdom he formed by combining his two inheritances. This kingdom, Ayodhyā—or Ayudhyā as it later became known—came into formal existence in 1351, when Rāmādhipati received his abhiṣeka there. But the preparations that brought it into existence had started several years earlier.

In 1349, says the Chinese writer Wang Ta-yüan, "Hsien submitted to Lo-hu." As Lo-hu means Lavo, and Hsien (Siam) means Sukhodaya in earlier works, the statement has generally been taken to mean that Mahādharmarājā I (Ḷīdaiya) became Rāmādhipati's vassal in 1349. But everything we have learned in recent years about Sukhodayan history shows that Mahādharmarājā I was never a vassal of Rāmādhipati, and that Sukhodaya remained independent until 1378. Professor O.W. Wolters, by demonstrating that Hsien means Subarṇapurī in Wang Ta-yüan's statement, has given us an explanation that fits the facts much better: Wang Ta-yüan is simply referring to Rāmādhipati's consolidation of his two inheritances (Wolters 1966:88ff. and esp. 95ff.). Alternatively we might draw a different conclusion from Professor Wolters's demonstration. It is possible that when Rāmādhipati went to reside at Labapurī after his father's death in 1344/5, Paramarājā tried to seize the throne of Subarṇapuri, and that Rāmādhipati crushed the revolt in 1349. That may be what Wang Ta-yüan means when he says that Hsien [sc., Subarṇapurī] submitted to Lo-hu [Labapurī] (Griswold and Prasert 1972:37–38 and n. 37).

In any case Rāmādhipati, when he received the abhiṣeka at Ayodhyā in 1351, appointed Paramarājā to rule over the Subarṇapurī domains at his vassal. In doing so Rāmādhipati was recognizing the entrenched power of the House of Subarṇapurī in its home territories, and was also doubtless attempting to assure himself of Paramarājā's loyalty.

At the same time Rāmādhipati appointed his own son Rāmeśvara as vassal ruler of Labapurī in recognition of the loyalty his father's house had established there, which he hoped Rāmeśvara would retain as his deputy. In addition the nomenclature offered auspicious perspectives. Rāmādhipati was named after the legendary Indian king, Rāma, the hero of the *Rāmāyaṇa* and the *Rāmakīrti*, who ruled a city of the same name, Ayodhyā. The legendary Rāma had a son called Lava or Laba, whose name reappears, perhaps by a play on words, in that of Labapurī, 'city of Lava', or as it is called in the inscription of Prah Khan of Angkor, Lavodayapura, 'city of the origin of Lava'. While Rāmādhipati gave Labapurī to his son for reasons of statecraft, magic would regard it as an apt choice.

These two appointments could not help perpetuating the dichotomy between the two halves of Rāmādhipati's kingdom. Paramarājā proved to be an unruly vassal, and a feud began between the House of Subarṇapurī and the House of Rāmādhipati that broke out into the open later on. As Professor Wolters has suggested, the feud was not only a matter of personal ambitions; it was also a matter of profoundly different views regarding the policy the Crown should pursue. While Rāmādhipati regarded Cambodia as the richest prize within reach, Paramarājā believed Ayudhyā should crush Sukhodaya before risking adventures elsewhere.

Rāmādhipati, who was probably related to Mahādharmarājā I by blood or marriage or both, was drawn to him by policy as well as inclination; each needed the other's benevolent neutrality to build up his own power; and there must have been an understanding between them defining their spheres of influence. Paramarājā was a potential threat to them both.

Sukhodaya in the Reign of Mahādharmarājā I

Six of Mahādharmarājā I's inscriptions survive, five of them in Siamese and one in Khmer. They all record donations to religion; but he discussess a lot of other things in them, as if he intended them to serve as a series of bulletins to his subjects on political and civil affairs as well as religious ones. The inscriptions were set up beside the monuments or other objects of worship whose founding they record, and they would be seen by crowds of pilgrims and participants in festivals. In a world without newspapers or radios, there could hardly be a better way to reach a large public.

Mahādharmarāja I writes in a clear, sober style that reminds us of Rāma Gāṃhèṅ. But he is more bookish and formal; and in keeping with the needs of the times he gives himself a more rotund title.

In his Khmer inscription he describes his accession: "He entered the capital to reign supreme in this land of Sukhodaya, as successor to his father and his grandfather. Quickly all the kings living in the four directions brought the crown, the sacred sword Jayaśrī and the white parasol, conferred the abhiṣeka on him, and gave him the name Braḥ Pāda Kamrateṅ Añ Śrī Sūryavaṃśa Mahādharmarājādhirāja" (Griswold and Prasert 1973a:136). The Khmer title Kamrateṅ Añ is that which his great-grandfather received from Phā Möaṅ, who had himself received it, together with the sword Jayaśrī and the other regalia, from the King of Cambodia. Braḥ Pāda (Sanskrit, 'sacred feet') is a Khmerism signifying "His Majesty". The epithet Mahādharmarājādhirāja, 'great king of kings in accordance with the Dharma', declares him to be the legitimate sovereign over a body of vassals.

Two of his Siamese inscriptions describe the same event. In them, as in the Khmer inscription, the rulers at the cardinal points confer the abhiṣeka (Griswold and Prasert 1973a:94f., 154). Their presence is not merely conventional, it is a magic formula. Like Mount Meru surrounded by its four lesser peaks, Sukhodaya had to be surrounded by a strong system of vassals in the four directions, which subsume all possible radii emanating from the capital. In plain fact the "rulers of the cardinal points" could hardly have been much more than the governors of four nearby cities; but the act of magic would be no less valid.

In one of his inscriptions Mahādharmarājā says he knows geography, medicine, and the *śāstras*; he knows how to play *skā* and *caturaṅga* [something like backgammon and chess], how to make *yantras*, how to ride elephants and capture them by lasso as prescribed in the *Vṛddhipāśaśāstra*, how to dig irrigation ditches and build weirs; and much else that is no longer legible.[18] In another he says he has studied the Three Piṭakas completely, including the Vinaya and the Abhidharma; from the traditional teachers of *Kṛtya* [non-Buddhist lore], such as the Brahmans and the ascetics, he has learned the Vedas, the śāstras and *āgamas*, the universal law and its applications, beginning with the treatises on astronomy (*Jyotiśāstra*); and that he personally made the calculations required to reform the calendar (Griswold and Prasert 1973a:137–138).

We do not think he is advancing these claims in a spirit of idle boasting: every one of them has a specific purpose connected with recovering the lost vassals and holding them. His understanding of Buddhism would mean they could rely on his sense of justice and mercy. His knowledge of the Vedas and astronomy would suggest that he possessed supernatural power and could foretell the future. In battle it was the custom for men of high rank to engage their adversaries in elephant duels; one who understood his animal thoroughly would be at a decided advantage over the other; experience in lassoing wild elephants would give him agility and confidence; and a study of the Brahmanical lore on training them would give him technical skill. In referring to yantras he probably had in mind some sort

[18] Griswold and Prasert (1973a:104–105). We are indebted to Madame S. Lewitz for an analysis of the terms *skā* and *caturaṅga*. The word *skā* (var: *pǎska*, from Skt. *pāśaka* 'a die') occurs frequently in Middle Khmer literature, meaning 'a game of dice' (whence Siamese *saḥkā*, a game something like backgammon, involving the use of dice and the movement of pieces on a board). The Skt. term *caturaṅga*, meaning "four limbs," i.e., the four branches of an army, assumes two forms in Khmer: (1) *caturaṅg*, meaning "an army"; (2) *catraṅg*, the usual word for chess.

of military mechanism. The games he refers to were not simply amusements, but games by which military tactics could be tested. Knowledge of geography would obviously help him, both in the field and in diplomacy. A vital part of his program to improve agriculture and ensure the prosperity of the kingdom was to dig irrigation ditches and build weirs; and he tells us elsewhere of his measures to encourage the planting of fruit.

Mahādharmarājā I's earliest surviving inscription dates from 1357, when he had already met with considerable success, having (quite recently, it seems) recovered the cities along the Ping. A mutilated passage in it seems to say that in Rāma Gāṃhèn's time the kingdom was vast, extending afar in every direction, and his vassals came to salute him and do him homage everywhere; but later on there was dissension; the country was torn into many fragments and pieces, whose rulers each acted independently. After Mahādharmarājā mounted the throne, however, the passage continues, he forced all those lords and rulers to submit; now the country is tranquil again; the people go by boat to trade or ride their horses to sell; and the king will stop anyone who tries to interfere with them (Griswold and Prasert 1973a:106–109). The text continues with a stiff lecture to the vassal lords: they must be good Buddhists; they must be nice to their brothers and sisters, respectful toward their elders, and considerate of the ordinary people, putting them to work only at tasks for which they are fitted (in other words he is setting limits to the corvée); they must keep abundant reserves of rice and salt on hand in case of scarcity; and they must not seize the estates of decedents but convey them to the rightful heirs. Any ruler who acts in accordance with these principles, he concludes, will rule for a very long time; any ruler who acts in violation of them will not last long at all (Griswold and Prasert 1973a:109–110).

In another inscription he says: "When he catches people who cheated or betrayed him, or people who tried to poison him, he does not kill them or beat them. Again and again he has taken mercy on those who did him harm" (Griswold and Prasert 1973a:155). The statement sounds like a reminiscence of something that happened early in his reign, when his enemies believed the kingdom was collapsing; no doubt quite a lot of people had been insolent to him, and some may have tried to poison him to hasten the kingdom's downfall. Mahādharma-rāja makes this statement in 1361, the same year the King of Nān—who had re-entered the orbit of Sukhodaya, not as a vassal but as an ally—was poisoned by a man "from the south," perhaps an agent of Paramarāja.[19] That crime may have sharp-ened Mahādharmarāja's recollection of earlier attempts on his own life.

The monarch Mahādharmarāja chose as his model was his grandfather, Rāma Gāṃheṅ, whose inscription he evidently knew by heart. In some of his own inscriptions he inserts a sentence or two borrowed straight from it, as if to produce a conditioned reflex in his readers. "When he sees someone's rice he does not covet it, when he sees someone's wealth he does not get angry," he says in 1361, using his grandfather's exact words (Griswold and Prasert 1973a:154 and n. 15). He goes on to say, but in his own words, that a decedent's estate is passed on to his heirs (a statement that might well make property owners in the defected states eager to return). Like his grandfather, he says that if he captures enemy warriors, he does not kill them or beat them; but he goes further, saying that he looks after them well so that they may not die (Griswold and Prasert 1973a:154–155 n. 18). Yet it does not follow that none of them were enslaved.

Upon returning from an expedition against Brè, says an inscription composed by the Saṅgharāja of the Forest Dwellers, Mahādharmarāja donated fifteen families to a monastery near Sajjanālaya (Griswold and Prasert 1974). These slaves were evidently prisoners of war; but others were fugitives from

---

[19] Wyatt (1966b:11); Griswold (1967:37); Griswold and Prasert (1969a: 63; for "November" in line 1, please read "September").

Ayudhyā. It appears from the preamble to Rāmādhipati's Law on Abduction that slaves often fled to the kingdom of Sukhodaya, where they might join a new master; and that there was a flourishing business of abducting slaves or even free people in Ayudhyā and smuggling them across the border to sell (Lingat 1931:360ff.).

While Mahādharmarājā based his method of governing on his grandfather's, it is likely that he made more use of Brahman advisers, and that he expanded the bureaucracy to some extent. His inscriptions, with their considerable use of Khmer and Sanskrit expressions, show his respect for Khmer traditions of order and Brahmanical learning. Two magnificent bronzes in the National Museum, Bangkok, one of Śiva (Figure 2) and one of Viṣṇu, are probably the statues his Khmer inscription tells us he founded in 1349 (Griswold 1967:32 and figs. 25–26). He was about thirty years old at the time, and the statues are very likely idealized portraits of himself. He appears stately and confident, with a friendly but somewhat reserved expression, while a pair of dimples gives the face unexpected liveliness.

Though his inscriptions make no mention of the Dharmaśāstra or the treatises on the science of kingship, he must have known them well. How could a monarch who studied other śāstras overlook those that were the most pertinent to the business of ruling? But though they might color his decisions on specific cases there is no reason to think that his system of administering justice differed in any important respect from Rāma Gāṃhèṅ's.

The arts of architecture and sculpture reached the peak of the classic style in Mahādharmarājā's reign. His most characteristic monuments (Griswold 1967:figs. 27, 32) are replicas of the central tower of the Mahādhātu at Sukhodaya as remodeled near the end of his father's life (Griswold 1967:20–21 and figs. 15–17). By building them in his chief cities he established a magical circuit between them and the capital; and the system reminds us of the cetiya cult in Lower Burma which, as Pro-

Figure 2. Mahādharmarājā I
as the god Śiva. National
Museum, Bangkok.

fessor H. L. Shorto (1963:573f., 589f.) tells us, held the Mòn
kingdom together. The holy relics enshrined in the Mahādhātu,
and those deposited in the copies of it, would generate a spiritual charge, which would transmit messages of benevolence
and protection from him to the rulers of the cities, and of
allegiance from them to him.

The bronze images of the Buddha of high classic style throb
with spiritual energy (Griswold 1967:figs. 44, 47). The stucco

reliefs of scenes from the Buddha's life are remarkably subtle; the composition is orderly and harmonious; the gods and princes are all individuals, as if shaped by the sculptor's recollection of real persons, and with faces expressing a variety of emotions (Griswold 1967:figs. 42, 45).

The potteries at Sukhodaya and Sajjanālaya continued to flourish, as indeed they were to do until the middle of the fifteenth century. The "Svargaloka" figurines from Sajjanālaya give us a lively glimpse of the people (Figure 3). The men are

Figure 3. Figurines of Svargaloka ware. Private collection, Bangkok. *Top row:* a hermit holding a cock; a pair of wrestlers; a man holding a fish. *Bottom row:* a pair of children (?); a woman holding a child; a hunchback; a loving couple; a woman touching her breasts; a woman holding a bird; a child riding a goose.

merchants, soldiers, wrestlers, farmers, and so on; some carry a fighting cock or a musical instrument; the women carry a child or a fan. These people too are individuals, sharply observed and rapidly sketched.

Mahādharmarājā's revenues must have been large. Among the gifts he distributed to the monks in 1361 before his ordination are the following: "Ten thousand of gold, ten thousand of silver, and ten million cowries" (Griswold and Prasert 1973a: 141). Evidently there was still no coinage. It is curious to find such a huge number of cowries mentioned as actual objects, not merely as theoretical counters of value. The weight of the metals is given in ticals, approximately half-ounces. At the world price on November 5, 1974, 5,000 ounces of gold would be worth nearly $850,000. If the information an Englishman received in 1608 regarding the Siamese market is at all relevant, the value of silver was something like one-third that of gold (Anderson 1890:46). In any case the purchasing power of both metals was far higher then than now.

We have already suggested the likelihood that there was an understanding between Mahādharmarājā I and Rāmādhipati.

Nagara Svarga was a place of vital importance to Mahādharmarājā, for it controlled the riverine communications between the two halves of his kingdom. But its position was dangerously exposed, for it was all too easily accessible by river from Subarṇapurī. Apparently it had broken away from Sukhodaya in Lödaiya's reign, maintained a precarious independence for some years, and finally returned to the old relationship when the ruler of Gandī and Nagara Svarga sought Mahādharmarājā's protection and became his vassal shortly before 1357.[20] It is hard to see how Mahādharmarājā could have recovered Nagara Svarga unless Rāmādhipati laid a restraining hand on Paramarājā, who must have been furious when the place escaped him.

In September of 1361, the same year the King of Nān was

[20] Griswold and Prasert (1973a:106–109); for an inscription commemorating the erection of a monastery at Nagara Svarga by Mahādharmarājā I and the dedication of the accruing merit to a deceased ruler of the province, see Griswold and Prasert (1973a:112–118).

poisoned by the man "from the south," Mahādharmarājā was ordained as a monk. There is some reason to believe that while he was in the monkhood, and while Rāmādhipati was busy elsewhere, Paramarājā seized Biṣṇuloka, which was one of Sukhodaya's principal cities.[21] In 1362, after resuming his throne, Mahādharmarājā conducted a military campaign to Nān and the valley of the Sak. The purpose of the campaign to Nān may have been to restore order there; at any rate we know that the murdered king's son Phā Kòṅ succeeded to the throne, which he might not have been able to do without Mahādharmarājā's intervention. The continuation of the campaign to the Sak Valley may have been intended not only to regain lost territory but also to outflank Paramarājā at Biṣṇuloka and show him that his position was untenable. That, plus a reminder to Rāmādhipati that his understanding with Mahādharmarājā was being violated by his vassal's greed, may have been enough to make Paramarājā withdraw. Mahādharmarājā then went to reside at Biṣṇuloka. As he tells us in the same inscription, he stayed at Biṣṇuloka for seven years [i.e., in the traditional arithmetic, anything over six years and up to seven]; and while he was there he built an irrigation canal from Biṣṇuloka to Sukhodaya to feed water to upland and lowland farms, so that areca palms and other trees could be planted, fish could be caught for food, and the people made happy and contented everywhere (Griswold and Prasert 1973b:116, 121–122). The passage shows Mahādharmarājā's constant concern for his people's well-being, and his wish (like Rāma Gāṃheṅ's) to encourage them to increase their income. Though he does not say so, the earth removed to make the canal would naturally be built into an embankment alongside and a road made on top, which would be useful not only for commerce but also for defense.

[21] Griswold and Prasert (1973b:106–108). For the date of Mahādharmarājā's ordination, September 22, 1361 (Julian), see Griswold and Prasert (1973a:122).

When he went to Biṣṇuloka, according to some of the
chronicles, he took with him an image called the "Ceylon
Buddha," which was evidently regarded as the palladium of
Sukhodaya: if he really took it to a city that had so lately been
lost and recovered, his action was a singular mark of confidence
in Rāmādhipati's word.[22]

Ayudhyā and Sukhodaya from 1369 to 1396

Rāmādhipati died in 1369, leaving the throne of Ayudhyā
to his son Rāmeśvara, the ruler of Labapurī. Less than a year
later Paramarājā seized the throne from him, and sent him back
to Labapurī to rule as his vassal.

About this time Mahādharmarājā withdrew his army from
Biṣṇuloka and returned to Sukhodaya to live, we do not know
why. Perhaps he thought Paramarājā would be too busy consolidating his own power at home to threaten Biṣṇuloka. Perhaps, on the contrary, Paramarājā forced him to demilitarize
the place: if so, Mahādharmarājā must have known that Biṣṇuloka was doomed and Sukhodaya in great peril.

In fact Paramarājā soon began a series of attacks on Sukhodayan cities. He took Nagara Svarga in 1372; the next year
he attacked Kāṃbèṅ Bejra, inflicting heavy losses, and then
retired.

Mahādharmarājā I, who died some time between 1370 and
1374, was succeeded by his son Mahādharmarājā II. In 1375
Paramarājā attacked Biṣṇuloka; in 1376 he again attacked
Kāṃbèṅ Bejra, again inflicted heavy losses, and again retired.
In 1378 Mahādharmarājā II, learning that Paramarājā was
about to attack Kāṃbèṅ Bejra for the third time, hastened to
the defense of the city; but his forces were overwhelmed and he
was obliged to surrender. In accordance with the usual custom,

---

[22] Griswold and Prasert (1973b:106–108). In the inscriptions Biṣṇuloka
is called Sòṅ Gvè 'two branches' (of a river), i.e., a confluence. In some of
the chronicles it is called Dvisākhā, the Pali translation of Sòṅ Gvè, in others
Jayanāda, an old name for Biṣṇuloka, not to be confused with the present
province of Jayanāda.

Paramarājā did not depose him, but made him swear allegiance and sent him back to rule Sukhodaya as his vassal.

By this means Paramarājā got the suzerainty of a kingdom he was unable to conquer. He also got its palladium, the "Ceylon Buddha," and sent it back to his capital. Though Mahādharmarājā II remained faithful to his oath, the ruler of Kāṃbèn Bejra, who had been appointed by Mahādharmarājā I and was still in office, began laying plans to revolt. He got hold of the palladium by a trick, but Prince Mahābrahma of Jian Rāy, the brother of King Kilanā of Lān Nā, learned of its virtues, led an army to the gates of Kāṃbèn Bejra, and demanded that the ruler yield it up to him. The latter thereupon made a secret alliance with Mahābrahma and gave him the image (or should we understand that he gave him a copy of it and kept the supposed original for himself?). Mahābrahma took it back to Jian Rāy, where he cast a copy of it, and later gave Kilanā either the image he had obtained or the copy, it is not clear which. Upon Kilanā's death in 1385, the throne of Lān Nā went to his son Sèn Möaṅ Mā. Mahābrahma tried unsuccessfully to wrest it from him, then fled to Ayudhyā to ask help from Paramarājā, who invaded Lān Nā at his instigation but was defeated. Paramarājā, who had meanwhile become disgusted with Mahābrahma, transferred his support to Sèn Möaṅ Mā and asked for his help against Sukhodaya, where he thought a revolt was brewing. Apparently Paramarājā and Sèn Möaṅ Mā agreed to make a concerted attack against Sukhodaya, but Paramarājā was delayed by the revolt of Kāṃbèn Bejra; Sèn Möaṅ Mā arrived at the gates of Sukhodaya first, and while he was hesitating whether or not to attack, the King of Sukhodaya fell upon him and routed his forces. This was a stroke of luck for Sukhodaya: while Mahādharmarājā II had sworn allegiance to Paramarājā, he was under no obligation to Sèn Möaṅ Mā; and by putting him out of action he ruined Paramarājā's plans without violating his own oath (Griswold and Prasert 1968:210–212).

In 1388 Paramarājā attacked Kāṃbèn Bejra for the fourth

time; but he was taken ill and died on his way home. His attempts to pacify the kingdom of Sukhodaya had ended in frustration. He was no military genius, as is obvious even from the laconic accounts of his campaigns in the Annals of Ayudhyā. He had not reckoned with Sukhodayan courage; and he died without getting any advantage from the oath of allegiance he had exacted from Mahādharmarājā II.

A few days after Paramarājā's death the ex-king Rāmeśvara seized the throne of Ayudhyā. No doubt his success was helped by the frustrations of Paramarājā's policy and the confusion of the Subarṇapurī faction when Paramarājā died.

Rāmeśvara and Mahādharmarājā II were drawn together, as their fathers had been, by friendship as well as self-interest. Mahādharmarājā II, whose oath of allegiance had expired with Paramarājā's death, almost certainly swore a new oath to Rāmeśvara, which would allow Ayudhyan boats to sail in Sukhodayan waters; and in that case who could complain if his own boats sailed past Nagara Svarga? But he was practically an independent monarch, so lightly did Rāmeśvara hold the reigns of suzerainty; and he ruled all the territory that had belonged to his father at the height of his power except Nagara Svarga (Griswold and Prasert 1968:213–216; 1969a:50–52).

On February 27, 1393 (Julian), Sukhodaya made a pact of mutual defense with the kingdom of Nān. It was presumably intended to be kept secret, being a precaution in case the House of Subarṇapurī should regain power at Ayudhyā. The person who subscribed to it on behalf of Nān was King Gāṃ Ṭăn, who had succeeded upon the death of his father, Phā Kòn, six years earlier; he was related by marriage to Sukhodayan royalty; and he had good reason to fear the Subarṇapurī faction, as he was a grandson of the king who had been murdered. Mahādharmarājā II, because of his oath of allegiance, doubtless felt disqualified to act on behalf of Sukhodaya, so he probably stepped aside by entering the monkhood for a few months; and

his son Sai Ḷīdaiya, evidently acting as regent in his place, subscribed to the pact on Sukhodaya's behalf (Griswold and Prasert 1969b:65–98). To bear witness to it, he and the King of
Nān called on an impressive list of ancestors, legendary heroes,
gods, guardian divinities of mountains and streams, and forest
divinities (Griswold and Prasert 1969b:80–84, cf. 86–89 and
n. 34). Among those invoked by Sai Ḷīdaiya was the Braḥ
Khbuṅ spirit who, as Rāma Gāṃhèṅ had said a long time
before, was more powerful than any other spirit in the kingdom
of Sukhodaya. The pact was soon put to the test. In 1396 Gāṃ Ṭăn himself
was poisoned by an emissary from "the southern ruler"—perhaps a Subarṇapurī man. Soon afterward the throne of Nān
was usurped by a prince from Brè, while the rightful heir, Gāṃ
Ṭăn's nephew Huṅ, fled to Sajjanālaya. There he raised an
army, with which he returned to Nān and regained the throne.
The ruler of Sajjanālaya who engineered Huṅ's restoration was
almost certainly Sai Ḷīdaiya (Griswold and Prasert 1969b:99–
101).

Ayudhyā in the Second Half of the Fourteenth Century

Ayudhyā was considerably less T'ai than Sukhodaya.
Rāmādhipati was perhaps the only Ayudhyan king, until much
later, who was thoroughly T'ai; and the T'ai were a minority
among the population. Ever since the Dvāravatī period the
region had been predominantly Mòn. To a great extent it must
have remained so during the years when it was ruled, through
the usual system of vassalage, by Khmer viceroys or by independent but Khmerizing kings. Khmer ideals of order and
ceremony were more deeply rooted than at Sukhodaya; the
Brahmans were more influential; and the Hindu cults, without
being in any sense a rival of the Theravāda or ever becoming a
popular religion, shared the general honor.
    Perhaps Ayudhyā's social organization in the fourteenth
century was already similar in many ways to that which the

Europeans observed in seventeenth century Siam, which is admirably summed up in the wood carving in Figure 4. The composition, occupying a triangular pediment, depicts a scene in heaven reflecting the hierarchy of an ideal kingdom. At the top is the god Viṣṇu, sheltered by an honorific parasol and carrying his ritual weapons. The sun-bird Garuḍa, supported by another solar symbol, the Kīrtimukha, bears him aloft, while a three-headed Nāga, ruler of the waters and of subterranean treasure, rears up between the bird's legs, producing a dynamic tension that will assure the kingdom the right proportion of rain and sunshine for a prosperous agriculture. At either side of the god, but at a slightly lower level, hovers a flying divinity holding a ceremonial sun-shield. Below are more divinities, disposed in orderly tiers, four in the top tier, eight in the next, and eight in the third, all with their palms pressed together in worship. Each member of the hierarchy has his

Figure 4. Scene in Viṣṇu's heaven. Pediment of the ordination hall, Văt Hnā Braḥ Meru, Ayudhyā. Seventeenth century.

allotted place in the composition: all are completely conformist, all are perfect "organization men," and none has a trace of individual personality. The other denizens of heaven, creatures of lower rank, are not even admitted to the happy scene. This composition is in startling contrast to the relief depicting the T'ai soldiery from Sukhodaya (Figure 1) and to the Svargaloka figurines (Figure 3); instead it reminds us of countless reliefs in Khmer temples portraying scenes of worship. Since many of the known features of Angkorian social organization were also present in seventeenth-century Ayudhyā, it might seem a fair guess that Ayudhyā had been like that from the beginning. For some things it is a virtual certainty. The special vocabulary used when referring to royalty was inherited from Angkor, having been transmitted, probably in an unbroken tradition, since the days when a son of Jayavarman VII was viceroy of Lavo. The Annals of Ayudhyā, when recording the death of Rāmādhipati and his successors, say they "entered Nirvāṇa," as if they were Bodhisattvas of the Mahāyāna pantheon. As they themselves were followers of the Theravāda, it seems likely the expression was a survival from the reign of Jayavarman VII, automatically taken over with the rest of the special vocabulary. A king's sacred feet were worshiped. He would expect his subjects to prostrate themselves when he passed through the streets in a palanquin or on an elephant, and to remain in that posture until he had gone by. The Brahmans were strongly entrenched as advisers to the monarch, as astrologers, as performers of ceremonies that would produce results by supernatural means, and as technicians of all kinds.

It is also quite probable that there was little personal liberty; that the bureaucracy was large and highly organized; that government officials received no salary, but a share of the personal services and crops of the people who were in their charge, or a share of the taxes, fines and so on, while those above a certain rank also received a life tenancy in landed property and animals as gifts of the sovereign; that even the officials lived in fear of being arrested and punished by confiscation or flogging; that the property of persons who died intestate went to the Crown; that there was no certainty of inheritance for anyone; that the most profitable businesses were monopolized by the Crown; that enterprises not forbidden to ordinary people, such as rice farming, fruit growing, fishing, and small trade, were subject to vexatious taxes; and that commerce was hampered by a network of tolls and octrois. All these things are attested at Ayudhyā in the seventeenth century, and most of them in Cambodia in the Angkorian period. As they are the very things Rāma Gāṃhèṅ prided himself on avoiding, we can guess they were standard practice in the monarchies of the thirteenth and fourteenth centuries, with Sukhodaya forming the most notable exception.

We can get much information on Ayudhyan institutions and behavior from the old laws preserved in the Recension of 1805 A.D. The only trouble is that there is no way of knowing how much of any given law, in the form in which it has come down to us, was really the work of the king to whom it is ascribed, and how much is due to amendments made by his successors.[23] But as we can hardly doubt that the laws ascribed to Rāmādhipati were really enacted by him, though not necessarily in the form in which we now have them, it seems likely that at least the preambles and the first few articles of those laws reflect the state of affairs in the second half of the fourteenth century.

The population, which was probably several times as large as that of Sukhodaya, was kept under tight control. Apart from slaves, officials above a certain rank, and monks, every man was subject to the corvée, owing six months' service to the Crown out of each year; he would be assigned to the army or one of the

---

[23] See Lingat (1938a:19f.). Lingat's (1938b) edition of the laws is based directly on the official manuscripts of the Recension of 1805 and is the only printed version that reproduces their spelling faithfully.

public services, digging canals, making roads, building temples, and so on; and as he received no pay or even food, he had to earn enough in half a year to keep himself alive the other half. To make sure that no one shirked his duty, the people were divided into territorial groups headed by Crown-appointed officials called *mun nāy*. At least that was true in the portions of the kingdom ruled directly from the capital; as time went on, the system was extended progressively to territories ruled by vassal princes, strengthening the authority of the Crown at their expense; but we do not know just how far it extended in the late fourteenth century. Wherever it was in force, the whole population were registered in lists called *hāṅ vāv*, 'kites' tails' (because they were so long), recording each person's name, the group he belonged to, and the service he was assigned to. Certain services were burdened with oppressively hard work, while others had much less, so there was always the danger that one group might be depleted by desertions to another; in some, conditions were so bad that people tried to escape by selling themselves into slavery. Freedom of movement was severely restricted. As it was the mun nāy's duty to supply as many men out of his group as might be required for service, he had to prevent desertions, keep track of his people, and know exactly where everyone was at all times.[24]

The *śakti-nā* system, though not perfected until later, was already in effect. Everyone in the kingdom had a specified number of "dignity marks," depending on his rank, and on his position, if any, in the government. It was an outgrowth of an earlier practice in which rulers, as absolute proprietors of the land, distributed specified amounts of it to their subjects to cultivate for their own advantage; the earlier practice survived among some of the T'ai peoples of Tongking and Laos until modern times; but in Ayudhyā it took a different turn. If, as seems likely, the systematic distribution of land to the general

[24] See Lingat (1950a:215f.; 1931:82ff.); Wales (1934:46–48, 94, et passim).

population had been discontinued, nevertheless the number of dignity marks still corresponded to the number of rai of land a person was theoretically entitled to. This number, which in the fully developed system of the fifteenth century, ranged from 5 for the humblest citizens up to 10,000 for the highest officials and 20,000 for the highest princes, was a measure of his "value"; and the fines for certain offenses were calculated in proportion to the dignity marks of the culprit and the victim. A major wife was considered to have half the number her husband had; a minor wife, one-quarter; and a slave wife who bore him children, one-eighth.[25]

A substantial portion of the population were slaves. They were of diverse origin: insolvent debtors or their sureties, sold into servitude for the benefit of creditors; criminals who could not pay their fines; persons who sold themselves, or were sold by their parents, in time of hardship; tribespeople imported by itinerant dealers; prisoners of war; the children of slaves; and so on (Lingat 1931 :ch. 1). Debt-slaves could buy their freedom if they could pay the debt, or else they could transfer to a new master who was willing to put up the money. For persons born in slavery there was a fixed redemption price, up to 1,400,000 cowries for a male and 1,200,000 for a female when they were in the prime of life, less for those under or over age (Wales 1934: 191f.; Lingat 1931 :61, n. 1). (At the legal rate these figures were equal to twenty-eight or twenty-four ounces of silver, but the actual rate of exchange between cowries and silver varied enormously from time to time.)

Ayudhyā's code of civil law was a unique institution, the origin of which has been admirably studied by the late Professor Robert Lingat (1950b; 1951). There was nothing like it at Sukhodaya, where the king decided cases in accordance with his own sense of justice, and nothing like it in Cambodia, where he decided them in conformity with the Hindu Dharmaśāstra;

---

[25] See Wales (1934:25–50, 60, 75–78) for the origin of the system. See also Lingat (1950a:232–234).

the kings of Sukhodaya and Cambodia did not legislate, but simply issued *ad hoc* commands. Only a small part of the Dharmaśāstra has any connection with civil law; the rest deals with Brahmanical religious observances, such as rites and sacrifies, purifications and penances; its authority rests on the legend of Manu, and its sanctions on Brahmanical belief. Cambodia and other countries where the Hindu religions predominated had naturally taken over the system with little or no change; justice could be administered, and the rites observed, by reference to the Dharmaśāstra, without any fixed code of civil law. But whatever its virtues, the Dharmaśāstra was of limited use in Buddhist lands. A substitute was worked out by Mòn Buddhists: using the Dharmaśāstra as a model, but discarding all the Brahmanical matter and relying for sanctions on a Buddhist adaptation of the legend of Manu, they composed a series of works called *Dhammasattha*, the Pali form of the word Dharmaśāstra, as a guide for the administration of justice. The earliest Dhammasattha on record was written by a Mòn monk at Pagán in the twelfth century, though it may have had predecessors in Dvāravatī or some other Mòn land. Another, which was extremely influential, is attributed to the initiative of Rāma Gāṃhèn's son-in-law Fā-Rua (Waréru), the ruler of Rāmaññadesa.

Though Rāma Gāṃhèn seems to have paid no attention to it, Rāmādhipati adopted a Dhammasattha from Rāmaññadesa as his guide in deciding specific cases. He caused a record to be kept of his decisions, which were then reduced to general form and classified according to subject; and the collection, known as Rājasattha, taking on the sanctity and all-embracing character of the Dhammasattha itself, became an integral part of it. He and his successors were thus real legislators instead of mere issuers of *ad hoc* commands.[26]

[26] For the process by which the Rājasattha, though it remained distinct from the Dhammasattha in Burma, became an integral part of it in Siam, and the method given in Ayudhyā's Dhammasattha for transforming the king's commands into *mātrā*, see Lingat (1951:180–187).

An Ayudhyan Law at Sukhodaya

In 1395, upon the death of Rāmeśvara, his son Rāma-rājādhirāja succeeded to the Ayudhyan throne. Rāmarāja—to give the new king's name in abbreviated form—was in effect a captive of the Subarṇapurī party, and forced to do their bidding.

A stone inscription, discovered in 1930 in the center of the old city of Sukhodaya, bears the text of an edict issued by a king of Ayudhyā whose name is mutilated (Griswold and Prasert 1969a:109ff.). It is dated in a year of the ox, the numerical designation of which is completely illegible, on the full moon day of the month of Vaiśākha, a Thursday, the T'ai cyclical name of the day being *miṅ hmau*. The only day between the thirteenth century and the end of the nineteenth century on which these calendrical data coincided was Thursday, April 12, 1397 A.D. (Julian) (Griswold and Prasert 1969a:128, n. 8). Unless the astrologer or the engraver made some mistake, we are therefore compelled to accept this date as the right one.

In the following discussion we shall tentatively accept it; and as a corollary we shall read the mutilated name of the issuing king, "........rāja," as "Rāmarājādhirāja." Some collateral evidence in the text suggests this may be right, but it is not conclusive.

It would be unheard-of for a suzerain to impose any civil legislation on a vassal state: a vassal's duty to his suzerain was to pay tribute, to refrain from doing certain things, and so on; the vassal ruler could be removed at will, but as long as he remained in office he was free to run the internal affairs of his state as he wished. It was only when one country was annexed by another and incorporated into it that we should expect the annexing king to take control of its internal administration. It is generally agreed that Sukhodaya, though reduced to vassalage in 1378, was not annexed by Ayudhyā until 1438. But the events of 1397 are obscure; the Subarṇapurī faction may have learned of Sai Līdaiya's preparations to place Huṅ on the throne of Nān; and it is possible they hoped to reduce Sukhodaya to impotence by forcing Rāmarāja to annex its territories and impose Ayudhyan law on them. Aside from the uncertain implications of this inscription, we know of no evidence that Ayudhyā annexed Sukhodaya at this time; but our lack of information proves nothing: we should hardly expect Sukhodayan sources to tell us much on such a subject; and the Annals of Ayudhyā are peculiarly reticent for Rāmarāja's reign.

Rāmarāja, supposing he is the author of the edict, constantly cites the Dharmaśāstra and couples the Rājaśāstra with it; though he uses the Sanskrit terms, he obviously means the Dhammasattha and the Rājasattha (Siamese monarchs later on used the hybrid forms "Dharmasāstra" and "Rājasātra"). Even a superficial comparison with the Recension of 1805 shows that this law is largely based on Rāmādhipati's legislation, which perhaps as yet had not had time to require much amendment. In effect, therefore, when the edict says that certain judgments shall be made in conformity with the Rājaśāstra, it is referring the reader to Rāmādhipati's laws for further information.

The text is full of difficulties—lacunae, uncertainties of reading, and obscurities of language—which we have discussed at length in the translation we published in the *Journal of the Siam Society* (Griswold and Prasert 1969a). In the following analysis we shall skim over them as lightly as possible, supplying conjectural reconstructions and explanations where we think they are necessary. Such conjectures are admittedly risky; it is inevitable that we have made some bad guesses; but we have grounds for hope that they are not on very vital matters.

The text begins with the date, which we have already discussed. Then, if we have reconstructed the name right, comes the statement: "This capital is under the authority of His Majesty Mahārājaputra Rāmarājādhirāja Śrī Paramacakrabartirāja." In itself, the statement might mean he was reasserting his suzerainty over the capital, and hence over the kingdom; but as a piece of civil legislation is introduced a few lines later, it looks as if it meant he was annexing its territory.

Rāmarāja tells us something about his stately progress from Ayudhyā to Sukhodaya, accompanied by his retinue, his generals, and his army with four branches. Upon reaching Kāṃbèṅ Bejra he was waited on by a number of dignitaries, including the Lord of Traitriṅsa—a reference that tends to confirm the tradition that the House of Rāmādhipati originated at Traitriṅsa, not far from Kāṃbèṅ Bejra (see Map 2), and suggests that Rāmarāja still had ties with his great-great-grandfather's descendants there. The inscription adds that the officials "sat down to do homage to his sacred feet."

After that the king proceeded to Sukhodaya, where he made it known that he intended to cleanse the region following the example of King Rāma, "whose greatness is proverbial." Rāma, the hero of the *Rāmāyaṇa* and the *Rāmakīrti*, was the legendary "ideal king" whose example all monarchs were supposed to imitate; as Rāmarāja bore the same name, and his capital Ayodhyā (as it was then called) was named after the Indian hero's city, he may have felt the example was particularly apt. Perhaps at the same time he intended a paronomastic reference to Rāma Gāṃhèṅ, from whom he was very likely descended in the female line; if he could persuade the Sukhodayans that he was imitating him, so much the better.

His Majesty, the edict continues, "promulgated this law to all officials and group chiefs as well as their retainers and all citizens, in small towns as well as large ones, throughout this whole region. He promulgated it in the center of the city of Sukhodaya, which is the metropolis."

It is doubtful if the system of group chiefs—the heads of the territorial groups described above—was yet in force at Sukhodaya, though Rāmarāja was perhaps taking steps to establish it. He also addresses himself to the officials (*lūk khun*);

the latter would include the vassal lords, whom he probably looked to to exercise the functions of group chiefs until the system could be perfected.

Article 1 deals with matters in large towns, where there seems to have been a considerable bureaucracy. The text names two officials with special functions, a Chief Magistrate (*subhāpati*, from Skt. *sabhāpati*) and an Officer of Slave Affairs (*cā khā*). The article may be summed up as follows.

When a slave in one of these cities runs away to a person's house, if that person withholds the slave for more than two days, or does not hasten to give him up to the Officer of Slave Affairs, and if the Officer and the Chief Magistrate, happening to learn what has occurred, go to fetch the slave to return him to his master, the law provides that: if anyone fails to return someone's slave, or withholds someone's slave or wife, he shall be judged according to the rules of the Rājaśāstra and the Dharmaśāstra. A fine shall be imposed upon him exactly as if he were a thief who stole someone's people but, instead of taking them out of the city immediately, ran away and hid them inside the city.

In other words, in accordance with Article 1 of Rāmādhipati's Law on Abduction, the culprit shall be fined an amount equal to the value of the slave or wife, the fine to be divided equally between the Crown and the injured party. Abducted persons were in the same category as stolen goods; the "injured party" was not the abducted person, but the owner of the goods (i.e., the husband of the abducted wife, the father of the abducted child, or the owner of the slave). Under the Law on Compensation, the value of a male slave, beginning at 150,000 cowries at birth, rose gradually to 1,400,000 at the age of twenty-six, remained there until the age of forty, and then gradually decreased until it was only 100,000 at the age of ninety-one; and the value of a female slave, beginning at

100,000 cowries, rose gradually to 1,200,000 at the age of twenty-one, remained there until the age of thirty, and gradually decreased until it was only 75,000 at the age of ninety-one. The value of a citizen's wife or child was calculated by multiplying the value of a slave of the same age by a specified coefficient based on the number of dignity marks the citizen had.[27]

   Article 2 deals with matters in small towns and in the country-side.

   When a slave runs away to someone's home, or a third party takes the slave there, the slave must be returned at once; and if the person who took him there returns him promptly because he fears the law, he shall be excused. If the slave is withheld for more than three days but not more than eight, the abductor or the home owner shall be fined 11,000 cowries per day; if longer, he shall be fined in proportion to dignity marks in accordance with the Dharmaśāstra and the Rājaśāstra.

   Under Rāmādhipati's Law on Abduction the fine would range from one-and-a-half to three times the value of the person abducted, depending on how far away he was taken and whether or not he was returned. The slave, if he was over twelve years old, was to be flogged.

   Article 3. When a thief who has stolen someone's animals or people passes by a person's home, the homeowner must seize the thief and take him, together with the stolen goods, to the authorities. A reward shall be given to those who helped re-cover the goods. If an accomplice of the thief, or someone who accepted a bribe to let the thief go, later informs against the thief and claims a reward for it, he shall not only be denied the reward but shall also be punished as stated below [i.e., in accordance with Articles 5 and 6].

   Article 4. When someone catches a thief with stolen goods such as slaves, people or cattle, then if he withholds them for

---

[27] In the fully developed Law on Compensation, the coefficient ranges from 1.50 for the lowest grade of citizens to 58 for an official having 10,000 dignity marks.

even one day, he shall be denied a reward, and also be punished in conformity with the Rājaśāstra.

Article 5. When a thief who has stolen someone's animals or people passes by a person's home as stated above [i.e., in Article 3], if the homeowner fails to seize the thief; or if he lets him go because the thief bribes him, or because the thief is his brother, or because the thief is the servant of a powerful man who might intervene to protect him; or else if the owner of the goods and slaves, having chased the thief to the house, cries out for help to seize him and the homeowner fails to help; in any of these cases the homeowner shall be punished exactly as if he himself were the thief. He shall be made to pay the full value of the goods, equal to the fine imposed on the thief; he shall be made to pay the reward to those who helped recover the stolen goods; and he shall be fined in proportion to rank and dignity marks.

Article 6. A thief's accomplice, or someone who is aware of a theft but fails to inform the authorities, shall be fined as if he himself were the thief and punished in the same way.

Article 7. If a man starts to bully someone, or to take something from him by force, and if the person has no one to help him catch the bully, then even if the bully is armed, anyone who is nearby must seize him. A fine shall be imposed on the bully and given as a reward to whoever caught him. Whoever is guilty of nonfeasance, not helping to chase and catch the bully, shall be fined an amount equal to the value of the goods the bully took by force.

Article 8 is to a considerable extent illegible. The gist of it seems to be as follows.

If any person, having some work to be done or a ceremony to be performed, plans to kill an ox or buffalo in order to feast the neighbors who help with the work or attend the ceremony, then if he is a group chief he must inform the members of his group, or if he is a member of the group he must inform his group chief and his neighbors, pointing out the animal for everyone to see [so as to prove it was not stolen]. If he fails to do so, then even if the animal belongs to him he shall be fined an amount equal to its value, and forced to pay a reward to anyone who has informed against him.

To Sukhodayans, accustomed to personal administration of justice of the sort Rāma Gāṃhèṅ prided himself on, this law must have seemed preposterous. It made no allowance for loyalties or ties of affection; and its set formulas, leaving no room for human considerations, must have appeared to them as crude and unbecoming as a pair of ready-made boots to an Edwardian gentleman.

If a man ran away with someone's wife but changed his mind after a couple of days and sent her back, would a Sukhodayan husband forgive him? That would depend chiefly on how much he loved his wife and what the abductor did to her while she was in his power. If a wife ran away of her own accord and hid in someone else's house, her husband might take summary vengeance, or he might forget about the whole thing; if he was bent on vengeance, he would hardly be appeased by a whole cartload of cowries. Who would expect a man to betray his friends and relatives just because they happened to take something that belonged to someone else? Whether or not a man chased a thief would depend on his relations with him and with the victim of the theft; if he was under obligations to the thief, it would be contemptible to chase him in the hope of getting a reward. What would liberty-loving people think of punishing a man for killing his own ox without publicly pointing it out beforehand? If a Sukhodayan lord had to judge a case, would he take the trouble to wade through this text, to look up the references in Article 3 to Articles 5 and 6, and to search out the relevant provisions in the Ayudhyan laws on abduction, theft, slavery, and compensation? What would he think of rules that based the value of a slave solely on age and sex, and computed the value of a citizen's child at so many times the value of a slave depending on dignity marks—without reference to the person's character, past performance, or devotion?

A Declaration of Independence and Its Consequences

Mahādharmarāja II died around 1398. In 1400, after the cremation had been performed and the usual acts of merit in favor of the deceased had been completed, his son Sai Ḷīdaiya suddenly invaded Ayudhyan territory at the head of an army, seized Nagara Svarga, and declared himself an independent monarch.

The declaration of independence is recorded in an inscription composed by the Queen Mother, Mahādharmarāja II's widow, the nominal purpose of which is to commemorate the founding of a monastery in 1403 (Griswold and Prasert 1968:221ff.). In the Pali exordium, after saluting the Triple Gem, she exclaims: "May all my enemies be destroyed!" Then she continues in Siamese, saying that in Śakarāja 762 [1400 A.D.] she and her son Samtec Mahādharmarājādhipati Śrī Sūryavaṃśa, strong to subjugate their foes, bold and intrepid, led the army forth to fight and marched over the territories of numerous rulers. Her son, she adds, "has succeeded to the enjoyment of supreme sovereignty as King of the land of Sajjanālaya-Sukhodaya. Jointly they destroyed the host of their enemies, extending the royal frontiers to take in Braḥ Pāṅ [Nagara Svarga] with its hundred and twenty thousand lakes and streams, and Brè. . . ."

For the next ten years or so, Mahādharmarāja III (Sai Ḷīdaiya) ruled Sukhodaya as a completely independent monarch. Probably his bold action had succeeded chiefly because Ayudhyā was torn apart by the feud between the houses of Rāmādhipati and Subarṇapurī. While Rāmarāja himself might be virtually a prisoner of the Subarṇapurī faction, his house still had powerful supporters. Sai Ḷīdaiya's conquest of Nagara Svarga caught the Subarṇapurī faction by surprise. Having lost the key to Sukhodaya's riverine communications, they could not threaten Sai Ḷīdaiya's independence without

risking a war in which Sukhodaya and the House of Rāmādhipati would be pitted against them; and though they were
steadily building up their power, they were not yet ready to
risk civil war.

The Annals of Ayudhyā, which say nothing about the events
of Rāmarāja's reign, tell us somewhat cryptically how it ended:
in 1409, Rāmarāja quarreled with his Chief Minister and tried
to arrest him; but the Minister escaped and offered the throne
to Prince Indarājā of Subarṇapurī, whereupon their forces
seized the city of Ayudhyā and removed Rāmarāja. Though
the Annals do not say so, it can hardly be doubted that the
Minister was one of the Subarṇapurī faction's men whom they
had forced Rāmarāja to appoint; and when Rāmarāja discovered the plot it was already too late for him to save his
throne.

We know, though the Annals again fall silent, that Indarājā
(r. 1409–1424) acted quickly against Sukhodaya, for the inscription of Văt Sarasakti shows that the kingdom was again
reduced to vassalage before 1412, and that Indarājā sent one of
his own men to Sukhodaya as Chief Resident to keep the vassal
king under control (Griswold and Prasert 1968:229–240).

Upon Sai Ḷ̣īdaiya's death in 1419 his son Pāla Möaṅ disputed
the throne of the vassal kingdom with another prince. The
suzerain power intervened and awarded the throne to Pāla
Möaṅ (Mahādharmarājā IV). In 1438, when the latter died,
the kingdôm of Sukhodaya was abolished and its territories
incorporated into those of Ayudhyā.

But the Sukhodayan provinces long remained turbulent.
The descendants of Rāma Gāṃheṅ, in desperate gambles to
throw off an oppressive yoke, more than once joined Ayudhyā's
enemies. One of them—yet another Mahādharmarājā—allied
himself with the Burmese invaders who stormed the capital in
1569, and was then crowned King of Ayudhyā as their vassal.
His son and successor, Naresvara (r. 1590–1605), in whose
veins flowed the royal blood of both Sukhodaya and Ayudhyā,

united the country and expelled the Burmese. He could hardly have done so without a thorough understanding of both Sukhodayan and Ayudhyan behavior.

Conclusion

Even if Sukhodayans were temperamentally unable to see any virtue in the Ayudhyan system of administration, everything in it that was most repugnant to them—its laws with their set formulas, its disregard of freedom and human values, its swarms of busybodies intruding into everyone's affairs—had another side: more than any other single factor, probably, this system made Ayudhyā the strongest kingdom in Southeast Asia and kept it alive for over four hundred years in spite of defeats, *coups d'état*, dynastic changes, and the folly of more than one king. Though the successive rulers could make any appointments in the bureaucracy they wished, its sheer size and weight made it impervious to any sudden change of policy. If it hampered the initiative of vigorous monarchs, it limited the harm that incompetent ones could do; and it enabled the kingdom to recover quickly from overwhelming disasters. Though the bureaucracy was often corrupt and inefficient, it nevertheless must have contained many devoted civil servants whose names have long been forgotten. While it imposed a uniform mediocrity on the kingdom, it also imposed a uniform order; "organization men" tended more and more to replace strong personalities; and the vassals, whose territories at the beginning were far larger than those ruled by the Crown's appointees, were converted one by one into government officials.

By 1600 the kingdom of Ayudhyā, though still composed of peoples who differed in their language and their outlook on life, had achieved national stability on the basis of fixed institutions. That was something that Sukhodaya, for all its subtlety and brilliance, all its warmth and courage, never managed to do. It took Ayudhyā 250 years; Sukhodaya did not have time.

GLOSSARY

In this paper we use a single system of transliteration for Sanskrit, Pali, Khmer, and Siamese. This is the "Graphic" system in general use among scholars for Sanskrit and Pali, which has been extended by epigraphists to serve for Khmer and Siamese as well. See *Journal of the Siam Society*, 56, Part 2 (1968), 245–247. In transliterating Siamese we have omitted tone markers.

The entries in this glossary are given in alphabetical order, in the transliterated form used in our paper, usually followed by their equivalents in the phonemic transcription used for Thai elsewhere in this volume. Most of the entries are Sanskrit or Pali, or Siamese borrowings from those languages; some are Khmer; some are T'ai. The origin, when known, is indicated by an abbreviation: Skt. (Sanskrit), P. (Pali), K. (Khmer), or T. (T'ai). The glossary does not include such well-known names as Bangkok, Siam, or the rivers Ping, Yom, and Sak, for which we use the common spelling. Nor does it include the names of authors, which we have tried to transcribe in accordance with their own preferences.

abhiṣeka (aphisēk): Skt., consecration of a king.
āgama (ākhom): Skt., a term applied to the scriptures and theological manuals of the principal Hindu sects.
Anurādhapura: Skt., the old capital of Ceylon.
Ayodhyā (Ayōtthayā): Skt., (1) legendary city in India, ruled by King Rāma; (2) old name of Ayudhyā in Siam.
Ayudhyā (Ayutthyā): modern name of the city that was the capital of Siam from 1351 to 1767 (see Map 1).
Bejrapurī (Phetchaburī): Skt., *vajrapurī* 'adamantine city'; town and province southwest of Bangkok (Map 1).
Biṣṇuloka (Phitsanulōk): Skt., Viṣṇuloka 'world of Viṣṇu'; town and province east of Sukhodaya (Maps 1 and 2).
Bodhisattva: Skt., person who has made the "great resolve" to become a Buddha in a future incarnation.
bò khun (phōkhun): T., 'king', 'ruler'.

braḥ (phra): 'sacred', etc. (often used as an honorific); from Skt. *vara* (?).

Braḥ Khbuṅ (Phrakhaphung): braḥ + Khmer *khbuṅ* 'exalted'; name of a mountain near Sukhodaya on which the tutelary spirit of the kingdom resided.

braḥ pāda (phrabāt): Skt.; 'sacred feet'; (1) element in royal titles; (2) Footprint of the Buddha.

Braḥ Pāṅ (Phrabāng): old name of Nagara Svarga (Maps 1 and 2).

Braḥ Rvaṅ (Phrarūang): name by which several kings of Sukhodaya are called, in particular Rāma Gāṃhèṅ (Rāmkhamhāeng).

Brè (Phrāe): T., town in northern Thailand (Map 1).

cā khā (čhākhā): *cā* 'officer' + *khā* 'slaves'.

caturaṅga (čhatturong): Skt., 'four branches of an army' (elephantry, chariotry, cavalry, infantry). K., *caturaṅg* 'an army'; *catraṅg* 'the game of chess'.

Cau Ū Dòṅ (Čhao Ūthōng): T., 'Prince [of] Ū Dòṅ'.

Chòt (Chōt): old name of Mè Sòt (Māesǫt), town in west-central Thailand (Maps 1 and 2).

Debanagara (Thēpnakhǫn): Skt., *Devanagara* 'city of the gods'; (1) appellation of any capital city; (2) name given to Labapurī c. 1319.

Dhammasattha (Thammasat): P., Pali adaptation of a Sanskrit Dharmaśāstra.

Dharmaśāstra (Thammasāt): Skt., a treatise on the Dharma.

Dharmasātra (Thammasāt): hybrid form of Dharmaśāstra (Skt.) and Dhammasattha (P.).

Dvāravatī (Thawārawadī): Skt., 'possessing gates'; (1) legendary capital of the god Kṛṣṇa; (2) a Mòn-ruled kingdom in central Siam, c. 7th–10th century.

Dvisākhā: P., 'two branches'; sc., the confluence of two branches of a river. Used in Pali texts to translate the name Sòṅ Gvè (q.v.).

Fā-Rua (Fārua): T., 'the sky is leaking'; sc., pouring out blessings. Rāma Gāṃhèṅ conferred the title Prince Fā-Rua on his son-in-law Makado (q.v.).

Gāṃ Ṭǎn (Khamtan): 'solid gold'; King of Nān 1387–1396.

Gandī (Khonthī): perhaps from P. *gaṇḍī* 'tree-trunk' or 'wooden percussion instrument'. Name of a town on the Ping (Map 2).

Garuḍa (khrut): Skt., mythical bird associated with the sun's rays.

hāṅ vāv (hāngwāo): T., 'kite's tail'.

Haripuñjaya (Haripunchai): Skt. and P., old name of Lāmbūn (Map 1), capital of a small kingdom ruled by a Mòn dynasty from about the 8th century to 1292.

Huṅ (Hung): King of Nān 1398–1405.

Indarājā (Intharāchā): P., *inda* 'lord' (epithet of Sakka, king of the Tāvatiṃsa heaven) + *rājā* 'king'; King of Ayudhyā 1409–1424.

Jaliaṅ (Chalīang): K., (1) alternative name of the old city of Sajjanālaya; (2) the portion of Sajjanālaya that lay about 1.2 miles east of the walled city; see Map 2; (3) name commonly applied to a ware with a heavy dark-brown or dark-green glaze produced at the potteries of Sajjanālaya.

Jayanāda (Chaināt): Skt. and P., 'roar of victory'; (1) town and province north of Subarṇapurī; (2) one of the old names of Biṣṇuloka.

Jayaśrī (Chaisī): Skt., goddess of victory; in Khmer and Siamese, a sacred sword that was a part of a ruler's regalia.

Jiaṅ Hmäi (Chīangmai): T., 'new city'; town and province in northern Thailand (Map 1).

Jiaṅ Rāy (Chīangrāi): T., town and province in northern Thailand (Map 1).

Jyotiśāstra: a Sanskrit treatise on astronomy.

Kāṃbèṅ Bejra (Kamphāēngphet): K. *kaṃbèṅ* 'walls' + Skt. *vajra* 'adamant'; town in north-central Thailand (Maps 1 and 2).

kamrateṅ añ: K., 'our lord'; a Khmer royal or viceregal title.

Kāv (Kāo): T., branch of the T'ai living in the upper Nān valley.

Kīrtimukha: Skt., 'glory face'; a demon's head.

Kruṅ Deb (Krungthēp): K. *kruṅ* 'city' + Skt. *deva* 'god'; (1) appellation of any capital city; (2) Bangkok.

kṣatriya (kasat): Skt., member of the warrior or princely caste.

Labapurī (Lopburī): Skt., Lavapurī; town and province in central Thailand (Map 1).

Lavo: doublet of Labapurī.

Lāmbūn (Lamphūn): town and province in northern Thailand (Map 1).

Lān Nā (Lānnā): T., 'a million fields'; sc., a thousand districts, each of which was conventionally called *băn nā* (*phannā*) 'a thousand fields'; kingdom which formerly controlled northern Siam.

Līdaiya (Līthai or Lūethai): Sanskritized form of the personal name of Mahādharmarāja I of Sukhodaya, r. 1347–c. 1370.

Lödaiya (Lȫthai): partially Sanskritized form of the personal name of Rāma Gāṃhèṅ's son, king of Sukhodaya from 1298(?) to about 1347.

lūk khun (lūkkhun): T., term used in the Sukhodaya period for officials and vassal lords.

Mahābrahma (Mahāphrom): Skt. and P., 'Great Brahmā'; (1) name of a god; (2) name of a prince of Jiaṅ Rāy.

Mahādharmarājā (Mahāthammarāchā): abbreviated form of the title Mahādharmarājādhirāja (q.v.).

Mahādharmarājādhirāja (Mahāthammarāchāthirāt): Skt., 'great king of kings in accordance with the Dharma'; (1) title of several kings of Sukhodaya; (2) after 1438, title of the viceroys of Biṣṇuloka.

mahādhātu (mahāthāt): Skt. and P., 'great relic' or 'great reliquary'; term used for a major relic of the Buddha and for a monument in which such a relic is deposited.

mahāthera (mahāthēn or mahāthēra): P., 'great elder'; designation for a monk who has spent at least ten years in the order and passed a certain course of studies.

Mahāthūpa: P., 'great stupa'; a famous monument at Anurādhapura in Ceylon.

Mahāyāna (Mahāyān): Skt., 'Greater Vehicle'; the so-called Northern School of Buddhism, which is predominant in Tibet, China, and Japan, and which at times enjoyed royal favor in Cambodia.

Makado (Makathō): a trader from Martaban who entered the service of Rāma Gaṃhèṅ, rose rapidly, and eloped with his daughter. In 1281 he made himself king of Martaban; in 1287, having made himself king of all Rāmaññadesa, he received the abhiṣeka as a vassal of Sukhodaya, together with the title Prince Fā-Rua, which the King of Sukhodaya bestowed on him through ambassadors.

Manu (Manū): Skt., the Indian sage to whom the Dharma was miraculously revealed.

mātrā (māttrā): Skt., 'measure, quantity, size', etc.; in Siamese, a section or clause of law.

Mè Khoṅ (Maēkhong): name of the largest river in Southeast Asia; commonly written Mekong (see Map 1).

Meru (Mēn): Skt. and P., legendary mountain in India, symbolic center of the Hindu world. According to Theravāda tradition, the Tāvatiṃsa heaven was located on its summit. In Siamese, the term also means a royal funeral pyre.

miṅ hmau (muengmao): in the old T'ai calendar, the designation of a particular day in the 60-day cycle, or of a particular year in the 60-year cycle.

möaṅ (muēang): T., 'community, city, province, principality, kingdom'.

Möaṅ Rāt (Muēangrāt): T., Phā Möaṅ's capital, probably near Uttaratittha.

mun nāy (munnāi): in Ayudhyā's administrative system, a group chief.

Nāga (Nāk): Skt. and P., a class of supernatural creatures, part serpent and part human in form, usually living under the earth or the waters.

Nagara Paṭhama (Nakhōnpathom): P., 'the first city'; town and province west of Bangkok, named in honor of a famous monument, the Paṭhamacetiya (P., 'first monument'), built in the 19th century on the remains of a monument regarded as the oldest Buddhist structure in Siam (see Map 1).

Nagara Śrī Dharmarāja (Nakhōn Sīthammarāt): Skt., 'city of the glorious king of righteousness'; town and province in southern Thailand.

Nagara Svarga (Nakhōn Sawan): Skt., 'city of heaven'; town and province in north-central Thailand (Map 1).

Nān: town in northern Thailand and the river on which it is located (Map 1).

Nareśvara (Narēsūan): Skt., 'lord of men' (nara + īśvara); King of Siam 1590–1605.

Ñī Pā (Yība): the last Mòn king of Haripuñjaya.

Ñua Nāṃ Thaṃ (Ngūanamthom): T., a usurper who reigned over Sukhodaya for a short time in 1347.

Pāla Möaṅ (Bānmuēang): 'guardian of the kingdom' (Skt. and P., pāla 'guardian' + T., möaṅ); Mahādharmarājā IV, vassal king of Sukhodaya 1419–1438.

paṇḍita (bandit): Skt. and P., a learned man.

Pāṅ Klāṅ Hāv (Bāngklānghāo): T., name by which Rāma Gāṃhèṅ's father (Śrī Indrāditya) was known before becoming king of Sukhodaya.

Pān Möaṅ (Bānmūeang): king of Sukhodaya, elder brother and predecessor of Rāma Gāṃhèṅ.

Paramacakrabartirāja: Skt., *parama* 'most excellent' + *cakravartirāja* 'a ruler whose chariot wheels roll everywhere without obstruction', a 'universal king'; part of the titulature of several kings of Ayudhyā, who probably adopted it from the kings of Lavo.

Paramarājā (Borommarāchā): Skt. and P., 'most excellent king'; Paramarājā I was King of Ayudhyā 1370–1388.

Phā Kòṅ (Phākǫng): T., 'mass of rock'; King of Nān 1361–1388.

Phā Möaṅ (Phāmūeang): T., 'rock of the kingdom'; ally of Pāṅ Klāṅ Hāv in liberating Sukhodaya from Khmer suzerainty in the first half of the 13th century.

Piṭaka (pidok): Skt. and P., 'basket'; one of the three main divisions of the Pali Canon (Vinaya, Suttanta, and Abhidhamma). They are collectively called Tipiṭaka (P.), Traipiṭaka (Skt.) or Tripiṭaka (Skt.) 'the three baskets' (as containers of tradition).

puñña (bun): P., 'merit'.

rai: T., a measure of land, now standardized at 1600 square meters (about 2/5 of an acre), but formerly a little smaller.

Rājapurī (Rātchaburī): Skt., 'royal city'; town and province southwest of Bangkok (Map 1).

Rājasāstra (Rāchasāt): Skt., term used in the early Ayudhyā period for a law promulgated by the king.

Rājasātra (Rāchasāt): hybrid form of Rājasāstra (Skt.) and Rājasattha (P.).

Rājasattha (Rāchasat): P., (1) in Burma, a class of literary works dealing with the art of kingship; (2) in Ayudhyā, a term used for a law promulgated by the king.

Rāma (Rām): Skt., legendary Indian ideal king, whose example all monarchs were supposed to follow. Numerous Siamese kings were named after him.

Rāmādhipati (Rāmāthibodi): Skt., Rāma + *adhipati* 'lord'; Rāmādhipati I was King of Ayudhyā 1351–1369.

Rāma Gāṃhèṅ (Rāmkhamhaēng): Rāma + K. *gāṃhèṅ* 'bold'; King of Sukhodaya 1279(?)–1298.

Rāmakīrti (Rāmakīen): Skt., 'the fame of Rāma'; name of several

Siamese poetical works dealing with the legend of the Indian hero Rāma. They are only vaguely related, if at all, to Vālmīki's Rāmāyana.

Rāmaññadesa: P., name for the Mòn country of Lower Burma; from the Mòn word *rmeñ* 'Mòn' + P., *desa* 'country'.

Rāmarājādhirāja (Rāmrāchāthirāt): Skt., 'Rāma, King of Kings'; King of Ayudhyā 1395–1409.

Rāmāyana: Skt., Rāma + *ayana* 'goings'; celebrated Sanskrit epic by Vālmīki, of which the legendary Rāma is the hero.

Rāmeśvara (Rāmēsūan): Skt., 'Rāma the master' (Rāma + *īśvara*); King of Ayudhyā 1369–1370 and 1388–1395.

sahāya (sahāi): Skt. and P., 'companion, friend, ally, follower, helper', etc.

Sai Ḷīdaiya (Sailīthai, Sailūethai): personal name of Mahādharmarājā III of Sukhodaya (c. 1398–1419). He was evidently named for his grandfather Ḷīdaiya (Mahādharmarājā I); the term *sai* shows he was the fourth son of his father.

Sajjanālaya (Satchanālai): P., 'abode of good people', or perhaps P., *sajanālaya* 'abode of the kinsmen' (the king usually appointed one of his sons to rule the city); the second most important city in the kingdom of Sukhodaya, surpassed only by the capital (Maps 1 and 2).

śakarāja (sakkarāt): Skt., 'era'. The Buddhist Era (Buddhaśakarāja), as used in the inscriptions of Sukhodaya, begins in 544 B.C.; the Great Era (Mahāśakarāja) begins in 78 A.D.; the Little Era (Cūlaśakarāja) begins in 638 A.D.

śakti-nā (sakdinā): Skt., *śakti* 'energy, power', etc. + T., *nā* 'ricefields'; in the Ayudhyan system the term refers to "dignity marks."

samtec (somdet): K., *saṃtac*, a title of high rank.

saṅgharāja (sangkharāt): P., *saṅgha* 'monkhood' + *rāja* 'ruler'; in the Sukhodaya period the title signified the head of a monastic order or sect in a given province.

Saraśakti (Sǭrasak): Skt., *sara* 'motion', etc. + *śakti* 'power'. Nāy Saraśakti was the title of an Ayudhyan official stationed at Sukhodaya in the second decade of the 15th century. He built a monastery there.

śāstra (sāt): Skt., a technical manual on any aspect of Hindu learning and science, both religious and secular.

Sèn Möaṅ Mā (Saēnmūeangmā): T., King of Lān Nā 1385–1401.

skā (sakā): K., *skā* or *pǎskā* (from Skt., *pāśaka* 'a die'), a game of dice. In Siamese it means a game something like backgammon.

Sòṅ Gvè (Sǭngkhwāē): T., 'two branches'; sc., the confluence of two branches of a river; name of Biṣṇuloka in the Sukhodaya period.

Sralvaṅ (Salūang): K(?), town between Sukhodaya and Biṣṇuloka.

śrī (sī): Skt., 'luster, glory, fortune', etc.; an honorific used in many contexts.

Śrī Indrāditya (Sī-intharāthit): Skt., *indra* 'king' or 'god' + *āditya* 'Sun'; first ruler of the independent kingdom of Sukhodaya.

Subarṇapurī (Suphanburī): Skt., *suvarṇapurī* 'city of gold'; town and province in central Thailand (Map 1).

subhāpati (suphābǫdi): Skt., *sabhāpati*, president of an assembly or court.

Sukhodaya (Sukhōthai): Skt., 'resulting in happiness' (*sukha* 'happiness' + *udaya* 'creation'); town and province in Central Thailand (Maps 1 and 2). This town was the capital of a kingdom of the same name which gained its independence under a T'ai dynasty in the first half of the 13th century.

Śukranīti: Sanskrit treatise on political science.

Sūryavaṃśa (Sūriyawong): Skt., 'the solar race' (*sūrya* 'the Sun' + *vaṃśa* 'race'. According to legend, the dynasty of the Indian King Rāma belonged to this race.

Svargaloka (Sawankhalōk): Skt., 'realm of heaven'; (1) a town, formerly the capital of the province in which the ruins of Sajjanālaya are located; (2) name commonly applied to the glazed celadons and painted wares produced at the Sajjanālaya kilns.

Syām (Sayām): an old name of the T'ai people, first attested in an 11th-century inscription from Champa; more particularly, the group of T'ai who settled in the Sukhodaya region.

Tāk: town and province in northern Thailand. Old Tāk is located on the right bank of the Ping, about 15 miles upstream from the present town of Tāk (Maps 1 and 2).

Tāvatiṃsa (Dāwadueng): P., 'thirty-three'; the heaven of the thirty-three gods whose chief is Sakka (Indra), located on the summit of Mount Meru.

Theravāda: P., 'Doctrine of the Elders', the Southern School of Buddhism, predominant in Ceylon, Burma, Siam, Cambodia, and Laos; Pali is its sacred language. Also called Hīnayāna (:'Lesser Vehicle') in contrast to the Mahāyāna.

Traibhūmikathā (Traiphūmikathā): Skt., 'Discourse of the Three Worlds', treatise on Buddhist cosmology and ethics composed by Prince Ḷīdaiya at Sajjanālaya in 1345.

Traitriṅsa (Traitrueng): town on the Ping (see Map 2). The name is a hybrid between Skt. Trayastriṅsa and P. Tāvatiṃsa, both of which refer to Sakka's heaven.

Ū Dòṅ (Ūthǭng): T., 'source of gold'; town west of Subarṇapurī, formerly called Carakhe Sām Băn (Čhǫrakhēsāmphan), T., 'three thousand crocodiles'.

uparāja (upparāt): Skt. and P., a viceroy.

Uttaratittha (Uttaradit): P., 'northern ford' or 'northern river-crossing'; town and province in northern Thailand (Maps 1 and 2).

Vaisākha (Waisākha): Skt., the sixth lunar month (April–May).

văt (wat): temple or monastery; perhaps from P., vatta 'religious service', or from P., vatthu 'place, property'.

Văt Hnā Braḥ Meru (Wat Nāphramēn): 'monastery in front of the sacred funeral pyre'; a monastery at Ayudhyā.

Viaṅ Căn (Wīangchan): town in Laos (Map 1).

Vṛddhipāsaśāstra: Sanskrit treatise on elephant hunting, Skt., vṛddhi 'success', etc., + pāśa 'noose' or 'trap' + śāstra 'treatise'.

yantra (yon): Skt., 'instrument, apparatus, device, machine, engine', etc.

Yvan (Yūan): branch of the T'ai who settled in Lān Nā.

2. Clientship and Class Structure in the Early Bangkok Period[1]

AKIN RABIBHADANA

This paper considers two aspects of the relationship between clientship and class structure during the Early Bangkok period, 1782–1873, when Thailand was in the last stages of its indigenous development and had been little influenced by Western ideas and standards. Clientship refers to a dyadic relationship in which one party, the patron, is clearly superior to the other, the client; it is an instrumental friendship, in which striving for access to resources, whether natural or social, plays a vital part (Wolf 1966a:10–17). First, clientship is considered as part of the class structure itself. Second, its development during the period in question is traced and the impact of changing patterns of clientship on stratification is explored.[2]

[1] This paper is a by-product of research carried out under Professor Sharp's supervision for the master's degree at Cornell University. I am grateful to Bernd Lambert for a critical reading of the first draft of this paper and to Richard D. Cushman and G. William Skinner for help in improving the language.

[2] The main sources for this paper are the royal decrees, royal proclamations, laws, and annals of Ayutthayā and Bangkok. Many if not most royal decrees and proclamations cite or discuss the events which give rise to them, and these events, even more than the legal content of the documents, lend empirical substance to this study. The correspondence of King Mongkut; the writings of King Chulalongkorn, Prince Damrong, and Khun Khachōn Sukkhaphānit; and the journals of foreign visitors of the period have also proved valuable. These sources are supplemented by the writer's own experience and observation of modern Thai society. This is an anthropological study of a past society, a reconstruction based on documentary evidence. The

The Control of Manpower

An important feature of society throughout the history of mainland Southeast Asia was the need for manpower, well illustrated by the events following each war between Thailand and her neighbors. The victorious side always carried off large numbers of people from the conquered country. Whole villages were often moved into the conqueror's territory, where they were eventually assimilated into the local population. The Thai in particular were keenly aware of the importance of maintaining a large population. King Rāmkhamhāēng's inscription of 1292 (Coedès 1924:51–60) can be interpreted as an advertisement inducing people to come and settle within the Sukhōthai kingdom.[3] The rules given to the governor of Nakhǭn Sīthammarāt in 1784 emphasized the duty of the governor to commit to memory the number of *lēk* (male commoners) in his province, and to prevent pirates and enemies from carrying off any of the population.[4] The sensitiveness of the Thai in regard to their lack of manpower is reflected in a metaphor used by Somdetčhaophrayā Sīsuriyawong, as re-

sources themselves inevitably shape our perceptions. Data are much fuller on nobles and princes than on the peasants who constituted the bulk of the population. Furthermore, the view of society as recorded in documentary sources is biased by their authorship: the great majority were written by members of the upper classes. Given the limitations of evidence, the conclusions presented here must be considered tentative.

[3] Professor O. W. Wolters, to whom I owe this observation, tells me that he is grateful in turn to E. H. S. Simmonds of the School of Oriental and African Studies, University of London.

[4] The rules stated: "He [the Governor] should frequently read the list of lēk, and commit to memory their number so that, when needed for government duty, they can be readily called into service. Should lēk of any *mū* [platoon] or *kǭng* [battalion] out of laziness run away to hide in forests or hilly areas, thereby avoiding marking and government service, the Governor should appoint loyal officials to go out to them and persuade them to come and settle down in an inhabited area and contribute to its prosperity."

"If the Yūan [Vietnamese], pirates, or [other] enemies come to take away our people, the Governor must resist. . . . Do not let the enemy take away any of our people" (*Prachum phongsāwadān* 1963, part 2, vol. 1: 475, 477).

ported by Sir John Bowring: "In a large house with many servants, the door may safely be left open; in a small house with few servants, the doors must be shut" (Bowring 1857, vol. 1 :465).

By the Early Bangkok period the core of the Thai kingdom was the large alluvial plain of the Čhaophrayā River, which was regularly flooded each year. But while the country was well endowed with fertile arable land, its population remained small and relatively mobile.[5] The crucial problems in establishing a viable kingdom in the area revolved around the mobilization and control of manpower. Manpower was necessary not only to develop and cultivate the land but also to fill the ranks of the military, for the area was subjected to continual warfare, success in which depended on the amount of manpower a state could mobilize rapidly. The Thai response to this organizational necessity was to require that everyone be registered under a *nāi* 'master', one of whose duties was to lead those registered under him into battle at the command of the king.[6] The category of persons obligated to register under a nāi was called *phrai*, consisting for the most part of ordinary peasants, while people of the nāi category were princes and the nobles.

The most important duty of a nāi was to produce the phrai registered under him when so ordered by the government, and not only in time of war. As there was no organized police force, the nāi was also required to produce his phrai for trial in a court of law. Thus, whenever anyone instituted a legal proceeding

[5] For estimates of Thailand's population, see Wales (1934:8); Crawfurd (1915:102); Pallegoix (1854, vol. 1 :7–8).

[6] Clause 10, Laksana Rapphǫng (Law on the Reception of Plaints), states: "When anyone institutes a legal proceeding who is not registered under any nāi, do not examine the case or give judgment. Send that man to the *satsadī* [registrar] to be registered as a phrai lūang." Clause 4, Laksana Āyā Lūang (Law on Crimes against the Government), states: "In the event of a royal order to mobilize men for war, if any nāi fails to bring his men to battle but takes money from them instead . . . , one of the eight types of punishment shall be imposed" (Lingat 1938b, vol. 2 :373).

against a phrai, the court sent a warrant of arrest to his nāi, and punishment was prescribed for a nāi who disobeyed the court's order (Lingat 1938b, vol. 1:297; vol. 2:296–298).

Originally, all phrai were considered the property of their nāi (see Lingat 1938b, vol. 2:125–126). Later, however, they were distinguished into two types, *phrai som* and *phrai lūang*. Phrai som constituted a part of the property of an individual nāi in the sense that he could sell them or give them away (see Sīwǫrawat 1963:371; Lingat 1938b, vol. 3:370). Phrai lūang, on the other hand, belonged in theory to the king. In fact, however, a given phrai lūang was registered as belonging to a particular office whose incumbent became his nāi. Being the king's phrai, phrai lūang were obligated to do corvée labor, called *rātchakān* (royal service), for six months of each year,[7] and it was the responsibility of the nobles, their nāi, to produce them for this purpose. One subset of phrai lūang, called *phrai sūai*, were exempt from corvée. This class of clients lived in areas that produced products (such as gunpowder) of particular importance to the government. Phrai sūai were required to supply the government with a fixed amount of the product each year in lieu of corvée (Damrong 1959:12). What distinguished phrai lūang from phrai som, then, was the service directly owed the government, plus the fact that their nāi had power over them only as long as he held the relevant official position.

Broad powers were given by law to the nāi over his phrai. In all cases, phrai had to obey the command of their nāi (Lingat 1938b, vol. 2:418) and could be punished by them. Thus a royal proclamation of King Mongkut specified that a nāi should put into custody any phrai lūang who had misbehaved or was of bad character, securing him with chains in the case

[7] Only the male phrai were required to serve corvée. Every phrai lūang had to serve every other month, for a total of six months a year. In the reign of King Rāma II, this requirement was reduced to one month in every four, for a total of three months a year. A phrai began to serve corvée at the age of twenty and was allowed to go into retirement when he reached sixty, or when he had three sons serving corvée.

of a phrai som[8] (Mongkut 1960–1961, vol. 2:254–257). Because the nāi had to produce his phrai at the demand of the government, the movements of phrai were restricted. They could travel from one province to another only with the permission of their nāi (see Lingat 1938b, vol. 3:352). Further, it was laid down by law that no one should hire or use the services of a phrai without the permission of his nāi (Lingat 1938b, vol. 2:237–239). Thus John Crawfurd (1915:135) complained that in 1821 there was no free labor in the capital, for the labor of every person was appropriated by some chief or other, without whose approval he could not work; (see also Mongkut 1960–1961, vol. 1:231).

The group consisting of a nāi and his corps of dependent phrai constituted the basic unit of political organization. Such units were combined to form larger ones, extending in many cases to several nested levels: large *krom*, small *krom*, *kǫng*, and *mū*. This structure may be compared to an army: large krom were comparable to divisions, small krom to regiments, kǫng to battalions, and mū to platoons. Nāi were the equivalent of officers, phrai the counterpart of ordinary soldiers. This comparison is apt, for the Thai themselves conceived of the system in military terms. The original meaning of the word for minister, *sēnābǫdī*, was "army general" (Damrong 1959:10). As with an army, too, the hierarchical structure was expressed in chains of command, the phrai being obligated to obey the orders of their nāi, who in turn were responsible to their superiors (Lingat 1938b, vol. 2:418). It should be noted explicitly, however, that the premodern Thai system was used for civil administration as well as for warfare.

In keeping with the differences between phrai lūang and

---

[8] This royal proclamation of 1860 contains advice directed to the nāi of Bangkok. The nāi of phrai lūang were told to put those of their phrai who showed bad character in the main prison at Krom Mūeang, while the nāi of phrai som were told to put such a phrai in chains or in the prison of any krom that maintained one. It was a function of Krom Mūeang to keep the peace within the area of the capital.

phrai som, there were two types of krom. In the Early Bangkok period, the majority of phrai were phrai lūang in the various krom of the central and provincial administration. Phrai som, on the other hand, belonged for the most part to princes, and these too were often organized into krom. Rather than services for the king (corvée), phrai som rendered services for their nāi, the prince. This system developed in the days when princes governed townships as tributary states, as was standard practice during the Ayutthayā period up to 1569. In the traditional concept of *mūeang* (princely township) as opposed to the modern concept of *čhangwat* (province), the emphasis was on people rather than territory. Even after mūeang were brought under direct central control, princes continued to be given men as their phrai som to perform services comparable to those rendered by the populations of the townships they once ruled. In Thai law, a mūeang was equated with a krom.

The most exalted and important of the princely krom was that of the Upparāt, normally an uncle, brother, or son of the king. The system of ranks and titles of the Upparāt's officials was a close replica of the king's, albeit on a much smaller scale (Damrong 1963a:153–155). While the number of princely krom varied from one reign to another, it was always sizable. These krom had no administrative function. When a prince, the owner of a krom, was sent out to do battle, the men belonging to that krom went with him under his direct command. In peacetime, a prince's krom existed only for his upkeep and dignity.

The krom of phrai lūang were organized into a single hierarchy, culminating in the person of the king. Below him, there were two chief ministers. The Samuha Nāyok (Chief Minister of the North) controlled the northern provinces, and the Samuha Kalāhōm controlled the southern provinces. (Here, the provinces may be seen as a special type of krom whose importance was a function of population size.) Besides the two chief ministers, there were four others, each of whom headed a major krom. They were the ministers of Khlang (Treasury Department), Wang (Palace Department), Mūeang (Department of the Inner Kingdom), and Nā (Department of Land). By the beginning of the Early Bangkok period, the duties of the minister of Khlang had undergone many changes. The position originated as comptroller of the royal treasury. To this responsibility were added the duties of outfitting the royal cargo ships and dealing with foreign emissaries and merchants. Toward the end of Ayutthayā period, the minister of Khlang was given administrative responsiblity for a number of coastal provinces. Thus, in the Early Bangkok period, the Samuha Nāyok, the Samuha Kalāhōm, and the minister of Khlang each governed provinces, collected taxes, and maintained law and order in a section of the country. Central duties of the other three ministers were supervising the royal household (Wang), promoting agriculture and collecting the land tax (Nā), and keeping law and order in the immediate vicinity of the capital (Mūeang) (Chulalongkorn 1927). In addition to these six major krom, others of less importance were attached directly to the king, and of course each of the major krom comprised numerous subsidiary krom.

The above description overemphasizes functional differentiation among krom and might suggest that, like a department in a modern bureaucracy, each was established for a particular specialized purpose. This was hardly the case. Not only were the functions of a particular krom continually shifted, but within a single higher-order krom, it was not uncommon for several subordinate krom to have similar or overlapping functions, while others lacked functions altogether. Of the five subsidiary krom within Krom Mahātthai, Prince Damrong found that three had identical functions, while officials of the other two had no particular duties apart from controlling the krom's phrai lūang. (1959:33–36). Furthermore, during the Early Bangkok period, when the phrai som of a deceased prince were transformed en masse into phrai lūang, the usual procedure was to establish a new krom as a subsidiary to one of the major krom (Chulalongkorn 1927).

That the main purpose in establishing a krom was to exercise control over manpower may be seen in the various regulations applicable to all krom and their members. Every male phrai had to be marked with the name of his nāi and the name of the province where he resided.[9] The marking of the phrai was considered one of the most important affairs of the state. It was carried out at the beginning of each reign, supervised by one or more officials appointed especially for the purpose. In the reign of King Mongkut, the two nobles of highest rank in the realm, *somdetčhaophrayā*, were appointed to oversee the marking of the phrai (Mongkut 1960–1961, vol. 1:136–140). Every krom was required to maintain a list of its phrai, and the registrar (Samuha Banchī) who kept the list was considered one of its major officials. Any change in the list had to be made in the presence of the three most important officials of the krom and witnessed by the impression of their seals (Lingat 1938b, vol. 3:303; vol. 1:289). A central registrar (Phrasuratsawadī), who held the rolls of all phrai of all krom, was responsible directly to the king. Moreover, the two chief ministers held the rolls of all phrai of all krom within their respective sections of the country. Keeping track of the precise number of men and their distribution among the various krom within their jurisdiction appears to have been their major duty.[10]

[9] Damrong (1962, vol. 2:353) places the institution of the marking of all phrai in the year 1773 (see also Thailand, Krom sinlapākǭn 1964:689). This was followed by a royal decree of 1774 (Lingat 1938b, vol. 3:231–232) laying down the death penalty for those making counterfeit tattoo needles.

[10] King Chulalongkorn states: "The administration of our country traditionally had six ministers of whom two were designated chief ministers. The Samuha Kalāhōm had authority over all military krom; the Samuha Nāyok had authority over all civil krom. . . . It might be expected that the former had responsibility and authority over all military affairs, while the latter had responsibility and authority over all civil affairs. But from the events recorded in the Annals, it does not appear to have been so. They appeared rather to be registrars of the population of the military and the

In sum, manpower was the critical resource in premodern Thailand. Control of a substantial amount of manpower brought in wealth, and nobles and princes were dependent for their livelihood on the gifts and services of their phrai. Furthermore, in the absence of sophisticated weapons, control of manpower was the base of all military and, by extension, political power, and balance in its distribution was essential for the security of the king. In order to prevent high-ranking officials, who necessarily commanded a large aggregation of manpower, from joining forces against the throne, there were laws forbidding their private contact with one another. Moreover, each was encouraged to inform the king of any illegal action committed by another. To further ensure their loyalty, such officials were required every year to imbibe the imprecated water in a ritual of allegiance to the king (Lingat 1938b, vol. 1:84–85).

Stratification

Control of manpower and its distribution was built into the ranking system, which covered the entire population. Four related methods of ranking were used: *yot* (titular rank), *tamnaēng* (government position), *rātchathinnām* (honorific name), and *sakdinā*.

The yot for princes (*čhao*) were *čhaofā* (royal offspring of a queen or a princess), *phra-ongčhao* (royal offspring of a concubine), and *mōmčhao* (offspring of a čhaofā or phra-ongčhao). The titles of *mōmrātchawong* (offspring of mōmčhao) and *mōmlūang* (offspring of mōmrātchawong) were established in the reign of King Mongkut and were not considered to be full-fledged čhao (Damrong 1929:4–5; Mongkut 1960–1961, vol. 3:235–237). A čhaofā or phra-ongčhao could be given a pri-

---

civil groups, respectively. Moreover, as to the division into the military and civil groups, although the laws in some respects distinguished between phrai lūang in the military and civil groups, in war both groups were used equally and in the same manner, so that the original purposes of such division are obscure" (1927:2–3).

vate krom, thereby attaining krom rank. The yot for nobles and petty officials, in descending order of importance, were *somdetčhaophrayā* (established in the reign of King Mongkut), *čhaophrayā, phrayā, phra, lūang, khun, mūen,* and *phan.*

The tamnāeng were the various positions in the organization. The three top positions within a krom—chief (Čhao Krom), deputy chief (Palat Krom), and registrar (Samuha Banchī)—were hierarchically ranked. Their counterparts within the administration of a province—governor (Čhao Mūeang), deputy governor (Palat), and registrar (Satsadī)—were similarly ranked. While the number of other positions within a particular krom or provincial administration varied according to its size and importance, all were unambiguously ranked in a single system. Among the tamnāeng of supreme political importance were the Upparāt, the Akkhara Mahāsēnabǫdī (chief minister), and the Sēnabǫdī (minister).

The rātchathinnām were long, imposing names bestowed by the king on his officials. Each name was attached to a particular position in a particular krom. Thus, when an official was moved from one position to another, he would also be given a new honorific.

The sakdinā was the most important and refined index of status. By this system a certain number of points—Wales has glossed them as "dignity marks"—was assigned to every person in the kingdom. These points ranged from 100,000 for the Upparāt, to 10,000 for a nonroyal minister, to 20–25 for a married phrai, and 5 for a *thāt* (slave) (see Appendix). The basic meaning of *nā* is rice field, while *sak* or *sakdi* (*shakti*) means power in the sense of resources or energy. Thus, sakdinā must have referred originally to power stemming from landholdings (Wales 1934:49). Prince Damrong has suggested that sakdinā at one time specified the upper permissible limit in rai (2.5 rai = 1 acre) on a person's landholdings. Such evidence as we have suggests a close correlation between a person's sakdinā and the number of men under his control. In any case, by the Early

Bangkok period, the sakdinā of a person, wholly unrelated to landholdings, correlated only with the number of men under his command.[11] A person of high status was said to have *yotsak*: *yot* was the rank given by the king; *sak* was power or energy. A way of accounting for a person's high status was to say that he had *bun* (merit). Bun was identified with sak, because it was only through a person's ability to exercise power that his possession of merit could be recognized (Hanks:1962). Bun, however, also carried strong moral connotations.

Given the belief that a person's status in this life depended upon the amount of bun he had accumulated in previous reincarnations, the hierarchy of positions in society was seen as part of the natural order. At the apex of society was the king, in whom inhered infinite bun and infinite sak. Thai kingship was sacred because it represented the dharma, the moral order of the society (see Akin 1969). Ranking was part of the moral order, hierarchy being maintained through the royal distribution of awards in the form of rank (yot) in accordance with the merit (bun) of each person.

The Thai conceived of the kingdom as a populace owing allegiance to a single monarch rather than as a piece of territory. This cognition reflected the relative value of manpower, which was scarce, and land, which was plentiful.[12] In societies where land is of greater importance the polity is subdivided into

---

[11] The lowest sakdinā was 5, which was that of a destitute commoner or a slave. Whether a slave had a family or not, his sakdinā remained the same for his children belonged to his master. The sakdinā of a phrai was 15 before he married, but increased to 20 and 25 when he married and had a family. A retired official, if he still possessed phrai of his own, was allowed to retain half of the sakdinā he had possessed before retirement. Wales (1934:50) goes so far as to state that the sakdinā enables one to tell the number of phrai under a nāi. Thus, supposing each of his phrai had the sakdinā of 25, a nāi of the sakdinā 400 controlled sixteen men.

[12] This is succinctly expressed in the saying "rok khon dī kwā rok yā" (to have too many men is better than to have too much grass).

regions and provinces with definite boundaries, but the Thai, focusing on manpower, subdivided the kingdom into groups of men, each with a chief. Boundaries were left vague. Underlying this organization was the theory that the king was the owner of all manpower, which he distributed among his officials according to their yot and sakdinā. Sakdinā at once mirrored the moral order and mapped the formal system of stratification.

It has been said that Thai society had four classes, *čhao* (princes), *khunnāng* (nobles), *phrai* (commoners), and *thāt* (slaves) (Wales 1934). While the hierarchical order of these four status groups was obvious to all Thai, it should be emphasized that as strata they were by no means discrete.

Čhao were descendants of the king. Their ranks were subjected to a declining descent rule ranging from that of čhaofā to that of mǫmčhao. The position of the children and grandchildren of mǫmčhao was ambiguous. They were not considered čhao, and yet, unlike the phrai, they were not marked. Their position was similar to that occupied by sons of nobles. They could be presented to the king (through the ritual of *thawāitūa*) and appointed to occupy official positions with the ranks of nobles, e.g., lūang, phra, and so on (see Appendix for sakdinā).

During the Ayutthayā period, the princes of krom rank were so powerful as to constitute a danger to the king. Their strength was based on the possession of phrai som, who became numerous during the latter half of the Ayutthayā period. The marking of phrai and related measures were originally introduced to restrict the increase of phrai som, and in time the power of the princes was reduced. After the reign of Rāma I, although some princes still controlled a considerable amount of manpower, their political power appears to have been eclipsed by that of certain nobles.[13]

---

[13] The power of the Upparāt was probably also reduced by establishing double allegiances for his officials. Many were younger, close kin of the king's most important officials (see Akin 1969).

Officials of sakdinā 400 and above were khunnāng (nobles) and performed the role of nāi. In addition, royal pages of whatever sakdinā were considered khunnāng (Chulalongkorn 1887:2) for, like officials of sakdinā 400 and above, they had passed through the ritual of thawāitūa, which involved being led into the king's presence by a person in the royal circle and making an offering to the king of tapers, incense, and flowers. Only those who had undergone this ritual could be appointed to an official position or become a royal page in attendance on the king. Even if he was not appointed to an official position or assigned to serve the king personally, a person who had performed thawāitūa would be enrolled in the Royal Pages Corps and was entitled to attend the daily royal audiences.

Sons of nobles were not marked as phrai (Lingat 1938b, vol. 1:281). There was a general expectation that they would go through the ritual and obtain official positions. If one of them did not, he would eventually lose contact with people in the royal circle. Although he himself might not be marked as phrai, his son probably would be, since the exemption from marking was limited to sons of khunnāng.

The phrai status group included the bulk of the peasants who tilled the land and cultivated rice for their own consumption. Their surplus went to support the religious establishment and their nāi, the majority of whom resided in towns or in the capital. Although it is logical to assume that phrai who had a nāi in common would reside in the same village or village ward, no clear evidence can be found on this point, and Prince Damrong asserts that manpower was not controlled on a territorial basis. In addition to nobles, each krom had many petty officials (*khunmūen*), who lived in the area where the phrai of the krom resided. Each khunmūen was responsible for the group of phrai among whom he lived (Damrong 1963b:310). These khunmūen were themselves considered to fall in the upper ranks of phrai, and their appointments and promotions were made by their *nāi* in the *krom* (Mongkut 1960–1961, vol. 1:121–122).

"Slave" is an unfortunate gloss for *thāt*, for the category covered a wider range of statuses than the English word suggests (Akin 1969:127–128). Most slaves in Thailand were in fact debt slaves, who had the right to redeem themselves at their original sale price, or at certain prices prescribed by the government. Under no circumstances were masters allowed to kill their slaves. Nor could masters in general punish their slaves in such a manner as to cause permanent injury without enabling the slaves to redeem themselves at a lower price (Lingat 1938b, vol. 2:100, 115; vol. 3:404–405). Because it was easy for a dissatisfied slave to change his master, slaves were generally well treated.[14] Phrai lūang not infrequently sold themselves into slavery to avoid the burden of corvée (Lingat 1938b, vol. 3:365–371).

A comparison of sakdinā possessed by the princes and the nobles shows that the former by no means always ranked above the latter (see Appendix). There was a similar interpenetration of phrai and thāt. A destitute person who was a phrai was given the same sakdinā as a thāt, because the sakdinā was based on the number of people under one's command. When a phrai had children of his own, his sakdinā was raised (see Lingat 1938b, vol. 1:228). A destitute person, on the other hand, by definition had sold his wife and child into slavery, and thus was given the same sakdinā as a thāt. Moreover, because prestige also depended on who the master was, it was unthinkable that the thāt of a somdet čhaophrayā or a čhaofā would rank lower than the phrai of a minor official.

The line separating nobles and commoners was not wholly clear either. The ranks of khun, mǖen, and phan could be held

---

[14] Pallegoix (1854:233–234) states that slaves were as well treated as servants in Europe, and Sir John Bowring says they were better treated than servants in England. Bowring goes on to say: "Masters cannot ill-treat their slaves, for they have always the remedy of paying the money they represent; and he must be a very worthless character who cannot get somebody to advance the sum" (1857, vol. 1:193).

by either a khunnāng or a phrai. But in general, the stratifica-
tional line between princes and nobles, on the one hand, and
commoners and slaves, on the other, was the sharpest of all. For
the most part, the Thai themselves viewed their society in
dichotomous terms,[15] and Prince Damrong wrote of the fundamental distinction between the ruling class and the ruled
(1959:12–13). Both occupation and privilege were discontinuous at this point in the stratification system. Phrai and thāt
produced goods and services; khunnāng and čhao lived off a
portion of both and devoted themselves chiefly to government
service.[16] Furthermore, a number of privileges were given to
officials of sakdinā 400 and above. They and their offspring
were exempted from being marked (Lingat 1938b, vol. 1:281).
They were allowed to mark a certain number of phrai as their
secretaries or attendants (samīanthanāi).[17] To cross the gulf that
separated commoner from noble, one had to go through the
ritual of thawāitūa. The assumption that mobility rates were
high in traditional Thailand appears to have been valid only in
times of war. In peacetime, there seems to have been very little
upward mobility from the stratum of phrai into that of nāi
(Akin 1969:185–206).

[15] The key word here is *chan*, which may usually be glossed "class." It
occurs in such phrases as "khon chan phūdī, khon chan phrai" (men of the
class that has refinement, and men of the class of phrai), "khon chan sūng,
khon chan tam" (men of high class, men of low class), and "khon chan nāi,
khon chan phrai" (people of the class of nāi, people of the class of phrai).

[16] The Thai view of a nāi as distinct from a phrai is illuminated by an
anecdote in Fung Ritthākhanī (1959). A *mūēnanurak* (a position with sakdinā
less than 400) was called to King Mongkut and asked where he had been.
He replied that he had been building barns to store up rice to sell to the
European merchants as soon as the Bowring Treaty came into force. The
King was made to say that mūēnanurak need not have troubled himself for
he would be made a noble sitting on a *tīang* (an elaborately carved bench).

[17] A royal decree of 1810 states that officials of sakdinā 1,000–1,600
were allowed to mark only three phrai as samīanthanāi, those of sakdinā
2,500–3,000 were allowed nine samīanthanāi, and those of sakdinā 10,000
were allowed fifteen to thirty (Kotmāi Chamrā Lēk [Law in Connection
with Male Phrai], in Sathīan Lāiyalak et al. 1935, vol. 4:5).

The Basis of Clientship

An important dichotomy in Thai life was between *sūng* 'high' and *tam* 'low'. A child was taught early to distinguish between the high and the low ("rūchak thī sūng thī tam"). In terms of the human body the relevant distinction was between the head and the feet. In social relations, the distinction was between *phūyai* and *phūnǭi*. When contrasted with *dek* (the young), the term *phūyai* means grown-ups. When contrasted with *phūnǭi*, it means superordinate or superior. At the national level, the relationship was based on the relative amount of sakdinā and consisted of patterns of respect. Thus King Rāma I evaluated a quarrel between two officials in these terms: "Phrayā Rāmkhamhāeng is only a phūnǭi, yet he does not respect and fear *phūyai*. He walked freely into the residence of Phrayā Sīrātchadēchō and pointed his finger over the head of the latter" (Lingat 1938b, vol. 3:380–381; the sakdinā of Phrayā Rāmkhamhāeng was 5,000, that of Phrayā Sīrātchadēchō was 10,000).

The behavior a phūnǭi should exhibit toward a phūyai may be summed up in three words: *khaorop*, *chūeafang*, and *krēngchai*. Khaorop means respect, which should be shown in both manner and words. Although chūeafang is often translated "to obey," it is more precisely rendered as "to comply with the wishes of the phūyai." Krēngchai means to fear to do anything that would displease another. Breaches of these norms were condemned as *dūthūk* (disrespect) or *dūmin* (contempt), against which sanctions were often applied immediately and severely. Chūeafang and krēngchai together imposed an obligation on the inferior not to do anything against the wishes, expressed or implied, of his superior. As a rule a phūnǭi should avoid behavior that was considered suitable toward an equal or an inferior. Thus a phūnǭi should not argue against a phūyai or proffer gratuitous advice. At the construction of Wat Phrachēttuphon in the reign of King Rāma III, an ordinary royal page warned Phrayā Sīphiphat, the supervisor of the undertaking, that the rope used for hoisting logs was too long, creating a danger that a log might swing against the wall of the building. Phrayā Sīphiphat cut him down to size by saying, "You are young and know nothing. You should not tell phūyai what to do" (Prayut 1962:87). A phūyai, on the other hand, being a morally superior person, should behave in such a manner as to gain respect from his inferiors. This usually meant that he should be calm, kind, generous, and protective toward them.

The phūyai-phūnǭi distinction pervaded the whole of Thai society. Its essence is summarized in the word *phueng* (to depend on). The Thai view of a superior seems to have contained an image of a large tree in the shade of which he could rest and be content.[18] This image was symbolically related to merit (bun), for it was under a phō tree that the Lord Buddha attained enlightenment. The word *phō* or *phōthi* was used to mean great merit, as in the phrase "phueng phraboromma phōthi somphan" (to depend on the merit of the king). Phrayā Satchāphirom (1959:14) writes of Phrayā Sīsahathēp (Thǭngpheng), a rising noble of the reign of Rāma III, that the Mons came to settle on both sides of the canal near his home to depend on his merit (*phueng bun*). The concept of *phueng* (to depend on) was an important component of the relationship between a superior and his subordinate. A person who had no *thīphueng* (someone to depend on) was unfortunate indeed.

The role of the superior in this relationship was to give protection and assistance. When King Rāma I issued a decree explaining to the phrai why they had to perform corvée, he emphasized the role of the king as the protector of the people and the religion, and in return for this protection phrai should give services to the king (Lingat 1938b, vol. 3:349).

In Thai religion the word *saksit* is used with respect to sacred Buddha images as well as powerful spirits (such as *phraphūm*,

---

[18] In traditional Thai literature, the customary wailing at the death of a person on whom one had been dependent for livelihood compared the deceased to a phō (*Ficus religiosa*) or a sai tree (*Ficus bengalensis*).

the house spirit) to indicate the possession of inherent power or efficacity. The most important manifestation of saksit is providing protection; the next most important is giving assistance. *Bon* is a major ritual associated with deities and images that have saksit. To bon is to beseech the image to do something (to protect a relative during a hazardous journey or to give success in a private project, for example) and at the same time to promise that an offering will be made if the request is granted. The initial ritual involves worshiping with incense, and when the request is granted an offering of food is usually made. If the request is not granted, no offering is made, and the person normally turns to another image or spirit.

This relationship is closely paralleled by that between a man and his superior. As with the image, high status was expressed as having sak (power or energy). The manifest behavior involved in the ritual thawāitūa was strikingly similar to that in the bon ritual. Thawāitūa literally means to give oneself to (the king). Closely related to thawāitūa is the concept of *fāktūa*, which means literally to put oneself under the care and protection of another. At present, the term carries a narrower meaning: to curry a superior's favor by giving gifts, providing services, or otherwise gratifying his wishes. But originally it referred to the creation of a personal relationship with a superior that promised to yield benefits for oneself. It amounted to a dyadic contract. A man would fāktūa with the expectation that his superior would provide protection and assistance. If the expectation was fulfilled, more gifts and services would be given. Otherwise, the man would seek to fāktūa with another person. It is probable that fāktūa was a crucial element in most patron-client relationships in traditional times.

Continuity and a semblance of permanence might be given to this relationship by the operation of a dominant value, *katanyū katawēthī*, "to remember and eventually reciprocate favors." Essentially the same concept may be expressed by the term *bunkhun*. A person was said to have made bunkhun to another when he had done something to benefit him. The recipient of the favor was obligated to do something in return. The importance of this value can be seen in the belief that a person who lacked *katanyū* should not be associated with and in any case had no future.

Clientship lay at the core of the crucial nāi-phrai relationship. On the one hand, phrai provided the gifts on which the nāi subsisted. "In general, clients [male phrai] constituted an important source of income for their masters [nāi]. If the latter did not oppress his clients but let them earn their living in peace, they would give him not inconsiderable gifts of rice, fruit, vegetables, and fish" (Pallegoix 1854, vol. 1:298).[19] On the other hand, nāi settled disputes among their phrai and provided protection and assistance.

From the great concern expressed by King Mongkut, as well as from Wales's description, it appears that the administration of official justice was sadly deficient (Mongkut 1960–1961, vol. 2:174; Wales 1934). However, Thai law allowed the settlement of disputes by arbiters acceptable to both parties, and in instituting a law suit, the nāi had to make application on behalf of his phrai (Wales 1934:184–185). A nāi, therefore, was in an ideal position to arbitrate when disputes arose among his phrai.

The evidence provided by available documents in all probability reflects only a few of the many ways in which nāi gave protection and assistance to their phrai. It is clear, however, that nāi attempted to prevent their phrai from being brought to trial and argued on their behalf when they did get involved in litigation (Lingat 1938b, vol. 2:297–298; vol. 2:396, 411). A royal decree pointed to a common practice whereby a phrai on trial at a district court in the provinces would contact his nāi in the capital as soon as he realized the hopelessness of his case,

---

[19] Pallegoix, however, misunderstood the meaning of lēk. He thought it applied only to a subset of phrai when, in fact, it applied to all male phrai (cf. Khačhōn 1962).

whereupon his nāi would send an order to the district officer, who served as judge, to send the phrai to the capital. In this manner the trial was stopped in mid-course, and the phrai escaped punishment (Lingat 1938b, vol. 3:212–217). Certain important officials provided their phrai with sealed documents for exemption from certain taxes, even when the latter were not legally entitled to them (Mongkut 1960–1961, vol. 1:260–262). A royal proclamation of King Mongkut makes it clear that powerful nobles in the capital gave extensive protection to their phrai. "When any high-ranking person whose thāt and phrai cultivate paddy fields or orchards or pasture elephants, horses, oxen, or buffaloes in the provinces, requests in writing or by word of mouth solicitous attention to his men from the township governors and their officials in such terms that the governors and township officials fear . . . even to make a report about them to the chief ministers . . . , that person is disloyal to the country" (Mongkut 1960–1961, vol. 1:147–148). It seems that the nāi of phrai lūang tried insofar as possible to help their phrai, at least those who personally pleased them, to avoid corvée altogether or to obtain a light assignment (Akin 1969:84, 133–134).

Not all nāi were model patrons, and under the circumstances it became inevitable that dissatisfied phrai should attempt to change nāi. It was to control this mobility that all phrai began to be tatooed with the name of their respective nāi.

Similar to the relationship between a nāi and his phrai was that between the king and each individual noble. To become a khunnāng—that is, an official of sakdinā 400 and above—it was necessary to go through the ritual of thawāitūa, which brought a man into the clientele of the king. Although a khunnāng was likely to be assigned to a krom where he would be under the direct command of his krom chief, he was still a royal client. It was the king, therefore, and not his direct superior, who had the power of punishment and promotion (Lingat 1938b, vol. 2:390). Normally, Thai officials were in service for life unless they were punished and demoted to phrai status by the king.

A rising noble would normally give at least one daughter to the king to serve in the royal palace or become a royal concubine (see the genealogies of noble families in Akin 1969). This act served many purposes. First, the gift of daughter could be considered potent in maintaining and strengthening the clientship. The girl herself benefited whether or not she was made a royal concubine, for she received at court training in various accomplishments that could not be acquired elsewhere. Placing a daughter at court was a source of prestige for the parents as well as for the girl herself. There was, furthermore, always the possibility that the daughter would become a favorite royal concubine, and it was obviously advantageous, especially in such keenly competitive circles, to have a kinsman close to the source of appointment. Thus women given to the kings were so numerous that the king could remember neither the faces nor the names of the great majority (Mongkut 1960–1961, vol. 3:125–127). Giving sons to become royal pages likewise had multiple advantages to a noble client. In addition to those paralleling the gift of daughters, sons went through the ritual of thawāitūa and were eligible to be appointed to important official positions later on.

The society can therefore be seen as consisting of a hierarchy of clientships. It had two major levels. When the society is categorized as having two classes, the phrai, clients of the nāi, were members of the lower class, while the nāi, clients of the king, were members of the upper class. In this manner was clientship built into the class structure.

The Development of Clientship

For the sake of clarity in the following discussion of the various types of clientships, it is necessary to introduce some new terminology. The system described above will be called the "formal structure," and clientship within the formal structure, i.e., the nāi-phrai bond, will be called "formal clientship." Other forms of clientship, including that which grew up around or within the formal organization without being incorporated into it, will be called "informal."

The number of informal clientships began to proliferate during the reign of Rāma III, in particular. The increase came in response to exogenous factors, the most important of which were the economic changes that accompanied the increase in international trade, the influx of Chinese immigrants with its consequences for corvée and internal trade, and taxation reform in the reign of Rāma III.

We may distinguish three types of informal clientships. The first was informal clientship within the class of nāi. The causes for its rise may be found in the nature of the government and the intensifying competition among Thai nobles for advancement. Consistent with the personal nature of clientship, the conduct of government was extremely particularistic. In all appointments or duties given to any official, consideration was taken of his personal life, connections, and kinship ties. The king treated his officials as a father would his children (see Udom Sombat 1962). Sometimes even regional arrangements were affected by such private affairs. Thus the quarrels and friendships between the governors of Nakhǫn Sīthammarāt and the governors of Songkhlā led to changes in the status of Songkhlā from a township subordinate to Nakhǫn Sīthammarāt to a township subordinate to Bangkok and back again (Wichīan Khīrī 1962). Despite the best efforts of noble clients to strengthen their relationship with the king, very few maintained direct contact with him. When a position became vacant, the king might ask those within his close circle to suggest a suitable person. Thus King Mongkut appointed Phrayā Wichitchonlathī to be the governor of Tāk on the recommendation of Prince Wongsāthirāt, who had personally known Phrayā Wichitchonlathī well (Mongkut 1963, vol. 2:47–48). There must have been numerous clientships between officials in the immediate circle of the king and others more remote. We are told that the middle level of officials would give 3,200 to 4,000 baht to persons whom they thought could influence the king in their favor for appointments to governorships (Mongkut 1960–1961, vol. 3:152–155).

Informal clientship between members of the class of nāi was entered into for protection as well as for career mobility. Most nobles were judges of one type or another, for the administration of justice was divided among a variety of krom (Wales 1934:181–182). To be a judge was a lucrative business. According to Lūang Čhakpānī, when an official of the rank equivalent to a krom chief realized that his income was insufficient, he could request permission from his superior to conduct trials at his own home. During a trial, the parties to the litigation and their witnesses had to stay at the judge's home, and their relatives and friends would bring food and supplies to them there. To please the judge, they would give him gifts and food (Čhakpānī 1956:19–20). It was obviously tempting for a judge to let his judgment be swayed by the relative value of gifts. There was danger in pursuing this kind of squeeze, however, for either party could appeal the case, claiming that the judge had taken a bribe from the other party. Thus officials who were judges of low rank sought protection by fāktūa with (that is, by becoming a client of) those who would be sitting on the court of appeal (Čhakpānī 1956:19–20).

The second type of informal clientship was that between members of different classes. At the time when nāi-phrai clientship was formalized, the right of a phrai lūang to change his nāi was legally abrogated. The marking of the phrai made it difficult for a phrai lūang to circumvent the law and change his status into phrai som, or even thāt.[20] One way out for a

[20] During the Ayutthayā period phrai lūang, through bribing their nāi and other means, often managed to change their status to phrai som. The tattoo marking of phrai with the name of their nāi and the name of their township was instituted during the Thonburi period (see n. 9 above).

phrai lūang who could not get on with his nāi was to become a client of another person whose rank was superior to that of his master. Because of the relationship between phūyai and phūnǭi, the phrai thereby put his nāi in a difficult position. King Mongkut mentioned a village where phrai lūang simply could not be mobilized by their nāi (Mongkut 1963, vol 1:181).

The ineffectiveness of the administration of justice also encouraged the growth of informal clientships. Persons of wealth or high rank could manage to stop a trial by using their influence (Mongkut 1960–1961, vol. 3:208–209). Some persons, clients of foreigners or the wealthy, committed petty crimes and boasted that the foreign consuls could give them protection from justice or that their patrons could bribe the judges to avoid punishment (Mongkut 1960–1961, vol. 2:300–304). The phūyai-phūnǭi distinction also came into play. When a phūyai (superior) intervened in cases being tried by a phūnǭi, challenge became virtually impossible. At one point King Mongkut issued a royal proclamation prohibiting powerful persons from meddling in legal proceedings (Mongkut 1960–1961, vol. 1:98–99).

The third type of informal clientship was that between Chinese immigrants and members of the nāi class. This was associated with the form of tax farming that came into wide use during the reign of King Rāma III. Their business often involved Chinese tax collectors in litigation. For this reason they had to be made nobles, for only a person of sakdinā 400 and above could be represented in the courts of justice by another person (Damrong 1959:29–30). From minor positions as tax collectors with the rank of khun or lūang, a number of Chinese became Thai and climbed up to such positions as township governors (Akin 1969:136, 162–165; Skinner 1957:148–154). Although the position of tax farmer was given to the highest bidder, it involved much manipulation of clientship. Apart from paying the yearly contracted fee to the government, a tax farmer paid various sums each year to other high nobles and

princes (Mongkut 1960–1961, vol. 2:10–15). A royal proclamation of 1858 relates that a number of nobles and persons
in the court circle, wanting to help their Chinese clients, tried
to persuade the king to set up a tax on betel leaves (Mongkut
1960–1961, vol. 2:41–42).

Chinese immigrants were desirable clients because, as successful traders, they could afford large gifts. Phrai, by contrast,
found it difficult to accumulate wealth. Restrictions on their
movement meant that they could not engage in trade. And a
phrai could not labor for wages without the consent of his nāi.
Thus these two occupations were left open to the Chinese immigrants, who were exempted from corvée and from the obligation to register under a nāi (Skinner 1957:96–97). After
accumulating a certain amount of wealth, they then sought a
patron in the upper class, often as a step toward eventual status
as Thai nobles.

The growth of informal clientships was accelerated by a
number of developments accompanying the increase in international trade. One such development was noted by King
Chulalongkorn when he said that officials of Krom Wang
(Palace Department) and Krom Mūeang (Department of the
Inner Kingdom) had to suffer the consequences of a rise in the
cost of living because of the progress that had been made
(1927:10). It is likely that most officials were similarly affected,
for increased income occurred only in those few krom, of which
Khlang was the most notable, that dealt with foreign traders
and tax farmers.

Another change was the increased use of Chinese rather than
corvée labor. The practice appears to have begun in the reign
of King Rāma II (Thiphākǫrawong 1961, vol. 1:75–76), when
the duration of corvée was reduced from six to three months
per year [21] and payment in specie came to be preferred by the
government (Vella 1957:19). Yet another change of conse-

[21] See n. 7 above.

quence for clientship was the development and expansion of interregional trade. By 1850 the Chinese were found to have gained almost complete control of this trade, and their trading activities reached even remote interior villages (Ingram 1971:19).

Almost all relationships within the formal structure were affected by these changes. The rise in the cost of living forced officials to demand more gifts and services from their phrai. At the same time, the reduction of corvée reduced the instrumentality of the relationship between nāi and phrai. Phrai now found it less necessary to lavish gifts on their nāi in order to get such favors as light work or illicit exemption from corvée. Further, with the development of regional trade, surplus produce that would otherwise have gone to nāi as gifts could now be exchanged for the goods brought in by the Chinese merchants. And in any case, now that a larger proportion of phrai made payments in lieu of corvée, the demands made by their nāi for services might have appeared unjustified. This loosening of the tie between the nāi and his phrai occurred just as many nāi came to need and demand more gifts and services from their phrai.

Nāi who used the power that was legally theirs to exploit or oppress their phrai in practice lost out as their phrai sought protection elsewhere, namely, from powerful nobles feared by their nāi. Phrai lūang of Krom Supharat, although marked for that krom and easily identifiable, were said to have disappeared and joined other krom (Mongkut 1960–1961, vol. 3:27–28). The actual lists of phrai of a number of krom during the reign of King Mongkut also reflect the situation. If a krom had forty to fifty phrai, the number available for service might be no more than eight to ten men. The rest would be said to have died or escaped, or to be ill or otherwise indisposed.[22] This situation

---

[22] I am grateful to Professor Yeneo Ishii of Kyoto University, who kindly provided this information and showed me copies of the actual lists.

appears to have compelled the nobles to provide increased protection and assistance to their phrai in order to keep them. We have already noted that powerful nobles in the capital often extended protection to their phrai in the provinces, and that they even interfered in legal trials. Power was also abused by those who wished to attract informal clients. Thus high-ranking nobles allowed their names to be used by their clients to frighten the people, tax collectors, and other officials (Mongkut 1960–1961, vol. 1:145–149).

Power, however, stemmed not only from clients, but also from wealth. And wealth could be used to get clients, by giving assistance to impoverished officials and protection to those in jeopardy. Previously, wealth could come only from having phrai. However, the economic changes that came with modernization opened up new sources of wealth, particularly for officials of certain krom, notably Krom Khlang. It was not surprising, therefore, that this period saw a phenomenal growth in the power of the Bunnāk family, whose members had continued control of Krom Khlang from the reign of King Rāma II to the reign of King Chulalongkorn (see Wyatt 1968; Akin 1969).

Clientship and Stratification

We have seen that in Thai society manpower was the scarce resource par excellence and that control of manpower brought not only wealth but also political power. Thus the main function of the formal political structure was the control of manpower. In theory the king distributed manpower to his officials according to sakdinā. So long as the amount of manpower under a person's command corresponded to his sakdinā, the latter served as an adequate official map of stratification in the society. However, as a criterion for status differentiation, the amount of manpower under a person's command was more basic than the number of his dignity marks. Thus informal clientship could play havoc with the formal system. Informal clients were not distributed by the king, nor could the king control their distribution. The proliferation of informal client-ships in the nineteenth century rendered sakdinā increasingly invalid as a map of the actual social stratification and, more-over, undermined the system of offices established by the king. Informal clientship had the potential for bringing administra-tion to a standstill, for it inevitably disrupted the chain of command. During the reign of King Mongkut, informal client-ship had profoundly disturbed but not yet undermined the formal structure. Yet anyone who reads King Chulalongkorn's "Speech on Changes in the Administration" cannot fail to appreciate that deterioration in administration was fast ap-proaching the point where a complete overhaul was required (1927).

It is easy to see how informal clientships worked to create conflicts within and between the units of government. Informal clients of powerful patrons tended to disobey their own supe-riors. Thus a nāi could not mobilize those of his phrai who had become informal clients of patrons who outranked him. A krom whose phrai had all become informal clients of powerful outside patrons would cease to function. It is instructive to consider a hypothetical case in which a noble official of a krom had be-come an informal client of a powerful outside patron. Let us assume that the minister of Khlang had an informal client, a noble official of the rank of *khunklāng* of Krom Kǭngtrawēnsāi (a subsidiary krom of Krom Mūeang) and with the sakdinā 400. Instead of obeying the command of the chief of his krom, the khunklāng would obey that of the minister, his informal patron. If the minister was powerful and wealthy, and espe-cially if he was in direct contact with the king, not only would the chief of Krom Kǭngtrawēnsāi refrain from forcing his direct subordinate, the khunklāng to obey his command, he would also not even dare to report the matter to the king. On the other hand, the khunklāng, finding his direct superior to be powerless against him, could proceed to build up an informal clientele of his own to rival the formal clientele of his direct superior. His being an informal client of the minister would raise his status in the eyes of people within his krom and elsewhere. It apparently happened that officials would sometimes simply leave their own krom and go off to work in the krom of their informal patron, if we may judge from an 1858 proclamation of King Mongkut warning officials to work only within their own krom (Mongkut 1960–1961, vol. 2:104–105). How far the existence of informal clientships affected the rights and duties of the officials can be gathered from this passage in a royal proclamation of 1855: "His Majesty knows . . . that officials, both in the capital and in the provinces, always consider the future consequences of whatever they do. They look to the left and the right, taking care not only of the affairs of the king, but also fearing this or that prince, this or that official . . . , who are in royal favor. They calculate who is likely to become phūyai. If one were to proceed in a straightforward manner, these persons would become angry and take revenge" (Mongkut 1960–1961, vol. 1:155).

Since status was based on the number of men under a person's command, increasing a person's informal clientele also raised his status. Having a large number of clients was taken as evidence of a patron's kindness, generosity, and power. The state had deprived or sharply curtailed the right of formal clients to terminate the relationship, but no such external regulation affected informal clientship. Thus it was necessary for a patron to exert his influence more vigorously in protecting and assisting his informal clients than his formal clients. In this situation, the more unscrupulous among a powerful man's informal clients would oppress and exploit others, knowing they could do so with impunity. King Mongkut found it necessary to issue a number of proclamations in an effort to curb these abuses. For instance, to high-ranking nobles who allowed their names to be used by their clients to frighten other people, he said: "Do not think only of making people afraid of your name at the present moment. Think more of the future. The people will not later love and respect you and your descendants, for they will know that you favor bad men over good" (Mongkut 1960–1961, vol. 1:147). Regarding commoners and slaves taking shelter in the palaces of princes and the residences of high-ranking nobles, he said:

Although the phrai, slaves, and debtors who have sought shelter there may praise you and say that because of you they could escape the demands of their *čhao mū* [platoon leader], nāi, and creditors, others who hear of this are not likely to offer praise, for those [whom you protect] have committed wrongs. Some have stolen the property of their nāi or creditors. Whoever hears of this will say that phūyai cooperate with thieves, and this is no honor. A person who is important now, or who aims to become so in the future, should strive to maintain his honor, to earn the reputation of being kind to all, not siding [always] with his own followers, much less with bad men, but desiring to help only good men. When a patron and his clients build a reputation for such bravery and daring that no one can do anything to them, they may be following a long-standing method for seeking status, but it is poorly suited for the need of the country at the present time [Mongkut 1960–1961, vol. 2:63–64].

The growth of informal clientship affected the ranking system in a number of ways. Since nobles lived on gifts from their phrai, a noble whose phrai had become informal clients of other patrons would not be able to maintain a life style suited to his status; indebtedness could depress his standard of living to the level of a commoner. There was also a tendency for informal clientships to build up into a nested hierarchy similar to that of the formal organization. The more extensive of these informal hierarchies posed a threat to the security of the king himself. At the very least, it introduced ambiguity into the relationship between the king and the patron at the apex of such a concentration of power. Thus toward the end of the Early Bangkok period, the king's authority was beginning to erode for systemic reasons. It is in this perspective that we must interpret King

Mongkut's complaint of 1868 (from a private letter to Prince
Mahēsūan):

When the king promulgates an order, those of great power and high
position in the land who disagree simply refuse to obey. In doing so
they flout time-honored customs. They refuse because they are phūyai
and do not have to *krēngčhai* [to fear to do anything that would
displease] the king. Therefore they do what they like. They either
become overly enthùsiastic about the Europeans, just as the princes
of Ava were about the Ceylonese monks or, blinded by their own
position and power, feel that the king cannot refuse to let them do
what they will. Even the insignificant princes, phra-ongčhao and
mǫmčhao, follow their example, not fearing royal regulations laid
down by the king [Mongkut 1963, vol. 1:188–189].

APPENDIX
Yot, Status, and *Sakdinā*

Yot	Status	Sakdina
King		Infinite
Upparāt	Čhao (prince)	100,000
Čhaofā (royal sibling)		
with krom rank	Čhao	50,000
Čhaofā (royal offspring)		
with krom rank	Čhao	40,000
Somdetčhaophrayā	Khunnāng (noble)	30,000
Čhaofā (royal sibling)		
without krom rank	Čhao	20,000
Čhaofā (royal offspring)		
without krom rank	Čhao	15,000
Phra-ongčhao (royal sibling or		
offspring) with krom rank	Čhao	15,000
Phra-ongčhao (royal nephew/niece		
or grandchild) with krom rank	Čhao	11,000
Čhaophrayā	Khunnāng	3,000–10,000
Phrayā	Khunnāng	1,000–10,000
Phra-ongčhao without krom rank	Čhao	4,000–7,000
Phra	Khunnāng	1,000–5,000
Lūang	Khunnāng	800–3,000
Mǫmčhao	Čhao	1,500
Mǫm (achieved rank for royal		
relative)	(Čhao)	800–1,000
Khun	Khunnāng or phrai	
	(commoner)	200–1,000
Mūen	Khunnāng or phrai	200–800
Mǫmrātchawong	(Čhao)	500
Phan	Khunnāng or phrai	100–400
Petty official in the provinces	Phrai	100–300
Commoner with family	Phrai	20–25
Unmarried commoner	Phrai	15
Destitute commoner	Phrai	5
Slave	Thāt	5

3. Education and the Modernization of Thai Society

DAVID K. WYATT

Profoundly important to the modernization of Thai society was the introduction of modern education during the reign of King Chulalongkorn (1868–1910). New schools on the Western model and a curriculum greatly different from that of the Buddhist monastery education of a few decades earlier contributed substantially to the definition of new roles and groups in Thai society and to the formation of a new generation of modern men which by the reign of King Wachirawut (1910–1925) had assumed direction of the public life of a Thai nation becoming modern. The manner in which these changes were promoted and accomplished depended greatly upon the political and economic circumstances of the day, and resistance or indifference to modern education delayed its impact upon the masses of the population of Thailand until late in the reign and beyond. Similarly, the same circumstances, and the general state of Thai society in the latter half of the nineteenth century, were reflected in the responses of different elements of the society to modern education. These responses, expressed in the enrollments of the early schools as well as in isolated public and private statements of opinion concerning education, affected the composition of the Thai elite at a critical state in the nation's history, and their legacy remains apparent in many ways.

Both the introduction of modern education in Thailand and the responses of Thai society to it were rooted in the forms and content of traditional monastery education. As Phya Anuman has noted (1967a: passim), Thailand's Buddhist monasteries had been centers of instruction and learning since the beginnings of the kingdom in the thirteenth century. Certainly as an ideal, and as often as possible in practice, education was intimately associated with religious attainment in the lives of individuals and in the life of the society as a whole. Although slaves found it difficult to gain release from their obligations so as to spend a period of service in the monkhood or novitiate, a substantial proportion of the male population must have been able to do so, and thereby acquire rudimentary literary and general training in the principles of their religion. Although most monasteries doubtless confined their educational offering to such simple fare there is substantial evidence that some monasteries, particularly those in the capital and in major provincial towns, were able to offer more specialized instruction to serve the demands of both village and court for specialists in the arts and sciences. The informal, unstructured patterns of monastery instruction could allow young men to pursue their interests in acquiring such skills as medicine or astrology for use in their home villages or allow the especially talented young man a channel into the specialized branches of the bureaucracy. Royal patronage extended to selected monasteries enabled such specialized instruction to develop throughout the country and provided a framework of bureaucratic and personal contacts through which a few especially gifted monks might come to the attention of the king.

Although monastery education pre-eminently functioned within a religious context, the essentials of which remained stable over long periods of time, there was considerable religious and cultural development in the Ayutthayā and Early Bangkok periods which both grew out of and was reflected in the monasteries. The domestication of Indic arts and sciences was primarily the work of monks and their pupils, and their influence on the development of Thai vernacular culture must have been considerable. It is not surprising that the first textbook of Thai language and poetics, based on a desire to emulate French missionary education in the seventeenth century, was written on royal command by a former monk (Thailand, Krom sinlapākǫn 1961:149–50); nor was it perhaps unusual that a monk studied foreign languages early in the eighteenth century (Wood 1926: 223, n. 3). The range of interests covered by some monastery schools was considerable, and the best of these schools were by no means concerned only with narrowly defined religious pursuits. Because ambitious and intelligent men would have it so, and because the monasteries, so intimately bound up with the life of the society, could ignore neither the intellectual currents that swept the kingdom and the region nor the requirements of Thai society for specialized instruction, there seems to have existed in Thai monastery education a receptivity to change and a capacity for critical self-examination which the society could tolerate and, at times, encourage (Wyatt 1969:ch. 1).

As Akin Rabibhadana has demonstrated (1969:ch. 8), the extent to which traditional educational patterns served as avenues of social mobility was extremely limited as late as the reign of King Mongkut (1851–1868). The class of nobles, the *khunnāng* who served the king, was rigidly defined in law and practice, and few who were not themselves the sons of nobles could gain either entrance into the Royal Pages Corps or appointment to public positions. Accordingly, the education of the sons of nobles was by no means rigorous, and "the elders of families other than the royal family still believed in the old principle that the literate arts were subjects for clerks, and it was unnecessary for a person of high status to study them seriously" (Damrong 1922:iii). Although there were some exceptions, and some slight changes in the syllabus of monastery schools between the seventeenth and nineteenth centuries, most boys, whether the sons of nobles or of peasants, still were instructed in the 1850's as their ancestors had been two centuries earlier. The sons of nobles and craftsmen alike gained a basic acquaintance

with the rudiments of reading and writing during their period
in the monastery, and then learned the vocation of their family
by a period of apprenticeship as pages at court or in the establish-
ments of princes and nobles and by working beside their fathers
or male relatives and family friends. As long as the traditional
arts and sciences were essentially unchallenged, and as long as
the court and bureaucratic nobility remained unreceptive to
new educational qualifications, there was little inducement to
major changes in educational patterns and little demand for
such either from the court or from upwardly-mobile young
men.

   In the second quarter of the nineteenth century a few young
men already were unsure of the capacity of traditional ideas and
institutions to deal morally and intellectually with a world beginning rapidly to change around them. The prince-monk
Mongkut, passed over for the succession to the throne in 1824,
sought by a return to first principles a revitalization of the Buddhist monkhood and the religious life of the society so as to
counter the increasing materialism and moral uncertainty that
grew from important shifts in Asian trade and changes in the
organization of Thai society (see Akin 1969:ch. 7). These same
economic and social developments were promoted by and
worked to the benefit of a small group of the Thai nobility, of
whom the chief was Čhaophrayā Phrakhlang (Dit Bunnāk),
who served concurrently as minister of the Southern Provinces,
Finance, and Foreign Relations throughout the reign of Rāma
III (1824–1851) (Wyatt 1968). His son, Chūang Bunnāk,
sought to adopt for government and his family's use such tools
of modern economic enterprise as the square-rigged—and later
the steam—sailing vessel and Western-style bookkeeping and
established close relations with the growing Chinese mercantile
community and with Western merchants and missionaries.
Together with Mongkut, his brother Prince Čhuthāmani,
Prince Wongsāthirātsanit, and a few friends, colleagues and
retainers, he learned English; and some studied other foreign

languages and Western science and read European books and magazines and the Hong Kong and Singapore newspapers. All of them were men of assured status and promising prospects in their own society, and they must have come to this experimentation with new ideas and techniques more out of strength then from weakness. All were well educated in the arts and sciences of their own civilization, yet all were both sufficiently uncertain of the adequacy of their own intellectual inheritance and sufficiently confident of their own ability to master the possibilities of change, first to enquire and then to learn and to utilize these foreign ideas and instruments.

The immediate results of this early dabbling and experimentation were of limited consequence. The early exponents of religious change, Western learning, and foreign languages were the leading promoters of Mongkut's accession to the throne in 1851; but their positions in Thai society were such as naturally to lead them to take such a role, and they in fact played down their reformist sympathies in the last years of the reign of Rāma III so as not to jeopardize their political fortunes (cf. Tarling 1960:50, 58–59, 63). Their accession to power as a group in 1851 made possible the accommodation to Western demands embodied in the treaties of 1855–56; but it did not fully tip the balance of political power in favor of the reformers, nor was their success accompanied by any aggressive espousal of the principles of fundamental reform. Mongkut's generation, although indeed a very small portion of it, made good use of the tools of communication and techniques of organization introduced from the West both to perceive the rapidly rising challenge to the continued survival and identity of their nation and to act to strengthen its ability to resist such threats. These men, however, were sufficiently products of an earlier age, and of its successful surmounting of the clearly defined crisis of the 1850's, to feel that accommodation and pragmatic formalistic change were sufficient to ensure the continued survival of the kingdom without fundamental reform.

Perhaps symptomatic of the approach and expectations of Mongkut and the Bunnāks are the plans they made for the education of their own children. With perhaps one exception, none was sent to study abroad or to attend the early missionary schools in Bangkok. Many studied with American or English tutors hired primarily to impart a facility in English—like Anna Leonowens in the 1860's—but none was given any more systematic or comprehensive instruction than Mongkut and Chūang Bunnāk had obtained from the missionaries before 1851. The education of the sons and grandsons of these proponents of accommodation, at least prior to 1868, remained within the broad, loose framework typical of the traditional educational patterns of princes and nobles; and the occasional tutor in English fit within these patterns like a tutor in elephantry or boxing. Although a handful of young Thai were sent abroad during Mongkut's reign for training in naval academies or secondary schools, these for the most part were not men of noble families but rather their clients and retainers, and their subsequent employment generally was as interpreters or clerks in the households and offices of their patrons (Damrong 1964:338–45; Rātchawǫrin 1963:35–39). They and their patrons continued to work within a highly structured and tightly integrated political and social framework in which Western-style educational qualifications had as yet no place, in which the old bureaucratic structure encompassed the entire society and ranked individuals and groups in an elaborate hierarchical system of status and responsiblity, and in which social advancement lay through the Royal Pages Corps, admission to which still was restricted as before.

Although Thai society had begun to undergo some "modern" changes by the beginning of the reign of King Chulalongkorn in 1868, these were extremely limited in scope. Some small portions of the royal family and nobility, like Mongkut and the Bunnāks, had found new sources of power and strength in money and land, while the labor-based wealth of the remainder of the upper classes was being eroded by rapid economic development and their power sapped by unequal bureaucratic competition with the Bunnāks, who by 1870 had a virtual monopoly on political power in the major ministries and departments of government (Akin 1969:147–154). The successful nobles, like the Bunnāks, owed their position to policies of diplomatic and economic accommodation, which by 1870 had reduced the threat of the West to what they seem to have viewed as manageable proportions. The attitudes of the remainder of the capital and provincial elite toward modernizing change must have been shaped by their general lack of direct contact with the West, which may have led them to minimize the necessity for change, and by their experience of the Bunnāks and the innovations introduced or patronized by them. If, as seems likely, they resented the imposition of a system of farming tax collections out to Chinese, the growing disparity between their own financial situations and that of the Bunnāks, or the manner in which the Bunnāks competed so successfully for high office, well may they have yearned for a simpler past and resisted any further encroachments upon their social and economic prerogatives.

In a very real sense, King Chulalongkorn was a generation ahead of his contemporaries. Born in 1853 to a king who had spent most of his adult life in the monkhood, he was only fifteen years old on his accession to the throne in 1868, while his ministers and the elder members of the royal family had been born in the reigns of Rāma II and Rāma III and had come to maturity well before 1851. Chulalongkorn was thus of the chronological generation of Mongkut's and Chūang Bunnāk's grandsons, and his experience lay entirely in a world in which European trading ships and diplomats, foreign languages and newspapers, and international affairs were commonplace. His early reforming zeal suggests that he took seriously the injunctions and exhortations of Anna Leonowens and J. H. Chandler, his English tutors, although his father's deep moral convictions and values indelibly marked his thought. He clearly was determined to embark upon a program of fundamental reform that went far beyond that which his father had initiated. This course sent him into collision with both the progressives and the conservatives of his father's generation, and especially with the regent, Somdetčhaophrayā Sīsuriyawong (Chūang Bunnāk), who superintended the young king's acts until he came of age in 1873 and continued to be the single most important political figure in the kingdom until his death in 1883 (Wyatt 1969:ch. 2).

Almost immediately upon ascending the throne, King Chulalongkorn took a number of measures to provide for the education of younger members of the royal family and nobility. First, in 1870 a school was founded within the palace walls for the Thai instruction of young princes and nobles in the Bodyguard Regiment of the Royal Pages Corps. Second, on his way abroad for a visit to India in 1872, the king enrolled fourteen of his cousins in the Raffles Institution in Singapore, there to be educated in English until such instruction could be provided for them in Bangkok. Finally, late in the same year the king engaged an Englishman to instruct his brothers and members of the Royal Pages' Bodyguard Regiment in English, French, and mathematics. The manner in which these projects were received says at least as much about the state of Thai society and politics in the early 1870's as it does about early Thai attitudes toward modernization.

The Palace Thai School for the Royal Pages' Bodyguard Regiment initially was well attended, drawing its 150 students from many royal and noble families which had sent their sons to join the Royal Pages Corps in the hope that they might be singled out for preferment by the new king. They had responded to the Palace Thai School not as an educational institution but rather as a device for gaining the favor of the king in a manner not dissimilar to the way in which they tried to bring their daughters to his attention. For his part, the young king seems to have judged these young men harshly, finding them semi-literate and ill-schooled in "the customs and practices of government," and founded the school in the hope of improving the quality of the royal service (Sathīan et al. 1935, vol. 8:81–82).

A Palace English School was provided in 1872 for the same boys with essentially the same intentions. In both cases, the king was appealing for personal and political support, as well as attempting to mold his following in his own image; and he offered this special education only to those committed personally to him in the Bodyguard Regiment. The response of the boys and their families to this act must have been guided by their assessment of the king's political position and prospects. That this was indeed so is suggested by the fact that, following a major confrontation between the king and the more conservative of his nobles in 1875 (Wyatt 1969:ch. 2), the enrollments of both schools dropped dramatically as the king's position weakened; the Palace English School was left with three students, all younger brothers of the king, and it finally closed its doors a few months later. The Palace Thai School continued on into the 1880's with reduced enrollments, serving primarily to provide added Thai instruction for the young men of the Royal Pages Corps and Royal Scribes Department. Although it did inaugurate a change in the methods of Thai education, introducing printed textbooks for the first time and instructing its pupils in groups instead of individually, the content of the instruction offered was wholly traditional—and, indeed, it could have been little else, for the school's teachers all were former monks, trained in the traditional fashion. In institutional terms, the palace schools functioned within the traditional framework of the Royal Pages Corps, and they appear to have been responded to as such.

In the three years immediately following King Chulalongkorn's confrontation with the conservative nobles, he and his young advisers made two further attempts to introduce modern concepts of education. First, in 1875 a decree was issued calling upon the royal monasteries (selected monasteries that enjoyed royal patronage for Pali and religious instruction) to offer formal Thai instruction in classrooms, using the government textbooks prepared for the Palace Thai School, the expenses of such instruction to be borne by the Crown through the Department of Religious Affairs. In some ways the decree was revolutionary, for it constituted an attempt to formalize in the monasteries secular Thai education, never before a direct concern of government. In his decree, the king explained: "The Thai language is of great benefit to the study of the *Tripiṭaka* which works to the support of Buddhism and, if one is a layman, to the utility of the government service, so that it is an advantage to be literate" (*Rātchakit čhānubēksā* 1875/76, vol. 2:111–112). He expressed the idea that literacy and a general improvement in educational standards worked to the benefit of the society as a whole. It is possible that the schools the decree envisioned were intended to compete with and counteract the missionary schools then being founded in Bangkok. Whatever its intentions, the decree was an utter failure, for not a single school is known to have been founded in response to it. Why? In the light of the fact that an almost identical action was successful ten years later, with most of the same individuals involved, one can dismiss the possibility of monastic resistance or poor administration. What was lacking in 1875 was secure prestige for modern education and an established demand for its products in the offices of government.

Lacking institutionalized modern education for the young men of the ruling families of the capital, and having failed in his efforts to provide such by 1875, the king tried another alternative in 1878. He responded to a suggestion of Samuel McFarland, then an American missionary, and supported the foundation in Thonburī of a modern school to offer, "especially for those of noble blood" (*Siam Weekly Advertiser*, 27 Dec. 1879), Thai and English instruction in such arts and sciences as might be "useful to the country" (Wyatt 1965b:1–3). The school was put under the superintendence of a governing committee composed of several of the king's brothers, his private secretary, and teachers of the Palace Thai School. Initially the prospects of the project were good: in its first year it enrolled 100 royal and noble pupils, including many who had begun their studies in the Palace Thai School. These young men would have responded to the leadership of the king, as well as to the prominence of both the traditional scholars of the Palace Thai School and the more progressive of the king's brothers and supporters on the school's governing committee. McFarland, however, as an American and a missionary, took no cognizance of the social status of applicants for places in the school. Although scholarships were offered exclusively to applicants from the royal and noble families, there was no shortage of monied day-pupils from the Chinese families of Thonburī, and they soon came to dominate its student body.

Not long after the foundation of McFarland's Sūananan School, Prince Damrong Rajanubhab—then only nineteen years old—founded a new school for the Royal Pages' Bodyguard Regiment in 1881. The reasons he later gave for founding this school suggest what was happening to the sons of the royal and noble families during this period and may partially explain the poor response to the educational experiments of the previous decade (Damrong 1963c:26–27). With a natural growth of the government service in the early years of Chulalongkorn's reign, following upon rapid economic growth and increased demands for government services in the new specialized activities of a bustling port, and greatly increased military and administrative requirements, the demands of the civil service for manpower were considerable. Prince Damrong found that young men were being rushed through a rudimentary monastery education on the old model and through brief periods of service as royal pages directly into promising positions in the expanding bureaucracy. To many, it must have appeared that the traditional system of recruiting and training young men for bureaucratic careers was working better than ever before. The sons of nobles were finding employment without difficulty. Fathers had considerable opportunity to indulge the ambitions of their sons and sons-in-law. And most officials were seemingly slow to perceive the needs of their own departments for men with changed qualifications who could efficiently run a new postal service, survey new boundaries and telegraph lines, or train new soldiers. Although the king's initiatives in the 1870's show his awareness of the importance of foreign languages, modern mathematics, and high intellectual standards enforced through common instruction and textbooks, he was not in a good political position to ensure that his wishes were heeded in such a critical area as personnel when he was still clashing with his father's generation over national policies on which he felt the very survival of the state depended. It was left to the private initiative of the king and others, such as Prince Damrong, to promote a new educational standard, and to await a day when those who responded to such opportunities could be rewarded.

Acting on his assessment of the need for better-trained officers in the Royal Pages' Bodyguard Regiment, Prince Damrong founded Sūankulāp School in September 1881, with the full support and approval of the king. Although only ten students enrolled in the first months, the response soon became overwhelming, and by its second year the school was training nearly 100 young men for civil responsibilities as well as for appointments in the officer corps of the Bodyguard Regiment and ultimately in a new national army. Prince Damrong quickly introduced new methods of teaching Thai, new courses in elementary mathematics and geography, and specialized courses designed to meet the needs of modern civil servants, including accounting, telegraphy, and the writing of précis, letters, and reports. Notably absent in the school was the literary emphasis of the old Palace Thai School and the strong religious emphasis of conventional monastery instruction. Sūankulāp was a new sort of school, run on modern lines, strongly influenced by the earliest Western and Western-type schools in Bangkok, and introducing into Thai educational traditions and institutions a strong bureaucratic bias that was extremely slow to fade (Wyatt 1969:ch. 5).

Sūankulāp School may be taken as a sensitive barometer of change in Thai society during the two decades following its foundation in 1881. Of nineteen students gaining the equivalent of a secondary education there before 1890, seventeen were of royal descent. The prominence of royal students at Sūankulāp in its first decade may not have been wholly accidental. In a speech in 1884 (Chulalongkorn 1915:36–37), the king explained that his primary motivation in approving the foundation of the school had been "a concern for the future of the royal family." He stated that

the problem with all these *mǫm čhao* and *mǫmrātchawong* [the grandsons and great-grandsons of kings] is that there has been no avenue through which they could enter government service. It is not that there have been no openings for them, but rather that, being of royal blood, there have been no opportunities for them to be trained [through apprenticeships in government offices], because they are royalty and not [the sons of] officials. . . . I intend that this school shall be a means of preserving their positions, that they might not be ignored as they have been in the past.

Viewed in such terms, Sūankulāp might have been the king's weapon against the power of the old noble families who dominated government departments at that time; but he also made it clear in his speech that more than simple power was involved. He felt that the country's fate depended upon intelligent decisions made and executed by well-educated government officers; and with royalty generally willing to follow his lead, their proffered services were not to be refused out of any blind adherence to outmoded social conventions. The school's prestige was well established with this speech (which came only a few months after the death of the leading figure of the older conservative faction, Čhaophrayā Sīsuriyawong [Chūang Bunnāk]), by the fact that the king began to send his own sons to Sūankulāp for their Thai and English instruction, and by the open participation of several of the leading princes of the realm in the school's administration. By 1888 its enrollment included more than 400 students, among whom junior members of the royal family predominated. The king followed his special provisions for the education of princes with new schools within the palace walls for his own sons and daughters in 1893 and then with major efforts to have all his sons and many of his nephews educated abroad, to the point where there were at least fifty young Thai studying in England in 1897, of whom at least half were members of the royal family (Wyatt 1969:161–164, 200–201). Junior members of the royal family were among the first to respond to the initiatives of the king and others in founding such schools as Sūankulāp, and consequently were among the first to be educated abroad. Thereby they gained a head start over other elements in Thai society which assured their subsequent dominance in the bureaucracy, and this advantage goes a considerable way toward explaining their prominence in the reigns of Wachirawut and Prachāthipok, as late as 1932.

On the whole, the old nobility was much slower to respond to the opportunities for modern education, for reasons indicated above. That they were slipping behind is indicated by a curious document issued in 1890, a "Royal Decree Inviting the Sons of Government Officials to Enter the Service of Various Government Offices" (*Rātchakitčhānubēksā* 1890/91, vol. 8:195–97), wherein the king explained that the old system of apprenticeship in government departments, under which the sons of government officials had worked as clerks in their fathers' offices and gradually rose as they obtained experience, no longer was functioning even to maintain the position of the old nobility in government service. Young noblemen were wasting their time on idle pleasures, disdaining work as common clerks, and relying on their ancestry and family backgrounds to qualify them for public service. Meanwhile, others of common backgrounds were taking up paid clerical positions "out of financial necessity," and by their knowledge and experience were qualifying for promotion over the heads of young men of good breeding (*trakūn*). The king was apprehensive lest,

if this state of affairs continues, the sons of families which have maintained their status for generations will not be able to enter government service. . . .

Therefore, His Majesty issues this decree to advise those government officials who have sons and grandsons who should enter government service at the present time that His Majesty would much rather have the sons of government officials of noble family enter the government service in the departments in which their fathers have served or even higher positions than have those of no distinguished family enter the government service.

He urged the old nobility to have its sons and grandsons trained (presumably in schools) before entering government service, and to accept clerical positions so as to gain the experience in modern office practice which he deemed indispensable for promotion. But the king closed by warning the nobility that the old days of the hereditary dominance of the nobility were past: "His Majesty needs many more government officials at the present time, as there is more work to do than people to do it; and, good family or not, if a man has sufficient knowledge and ability, His Majesty will maintain him in government service without regard for his background; but if he is of good family, so much the better." The opportunities existed, particularly at Sūankulāp, for young men of the old noble families to educate themselves for positions which would allow them to maintain their status in Thai society. Only slowly did they respond to these, by swelling the enrollment of Sūankulāp in the early 1890's, and then by attending the new secondary schools that began to appear at the turn of the century (Wyatt 1969:chs. 6, 10).

Much more prompt and insistent in their response to modern educational opportunities in the 1880's and early 1890's were two other elements in the urban population of Thailand: the Chinese and the lesser nobility. It is clear that these were the groups who sent their sons to the early missionary schools in the capital, and it would appear that they soon were patronizing the private schools, the existence of which is briefly and obscurely referred to in reports of the Education Department in the late 1880's and mid-1890's. McFarland's Sūananan School was reported to be popular among the Chinese and "common people" of Thonburī by 1884 (*Siam Weekly Advertiser*, 22 Dec. 1883, 20 Dec. 1884); and many of the most prominent of the monastery schools founded under the auspices of Prince Damrong and the Education Department beginning in 1884 were in strongly Chinese neighborhoods of Bangkok and Thonburī, notably Wat Samčhīntai (now Wat Traimit). At one private school supported by the Education Department, the Bančhinyāēm or New School founded in 1888, Chinese instruction was offered (Wyatt 1969:119n.). In the following year, Sūankulāp instituted a twenty-baht tuition fee intended "to prevent common people (*khonlēo*) from attending the school" (Wyatt 1969:121); and the royal decree of 1890 mentioned above implied that large numbers of nonnoble young men were entering the government service as clerks. Chinese students became more noticeable on the student rosters of Sūankulāp, McFarland's Sunanthālai (formerly Sūananan), and the new School (later Bānphrayānānā School) in the early 1890's (cf. Anuman 1967b:244–263); and Chinese and nonnoble students from Bānphrayānānā and Assumption College (run by French Catholic missionaries) did extremely well in the competitive examinations for king's scholarships when these were introduced in 1898 (*Bangkok Times*, 10 March 1898: cf. Skinner 1957:168). These indications from a fragmentary record suggest strongly that the Chinese mercantile community of the capital and minor bureaucratic families were relatively more responsive to modern educational opportunities before 1900 than was the old nobility. The reasons for this are nowhere made explicit but may be inferred from the context in which these developments occurred.

This was a period during which the Thai bureaucracy was expanding rapidly. Its growth before about 1885 was relatively moderate, as most of it occurred within existing institutions. Once the revived royal program of reform gained momentum in the mid-1880's, however, and new departments and proto-ministries were created in preparation for the major reorganization of the administration in 1892, the demands of the state were overwhelming, as the decree of 1890 suggests. Government expenditures climbed at the phenomenal annual rate of nearly 14 per cent in the 1890's, and the staffs of the new ministries increased proportionately. School enrollments, however, owing primarily to political difficulties over the budgetary priorities for the various ministries, remained virtually static, at 2,000 to 2,500, between 1885 and 1897; and the shortage of manpower by 1898 was viewed by the king as desperately acute (Phrasadet 1961:292–300). Similarly, the demands of Chinese and Western mercantile houses, banks, and shipping agencies for educated young men with foreign languages were considerable. This was an ideal situation for ambitious young men.

In addition, not all social groups were equally open to respond to the possibility of mobility. Until the abolition of corvée labor in the years 1899–1905, commoners would have found it difficult to continue their studies at the secondary level, for these commonly came at an age when young men began to be subject to the corvée. (Indeed, in an attempt to increase school enrollments in 1901, it was proposed that the requirements of compulsory labor be waived for students in secondary schools [Wyatt 1969:252–253]). Royalty, the sons of nobles, and Chinese, however, were exempt from the corvée and free to pursue their studies as long as they wished. In addition, a great deal of control over recruitment and training for the public service lay in the hands of the king and his brothers, who probably felt less inhibited in hiring commoners and Chinese than the older conservative nobles might have been. With the availability of modern education from the mid-1880's, in public, private, and missionary schools in Bangkok and the provinces, the educational opportunities were present for those perceptive enough to recognize their value.

The motivational factor, however, is essentially unknowable: Why were members of the royal family, the lesser nobility, and the Chinese relatively more responsive to modern educational opportunities in this period before 1900? Mǫmchao and mǫmrātchawong could have responded to the king's call for education and public service on a personal level and with the rapidity which springs from a long-resented exclusion, if one is to accept the king's assessment of their recent status. One might be able to infer something of the same motivation on the part of the lesser nobility if one supposes that they suffered from bureaucratic competition with the Bunnāks in the 1860's and 1870's and/or took the king's patronage of modern education as an invitation to outstep and bypass their rivals. The chief government appointments of the late 1880's and the 1890's went mainly to those whose major qualifications were educational; and particularly noticeable is the manner in which Prince Damrong Rajanubhab brought into the service of the Ministry of Interior men who had done well at Sūankulāp School in the period when he had directed it (Tej 1968:chs. 4–5). Some of the Chinese who came through the new schools in this period might be classed as lesser nobility, although the fathers of many of those whose names appear in the school rosters and prize lists of the day are prefixed with the term *chīn* 'Chinese', rather than with a bureaucratic rank. The political circumstances of the period seem most adequately to explain the responses of the royal family and the lesser nobility, while more practical considerations and a degree of commitment to the values of Thai society must be assumed for that portion of the Chinese community which so responded.

A great deal changed in the few years spanning the turn of the century. The king began, after his first visit to Europe in 1897, to perceive that the manpower requirements of the state were more than bureaucratic, and he began to demand more of education in building the common knowledge and sentiments which could make of his kingdom a modern national unity. A great many more vocations than the civil service required a fundamental basis in modern education, and all of the citizens of the state required education of vocational and moral utility. With the assistance of Prince Damrong, Prince Wachirayān Warōrot, and Phrayā Wisut Suriyasak (Mǭmrātchawong Pīa Mālākun, later Čhaophrayā Phrasadet Surēntharāthibodi), he began to frame, elaborate, and put into operation a vastly increased educational program, including major expansions both in public elementary education throughout the kingdom and in general and specialized secondary education centered in the capital.

Two educational institutions founded around the turn of the century were of particular importance to the royal family and the nobility: King's College, a preparatory school run as an English public school, founded in 1897; and the Civil Service School, founded in 1900. Although heavily subsidized by the government, King's College required an eighty-baht admission fee (equivalent to four months of a teacher's salary), and its student body was drawn almost exclusively from the elite of the capital. Of a student body of seventy-one in 1898–99, twenty-seven were of royal blood (mainly mǭmčhao) and twenty-six were the sons of government officials of the rank of phrayā and above (equivalent to a department head). It primarily prepared its students for studies abroad with a thoroughly English curriculum and English teachers; and from its foundation it was extremely successful, almost completely dominating the awards of king's scholarships from 1899. Operating on a different level, but for much the same sort of clientele, was the Civil Service School, which had a student enrollment of 182 within a year of its foundation. Data on the social composition of the school are not available, but scattered biographies of its graduates suggest that its enrollment came primarily from what has been termed the lesser nobility. Prince Damrong, however, writing some years later, states that he hoped at the time the school was founded that young men of common backgrounds might through it gain entrance to the civil service (1956:88–91). The school's curriculum, though partly academic, was primarily practical, and its students went directly to positions in the provincial administration of the Ministry of Interior (Tej 1968:ch. 5). After a time, it came also to serve as a means of integrating the sons of the petty nobility of the provinces into the national administrative elite. These two schools, then, functioned primarily to re-equip the traditional elite and to enable them to maintain their social status in a country which in many ways had changed dramatically over the course of a few decades.

Power and social status were much more broadly dispersed and finely shaded by the end of Chulalongkorn's reign than they had been forty years earlier. The bureaucracy had become a national service instead of a series of local ones topped by the limited circle of the court; and its finely graded hierarchies were reaching down through governors and judges, clerks and schoolteachers, to remote country districts and villages. A new national army and provincial police force had been created, and specialist services proliferated. These were staffed, for the most part, with the graduates of a greatly expanded system of secondary and technical education that by 1910 included thirteen secondary schools with more than 1,250 pupils and at least eleven technical schools with more than 1,500 pupils studying such subjects as medicine, law, education, military and naval sciences, and agriculture. These drew their enrollments from all elements of society but predominantly from the urban centers and mainly from Bangkok. Through these schools came hundreds of civil servants each year, as professional services began to develop and become aware of themselves as new elements in Thai society. In the long run they would come to compete for power with the graduates of the elitist academies and with those whose status and power depended to some degree upon the advantages of birth.

As Skinner points out (1957:ch. 5), Chinese society in Thailand by 1910 was beginning to have a coherence and self-consciousness which involved an increasing emphasis on Chinese education. The growth of modern schools around 1910, sponsored by Chinese community and speech-group associations, reinforced what the Thai came to view as Chinese economic exclusivity; and it had the effect of slowing the rate of assimilation of Chinese into Thai society. To the extent that assimilation became less urgent for the life and prosperity of the Chinese in Thailand; and to the extent that commercial and economic development, as well as the interests of political and social cohesion, provided incentives to the development of Chinese education distinct from that beginning to be offered by the Thai government—to that degree was Chinese participation in Thai government education reduced. No information is available on the proportions of Chinese students in government schools in Bangkok around 1910, but there is evidence that the government was beginning to be concerned over a slowed rate of Chinese assimilation and hoped to use the schools to correct this trend (Wyatt 1969:337–339).

The major government concern in education by 1910, however, was rapidly to achieve universal elementary schooling, and specifically to incorporate into a national educational system the provinces in which more than 90 per cent of the nation's population lived. The revival in the mid-1880's of the policy of extending public secular education in the monasteries had elicited a small but important response in the capital and a few provincial towns; but the numbers involved were minuscule. Through the 1890's the number of monastery schools increased very slowly owing to a shortage of public funds and the lack of a clear commitment to mass education. The first major expansion in provincial education came at the end of the nineteenth century with the king's determination to base Thai nationality and modernity on an educated public. A program separate from the Ministry of Public Instruction was established in 1898 under the leadership of Prince Wachirayān Warōrot, the king's brother and patriarch of the Thammayut reform sect, to survey the educational and religious state and needs of the provinces and to found new schools and modernize the Buddhist hierarchy. The reports of the monks who served as provincial education directors provide revealing glimpses of provincial attitudes toward educational change (Wyatt 1966a:329–331, 344). They are dominated by statements such as the following:

"Laymen are satisfied with [traditional] education as it is. They feel no need for higher [i.e., improved] education, and desire only simple literacy" (Rātchaburī).

"There is little interest in education; more in gambling" (Samut Songkhrām).

"Only one monk and layman in four is dissatisfied with traditional education" (Uthaithānī).

"Two-fifths are satisfied with traditional education" (Tāk).

"Although most laymen are satisfied with education as it is, the monks are not satisfied" (Suphanburī).

"The progress of education will be difficult, as it has not yet been proven to the public that education can make a difference to their livelihood" (Nonthaburī and Pathumthānī).

"Apart from government officials and some Chinese, there is little faith in modern education. People think that there is no use to be served by educating their children" (Čhanthaburī).

"There is more demand for Pali than for Thai instruction. . . . The only support for schools comes from officials and local governing committees" (Nakhǫn Sīthammarāt).

With their supporting evidence, these statements suggest that the provincial demand for modern elementary education as late as 1900 was extremely small. Areas with strong Thammayut monasteries and areas where much modern economic development had taken place seem to have been more responsive to the founding of new schools than less well-developed areas; and government officials, Chinese, and monks generally were more receptive to change than the ordinary town-dweller in the provinces. The demand was beginning to be felt in numerous scattered areas, including some very remote provincial areas in the Northeast (for reasons essentially unexplained); but the numbers enrolled in the new monastery schools as late as 1907 remained relatively small: approximately 20,000 students in 340 schools.

New and clearer concerns motivated a more forceful effort to promote provincial education in the last years of Chulalongkorn's reign. New ideas about the purposes of mass education were articulated eloquently by Prince Wachirayān early in 1906. While he felt government efforts were essentially successful in preparing rapidly large numbers of young men for the public service, Prince Wachirayān was concerned at the government's neglect of vocational education, the result of which he saw to be the economic and technical dominance of the Chinese in Thailand. Education, he argued, was "an instrument of social mobility" (*khrūeang plīan phūen phē*) which the government was using too narrowly. He urged the king to expand the educational system to provide *all* boys with a good general and moral education, as well as to prepare young Thai men for specialized nongovernmental careers in commerce, technical vocations, the crafts, and the professions (Wyatt 1969: 325–328). The same objectives were urged on the government in 1910 by Phrayā Wisut in arguing for the establishment of a major new vocational school in Bangkok (Wyatt 1966a:591). The vocational aspect of these proposals was slow to be embodied in schools, perhaps from lack of demand; but the general desire to build an educated citizenry through universal (and eventually compulsory) education began to be pursued with vigor in 1909. The new schools in every province and town of the kingdom attempted to provide instruction to groups of children in a common national syllabus, using common textbooks and the national language, and overriding provincial dialects and minority languages (Wyatt 1969:328–329). The government was by no means immediately successful in attaining its object; but the institutional framework was created through which further innovations and qualitative improvements could be introduced.

The public response to this major and rapid expansion must have been mixed. The entire kingdom certainly was not induced overnight to accept the proclaimed virtues and value of modern education; yet more than 100,000 boys in Thai villages and towns were attending the formal monastery schools on the modern pattern in 1912. To some extent the idea of the moral, economic, and patriotic value of education may have taken hold quickly; but it would appear that much more crucial to the rapid acceptance of modern education once it was pursued aggressively by the government was the behavior of the leaders of Thai society at all levels. The patterns of authority in traditional Thai society remained relatively intact, and to a considerable extent even the individuals and families remained the same. The moral and political authority of the king, tried and proven over an extremely long reign, coupled with his effective control over the functioning of the civil administration and his strong influence over the Buddhist monkhood and buttressed by the traditional authority and prestige of the monarchy, imbued the royal policies and orders and commitments with a sanctity and "rightness" which made them extremely difficult to resist, particularly when the king had the power to enforce his will if necessary. The leaders of Thai society at all levels, ranged in hierarchies newly tightened and laced with improved communications, responded at least pragmatically to what was expected of them, and they often did so with a confidence born of shrewd self-interest and simple trust. And so provincial governors headed up public subscriptions to build new schools, and village headmen and monks persuaded parents to send their sons to attend them.

The importance of royal authority and "change from above" rightly has been stressed often in treatments of the beginnings of modernization in nineteenth-century Thailand. The delay in reform until the king had established his power over the claims of the conservative nobility attests to this fact. But the greatest advantage the king had thereafter was his control, through carefully selected ministers—most of whom were his own brothers—over the occupational structure of the kingdom. His reform program created a new governmental demand for manpower which could be met only through modern education; and the king and his brothers, partly for political reasons but primarily out of a rational commitment to the idea of government by men qualified through education for their new public roles, shaped the manner in which that demand came to be satisfied. They succeeded in transforming both institutions and values to suit their ends. The traditional association between education and the Buddhist monasteries was maintained, but the content of the new education was secularized and adapted to changed vocational demands and political and social ends. The traditional appeal of the bureaucracy remained, yet the nature of the bureaucratic structure and its roles were changed. The monkhood and the monarchy remained pillars of the moral authority of the state, yet that authority was employed in radically new ways. It was the skillful and creative blending of such "continuities and discontinuities," of which Professor Sharp spoke so eloquently and insightfully in his presidential address to the Association of Asian Studies in 1962, that was so distinctive in the modernization of Thailand and has given Thai society for so long such vibrant strength.

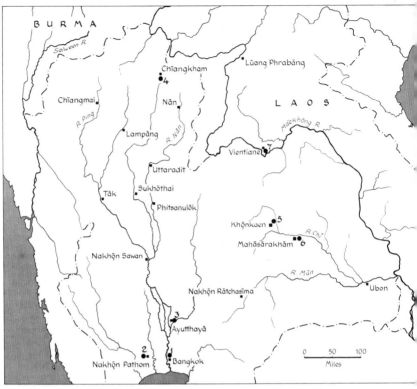

Map 3. Central and North Thailand and Central Laos, showing locations of the following villages: 1 Bāng Chan, 2 Sakathiam, 3 Bān Ǫi, 4 Bān Ping, 5 Bān Khok 6 Bān Nǫngtūēn, and 7 the group of villages studied by Georges Condominas, including Bān Hom, Hūakhūa, Mūēang Nǫi, Nāhai, Nākhwāi, Nǫnghēo, and Sīangdā.

4. Chīangkham's Trade
in the "Old Days"[1]

MICHAEL MOERMAN

One limitation of anthropology's usefulness is that ethnological information is produced about single communities but consumed by persons who are interested in peoples, regions, and nations. Despite Thailand's homogeneity when compared with much of Southeast Asia, those of us who have worked elsewhere than in the Central Plain often feel that the world's view of rural Thailand is biased by Bāng Chan. I have indicated elsewhere that the ethnic identifications (1965), clerical careers (1966), community loyalties (1967), and private irrigation systems (1968:50–53) of North Thailand seem to differ from those of the Central Plain, with the general consequence of making villages in the North more tightly organized and self-sufficient. This paper concerns late nineteenth- and early twentieth-century trade in part of North Thailand, contrasting it with Central Thailand (Siam).

As a prelude to his authoritative study, James C. Ingram characterizes the premodern internal trade of Thailand by these factors:

The Chinese seem to have gained almost complete control of the interregional trade of Siam. They carried the goods . . . even into the remote interior villages. . . . Native produce was thus exchanged for the goods of other regions and other nations through the medium of the [overseas Chinese] traders. . . . Most transactions were on a barter basis. . . . Most of the internal trade of Siam in 1850 was probably carried on through barter entirely within the villages. The movement

[1] Although I am grateful to Sidney W. Mintz and Leopold Pospisil for their comments on an earlier version of this paper, neither of them is responsible for its shortcomings.

151

of goods between villages and between regions must have been relatively small [1971:19–20].

According to the villagers of Chīangkham,[2] however, trade during what they call "the old days" featured the profit-motivated long-distance shipment of goods in the absence of Chinese merchants. The villagers' accounts suggest that one of the following is true. Either (1) the recollections of a few old informants are inappropriate data for doing economic history, or (2) Chīangkham was exceptional, even in the North, or (3) regional trade in the North—certainly in the vicinity of Nan, probably east of the Yom, and perhaps throughout the region—was distinctly different from regional trade in Siam proper. I hope that this paper will encourage students of Thai economic history to investigate these alternatives, to explore the differences among regional patterns of trade, and to suggest the implications of these differences (if any are documented) for subnational organization and peasant economies.

A sketch of local history must preface this account of trade in the old days. I worked in a Lue village called Bān Ping (see Map 3, location 4). The Lue are a T'ai people whose homeland is the Sip Song Panna state of Yunnan. Most of the Lue of Chīangkham district are the descendants of war captives brought from the Sip Song Panna between 1840 and 1860. They settled among another T'ai group, the Yuan or Khon Mūēang. Until 1902 all were under the immediate authority of the Čhao Mūēang Chīangkham who was subordinate to the Prince (Čhao chīwit) of Nan. In 1902, as a consequence of the Shan Rebellion (Curtis 1903:appendix; Moerman 1967: 405–406), the Siamese (Central Thai) conquered Chīangkham and began to administer it directly. Bān Ping's ethnic peculiarity, although unusually prominent, is not unique in that most Northern peasants are, like the Lue, conscious of the minor cultural differences which distinguish them from the Siamese

[2] Chīangkham is in Chīangrai Province (see Map 3, location 4). For two years of field work (1959–1961) there, I am pleased to be able to thank the Foreign Area Training Program of the Ford Foundation.

and so make them Yuan, or Shan, or Yang, and so on. In addition, awareness of a recent Siamese conquest is probably quite general in Chīangrāi, Lampang, Nān, and perhaps in other Northern provinces as well.

Although this paper's subject is historical, it makes use of a vague concept of "the old days" and provides few dates. Using the recollections of village informants makes accurate dating specious and enforces a sense of unpunctuated continuity with the past. The historical events which do provide punctuation can be stated briefly here. The Siamese conquest probably had an immediate effect on the Shan, but Haw trade seems to have persisted unchanged for another twenty years. Chinese shop-keepers apparently followed close on the heels of the Siamese, but the marketplace which the conquerors built seems only gradually to have altered intervillage trade. The old patterns of rice trade were unaffected until a railhead was built at Lampang in about 1917[3] and not completely altered until the use of ox carts became common in the 1930's. For purposes of this paper, then, "the old days" have a poorly documented beginning in about 1880 and taper off at about 1930. Another component of the private calendar which underlies this historical account is that "now" means 1960, the period of most intensive fieldwork.

Trade without Chinese

According to my informants, there were no Chinese in Chīangkham before 1902. They came to sell to the Siamese officials only after a stockade was built. Until the Siamese conquest, regional trading was done by the Haw, the Shan, and the local T'ai.

---

[3] I have been unable to determine the precise date on which the northern line reached Lampang from Bangkok. Investigations kindly undertaken by Boonsanong Punyodyana reveal inconsistencies in the relevant sources. A Thai source (Thailand) Krasūang khommanākhom 1954:232) reports that the railroad reached Chīangmai on 1 January 1921, while an American source (Transportation Consultants, Inc., 1959:49) reports that the route to

The Haw

Throughout the Shan Plateau (lat. 28° N, long. 98° E), long-distance trade was in the hands and on the ponies of the members of an ethnic category locally called Haw. In the recent literature, the Haw are considered to be "overland" Chinese from Yunnan. Even that literature, however, recognizes that they are sharply distinguished locally from the overseas Chinese of Southeast Asia (Skinner 1957:80–81; Halpern 1961:22; Mote 1967:490ff.). Their distinctiveness may be attributed to the fact that many of them were Moslem, or to the divergence of their language from that of any overseas Chinese, or to the complex ethnic origins which makes Leach (1954:59) suggest that the Haw "might well be called Min Chia or Chinese-Lisu." Whatever its basis, the fact remains that the Lue and many foreign observers (Colquhoun [1885] is an exception) did not consider the Haw to be properly Chinese. LeMay's description of their physical appearance (1926:231) as "Chinese and yet not Chinese—a sort of link between the Chinaman and the Shan [i.e., the Northern T'ai]" is an apt characterization of the way in which the Haw were categorized ethnically, and also of the economic and political functions of their north-south trade route.

The Haw brought Chinese silk and metal goods to North Thailand and returned to China with cotton, a surprisingly bulky commodity (Backus 1884:547; Bourne 1888:138, 140). My informants confirm this. Although some imported goods were available in the Chīangkham market before the Siamese conquest, most of what the villagers bought from the outside seems to have come through Haw traders, on their way to Mūēang Sǫng for cotton. The light blue silk ribbon often found on old-style women's jackets was bought from the Haw, as was

---

Chīangmai was completed in 1919. Sophit Sukkasem of Chīangmai told Mr. Punyodyana that he went with his parents from Lampang to Bangkok by rail in 1917. G. William Skinner, in a personal communication, reports that his research makes 1917 the most likely date for the completion of the northern line to Lampang.

the broad sickle with which rice was harvested. Before Yao and then Miao (Meo) tribesmen came to Chīangkham (about 1900), the Haw may also have provided the villagers with a little opium. In the Sip Song Panna, Haw lived in the hills and raised ordinary rice; the Lue grew glutinous rice in the valleys. Unlike their Yuan neighbors, the founders of Bān Ping could converse in Haw.[4]

Politically, the ethnic ambiguity of the Haw may have aided them in carrying goods between Chīangmai and the Shan states despite the enmity between Siam and Burma (cf. Colquhoun 1885:302–305). A British consul (Archer 1892:344) writing at about the same time as Colquhoun did not recognize as Chinese the many Haw caravans he encountered while touring the Shan Plateau and reported: "To show how little direct intercourse there is between China proper and the North of Siam, I may say that these Chinamen (a group of Szechuanese) are the first I had met anywhere in or close to Siamese territory other than immigrants by way of Bangkok."

In addition to their north-south trade, the Haw were responsible for more local movements of rice, tea, opium, and salt. This trade presumably contributed to the viability of the small regional states of the Shan Plateau.

Haw caravans, probably on both routes, used to call at Chīangkham every year during the dry season. Although their importance diminished after the Siamese conquest, they continued to come until the 1920's. LeMay (1926:188) confirms their durability: traveling in North Thailand after the Siamese conquest, he frequently encountered Haw traders. On the border of the Chīangkham district he "met Haw traders coming down from the Shan States—once a party driving a pack of mules, and at another time itinerant vendors, selling cloth, betel boxes and a miscellany of articles." The village theory

---

[4] Some contemporary villagers know the Haw language. The Chīangkham Lue seem to be friendlier with the Haw and more active in the hill trade than the Yuan are. Mote's report on Haw in Chīangmai (1967:512, 517) indicates that the obverse is also true, that the Haw get on better with the Lue than with the Yuan.

that the Haw no longer come only because China is now communist tends to support the idea that their trade ceased only recently.

The Shan

The other ethnic category whom villagers and Western observers consider the main traders in North Thailand were unequivocally not Chinese. According to my informants, "The Shan were the real traveling traders in the old days. No one packed as many oxen as the Chīangtung people." The importance of Shan traders is confirmed in accounts of the North (Dodd 1923:226; Graham 1924, vol. 1:172). Chīangtung's prominence came from its plentiful rice and opium and from the easy northern access which made it a great entrepôt for Chinese goods (Colquhoun 1885:302). Shan trade was less "international" in character than that of the Haw, for they did business mainly with fellow lowland T'ai. Their use of pack oxen, less hardy than the Haw ponies and mules, discouraged them from the tortuous mountain paths and also limited the speed of their trips.

In Chīangkham, however, the Shan were prominent more as merchants than as itinerant traders. Before Chinese shopkeepers came to the town, there were about ten impermanent Shan stalls where cloth, probably from Burma, was the main stock, but in which salt, dyestuffs, and kerosene were also available. These local Shan were petty merchants without political authority. But it must be remembered that they were able to ally themselves with the Shan, whose rebellion brought on the Siamese conquest. Their position was perhaps similar to that of the few contemporary merchants in Chīangkham whom the Thai government thinks are loyal to Communist China. Although the Shan families still in the town are not especially prominent, a lovely old Shan-style temple testifies to their former prosperity.

Long-Distance Trade for Profit

If the difference between Ingram's description of Siam in

1850 and my villagers' accounts was limited to the unimportance of the Chinese, it would perhaps be merely a historical curiosity. For our understanding of the economy of the North, it is more important to describe the ways in which villagers themselves traded. By concentrating on the rice trade I want to indicate that villagers, both before and well into the twentieth century, regularly pooled their resources and assumed entrepreneurial risks in order to move and sell large quantities of goods over long distances. They were motivated by a desire for profits, which they sometimes invested.

Physical Components

In much of North Thailand there are wide annual variations in rice yields, probably attributable to the rough terrain which creates shifting rain shadows and discourages large-scale irrigation works. In Chīangkham, however, the crop has always been bountiful. The local people ascribe this to the comparative superiority of the district's levees and ditches. Whatever the reason, Chīangkham has always had rice to export, and there have always been villagers who moved it.

All the rice that left Chīangkham was carried in the dry season. Traders might leave any time after the December harvest. They returned, at the latest, in time for the plowing that follows the April New Year. Prior to the introduction of carts, in Chīangkham and throughout the North (Backus 1884:434ff.), harvested rice was brought from the fields and milled rice taken for sale by trains of pack oxen. The lead ox, like the lead mule of Yunnanese caravans, often wore an elaborate mask of shells and feathers. In Chīangkham, follower oxen wore rattan muzzles to prevent them from disturbing the animal ahead. Many carried rattan frames containing huge bronze bells (illustration facing p. 222 of le May 1926) which announced the arrival of the caravan to its customers. When the middle-aged and older men reminisce about the fun of these trading trips, they often mention the melodious sound of these great bells, which also served to safeguard the venture and ensure its success. (Villagers believe that the protective spirits that live in the bells can still bring stray cattle home if one sacrifices a chicken to them.) Turbans, earrings, bright shoulder cloths, ceremonial swords, neat tucker baskets, and red shoulder bags made a pageant of the expedition.

Whatever the pleasures of using pack oxen, these beasts are clearly limited as conveyances. Three oxen are reckoned to carry about 100 kilograms[5]; an ox load of rice was worth less than two shirts.

The oxen set the pace of the trip. Ideally, one traveled only from the very early morning (perhaps 5:00 A.M.) until breakfast (10:30 at the latest) and let the oxen rest for the remainder of the day.[6] At this pace, a nonstop trip to Uttaradit, over 130 miles away, took twenty-six days. But it was very unusual to go so fast; the trips were leisurely and comfortable. One built a sleeping shelter and, if caught in the rains, the oxen too would be provided with leaf and bamboo coverings much like those now made for carts. The rice was always kept wrapped in leaves to protect it against the hazards of the journey.

The former traders are quite gleeful about the occasional large profits they made, but a more dominant memory is of the fun they had, of the sights along the way, of opportunity for song and riddle. Even in boasting of their success, they talk in this way: "I was a trading man. Whenever I made a trip, however far I went, I would sleep on a mattress every night. I never had to bring a mat or food because wherever I went, there were friends who would put me up. I would put them up when they came through here. A trading man must have a large house

[5] This capacity, which seems surprisingly small to me, is confirmed by villagers' unanimity and by Mouhot's (1966:143) estimate.

[6] Mouhot's ox caravan, traveling in the Northeast in 1859, rested daily from 10:00 A.M. to 3:00 P.M. because the oxen required it. Huts for this purpose were never more than twelve miles apart (Mouhot 1966:39f.). Elephant travel seems to have had similar limits of weight and distance; according to Mouhot (1966:143), "the load of three small oxen . . . is all that I ever saw the largest elephant carry easily. . . . Ten or twelve miles are the usual day's work."

because he has many age-mates [*sīo*]." Adventure, fellowship, popularity, and prominence—as well as profit—rewarded the trader.

Before the Siamese conquest, there was no road to Phayao. Only long after the Siamese conscripted Chīangkham villagers to clear a path was the route used for the rice trade. Until the railroad to Lampang was completed in 1920, the rice of Chīangkham was taken almost due south (see Map 4). It went through the valley of the Wāen and the feeder valleys of the Yom to Mūeang Ọi, Chīangmūan, Mūeang Sọng and, ultimately, to Phrāe, over 100 miles away. A trader returned when the rice was sold, although for reaching Phrāe there was a bonus of which many traders took advantage. At Uttaradit, nearly forty miles below Phrāe, one could obtain salt brought up from the Gulf of Siam. Since no one in Uttaradit eats the glutinous rice of the North, the Chīangkham traders would sell out no farther south than Phrāe and proceed with unladen oxen to Uttaradit for salt. Sometimes the traders of Phrāe were enterprising enough to bring up the salt from Uttaradit, but this was unusual.

During the ten or so years between the completion of the railroad and the advent of the cart, there was still an occasional trip to Uttaradit, in one instance for selling oxen. However, it seems to have been more usual in that period to have packed rice to Phayao. From Phayao, where rice seems always to have been plentiful, it was sent on to the railhead at Lampang. The advantages of the oxcart were greater speed and capacity. By pack train the round trip to Phayao took fifteen days; by cart, it took only four. While it required three oxen to pack 100 kilograms over dry roads, a pair of oxen could pull their driver and a cart laden with 300 kilograms through mud and water.

Social Components

Not all of the five great rice traders, of whom Thammačhai (born c. 1880) alone survives, went every year. According to a

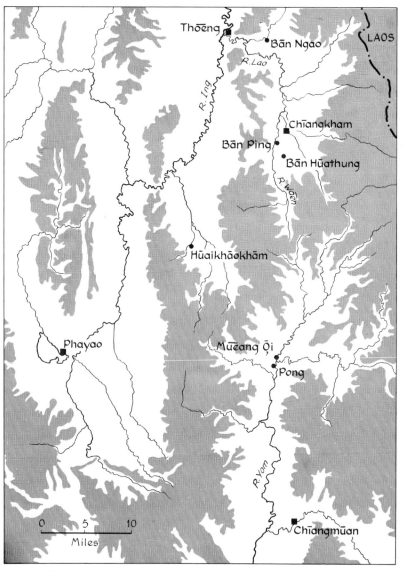

Map 4. Chīangkham and environs.

modern critic, the wealthy son of a trader, "Only when the money from the last trip was gone would they leave on another trip." Nevertheless, says Thammachai, it was often news of prices given them by trade-friends that inspired a trip. The trader would then go to one or two close kinsmen who also traded and together they would assemble as much rice and oxen as they could command. Every ten oxen required an assistant, and these were usually recruited from among younger relatives. I do not have enough information about the composition of these trading groups to know which kin principles, if any, were operative. I suppose, however, that assistants were selected on the nonexplicit principle of close- or co-residence. Some indication of this can be seen from the two former trading groups about which I do have information (see Figure 5). Today, assistants tend to be close kin.

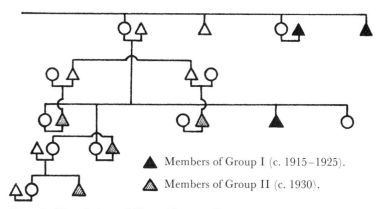

Figure 5. Kin relations of Chīangkham trading groups.

If there were not enough junior kinsmen, or if he "wished to help people poorer than he," the trader might take on some young and needy fellow villager, but even then the trade party is described in the vocabulary of kinship. In Chīangkham, and probably in all of Thailand, dependency relations are modeled

on kin principles. One frequently uses kin terms nongenealogi-
cally, and even where kin terms proper are not employed, the
kinlike terms of *lūknǭng*, literally "junior child," for subordinates and *phǭliang*, "nourishing father," for patrons and bene-
factors are used in Chīangkham by both villagers and officials.
There seems to have been no financial discrimination against
subordinates who were not close kinsmen. Regardless of
genealogical connection, those who contributed goods to the
expedition were partners, the others were more like employees.
Whether close kinsmen or not, these employees were paid according to the length of the trip: three baht to Chīangmūan,
six baht to Phrāē, ten baht to Uttaradit. Although the amounts
were the same, payments to a nonrelative were called "wages,"
payments to kinsmen, "gifts." "To make a gift" (*pan*) is applied
to exchanges in which the donor decides, often without specifically informing the recipient, how much is to be given. "To
hire" (*čhāng*) is reserved for situations in which both parties
have agreed, often by haggling, on how much is to be paid for
services. Even where the valuables in question are equal, the
villager in the nineteenth century and now (Moerman 1968)
uses "hire" and "give" to distinguish between commercial and
noncommercial transactions.

A young man might model himself on the trade exploits of
his father, just as Thammačhai remembers how his father, Tao,
sometimes went for salt to the city of Nān in the 1890's. More
often one learned from older collateral kinsmen, for father and
son rarely went together. One of them had to stay home to care
for farm and family, since no one was exclusively a trader.

Economic Aspects

Let us now consider the sequence of activities involved in a
rice trip in order to gauge the ways in which considerations of
straightforward economic advantage seem to have influenced
the form and scale of the trade. The trader's first task was
obtaining rice to move and sell. Although casual accounts make

it sound as if traders sold rice only from their own fields, much
of their stock was bought from fellow villagers or, less frequently, from neighboring Lue villages for a relatively stable
price. Throughout Thammachai's long career, he never bought
unmilled rice for less than five baht[7] and rarely for more than
six baht. The price at which he sold his rice was usually between
seven and nine baht though it sometimes went as high as ten
baht and, in one year, it reached twenty-three. Usually, the
more the trader got for his rice, the more he had paid for it. The
price was determined by scarcity and, although Chīangkham
was always comparatively fortunate, the same climate affected
its crop as that of its customers. In the disastrous year of Halley's
Comet, rice prices were fourteen times higher than normal, but
there were no rice trips in that year; "they would have made
for too much rivalry." Instead, people came to Chīangkham's
villages from as far away as Phayao or Chīangmai to buy or
beg or barter rice in small quantities.

The village trader, then, could safely anticipate a gross profit
but was unable to predict its size. He made use of ties of kinship,
neighborhood, and ethnicity to obtain his stock and might
therefore be said to be trading for his neighbors and community.
Nevertheless, it must be emphasized that the Lue rice trader,
like the Haw and the Shan, owned the goods he moved and
traded. When the trader transported rice, he assumed all economic risks. There were kinsmen to comfort him and trade-
friends to help him. But, whatever the prices, the rains, or the
health of his oxen, the profits were the trader's, and so were the
losses.

In normal times there seems to have been as much rice
available to the trader as he wanted to buy. Much of this was
dry rice for, like tractor-plowed crops today (Moerman 1968),
dry rice was cultivated as a supplementary source of cash and

[7] All prices are for one saen, equivalent to somewhat less than 100
kilograms.

not principally for subsistence. Transplanted rice seems to have always been viewed by the villager primarily as a subsistence crop. The extent of his cultivation is limited by the capacity of his carabao and by the labor available to the household at plowing time. A secondary crop of dry rice, though its yield was less, allowed more latitude. Its timing was not as firmly fixed by the rains, and it required intensive labor (for weeding and harvest) when one was not busy with irrigated fields. This permitted many households to grow dry rice which, through the trader, became a source of cash for consumption goods.

The trader took as much rice as he had cash to buy and oxen to carry. What, then, limited the scale of his operations? Since credit institutions were known as far back as my information goes, I asked a few old traders whether they had ever bought rice on credit for subsequent resale. The typical answer was, "Only very, very rarely did we *have* to buy rice on credit." Apparently, they viewed credit not as a normal means for expanding their scale of trade, but as something to be avoided.

An ox load weighs only thirty kilograms, but a trader can move as many loads as he has oxen. Since there was no scarcity of rice or labor, we must agree with Thammačhai when he tells us that "the number of oxen was the main limit on the scale of trade." An expedition might include fifty or sixty oxen, but rarely would any one trader have more than ten. Pooling their oxen was the main reason why traders went together. In addition, the villagers tend to equate the size of a group with the amount of fun it has; a large group also protects one against brigandage (which seems never to have occurred) and the evil spirits.

A trader's stature depended on the number of oxen he owned. But since traders realized that the scale of trade depended on the size of the caravan, did they attempt to borrow or rent oxen for the trading season? This question is relevant because at that time, as now, it was possible to rent carabao for plowing. But Thammačhai tells us: "No one rented oxen. For a short trip, say to Chīangmūan, one could sometimes ask to borrow the ox of a close relative." When pressed for a reason and presented with the analogy of carabao rental he could only suggest that "perhaps the owners were afraid the animals would come to harm." Renting oxen, like buying rice on credit, was not a normal way to increase the scale of trade.

It is still a prominent feature of the village economy that one does not consciously borrow in order to invest.[8] Given weak reserves and generally high interest rates, fear of debt is not irrational, but it is nonetheless a major influence on the sluggishness of peasant economies.

To avoid unnecessary weight, all the rice taken in trade was first milled in foot mortars. When I tried to see whether those hired for this tedious task were a sort of proletariat, Thammačhai's denial furnished insight into the villagers' motives for economic activity: "One often . . . hired unmarried girls who wanted to buy trinkets or young mothers who wanted things for their baby. Only very rarely did one hire poor people. Those who milled the rice were paid one bi for each shoulder load. This is equivalent to eight shoulder loads for one baht. But people usually stopped after milling two shoulder loads because two bi was enough to buy a jacket or whatever else they wanted." The traders, like those they hired, seem to have had limited economic ambitions. They viewed themselves principally as farmers and saw trade as but one of a number of sources of secondary income open to villagers. As Thammačhai puts it: "Other people spent the dry season in making gardens or in cultivating dry fields. If the gardens did well and one spent little, one could do quite well without trading. Similarly, with trading, there was no certainty of wealth, there was no lump sum of money. We were not like the Chinese now in the market.

---

[8] I stipulate conscious borrowing because villagers do not seem to regard the various credit and part-payment mechanisms which some of them have always used to obtain land as involving borrowing or indebtedness.

We went in part just to travel, in part to visit age-mates, in part to trade." These regular traders "spent the money they made on clothes and gifts for relatives, on liquor and gambling." Like the women they hired to mill, their uses for money limited their desire for it.

Then, as now, village standards of consumption emphasized conviviality and generosity. Then, as now, the purpose of economic life was "enought to eat, and enough to give the temple." Then, as now, all villagers saw themselves as farmers and the trading season was determined by the rice cycle. Presumably, this was not a reasoned choice among alternative sources of income, for it is quite unlikely that anyone considered whether he could make more by trading full-time. As Thammačhai explains: "A trip selling tobacco in Chīangmai would make [five to ten times as much as the usual rice trip] but I only made a few of these. The distance is so great I couldn't be sure of getting home in time to plow the fields. One can't give up farming. One has to eat rice. The money made in trade bought small luxuries. Rice farming provides rice to eat."

These curtailed aspirations were quite reasonable. Rice was an essential subsistence good and, given the local market, farming the only sure way to obtain it. Limited imported goods and sumptuary regulations restricted the consumption items on which wealth could be spent. Although land was always purchasable, large holdings had little incremental utility because the availability of virgin land made it difficult to hire the laborers who—given the intensive farming methods—would be needed for their cultivation. Moreover, the small market for Chīangkham's rice was perhaps the greatest single limit on the scale of the trade. The only customers were consumers. Now there are roads and railways for transporting rice to a market which, to any single peasant, appears infinite. But, "in the old days, it was hard to sell rice. One had to walk with it to the man who would eat it. Now, one merely takes it to the road or to the mill." When a caravan reached a village, its leader would tether the oxen and put up with a trade-friend. Customers came to buy only small amounts for their own consumption. Very infrequently a large sale might be made, to merchants in Mūēang Sǫng or Phrāē or to British lumber concessionaires in Chīangmūan. Even these rare large sales did not dispose of an entire caravan's load.

It would be wrong to exaggerate the pettiness of the rice trade, however, for it furnished steady income and distributed a basic subsistence good through a large region. In addition, the caravans traded in other goods, often at a substantial profit, and sometimes to provide young men with essential investment capital. Village rice traders occasionally brought hides, horns, sealing wax, and Chīangmūan tobacco south to Phrāē or Uttaradit.[9] On the trip home a trader would return with salt or, less commonly, kerosene. He might dispose of the salt in small amounts throughout the year, sometimes bartering it. In contrast to rice, it was also fairly common for customers, some of them Shan merchants, to buy large amounts of salt or kerosene for resale. However the trader disposed of these imports, his profits were substantial. About thirty years ago, he could buy salt for seven baht in Uttaradit and sell it in Chīangkham for fifteen. Many years before that, salt bought for four baht in Uttaradit could be resold locally for twenty-five or thirty. Having brought salt into the region, the trader sold it at the same price all the way from Chīangkham to Mūēang Thōēng (fifteen miles away) to both fellow villagers and strangers.

Although marketing salt and kerosene along the rice route may have contributed some investment capital, a more important source was the adventures in trade which young men— some of them trained by an elder on the rice route—made into alien lands. Although such trips were, for any set of individuals, infrequent, their contribution to the village economy was quite significant. My records of major land purchases in the old days are inadequate for sampling purposes, but it is nonetheless striking that most of them were made from the profits of a

---

[9] Rice, hides, and sealing wax are still Chīangkham's major exports.

young man's trade ventures. Trips to Laos for elephants to sell
to the Karen near Chīangmai, to North Laos for gold and jewels
to sell in the city of Lampang, to Northeast Thailand for ponies
to sell to the mountain peoples, to Burma with oxen, to Chīangmai with tobacco or carabao—these are prominent memories
for many villagers. Most men in Bān Ping have traded in the
surrounding hills, and not a few have organized complicated
ventures involving horses, cotton, fermented tea (mīang), and
opium. In the past, no one derived his regular income from
these interethnic transactions, but many now base their livelihood on their profits. A house, developed land, oxen for the
rice route, came from these dashing exploits in trade. They,
together with clearing virgin land, were the way in which young
men established themselves. While far less frequent than the
rice trips south, this type of trade expanded the village's capital
and helped pay for founding new households.

The regular southern rice route would not have existed without annual advantageous prices along its course. Price variation
from region to region was relatively stable, but traders were
often hindered by lack of market information and sometimes
refused to sell at one village only to travel five days farther and
discover the same price there. Price limits were set by past prices
and by relative scarcity, but for any particular sale "the price
was determined by haggling. The seller wants a high price, the
buyer wants to give a low one. The buyer threatens that the
seller won't be able to unload his product; the seller replies that
he'll go farther on and sell it there. [Haggling] then was just
like it is now."

Because he went to rice-poor regions, and because it had
always been that way, the trader expected to get more than he
had paid for his rice. Barter was unusual, credit discouraged,[10]
and minor charity occasional. That is, the trader insisted on

---

[10] The price for a credit sale was slightly higher—nine baht, say, instead
of eight.

selling all of his rice for profit in cash. When demand was too weak to permit this, he entrusted his surplus to a "kinsman" or age-mate (*sīo*), who sold it for him. Such men were themselves traders. They took no fee, but expected similar services in return. Because of these deposit sales, his need for hospitality, his vulnerability to thieves, and his desire for market intelligence, the trader could not do without numerous "kinsmen," age-mates, and other intimates along his route of trade. I do not want to claim that the warm human satisfaction with which traders describe the number and personal qualities of their age-mates is mere commercial chicanery. I merely want to suggest that the resources of manipulable kinship (Moerman 1966), sīo relations, and common ethnicity were important for successful commerce. The need for cooperation from other traders helps me to understand the lack of competition. If a trader came upon a village where another was selling rice, he would usually just move on. If the other trader's price was lower than what the first planned to charge, he might lower his price in the next village. But two traders would never compete in the same village.

The trader's need for hospitality, security, and someone to vouch for him in the villages he visited probably accounts for the conservatism of his trade routes. Since his customers were all consumers who knew no less about qualities of rice than he did, the absence of price competition would have made it important that his customers know and trust him (Mintz 1961). It is in such straightforwardly economic terms, and not as a conflict between commerce and comfort, that we must understand Thammachai's report:

Chīangkham rice was always taken to Mūeang Sǫng and Phrāē. Phayao traders took their rice to Lampang. Even if the Lampang price was better, a Chīangkham man wouldn't go there. Even if the Phrāē price was better, a Phayao man wouldn't go there. The length of the trip was not the only consideration. Where one's usual road went, there were kinsmen and fellow Lue as far as Bān Tāfā [in

Chīangmūan]. Beyond that, there were age-mates and friends and intimates with whom one ate and who would stay at one's home when they came selling salt. If strangers came selling rice, people wouldn't buy from them. They would wait for the men they knew. If we went on the Lampang route, people wouldn't buy from us. If Phayao traders took our route, our people wouldn't buy from them.

Conclusions

Chīangkham's trade "in the old days" featured the entrepreneurially motivated and economically active movement and cash sale of significant quantities of basic goods over long distances, without the participation of Chinese merchants. The differences between this trade and Ingram's (1971) picture of the Siamese are not trivial. The differences which the present paper sketches suggest that the Northerner was a different sort of economic man from the Siamese. Siamese villagers, as Ingram depicts them, would apparently have been too primitive economically to engage in enterprises of the scale, institutionalization, entrepreneurial acumen, and economic importance that characterize northern trade in the nineteenth and early twentieth centuries. Exploring this contrast requires more intensive economic history than Ingram or I have provided.

The economic history of Chīangkham suggests that the view of peasant economies as nonrational, conservative, and status-oriented is a basic error, presumably resulting from the analyst's reification of his ideal types. If intensive investigation of pre-modern Siamese economic activity discloses commercial ambitions and activities quite as rational, although perhaps on a smaller scale, as those found in Chīangkham, such a discovery would indicate that it is quite wrong to suppose that entrepreneurial views are an innovation for Thai peasants (cf. Ayal 1966:7). If, on the other hand, it turns out that the Siamese were, in fact, less commercially astute than the T'ai of the North, these differences might turn out to have been the consequence, and not the cause, of the activities of Chinese merchants, whose commercial superiority may have resulted from government policies encouraging differential economic opportunities (Skinner 1957:96ff.). Whatever the conclusions from a study of comparative regional economic history, they will have implications for programs and predictions of Thai economic development and for our notions of the rational capacities of peasant economies.

5. Economy, Polity, and Religion in Thailand[1]

A. THOMAS KIRSCH

The 1855 Bowring Treaty with Great Britain was perhaps the most notable of a number of treaties concluded between Thailand (then known as Siam) and various European powers in the mid-nineteenth century. Through such treaties the Thai were joined politically with the international community of nations and the Thai economy was linked with world trade and markets. From the mid-nineteenth century on, numerous social changes followed directly or indirectly from the implementation of these treaties. The Thai government itself was expanded, the administrative and legal systems were modernized (i.e., Westernized), and government assumed completely new functions such as providing a national secular school system. The Thai economy also expanded and was monetarized, while the mass of Thai citizens were freed from traditional corvée obligations. New ways of obtaining government revenues were developed as such traditional means as maintaining royal trading monopolies and selling exclusive rights to collect taxes on gambling, opium, and alcohol were gradually eliminated. Political centralization and internal commerce were facilitated by im-

[1] Sections of this paper were read at the meetings of the American Anthropological Association held in Denver in 1965. Earlier versions of this paper benefited from comments by Lauriston Sharp, G. William Skinner, Charles F. Keyes, and David K. Wyatt. Errors of fact or interpretation are exclusively my own. Lauriston Sharp (1968) has also called attention to a number of the points discussed here.

proved lines of transportation and communication constructed by wage labor under government sponsorship. The net result of these social changes was to create a host of new political and economic opportunities for Thai at all levels of society.

The changes in Thai society since the nineteenth century have highlighted several social patterns which appear to have deep historical roots in Thai culture. One pattern relates to the dominant role played by non-Thai ethnic groups in the Thai economy. Although elimination of traditional labor obligations freed Thai to take advantage of the new opportunities in the expanding economy, few in fact did so. Thai did increase their involvement in rice agriculture, but they were rarely attracted to the roles of businessman or merchant, or even to wage labor as such. Instead, non-Thai, particularly Overseas Chinese, assumed these roles and carried out these economic functions. While considerable historical evidence indicates that this is a long-standing Thai pattern (see Gervaise 1690:26ff.; Bowring 1857:241f.; and especially Skinner 1957:ch. 3), Ingram's summary of the period from 1850 on underlines the modern situation:

One of the outstanding features of the period . . . has been the general willingness of the Thai to leave the entrepreneurship function to foreigners. This was true not only in the case of middleman organization. In any new development which required the application of business methods and the use of individual entrepreneurship, the Thai were rarely to be found. Another striking feature of this period of Thailand's history was the existence of a supply of foreign entrepreneurship which was willing to flow into the country and allowed to [1971:37].

As Ingram indicates, the pattern of foreign involvement in the Thai economy was not fortuitous. Rather, it was actually promoted by official Thai policy. While Thai were not actively discouraged from taking advantage of the new economic opportunities, Chinese immigration and involvement in the economy was encouraged. An explicit official rationale for doing away with the traditional corvée requirements and creating wage-labor occupations, which were to be filled by Chinese, was to avoid the "vexation, misery and compulsion" of impressed Thai labor (cited in Skinner 1957:114) and to leave the "farming classes" undisturbed (Ingram 1971:210, n. 14). This situation suggests that in the nineteenth century Chinese control of strategic economic roles was not considered a threat to Thai society. Such a situation is of interest not only because it contrasts with the great concern expressed by contemporary European nations about foreign involvement in and potential control of domestic economies, but also because in the twentieth century official Thai policy underwent a change. Anti-Chinese feeling became manifest particularly after World War I and culminated shortly before World War II in a host of restrictive legislation aimed at limiting foreign (i.e., non-Thai) economic control and the increasing Thai-ification of the economy. That is, a pattern of economic specialization that had been encouraged in the nineteenth century was seen as a threat in the mid-twentieth century.

A second pattern highlighted by changes in Thai society since the nineteenth century also concerns Thai involvement in economic roles. While Thai are generally not attracted to economically oriented entrepreneurial or commerical roles, those who do get involved in such activities are disproportionately women. Occasional comments of early Western and non-Western visitors to Thailand indicate that this pattern also has a long history in Thailand (see La Loubère 1693:50, 73; Gervaise 1690:37, 52; Benedict 1952:3). Such historical observations about the role of Thai women in economic activities may be dismissed as the result of unsystematic impressions and therefore not reliable guides to the actual situation. More recent and more systematic data support the view that these impressionistic historical observations may reveal a long-standing pattern of sex role specialization in certain types of occupation among ethnic Thai. Skinner

(1957:301ff.) presents a model of occupational stratification in Bangkok as of 1952 that represents a reworking of 1947 census statistics and 1952 registration statistics. These statistics indicate "the Chinese preference for (and dominance in) commerce and finance, and industrial and artisan occupations" (Skinner 1957:302). But this census material also records the numbers of Thai men and women involved in a wide variety of occupations as well as the Chinese participation in the labor force surveyed; as many as three times more women than men held such positions as the following: large business owners and managers, small business owners and managers, market sellers in stalls, hawkers and petty market sellers, and market gardeners. More recent than the 1947 census figures is an article in Time magazine (1965:19f.) which reports that Thai women own about 90 per cent of Bangkok real estate and have heavy interests in transportation companies, construction firms, and restaurants. Thus the impressionistic observations of early visitors to Siam that Thai women are more active economically than Thai men receive support from more contempory observers.

Although these more recent data refer specifically to Bangkok, the pattern of Thai women specializing in economic activities is not confined to the relatively modernized or urban areas. In provincial towns and rural villages a similar pattern can be observed in which Thai women carry out the bulk of the petty marketing chores and are commonly the controllers of a household's pursestrings (deYoung 1963:24, 103f.).

Early observers sometimes attributed this pattern of economic specialization to the "laziness" or business "inefficiency" of Thai men. While the pattern is reasonably clear, such explanations are hardly adequate. But we might well ask: If Thai women are specialized with respect to economic activities, what are Thai men doing? Of course, the overwhelming bulk of the Thai population—both men and women—is engaged in agricultural production, most notably irrigated rice culture.

However, Skinner's statistics provide further evidence about the occupational specializations of Thai men.[2] His figures show they are active in a variety of skilled crafts such as carpentry, and in unskilled labor such as the construction trades. More significantly, Thai men are overwhelmingly involved in a variety of bureaucratic jobs and professional specialties. For example, more than ten times as many men as women were high-ranking government officials, high-status professionals, members of a high office staff or high-status industrial staff, lower government officials, government clerks, and business clerks. Thus the Thai pattern of occupational specialization follows a sexual division of labor, women specializing in "economic-type" activities, men specializing particularly in bureaucratic or "political-type" activities (Skinner 1957:302).

Just as the pattern of Thai women specializing in economic affairs can be seen in rural areas as well as in urban contexts, so too can the specialization of men in political activities. But this male pattern is obscured in the countryside, largely because small villages are not deemed to be arenas for political achievement, which in any event is limited at the village level. It becomes more evident at the district and provincial levels, and more so in the national administrative hierarchy.

[2] Two operations were performed on the statistics reported by Skinner to examine the pattern of Thai occupational specialization. First, assuming that occupations dominated by Chinese are particularly "economic," all occupations were classified as to whether the ratio of Chinese to Thai in each exceeded the ratio of Chinese to Thai in the total labor force surveyed. All occupations were further classified as to whether the ratio of Thai women to Thai men in each exceeded the ratio of Thai men to Thai women in the total work force. These operations yielded four categories: "Chinese dominated–Thai male dominated," "Chinese dominated–Thai female dominated," "Thai dominated–Thai male dominated" and "Thai dominated–Thai female dominated" occupations. The present discussion deals primarily with two of these categories, "Chinese dominated–Thai female dominated" and "Thai dominated–Thai male dominated" occupations. These two categories include over half the total number of Thai men and women reported in the statistics.

While this pattern of occupational specialization may not be uniquely Thai, it is well marked and distinctive, and can be shown to be both historically consistent and pervasive throughout Thai society. Yet there is no simple or obvious rule in Thai culture that immediately suggests why such a pattern should exist. Is there some general cultural factor operating in Thai society that subtly molds predispositions and attitudes of individual Thai and then leads to this pattern of occupational specialization? Surely, to account for such a widespread and persistent pattern we must seek out some cultural factor which has also had a long history in and pervasive impact on Thai society. One such factor is Theravada Buddhism, a potent influence on the Thai since at least the thirteenth century.

There are good theoretical and empirical reasons for looking to Thai religion to help account for these social patterns. Clifford Geertz (1966) has argued that religious systems, particularly in their symbolic and ritual aspects, may serve to induce predispositions and attitudes in religious contexts which influence activities in nonreligious contexts. In particular, Geertz sees the symbolic structure of religious systems as providing a model *of* society—making the present state of the world as experienced meaningful—and as a model *for* society—providing a set of images and patterns for constructing new modes of organizing social activities.

Aside from such general theoretical considerations there are a number of reasons for believing that religious values play some role in establishing the pattern of Thai occupational specialization. For one thing, it has sometimes been argued (see Ayal 1963) that the other-worldly focus of Buddhism generally discourages attempts at economic achievement, which is one aspect of the general pattern displayed in Thai society. Thus Buddhist values and attitudes may help us to understand a part of the Thai pattern, that part which singles out what Thai are *not* doing, i.e., operating in the economic sphere. Can an investigation of Buddhist values and beliefs broaden our understanding of the general patterns found in Thai society? Are there other elements in the patterning of Thai society we have overlooked but which may highlight further aspects of Thai social action? Can a study of Buddhism in Thailand help us to understand what Thai *are* doing—men specializing in political activities while women specialize in economic activities—as well as what they are not doing? Might the operation of religious factors provide insights into why Chinese control of the Thai economy was encouraged in the nineteenth century and strongly discouraged in the twentieth? I believe so.

By broadening our perspective to include the religious factor we can immediately discern yet another social pattern of specialization which is not revealed in conventional statistics on Thai occupations. This pattern, like that of political specialization, is associated particularly with men. Thai men have not only specialized in political or bureaucratic roles, but also in Buddhist ecclesiastical or "religious" roles. Indeed, there is an explicit ideal that each Thai man should spend at least a portion of his life in the Buddhist monkhood. While this ideal is not universally fulfilled, it is potent enough to encourage well over half the eligible Thai males to meet it.[3] It is noteworthy that in any one year as many as one man in every fifty may be in the Buddhist Order (Sangha). Women, of course, cannot be monks. In Thai society women's religious roles in general and Buddhist roles (e.g., the "nunhood") in particular are not only poorly developed but are also not highly regarded. Including the religious element, then, does add another dimension to our understanding of the patterning of Thai specialization. Economic roles generally are not popular and tend to be associated

[3] Thai statistics (Thailand 1965:509) report that over 95 per cent of the eligible males over fifty have served for a time as a monk. This figure seems to be inflated but does reveal the importance to the Thai of the ideal that all men should serve for a time as a monk. My figure of over half the eligible males meeting this ideal is derived from my own research in Northeast Thailand and the published reports of other fieldworkers.

with Thai women; men tend to specialize in religious and political roles. Perhaps consideration of the symbolic and ritual elements of Thai Buddhism may shed further light on these social patterns.

Nirvana, the formal goal of Buddhism, has often been characterized as radically other-worldly.[4] The Buddha taught about the transience of worldly things and the myth of individual personality, the dangers of desire and ignorance and a way of escape from the miseries of endless rebirth with its continued suffering in the world. Like Buddhists elsewhere, Thai Buddhists differ considerably with respect to their sophistication and understanding of the more philosophical elements of Buddhist doctrine. Sophisticated Buddhists may indeed repudiate sensual indulgence in the world and seek actively for "extinction"; less sophisticated Buddhists commonly claim to be seeking, not Nirvana, but a sojourn in some "paradise" after death and perhaps as improved status (as a rich man, for example) in a future life (Young 1898:277). If the explicit goals of the less sophisticated layman do not appear to involve a rejection of sensual enjoyments, neither can they be seen literally as inversions of the other-worldly element of sophisticated Buddhist belief. An enhanced rebirth status and/or "paradise" are not seen as *final* religious goals; they might better be seen simply as lower-order specifications of the abstract final goal of doctrinal Buddhism. When Buddhist laymen focus on such proximate religious goals as an enhanced rebirth they are recognizing implicitly what formal doctrine makes explicit: Nirvana is very abstract and distant and difficult for anyone to aspire to, much less achieve. Hence the layman aims at Buddhist-sanctioned goals which are more proximate and capable of achievement. In some respects one might compare this situation to the regime followed by Alcoholics Anonymous,

---

[4] The following discussion is elaborated and further implications are drawn in Kirsch (1973).

which recognizes that for an alcoholic to achieve "total sobriety" may be too abstract and distant a goal, focusing on it is to court backsliding. Instead, alcoholics are encouraged to focus on a more specific and proximate goal: to avoid taking a drink for twenty-four hours. We might view twenty-four hours in the experience of a Western alcoholic to be a rough equivalent of several lifetimes for the Buddhist attached to the world.

The religious goal of Nirvana is intimately connected with two central elements of Buddhist doctrine which are understood in some fashion by all Buddhists, sophisticated or unsophisticated. These two doctrines are karma and multiple rebirths (sometimes known as transmigration). Karma postulates that every act has some measure of religious reward or punishment attached to it and roots the cause of suffering in the world directly to the nature of acts themselves—hence the goal of Buddhist religious action, to escape from the world. The doctrine of multiple rebirths indicates that the path of escape from the world is long and difficult. These two elements of Buddhist belief are logically interconnected and form, in Max Weber's terms, "the most consistent theodicy ever produced by history" (1958:121).[5] Together they have far-reaching implications for a Buddhist world view.

The notion of a sacred hierarchy underlies the Buddhist world view. Each individual might be conceived to be a "balance" of his religious merits and demerits accumulated through his various actions in this and previous lifetimes. Inevitably, each person's balance of merits and demerits is unique, and there are wide divergences between the balances of different individuals. What Buddhist belief implies, then, is a view of men as intrinsically "unequal" with respect to their moral qualities or worth. From the perspective of achievement

[5] The logical relationship between karma and transmigration is also recognized by the Thai (see Poon 1931:iv). Obeyesekere (1968) has also discussed some of the logical implications of these key Buddhist concepts.

of the ultimate religious reward, we might say that individuals are conceived to be located at different points on a hierarchy leading to Nirvana. Often this hierarchical notion of the structure of religious reality has been crystallized in Buddhist thought by construction of elaborate cosmologies, such as that of the "five courses of existence" of the *samsara* (phenomenal) world (see Khemo 1957:33). Because the moral world of the Buddhist includes all animate life, the sacred hierarchy is seen to be discontinuous, composed of various "levels" including "gods" (*thewadā*) "human beings" (*manut*), "spirits" (*phī*), "animals" (*sad*), and "demons" (*prēt*). Discrete hierarchical distinctions are made even within these various levels of existence. Of particular interest is the level of existence occupied by mankind, which is subdivided into two levels connoting moral superiority and inferiority. One is occupied by the ordinary man, who is classed simply as a "person" (*khon*); the other is occupied by the Buddhist monk, who is classed as a "mana-filled object" (*ong*). The ong level is one of intrinsic moral superiority. These distinctions between the morally superior and the morally inferior are manifested in everyday life—linguistically by the use of numeral classifiers which are obligatory in Thai grammar, socially by well-defined canons of etiquette and respect behavior. The Buddhist world view, then, involves a model of a pervasive hierarchical order of differences in intrinsic moral worth; it provides a general paradigm for all human life.

Buddhist beliefs and values provide yet another perspective on the world of man, a perspective differing from the Hindu or Brahman systems from which Buddhism developed. Buddhism shares with Indian religious thought the doctrines of karma and multiple rebirths and the religious goal of escape from the world. The sacralized hierarchy implied in Indian religion was expressed socially in the caste order. Indian ritual action involved following the caste rules (*dharma*) of the particular caste into which one was born. While perpetuating the Hindu/

Brahman notion of a sacred hierarchy, Buddhism rejected the caste notion that linked together intimately or irrevocably one's birth status and one's moral status. In Buddhism various aspects of hereditary status might be taken as presumptive evidence of one's moral status, particularly in the case of royalty, but birth status was not to be taken as a sure or sufficient index of one's ultimate religious status. Buddhism fixed responsibility for determining religious status on the individual rather than on the group into which he happened to be born. Indeed, Buddhist belief emphasized that the individual's action can improve his moral status and his position on the sacred hierarchy vis-à-vis attainment of the ultimate religious reward. This was achieved most notably by making the status of monk, at least theoretically, open to all men regardless of birth, and more generally by providing a system of moral and ethical conduct and of ritual action which was available to all men. The pervasive hierarchical order of moral inequality implied by the Buddhist world view is not static or fixed. Also involved is the notion that individuals are free to alter their position in the sacred hierarchy by appropriate moral and ritual action; "activism" and "individualism" were integral to their conception of "hierarchy."

How is this religious notion of a sacralized hierarchy posited by Buddhism conceptually related to the actual world in which Thai live? We might say that Buddhist belief involves two levels of reality. At one level is the empirical world of everyday fact and experience, and at another is the world of the karmically conditioned. The latter level of reality is deemed to be the "really real." The world of everyday experience is defined as one of "ignorance" and "illusion," because in that world men are ignorant of their real place in the hierarchy of merit/demerit balances since their good and evil deeds from past lives "ripen" without their knowledge, thereby altering their moral balance. Aside from this, they are encouraged constantly in this life to improve their moral balance by religiously sanctioned action.

In Thailand the various elements of the sophisticated Buddhist belief system are tied together by the concept of "merit" (*bun*) and the ritual complexes associated with this concept, collectively referred to as "merit-making" (*tham bun*). Merit-making is so central a part of Thai Buddhist life that early observers such as Young (1898:274) considered such rituals to be "the sum and substance of their religious faith and worship." Indeed, it is within the context of Buddhist rituals that individuals most clearly manifest their commitment to Buddhist values and goals. As the name of this ritual complex suggests, the merit-making activities performed by the mass of laymen are directed at altering favorably the individual's merit/demerit balance, thereby improving (or at least maintaining) his relative position on the sacred hierarchy.[6]

Buddhist merit-making rituals are almost compulsively public, suggesting that more is involved in these rituals than individual religious striving. In fact, it might be argued that the various themes displayed in Buddhist ritual express, in symbolic forms, basic Thai social values as well as individuals' religious values. One common theme of Buddhist ritual activities, closely linked to formal Buddhist belief, is the symbolic "renunciation" of one's attachments to various kinds of objects. Let me note two key Buddhist rituals in which this theme is especially pronounced: giving alms to the monkhood, and entering the monkhood.

Giving alms, particularly food, to the monkhood is perhaps the most common merit-making act to be observed in Thailand. It is repeated daily throughout the kingdom, in city, town, and village. This ritual involves "giving away" objects and resources which the selfish or greedy person might like to keep.

---

[6] The ritual activities of the monkhood are more specialized than those of the merit-making complex. Through meditational exercises monks seek to break through to the karmically -conditioned realm, i.e., to the ultimate ground of reality which underlies the ignorance and illusion of the phenomenal world.

Needless to say, selfishness and greed are roundly condemned by both monks and laymen. In many respects, giving alms to the monkhood is a prototype for all acts of giving to the Buddhist Order. It is significant to note that this ritual act is rarely performed by men except on occasions of special significance such as birthdays, anniversaries, or special Buddhist holy days. Ordinarily, women perform the daily act of giving alms to monks.

Entrance into the monkhood is a particularly crucial ritual, one which not only ensures the continuation of Buddhist doctrine intact but also perpetuates the Buddhist hierarchical status order. The Buddhist world view postulates underlying differences in intrinsic moral value; the distinction between monk and layman manifests that underlying order in the midst of everyday life, in remote villages as well as towns and urban centers. The ideal that all men should serve for a time as a monk suggests how important the preservation of this order is for Thai society.

The ritual of entering the monkhood also displays basic themes enshrined in sophisticated Buddhist doctrine. In becoming a monk the individual not only "gives up" his old social ties and identity, symbolized by shaving his head, donning the yellow robe, and assuming a new monastic name, but his family formally "gives" him to the monkhood as well, by freeing him from any claims they might make on him as a kinsman. Through the ritual the young man is transferred from the world of ordinary affairs into a higher moral realm, and he is simultaneously shifted from the class of objects counted as "person" (*khon*) to the class of objects counted as "mana-filled object" (*ong*).

There is general agreement that becoming a monk is one of the most meritful acts a man can perform (Kaufman 1960:183; Tambiah 1968:69). The popular view of the way in which the religious merit stemming from this ritual is distributed is illuminating. Much of the merit involved is believed to go to the mother of the new monk. Indeed, since women cannot become monks themselves, giving a son to the monkhood is a prime source of merit for a woman. This popular view illustrates an important point with respect to merit-making: the more intimately one is attached to some object, as a mother is to her children, the more difficult it is to give up that attachment, and, correspondingly, the greater the merit involved when the object is given up in the interests of religion. This point provides a further clue to the Buddhist world view, for women are deemed to be more firmly rooted in their worldly attachments than are men; men are thought to be more ready to give up such attachments. In the secular sphere, for example, informants often claim that men are more ready to divorce or separate from their spouses and to give up their family ties than are women. The firm attachment of women to their secular relationships serves as both an "explanation" and a "rationalization" for the facts that: (1) women's Buddhist religious roles are poorly developed and not highly regarded, for women are "incapable" of tearing themselves away from their worldly attachments; (2) women tend to be specialized with regard to routine merit-making activities, for women "need" more merit than men; and (3) women may engage in types of activity (such as trade and other economic activities) which might pose threats for men in their merit accumulation, for if women "sin," it is only to be expected and the consequences are less.

Geertz (1966) has argued that it is within the context of ritual performances, such as the merit-making complex, that religious values are manifested. The structures of these Thai rituals incorporate abstract Buddhist values and beliefs, mirroring the religiously defined world view. Abstract values and sophisticated beliefs are translated into concrete acts and everyday situations and linked to the motives of individual actors. Thereby Buddhist ritual mediates between abstract ideals and the common-sense world. The strategic role of Buddhism in Thai society and the special emphasis placed on these rituals by

Thai individually and collectively supports the view that merit-making performances display general social as well as religious values. As Geertz has argued further, such ritual activities may be *more* than a manifestation of values already held; they may also function as "socialization mechanisms," inducing predispositions and attitudes which have their greatest impact outside the ritual, in nonreligious contexts.

To summarize, Buddhist rituals involve a theme of symbolic renunciation of attachment to objects. Further, men and women are radically differentiated and specialized with respect to such rituals: women are more rooted and fixed, while men are more free to be religiously mobile. Finally, it might be argued that repeated performance of Buddhist rituals may act as a socialization device, inducing attitudes and orientations toward activities which may then be generalized to nonreligious spheres of activity.

How might these religious factors be related to the Thai pattern of occupational specialization outlined earlier? As we saw, although Thai in general are not attracted to economic roles, leaving them largely to non-Thai ethnic groups, when Thai are involved in such activities, Thai women are overrepresented. Thai men appear to be overwhelmingly concerned with advancing primarily in the political sphere, seeking out a bureaucratic role or a government position. If there were no systematic cultural factor operating, we should expect the numbers of men and women in these different occupational spheres to be more proportional to their numbers in the total work force. Historical and contemporary evidence indicates that this is not the case, and for a variety of theoretical and empirical reasons it is likely that the Buddhist element of Thai religion is one key cultural factor that operates to mold individual choices resulting in such a pattern of specialization.

The "achievement" element enshrined in Buddhist values and enacted in Buddhist rituals may be one religious factor operating here. The emphasis on individual religious achievement may enhance attitudes toward all kinds of achievement and mobility—that is ideas about achieving religious merit may be generalized to achievement of social status. While measures of rates of *actual* status mobility are difficult to determine and still more difficult to interpret, considerable historical and contemporary evidence indicates that Thai society is one in which geographic and social mobility are at least normatively sanctioned to a striking degree (see Kirsch 1969:51ff.). Here we might underline once more that in terms of Buddhist role definitions (and popular stereotypes) women are disadvantaged with respect to religious achievements. While the achievement element in Buddhism may sanction social mobility generally, our empirical observations of the patterning of occupational specialization indicate that achievement is not sought uniformly in all spheres; Thai aspirations appear to be warped in certain directions more than in others. Let us consider the structure of Buddhist religious values and beliefs to see if they can shed further light on the pattern of occupational specialization.

The Buddhist religious hierarchy emphasizes the superior moral position of the monk, and monks also form a particularly important status group in Thai society. In religious terms, monks are closer to ultimate Buddhist religious values and goals than any other group. As a status group monks are viewed as superordinate, treated with special marks of deference and respect on all occasions by all Thai; in some respects they stand "outside of" and "above" the secular world in which most Thai live. On ordination a man is elevated from the category of ordinary person to the category of "mana-filled" monk. Thus, serving in the monkhood alters a man's religious *and* his social status, and this is both marked and rewarded linguistically and behaviorally.

One extremely important aspect of Thai religion and of Thai society is that any man can alter his status in this way and attain the "mana-filled" class; indeed he is encouraged to do so by the ideal that all men should serve a portion of their lives as monks. Of course, some men never enter the monkhood; most who enter do so for a brief period and then leave; some stay longer; a few remain permanently. It should be noted that, from the perspective of the Thai, being a monk is no fun; it is a serious business and an arduous experience. Monks are involved with difficult religious discipline, and monastic rules cut off the monk from activities that most Thai men enjoy—snacking at all hours, teasing girls, and so on.[7] Hence remaining a monk permanently or for an extended period implies a high level of religious commitment and, from the religious perspective, a particularly favorable balance of moral qualities. Those men who leave the monkhood after a short period are saying, in effect, "I do not have the stuff (i.e., the "merit") to remain a monk." But does this imply that the socially sanctioned religious emphasis on Buddhist-defined status mobility and achievement no longer influences their aspirations or activities? Not necessarily. It does mean that if these men are influenced by such religious factors they must achieve in the secular world and in secular roles. What spheres of life are invested with Buddhist-related value?

Buddhist values push men in the direction of achieving the status of ong, as a monk. Insofar as men working in the secular world are influenced by religious considerations we might expect that they would also be attracted toward achievement in the "ong direction." The ong category includes not only monks but Buddha images, high-ranking princes, and kings. If the aspirations of Thai men are shaped in the ong direction, then, there is one major sphere of life with which they can identify. They must seek to affiliate themselves with the polity, for the political structure is topped by the king, who also falls into the

---

[7] Phillips (1965) has shown how important "fun" (*sanuk*) is as a criterion for Thai social activities. Given the importance of the fun element in Thai life, the readiness of so many men to assume a monastic role is even more noteworthy.

ong class of objects. The king in his role of Defender of the Faith bridges the sacred and the secular spheres. In other words, the association of the political hierarchy with ongness invests it with positive affect which attracts men toward it. Or, perhaps more accurately, the interpenetration of the moral hierarchy and the political hierarchy drives men toward political achievement if they wish to achieve in the secular world. In this regard it may be relevant to note that achievement of the king's role by persons of relatively low birth—actually becoming an ong within the secular order—is not unknown in Thai history.

The king's role is perhaps the most direct structural link between the Thai polity and Thai religion, but it is by no means the sole link. Up to modern times there was an important relationship between the teaching functions traditionally carried out by the Sangha and the recruitment and advancement of government officials (Wyatt 1965a). The Sangha has also served as a haven for officials who were demoted, degraded, or retired. Historically, deposed kings were often allowed to enter the monkhood, for the role of monk is the only one which could be construed as a step *up* the status ladder for a king. Although contemporary constitutions have guaranteed religious freedom for all Thai, the king *must* be a Buddhist, and Buddhism is the state religion. Such direct linkages between Buddhist values and institutions and the Thai polity may help to shape religiously induced aspirations of individual Thai so that they seek achievement in political roles when they feel they lack the moral qualities essential for achievement in a religious role.

More generally, the Buddhist world view emphasizes achievement within a framework of hierarchical differences in moral status. Attitudes and orientations acquired in religious contexts may induce Thai men to seek out spheres of activity in which "hierarchy" plays a particularly prominent role, such as bureaucratic and political positions. It is notable that notions of hierarchical status difference pervade Thai society. There are virtually no roles or relationships in Thai society which carry connotations of formal "equality." All social relationships involve a degree of status superiority or inferiority expressed by pervasive standards of etiquette, linguistic markers, and status idioms.

Viewed from the perspective of the Buddhist world view, Thai society might be seen as a single, internally differentiated, sacred hierarchy, extending from the layman farmer, through government officials, nobility, and the king, and topped by the status group of monks. Presumably this hierarchy could be extended still further, to include the "gods" and other figures. Such a view of Thai society is suggested not only by formal Buddhist belief but by the coalescence of linguistic categories which carry sacralized connotations, lumping monks and kings into the same "mana-filled" class. While there have always been very close connections between Buddhism and the Thai polity, there has never been such a close association between religious categories and economic activities.[8] If anything, from the standpoint of Buddhist belief, participation in economic roles involves an attachment to the greatest of this-worldly symbols, money, as well as an ever present temptation to be greedy or selfish. It may not be fortuitous, then, that monks are formally shielded from contact with both money and women.[9]

[8] Historically the Thai king and high officials were often involved in trading ventures; however, their economic activities were a function of their political position, not vice versa. Commonly the individuals actually carrying out the economic activities for these officials were non-Thai, e.g. Indians, Malays, Chinese, and sometimes Europeans. A similar pattern might be discerned in contemporary Thailand where some Thai men occupy positions in economic enterprises because of their political connections.

[9] From the religious perspective both money and women may be viewed with ambivalence. Money can be used to gain merit, hence is not intrinsically evil. Similarly, women as routine merit-makers and givers of sons to the monkhood are not necessarily immoral. But women may pose a threat to Buddhist values. At times, for example, King Mongkut (Rāma IV) saw women to be a distinct threat to religion. He felt that some women looked on monks as "fattened hogs" and expressed the fear that monks were "likely to be driven crazy" by such women, i.e., induced to leave the monkhood and marry (Seni 1959).

The general hierarchical element in Buddhist belief may operate in another way to discourage Thai men from taking up economic roles. Participation in market activities—at least marketing which follows Western models—would involve a degree of formal status equality between buyer and seller which is not characteristic of Thai social roles. Thai generally feel uncomfortable in situations in which status difference are not clearly defined. The intrusion of such "noneconomic" factors as status inequality into economic activities can only hinder market operations.

Buddhist religious elements do throw some light on the pattern of Thai specialization outlined earlier. These religious factors play a positive as well as a negative role. Buddhist values and beliefs shape the attitudes and aspirations of individual Thai in the direction of "political" rather than of "economic" achievement. Economic activities generally have a "residual" character in terms of Thai aspirations. From this perspective we might say that Buddhist factors serve to rank various kinds of activities: religious highest, political next, economic lowest. Thai men have been so overwhelmingly committed to religious and political achievements that economic activities have been left up to non-Thai and to Thai women. Thai women are left with such economic roles because in religious belief, in the structure of religious roles and rituals, and in popular thought, they are deemed to be more deeply rooted in this-worldly activities and secular concerns than are men.

These religious considerations shed some light on why the Thai were willing to leave economic activities up to non-Thai, but why was this "foreign" control of the Thai economy not seen as threatening in the nineteenth century and viewed as a threat in the twentieth? Numerous factors both internal and external to Thai society undoubtedly contributed to this change. However, one important factor was that in the nineteenth century Chinese control of the Thai economy tended not to remain in the same hands for very long. The children, and, more surely, the grandchildren of Chinese immigrants were eventually lost to the Chinese segment of the population through assimilation to Thai society. Two features of nineteenth-century Thailand were especially important in this regard: the dearth of female Chinese immigrants, and the characteristics of Thai culture, which permitted complete acculturation.

In the nineteenth century the overwhelming majority of Chinese immigrants were men. If an immigrant wished to marry he was virtually forced to marry a Thai woman—and Thai women were not at all unwilling to marry the industrious Chinese men.[10] The children of these marriages were generally brought up speaking Thai and eventually adopted complete Thai ethnic identification. Summarizing the period prior to 1910, Skinner (1957:131) observed: "*lukjin* proper [children of a Chinese father and a Thai mother] more often than not considered themselves Chinese, but . . . the children of a *lukjin* [whether married to a *lukjin* or a Thai wife] considered themselves Thai."

The Buddhist element in Thai culture may have played a significant part in this process of assimilation. As we have seen, Buddhist values and beliefs place a premium on achievement and encourage the notion that it is possible and even desirable to bridge seemingly discrete social boundaries, such as those between layman and monk, between "persons" and "mana-filled objects." Similarly, Thai culture made it possible for Chinese immigrants, their children, and particularly their grandchildren to bridge the social boundary between Chinese and Thai, to achieve the status of an ethnic Thai by assuming the characteristics of a Thai and giving up the characteristics of a Chinese. Of course, differences between being "Thai" and being "Chinese" were recognized, but since achievement of

---

[10] Indeed, given the coincidence of occupational involvement shared by the Chinese and Thai women noted above one might speculate about a characterological affinity between the two groups.

Thai cultural status was not ascriptively closed to children of mixed Sino-Thai marriages, they could make the decision to identify as either Thai or Chinese. They could not be both. In this respect Thailand is in marked contrast to other areas in Southeast Asia, such as Indonesia, where Overseas Chinese also came to play an important economic role. In Indonesia an intermediate social status, that of the *peranakan*, developed to mark the unbridgeable gap between full Indonesian and full Chinese cultural status.[11] The barrier to full assimilation posed by Indonesian culture is reflected in contemporary conflicts between Indonesians and Chinese.

The process of assimilation of Chinese into Thai cultural status took place at all levels of society. In the countryside at least some Chinese immigrants quietly married Thai women, and they or their descendants eventually became farmers indistinguishable from other Thai villagers. At another level, Thai policy was to reward leaders of the Chinese community, particularly successful Chinese merchants, with noble titles and high-status positions within the Thai regime. Such rewards eased the way for their identification with Thai interests and their eventual assimilation. Thus the cream of the immigrant Chinese population was skimmed off the Chinese group and merged with the Thai elite. In contemporary terms, they were "co-opted" into the establishment.

Assimilation of successful Chinese to Thai cultural status involved their internalizing basic Thai values (for at least acting as if they had), in particular those values crystallized in Buddhist belief and ritual. The assimilated Chinese thus tended to turn away from purely economic endeavors and devoted themselves to advancement within the polity. Their place in the economy was taken by more recent immigrants, setting the stage for a repetition of this process and simultaneously ensuring

---

[11] Skinner (1960) provides a comparative discussion of some of the factors influencing the ease or difficulty of assimilation of Chinese in Thailand and Java.

the continued presence of a "foreign" group to carry out the essential economic functions. Skinner (1957:134) concludes: "The comparatively rapid assimilation of Chinese descendants in Siam also meant that the perpetuation of Chinese society there was dependent on continued immigration. The frequent references to the cultural persistence of Chinese in Siam during the nineteenth century . . . are witness not to a peculiar unchangeableness on the part of the Chinese but to the continual re-inforcement of Chinese society through immigration."

Encouragement of continued Chinese immigration coupled with the assimilation of large numbers of the immigrants within a span of three generations served as a safeguard for Thai society. On the one hand, in a period of general social expansion it provided a group of non-Buddhists willing to carry out the entrepreneurial tasks so unattractive to Buddhist Thai, freeing Thai to pursue activities more consistent with Buddhist-based values. On the other hand, it ensured that economic control was not vested in an ascriptively closed, self-perpetuating group which might potentially put its interests above the interests of Thai society. As long as immigration rates and assimilation rates achieved some sort of reasonable balance, no stable or enduring complexes of economic control or power might develop to threaten Thai autonomy.

This happy situation did not continue indefinitely, nor was it always so happy. Tensions developed periodically between the Thai regime and the Chinese community, particularly when the Chinese banded together as a group in opposition to the Thai. Such opposition was ruthlessly crushed (e.g., see Bowring 1857, vol. 1:87). However, in the period following World War I many Chinese immigrants were accompanied by their wives, and numerous single Chinese women immigrated to become brides of Chinese already established in Thailand. The effect in either case was to ensure that the children of Chinese would be brought up as Chinese, retaining their Chinese cultural identity and resisting assimilation to Thai cultural status (see Skinner

1957:253f.). Thus an imbalance developed between the immigration rate and the assimilation rate which posed a serious
threat to Thai autonomy. It is certainly no coincidence, then,
that anti-Chinese feeling became particularly manifest at this
time, resulting in the alteration of Thai policy, limiting foreign
control, and encouraging Thai participation in the economy
(see Skinner 1957:chs. 5–7).

The preceding discussion has postulated a relationship between sophisticated Buddhist values and beliefs and pervasive and long-standing Thai social patterns. Abstract Buddhist
values and ideas are encapsulated in the structure of common
Buddhist rituals participated in by Thai of all degrees of sophistication and at all levels of society. These religious values,
acquired and manifested in ritual contexts, are generalized to
nonreligious contexts and spheres of life, shaping the aspirations
and activities of individual Thai in certain directions rather
than others. Although no doubt many factors aside from the
religious have influenced the patterning of Thai society, this
hypothesized relationship sheds light on certain developments
in recent Thai history. It may also illuminate present and future
developments as well.

Two major problems face contemporary Thailand: political
integration and economic development. Buddhist values and
beliefs have some bearing on both problems. Despite the current expansion of the Thai economy and official encouragement
for greater Thai participation in economic activities, Thai do
not seem to have developed any notable attraction to entrepreneurial activities (except perhaps when they are influenced
by political considerations). That is, the traditional Buddhist-
influenced pattern still seems to hold. For economic development to occur, presumably some changes in that pattern will be
necessary, and thus some sort of change in the religious system
as well. The potential for such religious change is already
present. Even as the structure of the Thai economy and polity
have altered since the 1850's, so too have there been subtle

changes in the structure of Thai religion. The government has assumed the teaching functions once carried out by the monkhood, freeing monks to specialize more in their religious tasks. The Thammayut ("reform") order of the Sangha has gained official sanction. Such developments may allow a greater degree of economic participation on the part of Thai laymen while preserving Buddhist values intact.

6. The Thai Social Order as Entourage and Circle

LUCIEN M. HANKS

In trying to understand the social architecture of more than thirty million people, I shall show that the Thai social order is less specialized and differentiated than our own. At the same time I would like to avoid the implication that some societies are more "advanced" than others by dint of greater specialization and differentiation. Architecture exemplifies an impartiality of this sort, for few complain that a dome simply assembled from triangles and pentagons is more primitive than the many-faceted dome of Saint Peter's in Rome. I see the Thai social order as repeating a standard arrangement, the entourage and the circle, as if it were a geodesic dome. The American social order, like many of those capitol domes, is built from many differentiated specialized parts, implied in such terms as the "organs" of government, the economic "system," the residential "zone." In contrast the Thai have no specialized governing, economic, or residential institutions. The same institution governs, feeds, and shelters, as if it were a protozoan carrying out in one cell all functions needed for living. In sum the Thai social order comprises a collection of self-sufficient units rather than specialized and differentiated ones like ours; it is like a coral reef rather than a leviathan.

In what follows I shall describe the nonspecialized units out of which Thai society is built. Subsequently I shall show how these units form the social order by repetition and perform their social tasks. Finally, because these arrangements have not

197

become specialized after more than a century of contact with the West, I suggest that this is the particular nature of the Thai social order.

The Building Blocks

In Lauriston Sharp's Thailand seminar at Cornell we first talked about the patron-client relationship and later about the entourage. Let me review these discussions briefly here, though I have described them more fully elsewhere (Hanks 1962, 1966). Then as if we were at a new seminar, let me spell out my latest formulation.

Each Thai regards every other person in the social order as higher or lower than himself. The elder, more literate, richer persons tend to be higher due to greater virtue or "merit," as the Buddhist *bun* is usually translated. Based on these differences in social standing, a hierarchy arises where each person pays deference to all who stand above and is deferred to by all below. At the top is the king, and at the bottom some lone person who survives miserably in the dank jungle. Between these extremes fit the persons who carry out the tasks needed for living: the administrator, the merchant, the clerk, the peddler, farmer, laborer, and so on. The important thing to remember is that the Thai categorize not people but tasks. A person's merit varies when he does good and bad deeds, so that Thai, to a greater or lesser extent, as the Buddhist doctrine explains, move up and down the scale from job to job because of accumulated merit. Every person has the potential for changing from a laborious and painful occupation to a gentler one. Indeed, in Bāng Chan (see Map 3, p. 150, location 1) we have seen sons of farmers rise to positions of authority in government as well as securely placed teachers and farmers reduced to laborers.

In this society of unequals Buddhist doctrine urges each person to do what he can for the benefit of those who stand below him in the hierarchy. By helping others a man gains a helper, increases his own merit, and raises his standing in the hierarchy. The poor farmer provides to the best of his ability for his wife and children, while the wealthy mill owner cares for the larger group in his employ. This standard relationship of superior to inferior we have called the patron-client relationship. The superior gives from his greater resources something that will please an inferior, who returns the favor with such services as are at his disposal.

The particular relationship of patron to client varies with the degree of affection and trust. At its coolest the understanding resembles a piecework contract: twenty baht for digging two cubic meters of dirt or ten baht for each square meter of flooring laid in a building. When the work is complete and the pay given, the obligations cease. Yet more cordial relationships can develop from these beginnings, if repetition and familiarity lead to interest and affection. Thus the terms become less contractual, and the hired man not only works in the field but may cook meals, tend the children, and eventually perhaps bury the family gold. In return his patron treats him like a member of the family, not only feeding and sheltering him, providing money when needed, but helping find a suitable wife and defraying the costs of cremating a grandmother. So a patron may become the helper, protector, and symbol of confidence for his client, who in turn grows to become a cornerpost of the ménage.

Unlike feudal relations of lord to vassal this particular liaison between patron and client is voluntary and may be terminated unilaterally by either party. It rests on reciprocity, serving the two as long as is convenient or until some grave incident detroys mutual affection. In practice this key to social intercourse seems to be breached no more often than a firm contract reinforced by law. In its very flexibility lies its strength. An employer meeting hard times tells his worker that he cannot pay the same wage as previously. It then rests with the worker to decide whether to leave for a better-paying job or possibly to suggest that the boss reduce his wage even farther in order to help during a lean period. Similarly, a worker need not feel embarrassed to explain to the boss his need for more money to meet some unexpected expense.

With the probable exception of the bond between husband and wife, every liaison between people in this society takes on some forms of this patron-client relationship. Parents are patrons of their children; older, of younger siblings; captain, over the men of his troop; and a guardian angel looks after the king. There can be no doubt: this relationship is not just the mortar but the rods and rivets that hold Thai society together.

A patron may have more than one client, in fact will have a group of them if he is a person of any standing. The face-to-face group of a man and his clients is what we called "entourage" at the last Cornell seminar. The Thai have no equivalent. Though they speak of patron (*čhao*) and client (*lūk*) with various modifiers, the closest to entourage is the term *bǫriwān* used by a patron in reference to his group of followers (Prāmōt Nakhǫnthap, personal communication). No word includes the patron together with his client.

An entourage is a group focused on a single person. The points to be noted about it are its individualistic rather than group character, its dependence on a particular patron for survival, and its multiple functions.

As the entourage arises out of personal loyalty to the patron, group spirit is lacking in the Western sense. Each of the clients has made his own particular contract with the patron, and between clients indifference or even hostility may prevail. As everyone participates in the entourage on terms arrived at by dealing only with the patron, such concerns as equal pay for equal work do not apply. If anyone senses a grievance, he may withdraw at that instant. Team work, if any occurs, depends on the direct supervision of the patron, and of course, since the patron alone has interest in the welfare of all his clients, decision-making for the group as a whole can never be left to a lieutenant.

An entourage endures only as long as a patron is able to continue providing for his clients. When a patron dies or is forced to curtail benefits, the entourage disappears. Because of the personal relationship of a man to his clients, there can be no successor to the patron. Most frequently, clients of a dead patron go their separate ways, and the most powerful among his clients seize the most valuable assets that remain. If someone new tries to take over the entourage, rarely can he hold all clients of the former patron and still recompense his own particular friends. Thus in troubled times entourages are frequently being formed and frequently disappear to be reformed.

Finally, an entourage is a nonspecialized unit in the sense that it can function successively in a variety of ways, rather than continuously in a particular way. A patron sets his clients to the specialized jobs of paddy farming, running a store, or filling out the forms of a government office. Should the patron change his own occupation from growing paddy to running a store or managing a government office, he brings his clients with him to carry on the new work. As in any other complex society, Thai recognize the need for certain special skills, though not to the extent that a person becomes fixed for life in an occupational station. A paddy farmer is happy to become an orchardist; a small shopkeeper gladly takes on the less arduous and more esteemed government clerk's work. More important, the patron who fails to bring his beloved clients along to less arduous tasks loses them.

The entourage is a face-to-face group for living in common proximity. On the same wooden floor the farmer sleeps, shares food, gossips, and plays chess not only with his kinsmen but with his hired man after tilling the field together. The households within a compound join together less intimately but no less enduringly in digging a well, rebuilding a house, taking turn with the buffalo, and setting off together to a nearby cockfight. However, the provincial governor does not ordinarily build an entourage from his scattered district officers, for the monthly meetings are too intermittent, attenuated, and prescribed.

We are prepared to find in entourages varying degrees of attenuation. At some point not yet precisely determined, group intercourse becomes so impersonal and contractual that I prefer to call it a "circle." An entourage grows only as large as the patron's ability to maintain a semblance of devotion to each of its members. So the provincial governor's entourage perhaps includes the agricultural officer, the police chief, a secretary, and the janitor. Though the governor may drink and gamble with a sequence of visitors from the ministry, they are not his entourage. He pays tuition at the middle school for the janitor's children, in whose world he is the sun.

The Circle

The group which I call a "circle" consists in the extension of an entourage. A patron who summons his clients may also find the clients of these clients responding to the summons. The immediate clients relay the call to their clients, and the call may reach not only to the clients of clients but several stages beyond. Similarly I may respond to the call of my patron, who has responded to the call of his patron, or of patrons several entourages beyond me. The entire range of persons who respond to a man's call, provided it extends beyond his own entourage, makes up his circle. Presumably the king's circle is the largest, the circles of his ministers next largest, and so circles of decreasing size occur in descending the hierarchy.

During our first year in Bangkok we established our household, and then hired a gardener, a laundress, and a cook. They formed our entourage. While the gardener worked alone, the laundress sometimes needed extra help to keep us in clean clothes; so she called in her granddaughter. The cook, charged with purchasing, preparing, and serving food as well as caring for the household, brought in two assistants to whom we paid wages. Since one of these girls was the younger sister of the other, it was apparent that the elder had drawn another hand from her own little entourage. The house then ran smoothly with persons from three entourages beyond the one to which we initially addressed ourselves. Instead of having only three workers, there was an effective body of six. Indeed, since kinsmen of these six also visited on occasion, there were many others. One used to arrive on a bicycle to make a chocolate cake which our cook could not trust herself to make. He was never on our payroll and appeared usually before birthday parties, evidently at the behest of our cook. In an emergency the call might have reached many others whom we never before set eyes upon. Such was our circle.

In turn we may have belonged to a circle. Above us the entourage extended uncertainly, for we never met the person who permitted us to occupy the house, let alone its ultimate owner. Rent was paid at a nondescript office on a downtown side street, a firm which advertised itself as an insurance and export business. The person who said we might occupy the premises, originally contacted by the Sharps, had moved away, but people told us we lived in Crown property. Another said the land belonged to a former police commissioner, who was once pointed out in a crowd and described as an aging eccentric. Unfortunately no summons came from above, so we never discovered the patron or the patrons to whom we were indebted.

The Thai word *čhak* means, inter alia, the group of people who respond to a command. Vishnu dances with such a circle in his hand, sometimes a discus, sometimes a wheel, and this circle contains the power to make the universe obey his commands. From this same root the name of the present ruling dynasty in Thailand appropriately derives its name, Čhakkrī, from the founder Čhaophrayā Čhakkrī, the general who defeated the king of Thonburī. Another Thai word for circle is *monton*, a word related through the Sanskrit to our word "mandala," geometric figures (squares, triangles, circles, and the like) standing within or behind each other in an indefinite series. These two words symbolize well the Thai social order. Each person stands in two orbits, one of command and one of obedience, and beyond the more or less familiar figures both recede extending in one direction to the beasts of burden, in the other direction to the gods.

Like an entourage, a circle is an organization for living but provides what we may call secondary arrangements. While we eat, sleep, work, and are merry in our entourage, the circle offers subsidiary benefits. If one's patron provides housing, by dint of this patron's circle one may ride free on the bus, enjoy reduced prices at a certain market, or attend theatrical performances without paying. These result from the less intimate and rather attenuated liaisons which a person to some extent forms from his own circle of command. Thus I obtained a free haircut from the husband of a former servant girl, though I had never previously met the man. In most cases the greater benefits derive from a patron and those above him, like our beautiful house in Bangkok.

To acquire secondary conveniences for living, a patron begins by claiming a fairly defensible monopoly. The monopoly may be one of the mercantile sort familiar to all of us, such as controlling the supply of oil and gasoline for a given population. Some monopolies appear more extortive, like issuing export or import licenses together with special stamps, particular signatures of approval, and other bits of red tape familiar to bureaucrats. Some verge on robbery, such as the confiscation of some portion of the goods that pass a given point on a highway or river.

After maximizing the returns from the initial monopoly, the patron must balance these gains with secondary arrangements that attract new and hold the old membership. The formula dictates acquiring secondary benefits at the same time as one extends monopolies. Thus the sage patron acquires a building firm at the same time as he provides new houses for a wider circle. When he needs money, he founds a new bank which lends also to circle members. If television is the rage, he gains the franchise for distributing a certain brand. Few, if any, circles can include within their monopolies all that is desired for modern living. A secondary manner of extending benefits occurs through deals with other circles. Thus the oil monopoly can grant special prices to the railroad for operating its trains in return for special freight rates. In such ways a well-managed circle can acquire special privileges at markets, restaurants, and theaters for its members, and the more varied they are, the greater is the power to attract and hold. One may note in passing that these secondary benefits do not automatically become accessible to all members of a circle. Astute patrons use them selectively to consolidate the circle.

Because it holds a precious monopoly, a circle needs protection against covetous predators. While we ordinarily depend on the police for this purpose, police in Thailand are neither protectors nor enforcers of the law. The Thai police was introduced at the beginning of the present century by foreign advisers but soon came to act as a circle with its own special interests. Each circle must defend itself for it cannot expect protection from police unless the interests of the two circles happen to coincide. At the frontier circles dependent on smuggling have their own armed followers, but near the country's center, defenses become more covert. The builder of a new market must run the gauntlet of the locality's purveyors of licenses, health authorities, building inspectors, controllers of produce and others, whose interference, as in American city halls, can be turned to approval by appropriate payments. Frequently a circle leader anticipates these hazards and can overcome them by allying himself with a local figure able to clear the path. Such a move enhances the authority and scope of the circle, an important step in its growth.

Despite these and other defenses, organizational takeover by another circle continuously threatens all circles, as if they were Western corporations struggling to retain control of the common stock in the face of an avid buyer. In Thailand a man had acquired a tract of forest land with the assistance of provincial authorities in order to develop tea and orange plantations. Several years later the Department of Forests suddenly ordered the presumptive owner to vacate the land, because the plantations, they declared, occupied land reserved for forest. Only by appealing through the provincial offices to the influential Minister of the Interior was it possible to address, at cabinet level, the Minister of Agriculture, superior of the Department of Forests, and request the withdrawal of the order to vacate. The plea against the Department of Forests might also have been addressed to a court, but Thai courts in civil cases serve ordinarily as mediators of disputes rather than as arbitors. Had the plantation owner gone to court, he would probably have had to sacrifice some portion of his land to mollify the Department. Instead he chose possibly a riskier way, which might antagonize the forest officials, though it gained his claim in full. Hapless circles unable to summon guardians superior to their assailants quickly lose their monopolies.

All circles, particularly the less protected ones, are constantly changing, as entourages within their orbits dissolve and reform. Any change in the flow of benefits to clients may alter the stations of its personnel. With the demise of an old entourage and the formation of a new one, clients may advance from the periphery toward the center, drawing with them their clients and clients of clients. Or they may drift off. So a continuous ferment sustains, invigorates, or weakens a circle depending on its particular metabolic moment.

We are concerned with the stability of a circle, which tends to increase when patrons hold their clients with larger and more dependable benefits. From this it follows that the least stable part of a circle lies at the fringe, where lean clients please their petty patrons with "nothing but their hands," as

Thai characterize the minimal service that a client can perform for his patron. These less valued clients of less affluent patrons receive fewer benefits, find themselves less securely affiliated, and hence are more readily lured by minor increments of benefit from other patrons. So the periphery of a circle is its most unstable area, undergoing frequent turnover, while at the stabler center more prosperous clients enjoy larger and more constant benefits.

A circle is also unstable because it tends to cleave. Like a chain, a circle is as stable as its most fragile entourage, and should this point of fragility lie near the center, a whole sector may fall away. We have observed farm families prospering during the years when their children were growing in strength and skill, so that new land could be rented to cultivate additional rice. Then, when the children moved to more alluring jobs or married out, the old folks were lucky to have one child remain. At a more spectacular level we may read of states collapsing with ruptures of this sort. Thus the regime of King Taksin fell when Čhaophrayā Čhakkrī became disaffected, mustered an army, and defeated his former patron, thereby establishing himself as the new king known now as Rāma I. The understandings that weld a circle must be reinforced with daggers as well as gifts. Ambition and covetousness near the center of a circle increase its fragility.

The Social Order

The Thai social order consists of a congeries of linked circles with minimal functional differentiation. The specialized institutions of our scene are lacking. No universals order all the people, and no special economic apparatus supplies the consuming public. Indeed, there are no publics, no masses, nor even a proletariat; instead of these, segments of the population are provided for more or less adequately according to the circle of their affiliation.

Because of the special characteristics of these circles, the

Thai social order faces unique problems. Circles, because they are ephemeral, provide few stable functions in the social order. As circles grow by extending their monopolies, internecine struggles occur which are undampened by specialized peace-making apparatus. From these two sources the social order often appears mortally wounded, but the quick regeneration of social units promotes recovery at a more rapid rate than with a more specialized organization.

For convenience I shall refer to certain large and fairly stable circles as "government" because one or more of their monopolies resembles the functions of a Western state. Indeed, the past 100 years of Western instruction have introduced types of monopoly previously unknown to heads of oriental states: providing transportation, communication, schools, and hospitals. In addition to governmental circles there are smaller and less stable ones which operate manufacturing, mercantile, processing, transportation, and handling monopolies. Be it noted, however, that no border divides the two; government operates businesses, and businesses carry on governmental tasks. The gradation continues toward scores of still more ephemeral and smaller circles occupying villages, operating small markets, growing produce, robbing the buses along the highway, and pursuing other more or less "legitimate" occupations. Finally at the outer fringe are only tiny entourages and individuals, the hapless families, misfits, and ne'er-do-wells who make their living as best they can. This even-textured social order of relatively undifferentiated units is thus well knit at the center but has a tattered and shedding fringe.

In this section I shall show that the Thai state, at the social center, operates in ways quite different from our own and functions as a series of circles. By observing the state, we may observe instances of what appears to be typical activity of circles in the larger social order.

Only recently, under Western influences, has the Thai state begun to realize that it must act as a territorial state. The boundaries were fixed during the late nineteenth century, not by the Thai but by the French in Indochina and by the English in Burma and Malaysia. Before this time the Thai state functioned like a chain store, operating where it had affiliates. Hall (1955:445–447) tells us of the British East India Company about 1820 in Penang making contact with Malay sultanates which were thought to be autonomous. To their surprise, the company representatives found Kedah, a state near the present Siamese border, willing to intrigue against Bangkok. However, remoter ones like Perak were firmly attached to Bangkok. So the influence of the Thai state ramified in all directions, sometimes reaching well beyond the present boundaries, sometimes contracting to a nucleus that extended only a few hundred miles from the capital.

Even today nonterritorial vestiges remain. As late as 1955 hill tribes living in many portions of the border areas had no contact with the Thai government and moved freely through the hills across international boundaries (Lehman 1965). Thai sovereignty extended up the valleys, but large sections of the hills lay for all practical purposes outside government interest. In some districts local officials made great efforts to bring remote tribal villages into their orbit, but elsewhere minority villages geographically closer to the Thai carried on without benefit of contact. At border points we found a curious set of independent boundaries established by various administrative groups. For example, at Mac Sāi and Chīangsaen in the northern tip of Chīangrāi Province, there are police and customs officers, but the immigration office is located in another village about twenty miles away, as if the territorial boundaries existed for goods but not for people. Indeed, small groups of aliens move through many parts of Thailand, and citizens pay little heed to them.

That strange people sometimes move about within the Thai territorial borders also reflects another aspect of the nonterritorial state. Formerly membership in the state occurred through voluntary affiliation, so that unaffiliated groups resided in all parts of the kingdom. Wales (1934:132) tells of many Thai who lived independently in unpopulated areas; they had "run away from their patrons," though these patrons seem not to have cared to track them down. Similarly Mon and Karen villages appear in the midst of what are now well-settled areas; some are old villages long in their location but which remained unnoticed until local officials needed manpower for military service or the corvée. If such minorities were the nonaffiliated, they differed little from the affiliated. From the point of view of most mortals in their villages, the king was even more remote than the authorities in Kafka's citadel. Whether or not one's patron enjoyed a liaison to the capital altered most aspects of life but little; besides, it was as burdensome to fight for as against the Thai king.

Today, despite nationalism, nonaffiliation still remains but has taken new form. A Thai national is not simply a person born within the boundaries or someone naturalized by due process. Ethnic Miao, Yao, and Lahu, whose forebears lived many generations in Thailand, do not enjoy the right to hold land, but recent T'ai immigrants from Laos and Burma have received land for settling from local authorities. Nor is the criterion purely ethnic, since Karen and Malay peoples have remained undisturbed in their villages, while Vietnamese have been deported. The Thai themselves are not universally obliged to pay taxes or to serve in the army, nor do all enjoy the right to appeal to government for protection. This diversity may be explained simply: the obligations and rights of citizens have never been defined.

It is somewhat anomalous for a government with no precise territorial jurisdiction and vague sovereignty to have at the same time an apparently unlimited authority. Nonetheless, Thai governmental circles do regulate what in our society might be called private matters. Bāng Chan farmers told of having to rent hats and shoes when they went to Bangkok in the late 1930's; the prime minister, striving for the appearance of progress, had forbidden people to enter the capital without suitable dress. Department heads often direct employees on where to spend their vacations or on the minutiae of serving important guests. A superior may further expect his office staff to assist at a private party or to drive his children home from school. Nor is the individual protected by writs of habeas corpus or due process of law. There is little delicacy in treating an "enemy."

We might expect these monopolistic circles to serve the social whole in functional fashion, but the total picture is mixed. To be sure the railway and air transport, as well as the rice export and tobacco monopolies, operate much like occidental corporations. Elsewhere functions overlap the various ministries and departments. In the 1950's the police aspired to simulate the armed forces with its own flotilla of gun boats, a squadron of air planes plus a fleet of armored cars and tanks. Several branches of government run their own banks, and more than one retains a professional dance troupe to entertain guests.

No less perplexing is to discover that the very canons of functional administrative design seem to be flouted. Departments and ministries do not carry out what they are apparently designed to do. Perhaps the railway and the police can offer functional reasons for housing their employees, yet it is difficult to explain on these grounds why the police run a television broadcasting station; why the Department of Religion maintains a hospital; why the army operates factories to produce batteries, leather goods, glass, woven cloth, and canned food (Wilson 1962:184). Nor does it seem compatible with high ministerial responsibility to learn that one highly placed official acquired a soft-drink plant; another a hotel; a third a movie theater. When no firm lines separate the flow of departmental cash from personal investment nor employees of one enterprise from another, one seems to disregard order itself.

At this point the concept of circles begins to make sense of the scene. Circles have no territorial limits, regulate no constant body of people, set no limits on the kinds of demands to make of the constituents, and may manage a host of unrelated enterprises. While I have no data to show the precise number and functions of these circles, on the basis of general activity I shall make the case for government consisting in a number of circles allied at the cabinet level.

Circles, as we have seen, are autonomous organizations which work for the benefit of their constituents. Expediency governs their actions, particularly in conflict, for at the top none can appeal to stronger allies for assistance. In the following paragraphs I shall present evidence for these points in relation to the branches of government.

The weakness of coordinating forces within government may be inferred from the absence of a centralized system of revenue collection. Though the Ministry of Finance is technically in charge of providing revenue, it does not control, for example, the state lottery or the eighty-odd governmental monopolies in such areas as rice export and tobacco (International Bank for Reconstruction and Development [hereafter IBRD] 1959:199–200). Indeed, most branches of government have their own peculiar sources of revenue, in addition to what may be received from the central government: the forestry department from the sale of lumber, customs from the issuing of export and import licenses, and so on. While all who enjoy civil-service standing may count on base pay for their salaries, this source of income is ordinarily insufficient and must be supplemented by cash or indirect benefits from sources available only to a particular department or ministry. Thus the operation of a centralized budget is all but impossible (IBRD 1959:201), and certainly establishing priorities for general development proved to be exceedingly thorny (IBRD 1959:208).

That each branch of government seeks to provide its constituents with maximum benefits may be understood by the personal care which department heads frequently show for their staffs. Persons from the office often occupy rooms in their boss's compound, attend festivities at his house, and join him on vacations. On one occasion Mrs. Hanks and I were privileged to be guests of the Police Department in a small town and found ourselves not only eating in local restaurants but attending a local fair at no cost to our affable hosts or ourselves. On another occasion we were introduced to the manager of a government monopoly who put us up at the guesthouse for more than a week and treated us like visiting constituents. The peculiar benefits of the Police Department have been frequent subjects for conversation owing to the necessary openness of many of their operations. Thus on the basis of salary alone a well-placed police officer could scarcely afford to own a small house in a back street, yet for a time many occupied handsome residences on the boulevard. Their benefits include not only special rates at amusement centers but reduced prices for food in the markets and high priority on public transportation. Government offices dealing with schooling or cooperatives would be hard pressed to offer comparable advantages.

Between the branches of government occurs a competition characteristic of circles seeking to extend their monopolies. Though the struggle itself usually takes place behind the scenes, the results clearly indicate the outcome of a predatory encounter between weak and strong circles. During the 1960's a government order simply announced that primary- and secondary-school teachers would hereafter receive orders through the Ministry of the Interior. Anyone familiar with the scene knew that this corps of many thousand teachers had been built over the years by the Ministry of Education, as it sought to extend education to more people in remoter areas of the kingdom. For more than half a century the Ministry of Education had managed the training, placement, and supervision of teachers, and reorganization broke this continuity. The event makes sense only as one circle extending its monopoly at the expense of another.

One might give little heed to such an event in itself, yet a year or two earlier the Ministry of Education had gathered funds and built a new provincial university. While they were preparing to staff it, the new university was suddenly shifted to the jurisdiction of the prime minister, with considerable disruption of plans and personnel. Such a spectacle of enfeeblement is by no means unique. Shortly after World War II the Ministry of Cooperatives was created to accelerate agricultural recovery. After a change of cabinet its efforts to extend credit were frustrated by competing suppliers of credit. For several years the Ministry of the Navy suffered a decline for having participated in the unsuccessful coup of 1949. It continued as a shadow organization that could scarcely send a single ship to sea until the reorganization of the cabinet in 1957.

New departments and even ministries are also founded. Thus in the 1950's the wife of Prime Minister Phibūnsongkhram was appointed chief of a newly created Department of Cultural Affairs, which built a handsome building and carried on programs of social service, cultural uplift, and modernization. The end of the Phibūn administration sapped the vigor of this department. On gaining governmental control Sarit Thanarat added the Ministry of National Development. Though many existing ministries were competent to manage the issuing of licenses to industries seeking to begin production in Thailand, whole sections and departments were transferred from existing ministries to round out this new organization of promoted worthies. After this prime minister's death, the new ministry disappeared.

The most open conflict between circles that I have witnessed involved not a major monopoly but subsidiary monopolies of government circles with heads at the cabinet level. These two circles held among their range of monopolies franchises for bottling and distributing certain widely advertised soft drinks. One day in the 1950's there suddenly appeared in the vast majority of Bangkok coffee houses a new soft drink which outsold its two competitors at identical prices. The sun had not set when the newly opened bottling plant was ordered shut on grounds of not having been certified by sanitary inspectors. While the newspapers reported that the plant would reopen within a few days, difficulties developed over procuring sugar and sufficient foreign exchange to import this necessary ingredient. Some three weeks later the new drink finally reappeared, but only in a restricted number of outlets and at a price that was no longer competitive. The soft-drink monopolies continued successfully until the 1957 *coup d'état* opened the barriers for additional competitors.

It is now easy to conclude that the cabinet is an alliance of persons placed in control over various monopolies. Its weakness is witnessed by the near absence of coordinated activity between ministries (Mosel 1957: 311–312). Wilson (1962:161–162), in addition, also remarks on the need for ministries to look out for their constituents and the allocation of general resources in a manner just to hold loyalties. The cabinet rather than a ruling body is one for consultation and communication.

Whether in government, commerce, or the paddy fields, circles of greater or lesser size act in much the same manner. In Bāng Chan, where small circles verge on entourages, persons within the group assisted each other with labor, equipment, buffalo, and available cash. A man entered the circle (or entourage) by marriage or by settling in the vicinity of an existing patron. Between small circles cooperation occurred ordinarily on a strictly contractual basis. The crops were uprooted prior to transplanting and later harvested by exchanging equal days of labor, an arrangement that could be terminated if a party failed to work his share. No organization oversaw the common interest of all villagers or acted for the public good. Even the temple under the head priest consisted in little more than his entourage of resident monks and a dozen or so elderly laymen whose concern over their next existence led them to merit-making before they died. This circle managed various festival occasions and work parties to maintain the temple, the numbers responding to a summons depending on the personal magnetism of the particular head priest. Coordinated action was only possible in those few years when someone became rich enough to coalesce certain smaller circles into his larger one. A local resident once became *kamnan* (commune head), and enjoyed the power to collect taxes; under him Bāng Chan built its temple anew and dammed the water in its creek for irrigation. He also arranged to hold the buffalo in a common corral to protect them against theft. As a rule these farming circles coexisted, even without such a patron, with minimal conflict, their only worry being that bandits from other villages might hold stolen buffalo and boats for ransom. For self-protection each householder usually dug a moat around his dwelling and guarded it with thorny bamboo thickets or vicious watchdogs.

Open conflict occurred in the North between the circles of Thai and those of other ethnic groups. A Lahu village which farmed on a tea plantation was constantly beset with vanishing livestock, destruction of fences, and even burning of crops. Local authorities were powerless to intervene, since village headmen themselves were members, or perhaps leaders, of the predatory circles. Elsewhere Chinese refugees told of the local police granting their village the right to grow crops on adjacent land. On the eve of the harvest their crops were destroyed by neighboring villagers, and the police could neither protect nor compensate the losses. In the end the refugee community did better by allying itself with commercial markets where other Chinese circles dominated. Together they built up a substantial egg business within the village to supply the markets of their cousins.

Epilogue

This portrait may seem to overemphasize macabre qualities. Certainly we are long accustomed to condemning what appears to be petty warlordism, corruption, and opportunism. At the same time I have tried to arrange these familiar features into something other than a state gone awry or a public betrayed by its leaders. Thailand's social order enjoys intimate living, acceptance of authority, and flexibility of arrangement; it has no lonely public, no self-seekers unencumbered by obligations to others, and no activities frozen until due process can slowly grind out an authorization. So each social order, as we have often been told, contains its peculiar advantages and disadvantages.

Current parlance, nevertheless, makes it easy for some sophisticates to argue that the Thai social order is less "developed" than our own and will eventually become transformed into something like Western society. Some rest their argument on a theory of long-range historical transformation, indicating how the simple and undifferentiated tend to become complex and specialized: out of home industry grow factories, out of local rule the welfare state. In Thailand as well the diffuse and nearly autonomous circles of the nineteenth century have coalesced into larger and more complex circles ruled from Bangkok. The hierarchy from bottom man in the provinces no longer ends with the governor but continues up many grades in the central ministry before reaching the cabinet and the king. Throughout these changes in complexity, however, the same pattern of entourage and circle has persisted.

A second group of "developers" asserts that specialization is inevitable with the advent of modern industrial arrangements which force a high degree of specialization on any society. So preindustrial societies must be completely transformed to train youth for lifelong jobs practicing their hard-won skills. The circles of Thailand respect special skills too, but as we have seen already, no one would allow mere skills to limit his social advance. So the well-trained young man practices his specialty in the Thai style, assigning the more pedestrian parts to his assistants and moving from direct involvement to command. In such manner Thai adapt the technological order designed by and for the Occident to the peculiarities of their society. We cannot be sure in advance whether a brewery borrowed from another land will turn out more brewmasters or sots.

Entourage and circle represent a style of social construction, one so far unaltered by a century of increasingly intimate contact with the West. The form seems as deeply rooted in Thai social tissue as joy in life and fear of death is in our own. The characteristic is not immutable, for, after all, irradiation can now change a leopard's spots. Yet here is something quite as basic.

To verify this formulation requires further study. Perhaps someone might be urged to study a branch of government without the assumption that it is an institution formed only to regulate a particular aspect of society. Though David A. Wilson's (1962:180–194) observations on the Thai military bureaucracy confirm certain points of the present formulation, a more detailed study of a newly formed civilian organization offers a better test case. Edward Van Roy's (1967) study of the tea industry in Chīangmai shows the presence of circles and entourages but tells little about changes due to Western contact. A modern factory employing the new technology recently imported from the West would be a critical case.

In carrying out these studies we must try for a vision of the scene less heavily framed by our assumption of social arrangement. Concepts of class, elite, and specialized institutions becloud our vision, transforming even Timbuktu into another Kansas City with slightly quainter costumes but inferior hygienic arrangements. Can we set aside our preformed categories and observe unadorned action before we characterize the actors? If so, Ecuador can emerge to its own birthright from humble station as another peasant society, and Baghdad celebrate with whole roasted oxen the end of preindustrial status.

7. Merit and Identity in Village Thailand

JASPER INGERSOLL

This paper focuses upon the relationship between merit-making and identity formation in Thai village life. Merit is a central, explicit cultural concept among Thai villagers, while identity is of similar concern to educated, individualized Westerners. The persuasive writings of Erik H. Erikson have explicitly formulated a long Western concern with the individual. The late dean of Thai anthropology, Phya Anuman, writing under the pseudonym Sathiankoset (1967:6), has only recently introduced a Thai term for identity, *ēkalaksana*. By contrast, the rich vocabulary of indigenous and borrowed words in Thai for merit has no counterpart in English.

I am not, however, proposing to examine a major pattern of Thai belief and behavior in relation to an alien, Western concept—hardly an appropriate approach in a volume honoring Lauriston Sharp. Rather, I am treating formation of individual and group identity as a universal human process which occurs in diverse cultural forms. The particular cultural form of this process in Thailand is not explicitly emphasized by villagers, but it is not therefore less interesting or instructive in understanding their individual and community life.

The formation among Westerners of individual identity (who I am) and of group identity (who the people are with whom I identify) involves mutually exclusive distinctions congenial with Western categorical thought. In-group and out-group distinctions are also familiar in the experience

219

of ethnic minorities in Thailand, which have been studied extensively by social scientists.[1] For these minority peoples, the boundaries of the in-group are quite clear, based on such differentiae as distinct language, habitat, religion, occupation, and kinship group. Thus a man in a Lao Song village in central Thailand referred to fellow Lao Song villagers as "my language."

Similarly, life in urban Thailand presents many of the social and cultural differentiae mentioned above. Whether positive, negative, or neutral, encounters with various types of individuals and groups is a common experience for young and old urban dwellers. Thai Muslims in the Bangkok vicinity refer to themselves as "Islam people" and to Thai Buddhists as "Thai people." Thai Buddhists frequently use the same terms. Casual conversation of city Thai is sprinkled with very frequent references to foreigners, stressing distinctions more than commonalities.

Village Thai, however, are not personally very familiar with the mutually exclusive cognitive categories of Westerners, the distinctive in-group experience of minority groups, or the heterogeneous contacts of urban people or of northern Thai. My hypothesis is that in a village setting of relative social and cultural homogeneity, formation of individual and group identity is likely to be based upon behavioral characteristics somewhat more and ethnic differentiae somewhat less than in settings of greater heterogeneity. Lacking comparative data to test my hypothesis, I can only illustrate it by presenting data on merit-making as an important element of identity formation among village Thai.

My treatment of social as well as individual aspects of merit and of identity is more communally centered than descriptions of village Thailand by some other observers. Herbert P. Phillips

[1] Records of the Thai National Research Council indicate that the Council approved at least twenty-five field studies of a year or longer in duration of various ethnic minorities between 1963 and 1968.

found the villagers of Bāng Chan, near Bangkok (see Map 3, p. 150, location 1), to be extremely individualistic: "the village is comprised of 1,771 individualists. . . . [They are] . . . free agents helping others—but also ignoring them—when they see fit. . . . Much of the time they fulfill each other's expectations, but this is only because they want to, not because others expect it of them or because the situation demands it. It is the individual that is primary, not the social relationship" (1965:23, 31, 60).

The difference between my emphasis and that of Phillips may stem from our different research interests and methods, types of exposure to village life, and perhaps our own personalities, as well as differences in the villages we studied. My data come primarily from the village of Sakathiam in Nakhǫn Pathom Province west of Bangkok (see Map 3, location 2) and secondarily from the village of Bān Khōk in Northeast Thailand in the province of Khǫnkaen (see Map 3, location 5). Sakathiam is on the western margin of the fertile flood plain in central Thailand. Bān Khōk is on the western edge of the Khōrāt Plateau. Although superficially somewhat different, the ecological settings of the villages are similar: both are nuclear villages with houses crowded together in a network of dirt streets. Children and adults are within a few minutes walk of most of their friends.

By contrast, Phillips described the settlement pattern in Bāng Chan as isolated farmhouses in their rice fields and houses strung along canals, and he added: "Although it is difficult to draw precise relationships between demographic arrangements and psychological characteristics, it is noteworthy that the isolated locale of so many Bāng Chan households is not out of keeping with the independent and individualistic propensities of the villagers" (1965:17).

I would agree with Phillips on the difficulty of delineating precise ecological-psychological relationships and on the likelihood of the relationship he finds in Bāng Chan. By the same token, I would expect a different social-psychological pattern in villages where people live their lives in constant proximity. My "professional intuition" remains somewhere between surprise and skepticism regarding Phillips's extreme individualistic emphasis, but I appreciate his perceptive work and his careful qualifications. Bāng Chan, however, is ecologically representative, not of the Central Plain, but only of the small though important *flood* plain of the lower Čhaophrayā River. The major area of Central Thailand actually lies outside of the flood plain, in a huge arc stretching to the west, north, and east. Having flown in six different directions from Bangkok, I have been surprised at how quickly the clustered villages begin in this arc outside of the flood plain. In this drier habitat, in which the village of Sakathiam is located, millions of Central Thai villagers grow up and grow old without stepping into a canal boat. Thus, my own treatment here may apply only to parts of Central and Northeast Thailand.

My general argument is simply that beliefs and practices of merit figure significantly in the formation and understanding of identity in Thai village life—both individual and group identity—and that these identities are intimately interrelated. The argument does not lend itself to separation into discrete segments, but I divide it here into four premises for simplicity of presentation: (1) Villagers make merit, acquire it, and assume responsibility for it in a manner both deeply personal and broadly communal. (2) A villager can identify himself largely in terms of his personal merit, and villagers can identify the nature of their community partly in terms of their joint merit-making. (3) Merit has important consequences for individual behavior and for the behavior of people in a community. (4) These consequences of merit for individual and communal identity assume added significance in the course of the long karmic cycle of births and rebirths.

Although I analyze first individual and then social dimensions of each premise, the subtle interpenetration of psychic and social processes is very significant in making merit as well as in molding and modifying identity. Indeed, stating my argument in four premises illustrates our conventional Western preference for examining reality in analytically distinct categories. We are more proficient in isolating segments for analysis than in restoring the examined parts to a synthesized whole. Although I separate individual and social dimensions of each premise, Thai villagers seem to form their identity in a blending of psychic and social processes (self-in-society) rather than in a separating of psychic and social processes (self-versus-society).

Making Merit and Assuming Responsibility

Like the Indian Hindu-Buddhist doctrine of karma from which it has derived, the Thai Buddhist doctrine of *kam* is a deeply personal one. In the course of daily living each individual commits both good (*bun*) and evil (*bāp*), thus acquiring appropriate merit (*bun*) and its opposite (*bāp*) for which he will eventually receive appropriate rewards and punishments. An individual's total accumulated bun and bāp from his current and previous existences constitute his kam.[2] This personal definition of moral sowing and reaping is emphatically stated in Buddhist scriptures:

> By one's self the evil is done,
> by one's self one suffers;
> by one's self evil is left undone;
> by one's self one is purified.
> The pure and the impure stand and fall by themselves;
> no one can purify another.[3]

[2] Since the original Indian term "karma" has become fairly familiar in English, I will use the term "karma" for kam and "merit" for bun. Although the English term "merit" connotes actions and feelings very different from the Thai term *bun*, it is conventionally used.

[3] This well-known passage, from the *Sutta Piṭaka* (the second main division of the *Tripiṭaka*), is quoted from E. A. Burtt, (1955:60).

Although ordinary villagers cannot quote this passage, they are familiar with the general meaning. They have heard in sermons that one's inner thoughts, like his most private words or acts, can be a source of bun or bāp. A person can make merit alone in his room by paying respects to the Buddha. Somewhat less privately, but still apart from human society, a person can make merit by saving or sparing the life of an animal.

Villagers showed also that they understand clearly the second aspect of the austere doctrine of karma in the passage quoted above. Each person can hold only himself accountable for his destiny. Just as each individual is free to make his own choices between good and evil, he is responsible for reaping his own results in the future. As villagers interpreted their fortunes and misfortunes, or those of others, they invariably spoke of the outcome from previous deeds, or kam. Thai folklore, poetry, and drama abound with examples of people quietly resigned to their fate *when the time arrives* to meet their death. Although these literary cases may be charged with ideal values held out to edify people, contemporary Bangkok newspapers also carry accounts of similiar behavior on the part of condemned criminals at the time of their execution. The freedom of individual choice, so widely emphasized in Buddhism, carries a counterpart responsibility to accept the consequences of those choices.[4]

The Thai doctrine of kam is deeply individualistic; but its practice in Sakathiam, as in other villages I have observed

---

[4] In speaking of "people quietly resigned to their fate" or the "responsibility to accept the consequences" of kam, I do not imply a passive resignation to fate before the fact. In an earlier attempt to trace the complex relationships between fatalism, divination, and merit, I contended that Thai villagers make strenuous efforts to avoid evil fortune prophesied by seers; that only *after* their best efforts have failed do they quietly resign themselves to their fate *when the time arrives*. See Ingersoll (1966), a contribution to a symposium entitled "Fatalism in Asia: Old Myths and New Realities." Other symposium contributors, particularly Richard W. Lieban on the Philippines and Arthur H. Niehoff on Laos stressed this same point.

more briefly in Central and Northeast Thailand, is deeply social. Although individuals acquire and possess merit and receive its consequences, they do so almost entirely in association with other people. The most common situations in which villagers make merit are ritualized acts of presenting goods or services to priests and, secondarily, to other laymen at life-passage ceremonies. Substantial merit-making is normally public, and some of its forms are very conspicuous. At large temple festivals people place their money contributions in slotted bamboo sticks gathered into the shape of a tree. Each contribution is conspicuously displayed, and large donations usually receive corresponding publicity. Public-address systems, now common in many rural temples, merely extend this traditional publicity. At a recent festival in Northeast Thailand a professional singer of traditional northeastern songs (*mǭlam*) frequently read from a long list the names of donors and their contributions.

Not only do Thai villagers commonly make merit in social situations, they enhance their merit by sharing it with others in the act of making it. Family members commonly share their merit-making. Members of the same village community frequently do also. Speaking of her grandchildren, one woman expressed her hope that their studies would enable them to bring more merit back to other members of their family. As people offer daily food to priests, they frequently describe it as an act done on behalf of their families. When they make merit in the weekly temple observances by placing rice in the priests' alms bowls, members of the family frequently form a tail behind the member distributing rice, each one touching the person in front of him, thus sharing the merit. Referring to their parents' efforts to bring them up, many people said that their parents had very special merit with them (*bunkhun*), which they expected to return by caring for their parents in their later years. Several people expressed the belief that a boy entering the temple as a novice offers his merit from this occasion to his mother, while a young man offers the merit from his ordination as a priest to his father. Others felt, however, that both parents share in the merit from both these actions.

Outside the immediate family circle, villagers often share their merit-making with each other. Before offering rice to priests at the temple, villagers often transfer some of their rice to the offering bowls of friends, thus expressing a desire to share their merit-making and their resulting fortunes. Of the many expressions I heard about the virtue of sharing merit, the most memorable came from a retired head teacher. He likened the making of merit to the light of a candle: people can obtain light from our candle and pass it on to others, increasing the light with their candles without diminishing the light from our own.

The doctrine of individual responsibility for making merit and receiving the results of merit is also very social in its village practice. In a conversation with a group of villagers in Sakathiam, I asked if we have responsibility for the merit of other people. After considerable thought they agreed on several points. We cannot accept responsibility for those not yet born; we cannot know who they will be. Insofar as some of those people will be some of us in future lives, it makes obvious good sense to accumulate merit for our own future existences. For people currently alive we do have responsibility. We cannot order them to make merit; but we can increase our own merit if we can persuade them to make merit and especially if we can turn them away from doing evil. In any case, we should invite others to make merit with us, which increases our own merit. It is the responsibility of parents to teach their children to make merit, and it is the responsibility of teachers to instruct school pupils about merit-making.

For those already dead we also have responsibility, according to the same group of informants. We should send our merit to our dead ancestors. The only ancestors who can receive merit sent from us are those wandering as spirits (*winyān*) not yet born into another life. Once they are reborn, we do not know who they are, and we cannot share merit with them any longer. But we cannot be sure when they are reborn, so it is better to continue sending our merit to them. In fact, most people continue doing so for their entire lives.

The individual and social aspects of merit-making and identity formation reviewed above are not simply the difference between doctrine (individual) and practice (communal). People in Sakathiam believe that each person must make his own way; but each villager makes his own way and forms his own self, partly through making and possessing merit, in intimate relationship with his family and neighbors. An urban practice just beginning to enter village life illustrates this traditional pattern in a new manner. A few village parents have begun teaching their children on their birthdays to offer food to priests. As one village teacher commented, it is a new custom, but it helps a child to know that the day is his birthday. The practice brings together in a single focus the formation of one's identity and the making of merit.

Individuality is important and frequently mentioned by villagers, but they prefer to achieve and maintain it only in a continuing series of mutual associations. In the aspects of identity involving merit, my contention is that Sakathiam villagers emphasize interdependence between individual and social dimensions of their identity, rather than putting the common Western stress on contrast and conflict between individual and society. Even as individuals create a significant facet of themselves by making merit, so they create a significant facet of their community life by making merit together.

Identifying Self and Village in Terms of Merit

A villager in Sakathiam can define himself largely in terms of his merit and can discern his current merit largely in terms of his current status and fortunes. His association between himself and his merit is significant and extensive, but the two are by no means synonomous. The association between joint merit and village community is also important but less extensive. Several considerations support this close association between merit and identity.

First, villagers in Sakathiam, as in several parts of Northeast Thailand, demonstrate the intimate, psychic dimension of merit with their frequent references to the importance of one's mind or disposition (*čhai*).[5] My questions regarding the sources or causes of merit commonly received the reply: "It depends on one's čhai; it's up to the individual." Although villagers saw large offerings to priests as conferring more merit than small offerings, they also said that merit made in a given act depends on the purity of one's mind while performing it. One's psychic condition, as well as one's externally visible actions, determine the quality of one's merit. The merit one makes is a product of one's inclinations and decisions. Correspondingly, the merit one has accumulated, as it affects one's fortunes, continuously contributes to what one is forever in the course of becoming.

A second consideration is the ancient Southeast Asian view of reality as relationships between forms with similar appearance. Consistent with the great Asian tradition that the world of man is a miniature reflection of corresponding forms in the larger universe, Thai villagers tend to associate life experiences with presumed karmic antecedents which are similar in appearance or form.[6] For example, a villager described a butcher who on his deathbed felt profound remorse for his

[5] Compared to Westerners, the Thai tend to make a less sharp distinction between "the thoughts of the mind" on the one hand and "the feelings of the heart" on the other. Thus the term *čhai*, used frequently in daily living and often combined with other terms to form compound meanings, rests upon a presumed unity of mental and emotional aspects of life rather than on the Western, presumed cleavage between these two. Given this presumed unity, we may think of *čhai* as "mind" and *čhitčhai* as "disposition" or "spirit."

[6] The general parallelism between the macrocosmos and the microcosmos was cogently described by Robert Heine-Geldern (1956). This parallelism

calling and died squealing like a pig. Similarly, several villagers in conversation agreed that the theft of a water buffalo implies that the victim must have stolen a water buffalo in a previous life. A young woman recounted the bitter but instructive story of her grandfather who, angry at his lazy ox, hacked off its legs at the knees, subjecting it to a protracted, painful death. Correspondingly, he spent his own last months in misery as his legs became grotesquely swollen and useless below the knees. Perceptive to the parallelisms which life seems to reveal, these Buddhist villagers find many vivid examples of very close correspondence between one's merit and oneself.

A third consideration indicating the way in which Thai have identified themselves with their merit is found in a classical dance drama, *Sangthǭng*.[7] After strenuous efforts to bear the king a son, a young queen bore instead a conch shell. The court astrologer, bribed by a jealous minor wife of the king, interpreted this unhappy event as caused by bad merit accumulated by the queen in a previous life. The king accepted the astrologer's interpretation, and the queen was banished. As her maids prepared to follow her into exile, she bade them remain in the court: "Since I have little left from good deeds, we cannot stay together." Defining herself anew in her radically changed situation, the queen regarded herself as no longer worthy of being served by her former maids. As long as she was queen, by virtue of her merit, it was fitting that she be served by others. When, however, she ceased to be queen, she risked evil and danger by continuing to be served. She was

---

was ably applied to the traditional Thai state by Fred W. Riggs (1966). Although most villagers may not be aware of the elaborate cosmology contained in Heine-Geldern's analysis or the elaborate trappings of statecraft discussed in Riggs's study, they do tend to regard life in these terms; notably, aspects of life which resemble each other in appearance or form tend to be associated with each other, sometimes in causal-like relationships.

[7] *Sangthǭng* is one of six plays in *lakhǭnnǭk* style gathered and written by King Rāma II and his court poets. For the episode in question, see Phraphutthalōetla Naphālai 1973:47–72, in the translation by F. Ingersoll.

forced to redefine herself in the light of her evidently diminished merit. This process of reassessing one's merit and oneself in the light of experience is lifelong.

The same process of reassessment, though with a happier outcome, was also illustrated by a lady in Sakathiam whose buffaloes were stolen. After an energetic search, a village posse was able to return the animals to her. "Oh, I still have merit," she said with great relief. Her buffaloes were essential to her farming, but she had become even more worried about the ominous indication that her store of merit must be precariously low.

Villagers in Sakathiam fashion to a large extent their future, and to a smaller extent their individual identities, as they continue accumulating bun and bāp. Each person is what he is largely because of his merit, and his merit is what it is because of his conduct. These villagers speak of this process as one that continues in a highly socialized context. A person inclined to make merit (čhaibun) is sensitively dependent upon, or at least likely to be found in the company of, other people with similar inclinations. The total results of their collective meritorious efforts are plainly visible to them in the form of their temple, school, and other community facilities. In a less material sense, they also believe that their meritorious activities have significant social consequences. These consequences, discussed in the next section, help to stamp the character of their village society.

It would be overstating my argument to assert that villagers identify their communities with their presumed communal merit to the same extent individuals identify themselves with their personal merit. I would, instead, merely stress some important communal aspects of merit-making. Like Thai villagers elsewhere, most people in Sakathiam prefer to make merit at their own temple where it will be more visible to people who matter. A layman can gain merit by acts of service to any priest, but villagers often showed less solicitude and deference outside the village for priests whom they did not know. Villagers riding in my jeep along the highway evinced no interest in contributing to numerous solicitors for temple building funds at relatively remote villages. One morning in the Nakhǭn Pathom market a priest from a village near Sakathiam requested a ride back in my jeep. When I asked my village passengers, busy buying food for a festival, if we had time to wait for him, they said we would always have time to wait for our own priest, but not for one from elsewhere.

These same village passengers said people normally prefer to make merit in their own temple where their contributions of money and labor make for improvements in their own community. Another group of villagers expressed essentially the same position in a long conversation in the temple one day. One perceptive headman, nearly paraphrasing Durkheim, said, "People must rest on religion, and religion must rest on people." All the men in this conversation saw a very clear interdependence between people and their religion, which they expressed largely in terms of wealth: "When we make merit we help both religion and ourselves. We help religion and religion helps us, which makes for well-being and money later. Wealth makes for merit, which makes for prosperity for the temple and gold for the people."

In a conversation about secularization, one astute village observer distinguished Sakathiam from other villages nearby where people do not seem to think much about the implications of merit-making for the future. He found that people in such villages say, "Once we die we don't know what it will be like," and he observed that they tend to argue and fail to maintain decent social order. If people lack Buddhist principles for appropriate social conduct, they are not happy, he said.

Such comparisons are doubtlessly idealized and also tinged with local patriotism, but the point remains that villagers account for communal differences as differences in communal merit. If not the identity of their village, at least something of its character is, in their view, shaped by their own acts of making merit together.

Merit as Cause and Effect of Conduct

The argument that villagers in Sakathiam tend to identify themselves largely in terms of their perceived merit and to identify their community life somewhat in terms of merit which they make jointly becomes more tenable in the light of a third major consideration: acquisition of merit is the cause *and* effect of much of people's behavior. In their daily conversation people frequently cite events as consequences of past merit. Consequences of merit accruing to both individuals and the community at large are numerous and significant. This third point is a particular explanation for the previous section: merit is significant in assessing individual or social identity precisely because merit derives from and shapes individual as well as community lives.

The causes and consequences of merit-making to the individual are a matter of common experience. While waiting for a ceremony to begin, I asked a small group of men assembled in the Sakathiam temple if we have any way of knowing when we have much merit. One man replied confidently, "Yes, we must know." They readily agreed that a big house, a good deal of money, eyeglasses, good clothes, or good health were all obvious indications of much merit. Such signs make abundantly clear the condition of one's merit. Equally clear, these signs are themselves the natural results of good conduct at some earlier time. An increase in a person's fortunes would be happily accepted as reward for past merit, though he might modestly characterize it as a matter of good luck.[8]

Second, a person's position in society is one which villagers

---

[8] In the symposium on Asian fatalism cited above, James Mosel (1966) and I noted the close relationships between the deeply moral Thai concept of karma and the less morally charged concept of luck (*chōk*). The two concepts are more distinct among urban than among village people. See Mosel 1966 and Ingersoll 1966.

tend to see as the result of past conduct—mainly, but not entirely, in previous lives. As Lucien M. Hanks has presented it, from the king at the pinnacle down to the lowest hunter wandering alone in the forest, Thai society is comprised of people occupying positions of influence and power over others commensurate with their merit (1962:1250).

Some of the more pious people in Sakathiam point to another cause and consequence of merit which is deeply personal and thoroughly interpersonal. They said that in the course of making merit one acquires a greater interest in doing so. One becomes čhaibun: inclined to make merit and to be associated with other like-minded people, who, in turn, reinforce his inclination toward the meritorious. By associating with such people one has more opportunities to participate in merit-making. One acquires a reputation for this manner of living, and one comes to see himself as a person for whom this value is important. Two especially capable village informants stated this personal-social field very succinctly when they said, "If one is good, other good people will come to him."

Another aspect of merit-making with important consequences for the assessment of one's identity is the accumulation of prestige. Although villagers commonly define their current social status as the product of previous accumulated merit, they also seek to enhance their current prestige. One elderly lady said, "The results of merit are in our own mind [čhai]." But this inner feeling of well-being is greatly reinforced by other people's awareness of one's merit. In the intimate village world, where secrets are few and short-lived, individuals establish reputations for goodness and honesty as they make merit together. Individuals attain prestige somewhat in proportion to their known record of merit-making. They then enjoy a sense of personal worth as well as an enhanced reputation for honesty and reliability, including a better financial credit rating.

By examining the belief that people can simultaneously

earn merit and prestige in the presence of others, we may better understand the openly utilitarian view of most village Thai toward their merit, an openness which has seemed naïvely self-centered to many outside observers. The karmic tradition contains no injunction against letting the left hand know what good works the right hand is doing. This overt, self-centered interest in accumulating merit is perhaps best understood as a *validation* of the very existence of merit by its becoming public knowledge. The gathering of one's reputation and karma are aspects of the same interpersonal-spiritual process. Thus one can ill afford to be secretive or coy about good works.

In this perspective the statement of an elderly temple leader in a village near Sakathiam becomes less self-centered. He told happily of his generous contribution for a new meeting hall in his own temple as well as his contributions to other nearby temples. He contrasted his own generosity with that of a wealthy village headman who had given nothing for the new temple meeting hall, an obvious indication that this headman had no self-respect and did not even care about himself since he was giving himself no advantage for the next life.

I have contended that most Thai villagers are keenly aware of the important consequences of merit in the life of the individual, in respect to his possessions, his status in society, his inclinations to make more merit, and his prestige. I have further contended that these consequences are intimately bound up with relationships with other people in society. It is equally true that villagers also see important consequences to their community as a whole from their making merit together.

Since merit is so deeply imbedded in interpersonal relations, it is difficult to speak of the consequences of merit at only the "individual level" or the "community level." Either one is, for the villagers, an arbitrary selection from the essentially unitary, personal-social process of living and making merit.

Some people in Sakathiam regard merit as involved in any act which enhances positive relationships among people. The village head teacher expressed this view most clearly when sitting several years ago with the head priest and a group of laymen after an evening ritual in the temple. His simple statement of the case found agreement among all the people in the conversation. His opinion has the further weight of his influence on schoolchildren for over forty years. He regarded bun as deriving from those things we do which give other people happiness, gaity, laughter, or fun, or which improve them materially or physically; bāp, on the other hand, comes from the opposite: those things we do which cause other people distress, sadness, inconvenience, disturbance, or harm. The social consequences of merit are thus wrought by the efforts of people making merit together—consequences which they understand accrue to the village community as a whole and to themselves individually. Some of these major social consequences are unity, peace, reciprocity, and enjoyment of living.

Unity. A villager in Sakathiam was seeking contributions one day for a temple building fund in a nearby village where some of his wife's relatives lived. He explained that these contributions would be for merit and for social unity. He was stressing unity and harmony between the two villages, but the same dual values of merit and social unity are frequently invoked for merit-making within a single village. Solicitations for the temple or invitations to weddings and cremations often call for contributions in the name of merit and social unity. In making merit the contributors create to some degree an atmosphere of harmony and social unity.

Peace. Since only limited authority is vested in hamlet headmen and police protection is too far away to help, villagers in Sakathiam naturally place a strong value on peace. Although they have to depend largely on neighbors' desire for bun and fear of bāp, they nevertheless understand that their merit-making produces, among other good things, peace in the village. They sometimes contrast their own village favorably with others in this respect. A carpenter mentioned another village in which, he said, the people are inclined toward evil and disorder. He heard shooting almost every night he was there, and he gave a vivid impression of social breakdown in a village near an urban center. In contrast, the carpenter felt that people in Sakathiam tended more toward making merit and enjoying peace. Other people made similar though less explicit contrasts: their own village enjoyed peace as a consequence of their efforts to make merit.

Reciprocity. Villagers normally make merit in some form of reciprocal relationship between two or more people. The village laymen have an exchange relationship with priests: the laymen offer priests goods and services and receive the manifold values of merit in return; a priest offers laymen occasions to acquire the blessings of merit by making their ritual presentations to him. The laymen's offerings enable the priests to continue cultivating virtue and providing further occasions for laymen to acquire merit.

Villagers depend on each other to finance the expensive family rituals celebrating life-cycle events. An expensive wedding or cremation costs more money than most farmers make in a year. Villagers spread these costs among themselves by helping each other finance their celebrations. Closer relatives and friends contribute more money and labor, but everyone who comes brings money or food. Every contribution is carefully recorded in a notebook to guide the host in his future help to these same contributors. If someone gave me twenty baht at my housewarming ceremony last year, he would expect me to give at least the same amount for a cremation in his family this year; and he would think very well of me if I were to give slightly more than his gift of last year. Indeed, he would try to follow my example if I should invite him to an ordination ceremony in my family next year.

The constant round of family celebrations, especially after the rice harvest, requires considerable expenditure. Each family, however, is protected by mutual help against a catastrophic expense when it sponsors a large celebration. Villagers treat this mutual help as a kind of debt insurance, but they also regard these life-cycle celebrations as occasions of great merit-making. The family sponsoring a ceremony makes considerable merit by inviting priests and other laymen to join in the celebration.

Merit made by hosts and guests at family life-cycle ceremonies also affects their social relations. They reaffirm their dependence on each other for financing these celebrations; and this financial interdependence contributes, I believe, to maintaining a higher level of social solidarity than might otherwise exist. Rather than borrow money at high interest rates and depend on a particular creditor, villagers are dependent on each other in a diffuse manner. Further, this pattern of reciprocal merit-making and financing of family ceremonies tends to reinforce, and be reinforced by, the pattern of reciprocal activities in farming, house building, and other interpersonal relations.

Enjoyment of living (sanuk). Thai villagers generally regard temple and family rituals as occasions for enjoyment. A teacher's wife recently described preparations for a temple festival in a village near Sakathiam. Her eyes glistened as she spoke of the fun of dressing up and joining the dance procession accompanying the presentation of robes and offerings to the priests. She added, "It does not seem complete if we only make merit without having enjoyment, but if we combine merit and enjoyment it is very good." Her evident relish in telling of this occasion was more expressive than her words. Still more expressive was her very lively group of dancers in a *Thǭtkathin* ceremony in Sakathiam. Supported by a loud percussion band, the dancers accompanied the offerings into the temple hall, danced there with raucous gaity, and then withdrew to continue their nearly frenzied joy outside.

We might consider this enjoyment an individual aspect of merit-making since individual participants experience it; we might also regard it as a social consequence of merit-making because of its communal setting; but we may perhaps more profitably regard it as rooted in the interpersonal process in which people associate, make merit, and enjoy the fun that emerges. As with the other consequences of merit examined above, the element of enjoyment is one which villagers consciously use to characterize their condition—indeed, I would posit, to identify themselves and their community in the context of merit-making festivals.

In sum, I have argued that the merit of an individual is the result of his previous conduct and an important influence on his future conduct. An individual's merit is a very personal intrapsychic phenomenon, but its validation rests mainly on its becoming public knowledge. As villagers make merit in communal rituals they also enhance community unity, peace, and the opportunity for enjoyment of life. Their mutual help in financing each other's family ceremonies—combined with their reciprocal help in agriculture and other social relations—result in a molding and sharing of economic, social, and spiritual values in a continuing series of reciprocal exchanges.

I should mention one urban example of merit as cause and effect of communal behavior: a special ritual which occurred in Chīangmai in June 1968, when the city revived an ancient ceremony of making merit for its destiny, *Thambunsūepchatā.* According to one explanation, the people express their gratitude to the guardian spirits of the city and invoke their blessing for the well-being of the city and of its people. These guardians include former kings and heroes as well as deities. The ritual was traditionally held when the city was in danger or had suffered bad luck. The 1968 observance came in the wake of what some people regarded as ominous conditions. In the course of the ritual, eight traditional evils were expunged from the city.

According to a second closely related explanation, the ritual is a form of supplication for long life for the city and for its governing leader, similar to merit-making rituals to ensure long life to individuals. Accordingly, the number of priests invited to the ceremony was equal to the number of years since the founding of the city—or perhaps even greater, symbolizing the hope for its long existence.

A *bangfai* rocket fired from the center of the city started special chants by priests at each of the four city gates, each of the four corners of the city wall, and at the center of the city. After propitiation of the city's guardian spirits, people made offerings to them under small replicas of the po tree at each of the nine locations mentioned above.[9]

Although individual citizens present offerings and make merit, they do so as fellow citizens of Chīangmai; and they intend that the merit acquired in the course of this civic ritual should be for the common good of their city. Individuals would receive the benefits of safety and health, but only as members of the community which is blessed by its guardians. The blessing of long life is sought for the city itself as a continuing social entity.

Identity in Karmic Perspective

Thai villagers believe that merit made in the current life will have consequences within the same life. But the major significance of merit-making for individual and community identity formation emerges from a deeper examination of people's experience as they themselves trace it through successive incarnations.

In the course of conversations with priests and villagers in Sakathiam, I gathered many explanations regarding the

[9] I am grateful to Rose Frutchey, who was living in Chīangmai when this ritual was held in 1968. She recorded her observations of the ritual and secured written accounts in Northern vernacular and Central Thai of the background of the ritual.

workings and results of karma but very few on its sources. Villagers generally understand canonical doctrines regarding the formation of karma, but they are much less concerned with theological explanations than with their religious implications. Village explanations on the sources of karma are a simplification of the written texts: karma emerges from our misunderstandings of the nature of reality and from our consequent cravings and ambitions for possessions and experience, including our craving for life itself. These strong desires and our many choices based on them create a kind of energy or moral force, the consequences of which are worked out and continually supplemented by a person through his many incarnations.

What concerns villagers far more is that karma follows a person through his many lives, in human and in animal form, in hell and in heaven. The great wheel of existence, to which all creatures are bound, ensures that each person shall return again and again to be rewarded appropriately for his good and evil. Thus in any given life a person's status and hence his identity is fundamentally established by his accumulated karma from the past, which would serve to distinguish the more fortunate villagers from those less fortunate, man from animals, and animals of higher form from those of lower form.

This doctrine of successive lives receives constant reinforcement from stories people recount, from sermons they hear in the temple, and from the vivid pictures painted locally or brought from Bankok which line the walls of temple meeting halls. These pictures are usually interpretations of Jataka tales, especially the last ten lives of Buddha before his incarnation as the Enlightened One. These temple pictures also vividly depict the vision of Phra Malai, a later follower of Buddha, whose Dante-esque pilgrimage exposed him to the excruciating tortures in hell of those who had chosen evil, as well as the heavenly bliss of those who had acquired rich merit.

Although villagers speak rather generally and somewhat vaguely about the karmic process by which human conduct and its moral consequences continue through many existences, their conviction is still very strong that our kam follows us from life to life. The most important mechanism in this process is the *winyān*, a form of spiritual essence or soul which inhabits the body and survives its death.

A policeman who told of the sudden death of his prized horse recounted the general process in a widely familiar manner. The soul leaves the body at death and awaits rebirth for an unfixed period. The appropriate time of rebirth for an individual arrives when a couple in a position to provide status commensurate with the accumulated merit of the dead individual conceive an offspring. At that moment, the winyān of the dead individual enters the womb of the new mother to begin his next existence. In this manner any creature may be reborn in any part of the entire animal kingdom.

Thai informants of widely varying backgrounds agree that the soul is a spiritual essence without form or substance which exists in the body, survives death, and passes into a subsequent life. In referring, however, to their spiritual or psychic essence during the current life, villagers usually speak of their *čhitčhai* 'spirit', in terms of which they account for their inclinations, dispositions, or motivations. The spirit dies with the body, but the soul flies free though not yet fully aware, according to folk tradition, that its body is dead. It returns three days after death (according to some, seven days) to find that the body has indeed ceased to function. The soul is saddened at this discovery and weeps. It then moves on, spending an indeterminate time perhaps in heaven, perhaps condemned to hell, perhaps wandering over the face of the earth. During this interim the soul of a person who has died violently or has committed evil is likely to take the form of a ghost or *phī* that haunts and disturbs other people in its uneasy quest to right old wrongs. According to folk tradition still accepted in villages but apparently declining in the city, if a falling star passes the star of a woman as she is impregnated with a new offspring, he will probably be someone of high status.

In this continual process of reincarnation the factor of crucial significance for identity is the continuity of the soul from life to life. The soul which flies free from a dead body and eventually is embodied in another life, only to survive that one and the next, is the self-same soul. A large number of priests and laymen agree on this point.

The soul thus has a sort of continuing identity, but it is not entirely the same as a continuing self. Villagers seem to regard the spirit as the self. The spirit passes from existence at death, while the soul survives and later exists in a new individual.

For many rural Thai, however, the soul is an important aspect of self. Many individuals seem to identify themselves with their souls in previous existences. Some people, for example, can recall themselves in an earlier life—usually the immediately preceding life. Stories of this sort are frequent. A man in Sakathiam by the name of Rūeang was shot to death while stealing an ox. He was subsequently reborn as a boy with the name of Sao in a village a few miles away. At about the age of seven, he suddenly recalled his previous life and death. He returned to Sakathiam and was able to identify the house in which he had lived and some of his Sakathiam relatives of his previous life. As further indication of the continuity of his identity, he had a scar on his head in the same place where he was shot in his previous existence. Now about thirty years of age, Mr. Sao no longer speaks of his past life, but his remarkable performance gave strong support to the general folk belief in the continuity of self in successive lives.

Similarly, several people have recounted a story which appeared in a Bangkok newspaper. The husband of one informant knew about it personally. A young girl died in Lopburī Province. She was later reborn in a village about thirty miles away. After several years in her new family she suddenly recalled her former life and family and wanted desperately to return to her former parents. She was able instantly to identify the earlier parents upon meeting them and longed to rejoin them. Both sets of parents felt she was their "own." Despite her unhappiness she remained with her second set of parents, who could not bear to see her leave.

Another similar, widely known story is that of a priest who had advanced to studies in Pali. He died and was reborn as a boy who was able at the age of four or five years to recall his previous knowledge, including reading and chanting in the Pali language.

Such stories are common knowledge in urban and rural Thailand. As support for the traditional view of rebirth, they receive wide attention and provoke lively discussion. My impression is that urban, educated people regard these stories with more skepticism than do rural, farming people. Everyone seems to view them as rather extreme phenomena: the sort which most people have heard about but few have experienced directly.

Both urban and rural Thai seem to find these stories arresting, but they spend little time thinking and wondering about their own previous lives. Although current life experiences are clues to past lives, most people are more concerned with the moral implications for this life than with pondering who they themselves may have been in previous existences. My inquiries have thus far revealed no one dreaming about who he was or what he was in past lives. If such people exist, I would expect their motivating force to be a practical, religious one rather than a philosophical, speculative one.

My impression is that most villagers see their current place in life as almost entirely the product of previous conduct.

Their status and their very identity are the result of their merit from past conduct. Villagers frequently consult a medium who can establish contact with the souls of relatives who have died. But people normally do so only in times of stress, uncertainty, or practical need. Thus, I would say Thai villagers assume that they themselves have existed in the past as they will in the future and that their souls have a continuing identity, but their main interest is the practical one of living well in the present.

Whatever their views on the soul and the spirit in relation to the self, several informants, including three village priests, agreed on a point central to our interest in identity in karmic perspective: the person committing an act (*phūtham*) in one life is the same person as the one receiving the karmic consequences (*phūrap*) in a later life.

How does this popular view of merit and self relate to one of the basic doctrines of canonical Buddhism: *anattā*, the doctrine of the unreality of the self? Winston King has stated it succinctly. Beginning with the doctrine of dependent origination—that all items of experience are compound structures made up of other elements—King noted that in the Buddhist view no actual self exists beyond, beneath, or within the five aspects of existence: physical form, feelings, perceptions, thoughts, and consciousness. Rather than some unitary essence which possesses these five attributes, a self is merely a psychosomatic event which is a continuous flux of these five elements. No immortal soul or continuing self passes from one rebirth to another. The five aspects of existence fully disintegrate at death, but the force of their disintegration produces a sort of continuing effect. That which continues is not identical with a former self but is a sort of personality-producing karmic energy, based on a craving to continue experience, a craving in turn based on ignorance of reality. Enlightenment thus consists of intellectually apprehending the nonreality of the self and finally directly experiencing this nonreality through sustained, disciplined meditation (King 1962:186–195).[10]

This austere, arcane doctrine is distantly removed from the beliefs and behavior of Thai villagers. King himself sees little relationship between canonical doctrines and those of the masses of village people: "Most of these many millions practically speaking *deny* the denial itself by immersing themselves in the pursuit of better self-rebirth and by consoling themselves with the fellowship of devas and a personalized and living Buddha" (1962:193).[11]

My field inquiries reveal that Thai Buddhists do not explicitly deny any doctrines of their religion. They seem largely unaware of the anattā doctrine. One reflective young woman with experience in both village and Bangkok life was familiar with the term but did not know what it meant. She said one would have to ask a layman well-versed in religion or a priest to understand it. A priest in Northeast Thailand was familiar with the doctrine and discussed it easily. He said, in effect, that there is no self but that the doctrine has a second aspect, namely that we have no control over our lives. We wish to be happy, we are not; we wish to be healthy, we are not; we wish to avoid growing old, we cannot. Thus no self exists in the sense of the kind of self-control that we would like to have in life. But this doctrine is very complex, and most of us do not understand it, he added.

[10] Although King's principal sources are canonical writings and scholarly commentaries, he very carefully and sensitively places them in the cultural setting of his twenty-month stay in Burma and his extensive interviewing and participation in meditation centers. By explicitly comparing God, love, guilt and Dukkha, prayer and meditation, and self in Buddhism and Christianity, he succeeds in presenting both traditions sharply and succinctly. He does not seek to present the village tradition, but he consistently seasons his textual interpretation with pinches of Burmese urban cultural context.

[11] If the practical effect of folk Buddhism is to deny the anattā doctrine, it is neither the villagers' intention to do so nor their understanding that they are so doing. This distinction between intentions and effect is irrelevant to King's interest but not to mine.

Thai villagers, aware of the more elementary teachings of the vast Buddhist canon, practice their religion in the light of their understanding of the doctrines and their intimate experience of community life. Even though most of them do not know the term *anattā*, their thinking and behavior are still somewhat informed and influenced by the doctrine—rather like the majority of Westerners who accept as natural certain human rights without ever having read John Locke's treatise.

We turn now from examining the long karmic process in its implications for the self, to its implications for interpersonal relations, starting with those between husband and wife. *Bupphēsanniwāt* is a widespread belief that the relationship between a man and a woman reflects their relationship in a previous life. Many university students in Bangkok ponder this matter when considering a spouse. Within this pattern at least three sorts of couples exist. The first, *khūsāng khūsom*, is a couple who have made merit together in a past life and now have a good marital relationship. The second, *khūwēn khūkam*, is a couple married in a previous life who were not good to each other. Either spouse may have suffered at the hands of the other. They are now reaping the rewards of that previous relationship, the previously injured spouse causing the other to suffer in turn. After being divorced from her husband for some time, one young woman decided that they must have been a couple of this sort. The third type, *khūlāng khūphlān*, is a couple with a very bad relationship in a previous life. One spouse may have tried to kill the other, and in this life the other spouse is trying to even the score.

The particular emphasis in this belief is upon the relationship between spouses rather than the behavior of either one. The significant point is that karmic consequences arise from such relationships as well as from individual behavior.

Villagers in Sakathiam develop their strongest sense of communal solidarity in the relationships among people who continue to make merit together in their temple: these relationships reach outward toward each other in the present life, backward toward their (frequently shared) ancestors, and forward toward descendants as well as their own future lives. Before the end of each merit-making ritual the priests recite a special chant, *truatnam*, during which the people review their merit and reflect upon it and share it with others. Informants tend to agree that they think first of themselves as receiving the merit from participation in the ritual and then of their parents, their grandparents, their ancestors more widely, the entire village community (especially that represented at the ceremony), and then all beings in the world. The sequence of beneficiaries upon whom they reflect may not be very uniform, but they do think, they said, of sharing merit with other members of the village assembled.

Compared with the great importance of sharing merit with members of one's family, alive and dead, sharing with fellow villagers may not be of the highest importance; but it takes on greater significance if we regard it, as villagers do, in the perspective of the karmic cycle of many lives. As I have stated, villagers feel a bond of unity between those who make merit together. They feel that their bond is older than this life, that they are making merit as members of a community now because they have made merit together in a past life.

By the same token, Thai villages consider that their accumulated merit has implications for their future as members of a community. When my family sponsored a sermon one afternoon, by providing gifts for the priests and coffee for priests and congregation, several villagers interpreted our inclination to live in Sakathiam and make merit with them as signifying that we must have done so with them in a previous life. They also said that in a future life we would probably be born in Sakathiam and live there making merit with the people again. Our collaborating in sponsoring a similar sermon some seven years later merely confirmed this interpretation in the minds of several villagers who again discussed it.

An elderly lady emerged from the darkness one evening with a startling greeting: "In order that we may meet again in the next life." My initial confusion passed when she entered the lamp-lit area of our porch carrying a small silver bowl and announced that she was collecting contributions for our hamlet to sponsor the sermon on the following sabbath. Although a person may be born anywhere in his next life and although some may hope for a much better station than that of his current life, most villagers hope to be reunited in the same community of fellow merit-makers.

The significance of accumulated merit through a succession of lives is not the same for individual identity as for communal identity. My data suggest that most villagers in Sakathiam do not anxiously ask themselves who they are. Their beliefs and practices of merit-making seem to provide a partial but important answer: a person is who he is and where he is because of who he has been and what he has done. In the continuing karmic process, a villager's significant concern is not so much to examine his identity as to strengthen it with proper conduct for future betterment. I doubt, however, that villagers see communal fortunes and misfortunes as a consequence of the sort of village Sakathiam has been during past lives. They do not regard the village itself as having a series of lives, only its individual members. Rather, they perceive that their interpersonal associations are affected by their previous associations and will, in turn, have important consequences for their future associations—and thus for the quality of their community life.

One elderly lady, with whose family we have been particularly close, pondered the question of whether her family and ours had made merit together in a former life because, as she and other villagers observed, we had been drawn to her family in two different periods of time. Believing that their joint efforts of merit-making have communal as well as individual consequences, villagers in Sakathiam see these consequences as having long shadows stretching from one generation to the next through the karmic cycle. Individuals make merit, not the community as such. But each person does so as a member of a significant community and thus makes it a different sort of place in which to live. As he makes merit and shares its consequences with other people with whom he identifies, he gradually fashions an image of who he is and of the village community of which he is a part. As he sees this same process extending to past and future existences, he sees how deeply merit-making helps fashion communal as well as personal identity.

My argument here on the significance of merit-making for communal aspects of identity is partly based on the premise that for Thai villagers the personal, social, and cultural aspects of life traditionally have been intimately related. Our visits to Sakathiam during 1967–1969 and briefly in 1972 and 1973 have strengthened my earlier suspicion from 1959 60 that the very rapid pace of modernization and secularization is tending to segment and reduce that traditional intimate relationship. Commercialized agriculture, monetized social relations in the village, individually owned motorcycles and radios, an increase in the number of people who seek higher education and occupations outside the village, erosion of supernatural sanctions, reduction of authority relationships within the village—all these trends seem to be creating new conditions in which younger people will mold and interpret their identity. The individual villager used to recognize pervasive moral strands in his relationship to other villagers and to nature largely in terms of karma. He identified himself in a moral sense with his community, especially his temple, and with his nation, especially his king.

That the king and queen personally identified with the kingdom in a reciprocal fashion was vividly illustrated in the drama previously cited, *Sangthǭng*. If the birth of a conch shell resulted from the queen's past deeds, then the entire kingdom faced destruction and ruin unless she were banished. The karma of the queen touched not only her own and her family's lives, but reached out to the entire realm, threatening the very survival of the state.

In a diffuse but significant sense, ordinary people are connected with the survival of the entire human race in the karmic process. An example of this moral connection arose in a conversation with the Sakathiam head teacher and several farmers. The teacher remarked, as Thai Buddhists frequently do, that all religions are basically the same. When he asked about Christian ideas about the next life, I pointed out the similarities but also a difference: no one ever returns to earthly life from the Christian heaven or hell. The head teacher's habitual composure dissolved in an exclamation of shocked incredulity at such an unworkable, even unthinkable scheme. If people did not come back to this earth, then where would human population come from? Where would the people be to populate the earth? In the course of being reborn and working out the effects of his own karma, the individual actually participates in maintaining the population of the earth.

I began with the hypothesis that in a relatively homogeneous village setting, lacking clear-cut ethnic differentiae, the formation of individual and group identity is likely to emphasize behavioral characteristics. I have argued that the patterns of merit-making figure prominently in the manner in which many Thai villagers identify themselves and their village society: (1) making merit and assuming responsibility for it personally and socially, (2) identifying self and village community in terms of merit attained, (3) reaping the personal and collective consequences of merit, and (4) deepening these consequences in the course of the karmic cycle.

I have tried to indicate the place and importance of merit in identity formation among village Thai, *not* to present merit as the only ingredient in individual and group identity. Despite the close relationship between the social and psychological processes of accumulating merit and formulating identity in Thai villages, the two processes are by no means identical. The formulation of identity involves many other ingredients besides the single process of merit-making discussed here.

At the outset I contrasted the strong Western emphasis upon individual identity with its relative absence among village Thai. Terms like "the search for identity" and "identity crisis" have become familiar expressions in American life, while the recently coined term in Thai for identity is scarcely known. The contrast is *not* that Westerners form clear identities and Thai villagers do not, but rather that Westerners are much more explicitly and strongly concerned with this universal human process. Do my limited data suggest any explanation for the seemingly low level of concern for identity among these Thai villagers? I might proffer one partial interpretation. Their profound doctrine of karma and elaborate patterns of merit-making have given them a very thorough, moral explanation of who they are individually and communally, and they reinforce this identity in daily community life. Perhaps the deepest significance of karma and merit-making for their identity formation is that with these beliefs and behavior patterns they have achieved a comprehensive enough image of their own humanity to be relatively free of disquieting uncertainty or doubt about who they "really" are.

8. *Phībān* Cults in Rural Laos[1]

GEORGES CONDOMINAS

Theravada Buddhism is the official religion of Laos, of its neighbors to the south and west (Burma, Cambodia, and Thailand), and of Ceylon.[2] In all these countries a cult of the "spirits" (*phī* in Lao) remains strong, having mingled so profoundly with Buddhism that the religion as actually practiced by the people represents a syncretism of the two. However, in all these countries Buddhism is predominant in the ideology and is the religion professed.[3]

The introduction of Theravada Buddhism to Laos is known to antedate the mid-fourteenth century, the era of the foundation of Mūeang Lānsānghomkhāo, "The Land of the Million Elephants and the White Parasol," by King Fāngum (Lévy 1940). Thereafter Lao kings vigorously supported Buddhism, the religion of the Perfect One. One such king, the great

[1] This essay was written in December 1968. Much of the material on which it is based was previously presented in two ethnographic reports (Condominas 1959, 1962); these data have also been used in a general analysis of popular Lao Buddhism (Condominas 1968). I wish to acknowledge the assistance of Ward Keeler and G. William Skinner in preparing this paper from an original draft in French.

[2] See Lebar and Suddard (1960) for an overall picture of Laos, and Condominas (1970) for a general view of Lao culture. Berval (1956) has assembled a rich collection of articles dealing with the topic of this paper. It would also be useful to compare the research on Laos with the pioneer work on Thailand done under the direction of Lauriston Sharp.

[3] For Laos see Condominas (1968), and for the other Buddhist countries see the collection of articles edited by Nash (1966).

Pōthisārāt, even issued an edict in 1527 that banned spirit worship and ordered the destruction of all sanctuaries associated with the phĩ cult. Even the sanctuary of the guardian spirit of the then capital city of Lūang Phrabāng was ordered destroyed, and on its site the king constructed a Buddhist pagoda (Le Boulanger 1931:72–73). During subsequent reigns, most notably the glorious reign of Pōthisārāt's son and successor Sētthāthirāt—a great builder of religious monuments—a large number of Buddhist monks came from Cambodia and Siam to study in the kingdom of Lānsāng. The kingdom became a center of Buddhist learning, and Buddhism increased its hold on the Lao people.

In Laos today Buddhism affects each stage of the life cycle and pervades the daily routine of the common people, as in the daily offering of alms to the monks (*čhaohūa* or *khūbā*). Similarly, the lunar cycle of Buddhist holy days (*vansĩn*) and regular calendrical ceremonies, such as the New Year's festival, as well as variable ones, such as the Bun Phavēt, the annual ceremony in honor of Vessantara, serve as focal points for the village collectivity. These Buddhist ceremonies, whether individual, familial, or villagewide, are occasions for offering gifts to the monks and thereby "acquiring merit" (*hāetbun*). The "merit" acquired in this way will influence one's future place in the hereafter and in the cycle of rebirths. The desire to make merit is unquestionably the chief motivation in the spiritual life of the Lao peasant.[4] Since the best way to gain merit is for a man

---

[4] See Hanks (1962:1247–1248) on the significance of merit (*bun*) for the Thai. Tambiah (1968:49–53) deals with the Lao of Northeast Thailand. The latter emphasizes the notion of "error" (*bāp*) as an opposition to "merit" (bun). In my opinion, for the Lao peasant at least, the notion of bap has only limited importance, certainly in no way comparable to the opposition between Good and Evil found among Christians. The essential preoccupation of the Lao is with bun, individual merit, even if the ritual involves several persons and takes the form of a collective expression. A notion more commonly employed by the Lao is *khalam*, "contrary to the rules," "forbidden," which does not have the same connotation as bāp but which seems more appropriate in this context (see Katay 1955:554–556).

to enter the Buddhist monkhood, even if only for a short time, one can understand why the residence of the monks, the local monastery (*vat*), is of central importance to the village community. However, the village monastery has multiple functions, serving not only as a religious structure, but also as a warehouse for the village, its forum and community center, a shelter for travelers, and so on. But above all, the monastery is an expression and a symbol of the village unit, for in most cases the village has either conferred its name on the monastery or taken its name from it (Condominas 1959:80–96; 1968:91).

Despite the attacks by various Lao kings on the cult of the spirits and the primary role played by Buddhist monks and monasteries, the pattern of Buddhism as such does not exclude either the belief in spirits or the cult of the phī. The term phī encompasses a number of diverse notions such as "soul of the dead," "malevolent spirit," "guardian spirit," "nature deity," and the like.[5] In fact, the majority of the Lao devote considerable attention and effort to the phī, whether asking them for favors or simply for their protection, escaping their pranks, or repairing the damage and curing the ills they have caused. In general, the phī do not require any substantial public ritual structures comparable to the Buddhist monastery.[6] And, apart from *hǭ khāo padap din* ("ceremony of the rice cakes to decorate the earth") and *hǭ khāo salāk* ("ceremony of the rice packets drawn by luck"), both directed primarily to ancestral spirits, there are few large ceremonies dedicated to the phī. Important exceptions are ceremonies and altars directed toward higher-order territorial spirits, such as the *phīmūeng*, which may be quite large and ostentatious. This essay is concerned primarily

---

[5] Some idea of the variety of meanings subsumed by the term phī can be obtained by consulting Anuman (1954).

[6] Such as those practiced for the *phraphum čhaothī* ("spirit of the place") to be found in front of every house in Central Thailand. One could apply to Laos and the Vientiane Plain Moerman's comment (1966:138) about the Thai Lue: "Unlike the Siamese, Lue personal and household spirits are of minor importance, for the village spirit claims much more attention."

with one type of lower-order territorial spirit, namely, the "spirit of the village" (*phīban*), also known as the "spirit who loves the village" (*phīhakbān*) or the "spirit who protects the village" (*phī laksābān*).

The cult of territorial spirits is common to the T'ai peoples of Southeast Asia, whether Buddhist or not, and bears some resemblance to the Chinese veneration of the earth god (Maspero 1950; Chavannes 1910). Under a variety of names, this cult is so widely spread among the different peoples of Southeast Asia that Paul Mus (1934:8) saw in it a "form of religion which was at one time common to the diverse parts of Monsoon Asia."

Properly, the term phīmūeang refers to a spirit who resides in the capital of a principality (*mūeang*) and whose jurisdiction is its entire territory. The phīmūeang was initially brought into being by the construction of a *lakmūeang* ("pillar of the principality"), which involved the voluntary self-sacrifice of a pregnant woman who was thereby transformed into the guardian spirit of the principality.[7] Hence, the construction of the lakmūeang involved the creation of the guardian spirit of the kingdom, and one might say that it is this spirit who received the subsequent annual sacrifices. It should be noted that subsequent sacrifice to the phīmūeang involved no human sacrifice; rather, the cult called for the annual sacrifice of a water buffalo. This rite is officially celebrated to this day with great pomp at Vat Phū in the old kingdom of Champassak (Archaimbault 1956a). The phīmūeang ceremony was celebrated in Vientiane as recently as thirty years ago (Lévy 1943), though it disappeared somewhat earlier from Lūang Phrabāng (Lévy 1943:301, n. 2). It was at one time celebrated regularly at Chīangmai (Notton 1926:205, n. 2), and Kraisri has recently

---

[7] See Notton (1926:176, n. 3; 205, n. 2) on the Lakmūeang of Chīangmai; and on that of Vientiane see Lévy (1943:303, n. 3) and Nhouy (1956:963). A less bloody legend undoubtedly influenced by Buddhism explains the origin of the Indakhila Column at Chīangmai (Notton 1926:26ff.). The spirit protectors of the city gates born of involuntary human sacrifices are more similar to the first situation (Pallegoix 1854:50–52).

described such a sacrifice in the pre-Thai protector spirits of Chīangmai, though the cult there has lost much of its importance in recent years (Kraisri 1967:198).[8]

A considerable number of protector spirits also figure in myths of origin, such as that of Khun Bulom in northern Laos (Archaimbault 1959a). These myths indicate that numerous lesser territorial spirits also receive offerings during the annual phīmūēang ceremonies in the capital city, which Notton tells us was also the case in Chīangmai (Notton 1926:57–66). These origin myths together with observed survivals of the phīmūēang ceremonies point up certain political facts. The political dependence of the villages on the capital finds its counterpart in the cult of the guardian spirits, for protector spirits of the various villages form a symbolic hierarchy similar to that of the political groupings they protect. "Every year at the time of the sacrifice of the water buffalo, those in charge of the hǭ phībān [i.e., the altar of the village protective spirits] erected, near the great altar [to the phīmūēang] of Chīangkhong [Chieng Khouang], a temporary shelter, a reproduction in miniature of their village hǭ" (Archaimbault 1961:198; 1967:570). The hierarchy of protective spirits may be clearly discerned in the phīmūēang ceremonies of Chīangkhong, and this is by no means an isolated case. In fact, this pattern was introduced to Chīangkhong in the fifteenth century from Lūang Phrabāng, which has twelve altars to different lesser territorial spirits in addition to the main altar of the phīmūēang. The political implications of the origin myths are consonant with the symbolism of other rituals as well.[9] For example, the ceremonial hockey game called līkhī, performed at Thāt Lūang, appears to involve symbolic political confrontations between groups similar to those that arise at the

---

[8] Compare the ritual conducted in 1968 in Chīangmai, as described by Ingersoll at p. 238 of this volume.

[9] The myth of Khun Bulom (Archaimbault 1959a) could be cited in its entirety for the Black Thai, yet another T'ai group (Lafont 1955:798ff.).

level of the kingdom (see Lévy 1953; Archaimbault 1956b, 1961, 1966).

This essay focuses on the cult of protective spirits at the village level—that is, on the phĭbān[10]—rather than on the phĭmūeang. Because of this restriction, the hierarchical element in the cult of the phĭmūeang recedes from view.[11]

Sanctuary of the Phĭbān

The sanctuary of the village's guardian spirit is the *hǭ phĭbān*. the hǭ is generally built in the forest and hence stands apart from the village complex, which is dominated by the spacious buildings of the Buddhist vat. (In general, this description holds for villages lying east and southeast of Vientiane; see Map 3, p. 150, location 7.) One might take the hǭ as one of the two sacred nodes unifying the village, the other being the vat. In terms of its unifying function the hǭ phĭbān might be viewed as something of an animist equivalent of the vat (Condominas 1962:82; 1968:130–131). However, the hǭ phĭbān by no means echoes the vat's outward appearance. It usually consists of a simple hut on stilts of wood and bamboo, approximately two to two and a half meters in height and one or two meters in width, depending on whether the hǭ is single or double.[12] The buildings of the vat, on the other hand, are centrally located, more substantial, and constructed of more permanent materials. If a sanctuary building (*sim*) is included in the vat complex, it may even be constructed of brick and roofed with tile. The different locations of the vat and the hǭ are understandable. The vat

[10] Other spirit cults may also be linked to the category of the phĭmūeang, such as the spirits of forested lands (Anuman 1954:154–157; Velder 1963) and of salt mines (Archaimbault 1956b).

[11] One sometimes finds a rigid hierarchy reflecting the structure not of the village but of the total society. This is the case for the spirits of the earth (Archaimbault 1956b:222).

[12] For an attempt to classify the different kinds of hǭ phĭbān found in Laos and North Thailand see Iwata (1962:401, fig. 2 and plates 1–12).

represents the Buddhist principles which govern men directly, whereas hǫ phībān represents the land on which the village is established and from which the villagers obtain their food and principal resources.

The functions of the phībān overlap somewhat those of Nāng Thōranī, a goddess of the soil, whose concern is the agricultural fertility on which harvests depend. However, whereas Nāng Thōranī is generic and functionally specific, the phībān is a *genius loci*, the god of a specifically defined area, the protector of the fields, the forest, and the ponds which make up that area, and also of the people who live off it. While the phībān can be a single individual, it is more often a married couple, whence the double hut.[13] In most cases the guardian spirit appears to derive from the first settler of the area or the founder of the village, together with his wife, but he can also be a high official, a king, or even a deity (*thāēn*).

Master of the Phībān Cult

The master of the cult of the village's guardian spirit is designated the *čhaočham phībān*. One might think that, because of his responsibilities to the village guardian spirit, the čhaočham might sometimes set himself up as a rival to the head of the village pagoda. This does not occur, however, for actually the čhaočham is usually a good Buddhist who would never believe that the rites he performs in honor of the village spirits run counter to his worship of the Buddha. In fact, before the čhaočham goes to the hǫ phībān to honor the spirit, he goes first to give alms to the monks. With respect to his personal qualities the čhaočham is in no way a marginal or occult person, nor is he any kind of sorcerer. Though villagers seem unaware of them, the functions performed by the čhaočham on behalf of the village collectivity make him one of its most influential citizens.

[13] The two people serving as phībān may sometimes be sisters (Archaimbault 1959b:413, n. 40).

The village headman (*nāibān*) participates in the selection of the čhaočham, as does the *sālāvat*, who is both deacon and beadle of the pagoda (Condominas 1962:82; 1968:108). The selection of a new čhaočham ordinarily follows numerous interviews and discussions between the nāibān and the villagers, and the final choice is usually ratified by the village assembly. However, in the village of Sīangdā, the abbot of the monastery pointed out that the čhaočham could be selected by the spirit itself, which is to say that the phībān might induce a trance in the person of its choice. This possibility is congruent with the instance, cited below, that concerns the erection of a sanctuary for a secondary phībān in the village of Nāhai.

The village of Mūēang Nǫi is unique, for there the village nāibān is simultaneously čhaočham not only of the village guardian spirit but also of the beneficent spirit of the monastery (*phīkhunvat*);[14] his selection as nāibān carries with it these religious responsibilities. In Mūēang Nǫi the same man acts as village headman and is charged with the protection of men and goods both as administrator and as religious leader. To characterize this situation in Western terms, one might say that this man holds both temporal and spiritual powers, which he exercises for the protection of his fellow villagers. However, it should be remembered that in the spiritual domain his role is limited to that of mediator.

The village of Mūēang Nǫi is also peculiar in another respect. Although the čhaočham in certain cases receives half of the

[14] The phīkhunvat is none other than the spirit of the original abbot of the monastery. This example indicates how two notions we consider distinct—"ancestors" and "guardian spirits"—may in fact be only one. It is the same in the case of the phībān who often appears to be the first settler and the founder of the community. By his origin the phīkhunvat could be said to constitute a link between the monastery and the phī cult. The altar of the phīkhunvat, called *hǫ phākhāo* or *hǫ čhaophaokhāo* ("altar of the Prince with white clothes"), is even more modest than the hǫ phībān and stands discretely fifty centimeters above the ground in a corner of the vat. In two of the five villages studies its čhaočham was also that of the phībān (Condominas 1962:84, 96; 1968:109).

offering made during *kaēba* (a sacrifice to the phībān in thanks for a wish fulfilled), the position is ordinarily without remuneration.[15] Not so in the village of Mūēang Nọ̈i, where the chaōcham receives the yield of a rice field in *ex officio* trust to support the phībān cult. Perhaps this remuneration is a surviving indication of the special importance of this particular area, as indicated by ruins of five old pagoda sites distinct from that of the modern vat.

The association of the chaōcham's and nāibān's positions in Mūēang Nọ̈i presented a thorny problem when the incumbent village headman was elected to the post of canton chief (*nāitā-sāēng*). The new canton chief continued to maintain the worship of the phībān, but the man elected village headman to replace him claimed that he bore the right to the post of chaōcham phībān and with it usufruct of the rice field. To settle the dispute the new canton chief decided to share the rice field with the new village headman, while he himself would continue as chaōcham both of the phībān cult and the phīkhunvat cult as well.

Another case of particular interest involves the inheritance of the chaōcham's duties within a single family. About twenty years ago, a healer was summoned in the wake of an epidemic which struck a group of homes in the village of Nāhai. The healer, a *mọ̈mon*, revealed that a spirit, a bachelor younger brother of the village phībān, demanded a họ̈ for himself, an altar whose upkeep was to be assured by Nāi Suk, the father of one of those stricken.[16] This spirit thus designated Nāi Suk to be chaōcham of the sanctuary, which was constructed that very day, though Nāi Suk moved its location on two later occasions. In 1959, feeling that he was growing old, Nāi Suk presented his son Nāi Muk to the spirit as his replacement. Though a group

[15] However, informants did not consider even this portion of a sacrifice as actual remuneration. They believed that if the chaōcham fulfilled his ritual functions properly his recompense would be the good health of his family.

[16] On the mọ̈mon or "doctor of mantras" see Condominas (1962:104; 1968:139).

of eight neighboring houses of Nāhai honor this celibate spirit, they continue to participate with the rest of the village in the cult of the phīban of Nāhai, a married couple. Only after they have contributed to the ceremony of feeding the phīban do these people go to the spirit of their neighborhood to make an identical offering. Although this spirit is considered by its followers to be of the same nature as the phīban of the village, it is hardly known to the other villagers. When he was asked about this spirit, the headman of Nāhai, who was otherwise knowledgeable about his village, thought it was only the guardian spirit of a rice field.

Phīban Rituals

In addition to maintaining the altar of the phīban, the čhaočham has responsibility for performing a number of regular services. For example, he must come to pray to the spirit for the prosperity of the villagers every fifteenth day of the waxing and waning moons, which schedule coincides with the cycle of Buddhist holy days (*vansīn*). This invocation follows the morning almsgiving to the monks and is accompanied by a simple offering of flowers, candles, husked rice, and saffron water. The čhaočham is always alone when he carries out this service. Similarly, when a villager asks the čhaočham to implore the phīban to heal either himself or a member of his family, or to protect him on his departure to a distant place, or to grant any such request, the čhaočham goes alone to the hǭ phīban to present the tiny offerings furnished by the sponsor. This second type of function ends with a sacrifice called *kāeba* when a sponsor's request has been satisfied. It represents an obligation that has nothing to do with the regular duty performed twice monthly by the čhaočham. The sacrifice offered varies according to the nature of the request and the sponsor, which can be an entire village. This was the case, for example, in Mūeang Nǭi, where a pig was offered only a week after one had been sacrificed during the sixth-month ceremony of feeding the phĩbān because the villagers' request in May 1961 that they be spared adverse effects from the civil war appeared to have been granted.

The chaocham's role as a mediator working on behalf of the entire village collectively is most strongly emphasized in the ceremony of Līang Phĩbān ("feeding the spirit of the village"). All villagers participate in this ceremony, which is performed twice yearly, in the first and the sixth lunar months. However, the Līang Phĩbān ceremony of the first month, essentially a thanksgiving for the stored harvest, is far less important than the sixth-month ceremony. The latter is essentially a request for good health among men and livestock on the eve of the rainy season and, above all, for good harvests at the time when work in the rice fields is just beginning. The ritual proceedings of this sixth-month ceremony vary from one village to the next. In some (all villages in the zone reported on here with the exception of the village of Nākhwāi) it consists of a collective sacrifice. Either each household annually offers at least one chicken to request good health for the members of the family, a second for the fertility of their rice fields, still another for the success of family businesses such as salt mines, or every three years households are levied a certain amount toward the price of a pig to be sacrificed and consumed at the foot of the hǭ phĩbān. On the morning of the sacrifice to the phĩbān, *talāeo* (strips of bamboo plaited to form a star) are posted at different entry points of the village to serve notice to outsiders that the village is closed.[17] The Līang Phĩbān sacrifice in these cases clearly symbolizes the unity of the village as a collectivity.

The Rocket Festival and the Sixth-Month Phĩbān Ceremony

In the village of Nākhwāi and the great majority of its neighboring villages, the Līang Phĩbān ceremony and the Rocket Festival (Bun Bangfai) are merged. In this case the village is

[17] On the talāeo see Robert (1941:39, 68, 179, and plates 37 and 38) and Anuman (1967c).

open to outsiders; powder is sent to surrounding villages so that the villagers may make fireworks, which they bring to the host village to be entered in a contest. Neighboring villages which have not received any powder may send only monks and, of course, spectators.

What does the Rocket Festival represent? For one thing, along with Bun Phavēt it is the equivalent of our fairs, bringing together large numbers of people. Bun Phavēt is a Buddhist ceremony consisting in the ritual reading of the story of Prince Vessantara, the penultimate incarnation of the Buddha.[18] Though the Buddhist associations of the Rocket Festival are less clear, it is still regarded by most Lao villagers as a Buddhist ceremony. They suppose that it commemorates the Visākha-būsā, the triple anniversary of the Buddha's birth, enlightenment, and death. However, some Lao see in this ritual "the survival of ancient pagan customs. . . . Occurring at the beginning of the rainy season, Bun Bangfai is nothing other than an invocation to Phanhā Thāen (God of Heaven) to ensure the fecundity of the paddy fields and the abundance of the harvests" (Trans. from Nginn 1961:9). Only in Vientiane can the Rocket Festival, which is celebrated there near the old site of Vat Kāng during the full moon of the sixth month (i.e., May), be confused with the Visākhabūsā. Everywhere else in the Vientiane Plain this ceremony (which, like the annual ritualized boat races, can take place elsewhere only after it has occurred in the capital) does not fall on a fixed day but varies over a one-and-a-half-month period; some villages may observe it as late as mid-June. In some villages—Hūakhūa is a case in point—the Rocket Festival is never celebrated; in a few it is celebrated as a ceremony quite separate from Līang Phĩbān. But in most, the Rocket Festival makes its appearance in conjunction with the sixth-month ceremony of the village guardian spirit under the direction of the čhaočham.

[18] On the Bun Phavēt in Laos see Condominas (1962:56–65; 1968: 119–125). For the Lao of Northeast Thailand see Tambiah (1968:77–87), and for the Central Thai see Anuman (1961).

Of the villages that customarily observe the Rocket Festival, some, such as Nākhwāi,[19] normally do so every year; others observe it less frequently, but in any case the decision on whether or not to hold it in a given year is made at a villagewide meeting. During this meeting the list of villages to be invited and the amount of the contribution expected from each household toward the price of the powder are fixed. In principle, powder (usually from one to four kilograms) is given to each invited village so that it will participate by making a rocket. But in 1961, Nākhwāi gave powder to only seven of the eleven villages invited because the village felt it could not afford to buy powder for more than seven villages, even though the participation of monks from all eleven neighboring villages was needed for the ordination which was to take place at the same time. The village of Nǭnghēo never offers powder to its neighbors; hence all the rockets which are set off on the day of Bun Bangfai are made by its own inhabitants.

The villages and other participating groups are given about ten days in which to make their rockets. They must prepare charcoal, construct the body of the rocket, find an appropriate "tail" (a good stick of bamboo, ten meters or so in length, and preferably from a single shoot), squeeze the explosive into the body of the rocket, assemble the parts, decorate the rocket with bands of brightly colored paper, and so on. Interestingly, monks are usually the best rocket makers in a village, and they are invariably the inhabitants with the greatest amount of time to devote to such tasks.[20] Oddly enough, in making the rocket to

[19] It does not seem likely that this is due to Nākhwāi's proximity to Thāt Lūang, where the Bun Bangfai is especially brilliant because the spirit venerated there is that of its founder King Sētthāthirāt. It is at Thāt Lūang that one of the major ceremonies concerning all of Laos takes place, a ceremony which seems more and more to be a national celebration. See Nhouy (1956) on the Thāt Lūang ceremony, and on the hockey game (tīkhī) which is its central episode see Lévy (1953) and especially Archaimbault (1956b, 1961, 1966).

[20] As early as 1900, Raquez (1902:115) remarked on the primacy of Buddhist monks as the makers of fireworks in Laos.

represent their vat, the monks play their most important role in the Rocket Festival.

The festival lasts two days, though most of the activity takes place during the two afternoons. The general outline is as follows: Late in the morning of the first day, bands of costumed youths and a few older men circulate in the village singing off-color songs, stopping to give special renditions to anyone who offers them drinks. Their disguises are imaginative and depend entirely on each man's fancy, though as invariably happens at carnivals several men disguise themselves as women. (No women actually take part in these goings-on.) One member of such a band always brandishes an object to remind everyone, even if unconsciously, that the Rocket Festival is a fertility rite. This object, a wooden phallus painted red and about half a meter long, is usually displayed intermittently to the crowd in a very realistic manner. The results can be very effective: the phallus rises suddenly in the form of a projectile when someone pulls the trigger of a bazooka used to threaten a group of girls. Or it is the "birdie" of an old plate camera with which a young man offers to take the picture of a pretty maiden. Of course, the disguised and soon tipsy young men, their faces streaked with soot, serenade proper young maidens as well as those who give them alcohol. Their songs are accompanied by clapping and the playing of musical instruments (see Figure 6): foot drum, Lao panpipe (*khāēn*), or even a petrol can used as a metal drum. These raucous activities ensure a large and lively crowd, which will join the later procession to the sanctuary of the phībān.

Early in the afternoon (or somewhat later if there is a Buddhist ceremony such as an ordination on the first day of the Rocket Festival) the čhaočham goes to the spirit's sanctuary. He is accompanied by a procession of villagers, who are also joined by the band of youthful revelers. At the sanctuary the čhaočham makes an offering to the phībān, accompanied by a prayer. The village's rockets are also presented to the phībān,

Figure 6. Musicians at Rocket Festival (Bun Bangfai), Nǫnghēo village, Laos, 1961.

their "heads" placed on the platform of the sanctuary. (If there are many rockets, only two or three may be presented to represent them all.) The tumult which follows the čhaočham's prayer is sometimes preceded (as at Nākhwāi) by the lighting of miniature fireworks and firing a gun into the air.

Though they play a prominent role in the later proceedings, the women mediums (*nāngthīam*) do not usually participate in this procession.[21] At Thāt Lūang, however, the nāngthīam who incarnates the great King Sētthāthirāt, the guardian spirit of the area, plays a major role. It is usually she who leads the procession and directs the ceremony. We did see women mediums in Bān Hom don their ceremonial dress near the hǫ phībān after having saluted in that direction, but in this village the sanctuary was right beside the road.

Leaving the sanctuary of the village spirit, the procession moves toward the vat. The rockets previously presented to the village spirit are then placed on a platform which stands in the court of the pagoda and on which the rockets from other villages have already been arranged. Before the arrival of the procession the nāngthīam have already begun to dance before the rockets. They are elaborately costumed in turban, scarf, belt, and tunic of silk. They dance individually or together in front of the rockets displayed in their bamboo mounts. On the bars of the rocket mounts lie the sabers used in the later dancing together with the traditional offerings, invariably including a bottle of alcohol. The principal musical accompaniment is provided by a drum (*kǫnghāng*) suspended from the shoulder and struck by both hands. A pair of little cymbals and one or more khāen often complete the ensemble. Nowadays this highly rhythmic music is often drowned out by a blaring loudspeaker, powered by a generator, which has been rented for the occasion by some pious soul. While they dance, the mediums swig alcohol from bottles which faithful clients offer them. The dance grows steadily wilder, stopping only as the nāngthīam are possessed by their respective spirits (phī). Only in the village of Nǫnghēo did we observe the čhaočham himself assume ceremonial dress and participate in the dances.

---

[21] In the area covered by this essay only two out of five villages, Nākhwāi and Hūakhūa, had nāngthīam, five and three respectively. In general, the nāngthīam were possessed by the local spirits of the ponds and swamps of the two areas. On the relations between nāngthīam and čhaočham see Condominas (1968:136–137 and n. 40).

At the end of the afternoon a procession takes place around the *sālā* (convocation hall) of the monastery. One of the nāngthīam armed with a pair of sabers dances at its head. She is followed by the orchestra, the čhaočham, and the other mediums, also dancing. Some of the men carry the mount on which the rockets have been placed, and if the invited villages have also made mounts to transport their rockets, the parade is quite spectacular (see Figure 7). Last of all comes the crowd, in which small groups of merrymakers continue to sing and play their instruments without regard to what is being played by the next group, by the orchestra in the lead, or over the loudspeaker.

Figure 7. Procession of the Rockets, Rocket Festival (Bun Bangfai), Nōnghēo village, Laos, 1961.

The procession circles the sālā clockwise three times; the rockets are then put back on the platform in the court of the vat. Night falls. The nāngthīam dance a few more steps, remove their ceremonial costumes, and withdraw. The first day of the festival is over.[22]

The second day's festivities consist principally of the lighting of the rockets. Early in the afternoon, after the monks and laity have eaten, the rockets are brought noisily to the "launching ground" at the edge of the village's largest tract of rice fields. A little cluster of trees serves as the launching ramp, with two or three large sticks of bamboo tied together by lateral rungs attached almost vertically to the trees. The rockets are lit one at a time. Their takeoff is watched closely by the crowd and provokes either the wild enthusiasm. of its makers and of those who have placed bets on it if it performs properly, or the equally noisy sarcasm of the crowd if it falls in a cloud of smoke a few meters from the launching ramp. The rocket that travels farthest wins a prize of two or three hundred kip, which is set out in a small moneybox at the vat.

This prize does not represent the only monetary interest involved in the competition. Long before the competition actually takes place, bets are opened both on the large rockets and on the much simpler rockets of smaller scale built by amateur pyrotechnicians. The bettors simply split into groups, each betting on the victory of a particular rocket. Or a man may claim that his rocket will cover at least a certain distance; others will call his bet by putting up an equal sum. Other bettors may then join in. In either case, the bets are placed in a kitty which the winning side takes and divides among its participants in proportion to the size of their bets. If the majority of the bets are on the order of several dozen kip, a rocket owner may lay out two or three hundred kip to support the reputation of his creation. In the village of Nākhwāi, bets went as high as

---

[22] A description of a Rocket Festival in the village of Sīkhai, located on the outskirts of Vientiane, may be found in Archaimbault (1961:196–197, n. 3).

three thousand kip, an exceptionally large sum for a rural area.

Despite the pious legend which would link the Rocket Festival to the Buddhist Visākhabūsā, the Buddhist elements involved in this festival are actually quite minor. The chief manifestations of Buddhism—that the monks are the principal makers of the larger rockets (those rockets which are taken to represent the villages), that the dances of the nāngthīam take place in the court of the pagoda, and that there is a ritual walk around the sālā of the vat—inform only a negligible portion of the entire set of events involved in the Rocket Festival.

The peasants are right, then, to believe that feeding the phīban on the first day, is the principal part of the Rocket Festival. Several aspects of the celebration underline its true nature as a ceremony for the village spirit. These are: the pre-eminent role of the Master of the Cult of the Village Spirit (mediator par excellence between men and the phīban), the almost equal importance of the nāngthīam (spokeswomen of the spirits related to the phīban), the symbolism of the rockets themselves, as well as their presentation to the phīban on the first day of the festival, the sexual content of the songs, the raucous displays and phallic symbols of the groups of revelers who lend the overall tone to the ceremony, and even the time of year the festival takes place (just before or at the beginning of the agricultural season). All of these elements point to the festival's crucial character as the outstanding celebration of the cult of the phī and as a fertility rite which Buddhism could not or did not try to eliminate.

Two aspects can be discerned in popular festivals and ceremonies in rural Laos. The contrast between them is sharply apparent when we compare the two largest village ceremonies, the Rocket Festival and the Bun Phavēt. Both festivals are noncalendrical, and in both the village expresses its collective unity. But each festival is an expression of one of the opposing poles of the rural religious milieu: the spirit cult and Buddhism. The former sings exuberantly of the fecundity of men and plants, the latter glorifies the meditation and charity preached by the Buddha. These contrasts, however, never trouble the peasants. Part and parcel of the symbiosis of the two religions are the elements that each has borrowed from the other, for example, the walk around the sālā during the Rocket Festival and the carnivalesque processions (minus the phallic symbols) in the Bun Phavēt.[23]

Conclusion

Travelers and anthropologists have often noted how well Theravada Buddhism has adjusted to the belief in phī and its associated cult—not only in Laos but in all the countries where this great religion holds sway. More often than not, the role of the phī cult has been considered secondary and even negligible—a collection of peasant superstitions surviving surreptitiously in the shadow of the Buddhist great tradition. However, in contemporary rural Lao society the cult of the phī is restricted to no such minor role. It is on a par with Buddhism, with which it forms an integrated whole. The general point appears to hold not only in other Theravada Buddhist countries[24] but throughout Southeast Asia. This is suggested by the in-depth studies of the spirit cult and its place in the overall religious system carried out in Mahayanist Vietnam (Cadière 1944–1957) and Muslim Java (Geertz 1960).

If the establishment of Theravada Buddhism or any other "great tradition" results from one of the major cultural discontinuities which Lauriston Sharp (1962:8–10) sees in the history of Southeast Asia, a certain uniformity in the various beliefs and rituals connected with the spirit cult can be discerned in the area as well. And this uniformity exists regardless of the great tradition with which the spirit cult is associated.

[23] One can even see during the course of the Bun Bangfai a very daring parody of the ritual reading of the story of Phavēt (Vessantara), see Archaimbault (1966:41–42, n. 55).

[24] See, for instance, Lingat (1939) and Textor (1960).

This situation would seem to testify not only to an ancient form of religion common to this area of the world (Mus 1934:8) but also to considerable persistence. In certain respects, this common religious core has been penetrated only superficially by exogenous world religions, and has been less than profoundly affected by other cultural elements taken over seemingly in toto by the peoples of Southeast Asia.

We have seen that the altar of the village spirit, the hǫ phĩbān, constitutes one of the two religious poles of the village community, the other being the Buddhist monastery, the vat. How is it that most authors have minimized the role of the spirit cult? For one thing, these observers were themselves followers of a major religious tradition and, in general, had little interest outside such great traditions and the evolved metaphysical systems associated with them. They regarded other manifestations of religion as so many curious and disparate superstitions. And, it is true, appearances offer some support to their preconceptions. Everyone identifies himself as a Buddhist, and the only religious monument, an outstanding one at that in terms of its size and the quality of its materials, is the vat, which clearly dominates the village community. The hǫ phĩbān, by contrast, is merely a little hut, hidden in the brush far from the other buildings of the village.

The vat serves many of the functions necessary to community life: primarily temple and monastery, to be sure, it is also town hall, ceremonial center, school, warehouse, and inn. The hǫ phĩbān is a place of worship and nothing else. The Buddhist ceremonies associated with the vat open the village to its neighbors who are invited to attend, while the Līang Phĩbān ritual closes it to outsiders (except when the ritual is accompanied by a Rocket Festival, which is characterized today as Buddhist). Differences between these two institutions express distinctive functions. The vat, an expression of the adopted great tradition, answers the needs of the people as members of a spiritual community, and it is the place of assembly for the

group as a social and political entity. The jurisdiction of the
họ phǐbān, on the other hand, is not the community as a social
entity but rather the natural ecological system that nurtures its
members, above all the land which provides food, shelter, and
clothing. The phǐbān belongs to the world of nature, and it is
there that it takes refuge.

9. Kin Groups in a Thai-Lao Community[1]

CHARLES F. KEYES

In this paper I discuss kin groups as they are found in Bān Nǭngtūen, a Thai-Lao community in Northeast Thailand. I follow Meyer Fortes in distinguishing "between the domestic field of social relations, institutions, and activities viewed from within as internal systems, and the politico-jural field, regarded as an external field" (Fortes 1962:2). In Bān Nǭngtūen, as elsewhere, the members of the domestic groups, who are held together by the need "to rear offspring to the stage of physical and social reproductivity" (Foster 1962:2) and by bonds of economic interdependence, are primarily kinsmen. Members of a domestic group need not reside together in a single dwelling, for at one "phase" (to use Fortes's term) in its development cycle the subgroups of the domestic group may have separate dwellings. Normally, however, members of the various units must live reasonably close together if they are to maintain an effective level of economic and social cooperation. Members of domestic groups away temporarily for purposes of work or

[1] Research on which this paper is based was carried out in Northeast Thailand in 1962–1964 with support from the Foreign Area Training Fellowship Program and the Foreign Area Fellowship Program of the Ford Foundation. The study here presented was substantially completed in 1967, and only minor changes have been made to take into account new findings made on my revisits to Bān Nǭngtūen in 1967–68 and in 1972–1974. I am indebted to Professor Sharp not only for introducing me to the subject of kinship and to Thai society, but also for providing valuable criticisms of my first attempts to make sense of data from Bān Nǭngtūen.

schooling are not really exceptions to this generalization. In some societies, domestic functions are occasionally carried out by such atypical institutions as orphanages or child-rearing cooperatives. These exceptions notwithstanding, domestic groups in almost every society can be defined as localized kin groups in which some members are connected by consanguineal ties while others are connected by affinal ties. In cases where extended family units of some type are domestic groups, rules of postmarital residence also directly affect the structure of domestic groups.

Given certain definitions of descent, domestic groups may be seen as predicated in part on a rule of descent, although most anthropologists do not treat them as being of the same order as descent groups. Descent groups usually do not include affinals, while domestic groups normally do. More importantly, descent groups lack the important function of providing for social reproduction. In short, domestic groups belong to the domestic realm of social relations while descent groups belong to the politicojural realm.

Where they exist, descent groups provide one type of solution to the problem of allocating power and authority to regulate social relations in the politicojural realm. Nonetheless, there is no necessary and sufficient reason, as there is in the domestic realm, why statuses in the politicojural realm should be allocated along kinship lines.

Descent groups can be structured according to a unilineal or a nonunilinear rule of descent. As Ward Goodenough has said: "Unilineal descent groups are only a special case of a type of group based on common descent from a real or imaginary ancestor, who remains a fixed point of reference down the generations until such a time as the group segments" (Goodenough 1961:1343). Descent alone may not suffice to define membership in descent groups (Goodenough 1955:72). Often, for instance, a person must reside in a particular locality to activate his rights (through descent) to membership in a descent group.

In addition to the domestic and politicojural realms in every social system, it is necessary also to recognize an individual realm. Fortes has argued that in societies "where the unilineal descent group is rigorously structured within the total social system there we are likely to find kinship used to define and sanction a personal field of social relations for each individual" (Fortes 1953:29). In societies that lack a unilineal emphasis, some members of an individual's cognatic kinsmen recognize an obligation to give him help and support in culturally determined ways (see Freeman 1961:209). This is true whether or not the society possesses definable "kindreds" and whether or not the society is "bilateral" (Goodenough 1961). Quite often affinals (particularly spouses) and "friends" also join in providing aid, support, or comfort for an individual. However, insofar as consanguineal kinsmen form the core of groups which act in concert to fulfill these functions of the individual realm, we can speak of the existence of ego-based kin groups.

It should be apparent from the foregoing discussion that not all kin groups can be defined according to the premise that descent principles are primary. Ego-based kin groups are predicated upon lateral extensions of kin ties, not lineal ones. Domestic groups are localized groups structured in reference to both consanguineal and affinal ties. In some societies, rules of postmarital residence are also relevent to the form domestic groups assume. Even descent groups may employ criteria other than descent (especially the criterion of locality) as a means for defining membership. Each society employs a variety of principles that may receive different emphases in structuring its kin groups. Let us now examine how these principles operate in the community of Bān Nǫngtūēn.

Bān Nǫngtūēn lies about eight miles east-southeast of the provincial capital of Mahāsārakhām (see Map 3, p. 150, location 6). In July 1963 it had a population of 703 people, almost half of whom were under the age of fifteen. Although the village, when I first studied it in 1962–1964, was divided into four (and for some purposes six) "neighborhoods" (*khum*) and although it subsequently was divided into two administrative villages,[2] it has a nucleated character with rice fields lying outside the area of settlement. The fields of most villagers are well situated, being subjected only rarely to the overflooding and drought that afflict many northeastern villages. This favorable situation may explain why the site of the village was also inhabited some 600 years ago when Khmer-speaking people dominated the area. The ancestors of the present-day Thai-Lao villagers, however, settled there no more than 150 years ago.

Bān Nǭngtūen villagers belong to the Thai-Lao ethnic group that predominates in the population of Northeast Thailand. Although sharing more aspects of social structure and culture in common with villages in Laos than with villages in Central Thailand (Keyes 1967:62–76), Thai-Lao villages have also absorbed some influences from Thai national society into their local social systems. For example, surnames, introduced by King Wachirawut, are possessed by all citizens of Thailand, Thai-Lao villagers included, whereas villagers in Laos continue to do without them. In addition, other Thai laws, such as those relating to property ownership, local administration, and registration of land and of vital statistics, have left their marks on on the social structure of Thai-Lao communities.

While Thai-Lao villages vary in ecological setting, in local custom, and in adaptation to the Thai national systems, the social structure of most such communities is basically the same.[3] The analysis presented here can, I believe, be assumed to be

[2] The political division of the village occurred in 1968 at the instigation of the leadership of one neighborhood which was physically most separated from the rest of the village. This administrative division of the village has not yet (1974) been followed by divisions of other community functions.

[3] For studies of village society in Northeast Thailand that are relevant to this essay see Amyot (1964), Kickert (1960), Kirsch (1967), Klausner (1972), Lux (1962, 1969), Madge (1957), Mizuno (1968, 1971), Prajuab (1971), Saund (1969), Suthēp (1968a), Tambiah (1969, 1970), Yatsushiro (1966), and Yatsushiro et al. (1967).

applicable to most Thai-Lao communities in the northeastern region of Thailand.

The Village of Bān Nǭngtūen as a Kin Group

As might be expected from the comparative study of peasant societies, part of the politicojural realm of Bān Nǭngtūen villagers lies outside the local environment (Keyes 1967). In Thailand kinship plays little role in structuring the supravillage sector of the politicojural realm, and even the local sector is structured in large part along nonkinship lines. Nonetheless, there is a kinship dimension to the village of Bān Nǭngtūen that gives it something of the character of a descent group.

Bān Nǭngtūen villagers consider all residents of the village to be kinsmen who either share a common ancestor in the tutelary or guardian spirit—*phīpūtā*[4]—or are married to some one who is a descendant of the spirit.[5] Ideally, it would be best if everyone in the village were descendants of phīpūtā, that is, if everyone were members of a group which approximates a non-unilinear descent group, since they would thereby be more likely to avoid those actions which offend the spirit. In fact, a significant minority of villagers, most of whom are men, were not born in the village and have moved into it only after marriage. As Table 1 shows, fewer than two-thirds of existing marriages in Bān Nǭngtūen realize the expressed ideal that marriages should be village-endogamous. Nonetheless, consanguineal kin ties do connect a large proportion of villagers.

In addition to the kinship element present in the structure of the cult of phīpūtā, kinship is also relevant to the structuring of the congregation of the village Buddhist temple, the *wat*.

---

[4] Literally translated, *phīpūtā* means 'spirit-paternal grandfather/maternal grandfather'. Despite the implied plurality, villagers treat phīpūtā as a single spirit of male sex. The term does indicate, however, the stress of both paternal and maternal sides in the tracing of descent from a common ancestor.

[5] For an extended treatment of the cult of the village tutelary spirit, see the paper by Condominas, immediately preceding in this volume. Also see the study by Suthēp (1968b) and the discussion in Tambiah (1970:253–254).

Table 1. Endogamous and exogamous characteristics of existing marriages*
in Bān Nǭngtūen, 1963

Characteristic	Number of occurrences	Percentage of occurrences
Endogamous marriages	74	64.4
Exogamous marriages	39	33.9
Husband from outside Bān Nǭngtūen	(33)	
Wife from outside Bān Nǭngtūen	(4)	
Both partners from outside Bān Nǭngtūen†	(2)	
Insufficient information	2	1.7
Total existing marriages	115	100.0

* Existing marriages are defined as those in which both partners are still living.

† In each of these two cases a man had first married into Bān Nǭngtūen to a village woman who subsequently died. Each man subsequently took a second wife from outside the village and brought her to live with him and his first wife's children.

Domestic groups, not individuals, are considered by villagers to be the constituent members of the congregation. Moreover, after the cremation of adult members of the community who have died "natural" deaths, their ashes are enshrined in reliquaries (*thāt*) located around the perimeters of the wat. These shrines are the foci of ancestral cults to be descussed later.

Finally, participation in the "town meeting" of the village which is called periodically by the village leaders is also determined on the basis of kin-group membership. The head of each domestic group is expected to be present at such meetings.

The kinship basis of village social structure, however, should not be overstressed. For example, the village has no power to enforce marriage regulations, a prerogative which is often within the power of descent groups elsewhere. In addition, statuses connected with wealth deriving from ownership of cattle and profits of trade, most nonagricultural skills and occupations, and religion are allocated to villagers along lines other than kinship. Most importantly, individuals who marry into the village have almost as many rights and duties of village membership as those born there. A man born in another village who has taken a wife in Bān Nǫngtūen is entitled, once he becomes the head of a domestic group (see below), to participate in village council meetings and to aspire to any leadership position save those of headman and keeper of the village shrine. He will be expected to contribute money, goods, or work to village undertakings in the same way as any man born into the village.[6] However, villagers feel that the roles of headman and *khaočham* (intermediary in the cult of the tutelary spirit) should be filled by persons who were both born in the village and have continued to live there after marriage. A man who had married or migrated into the village would not be suitable for filling these roles, villagers say, because he would not know enough about village affairs to be headman, nor would he be a descendant of the ancestral spirit. Beliefs in shared descent are also explicitly stressed in the annual rites of propitiation of the village ancestral spirit. On balance, kinship can be said to reinforce communal solidarity in villages such as Bān Nǫngtūen, but it does not permeate the fabric of the system in the same way as it does in societies with descent groups.

Bān Nǫngtūen is divided into four or six "neighborhoods" (*khum*)[7] which have little sociological significance in the structure of the Bān Nǫngtūen social system. Although one or more members of every domestic group in a specified khum can, if pressed, trace his genealogy back to a common ancestor who lived only five or six generations in the past, there is no belief

[6] In villages near Bān Nǫngtūen traders and schoolteachers who have settled in other than their natal villages have also been granted the same rights and duties of village membership.

[7] If villagers want to be very specific about where a particular person lives they make use of names for two smaller khum containing, respectively, five and six households. However, when general reference is made to parts of the village, these households are included within the larger "neighborhoods" on which they border.

that a khum is a kinship group.[8] The khum does not function to regulate marriage, control property, shape economic cooperation, or worship common ancestors. The only exception to this generalization is the occasional (not more than once a year) *aobunhūean* or "household merit-making" ceremony in which all households within the khum share in the preparations, cooperate in feeding the invited monks, and receive the blessings that result from the rituals performed.

Propinquity and recognition of consanguineal kin ties among the households of a khum do provide the basis for greater cooperation among kin living within a khum than among those living in different khum (or different villages). But these functions of kinship properly belong to the domestic and individual realms of social relations rather than the politicojural one.

Domestic Groups

The domestic groups of Bān Nǫngtūen are not definable, as they are in many other societies, in terms of those who live together in a single dwelling. That is to say, the domestic groups of Bān Nǫngtūen cannot be equated simply with "households." Villagers divide up the domestic realm into groups of kinsmen who cooperate in primary agricultral production. Some of these groups are independent household units while others consist of extended families living in two or more households.[9] To understand the variable structure of Bān Nǫngtūen domestic groups

[8] Villagers identify each khum with a particular surname. However, this identification is very recent (beginning with the introduction of surnames after 1913 when every household in a khum took the same surname), has no functional importance, and will soon become totally misleading through the loss of large numbers of carriers of the surname identified with particular khum through the practice of uxorilocal residence. At the present time, of the 119 heads of households in Bān Nǫngtūen only 31 have surnames which are recognized as belonging to the khum in which they live, while another 88 have surnames which differ from that of the khum surname.

[9] The Thai-Lao term for domestic groups, *langkhāhūean* (lit., 'roofhouse'), seems to suggest that such groups are independent households, as is the case

we need to examine the changes that occur during their developmental cycle.

Recruitment of membership in a domestic group can be a consequence of birth, postmarital residence, or "adoption." If we begin with the independent nuclear family, which structure characterizes almost every domestic group at one phase or another of its cycle, we can trace the ideal pattern of expansion, during which these recruitment principles are utilized, and of fissioning of domestic groups in Bān Nǭngtư̄en. Each child born into a nuclear family remains a member of it at least until it is time for him or her to marry (or in some instances until he or she is "given" to another family for "adoption"). On marriage a son normally moves into his bride's household while a daughter is expected to continue living with her parents and unmarried siblings in the same household. Thus the nuclear family is transformed at the marriage of a daughter from a nuclear family into what I call an "uxori-parentilocal stem family."[10] Before the marriage of a second daughter or after the birth of their first child the first couple must found a separate household, preferably in the compound containing the household of the wife's parents. Land on which a couple builds their new house should come from the wife's parents. This new household, again ideally speaking, should continue to be economically dependent upon the parental household.[11] The

---

in other parts of Thailand. However, as I discovered in my census work, and had confirmed in my work with records kept in the district office of births and deaths of villagers, villagers consider household units which are still economically dependent upon a parental household to be part of a single langkhāhư̄ean. It should be noted that this folk definition of the social units of the domestic realm does not accord with the official Thai one which defines those living in a single dwelling to belong to an independent unit (cf. Thailand, Samnakngān sathiti hǣng chāt 1962: Part B).

[10] I have invented this term because I feel that none of the established terms adequately describes the situation in which a man follows his wife after marriage and moves into the household of her parents (not the household belonging to her mother's side or her father's side).

[11] Most new households of this sort do not have granaries of their own. When eventually they do have, they are filled from the wife's parents' gra-

foundation of a new household prior to the marriage of a second daughter leads to the formation of an uxori-parentiloced extended family consisting of two nuclear families, the senior of which becomes an uxori-parentilocal stem family after the marriage of the next daughter. The process continues until the marriage of the last (usually the youngest) daughter, who is expected not to move out of the parental household at all. Meanwhile all sons have married out and joined their wives' parents' domestic groups. Fissioning of the domestic group begins with the founding of separate daughter households, but it is not completed until the last surviving parent in the parental household has either died or joined another domestic group through remarriage. Upon the removal of the surviving parent, the domestic group fissions into as many domestic groups as there are daughter households (the parental household having now been turned into the household of the last daughter married).

During the course of the developmental cycle of a domestic group, children may be "adopted" into the group. In Thai-Lao terms the status of *lūklīang* (lit., "child to nourish and look after") is not quite equivalent to that of "adopted child" in the American sense, and is perhaps better translated in most cases as "foster child."[12] Lūklīang are quite often either grandchildren or newphews/nieces of one member of the senior couple in a domestic group. Boys will eventually marry out and join the domestic groups of their wives; girls may at marriage claim membership either in the domestic group of their true parents or in that of their foster parents. In the latter case, excepting

---

nary, not directly from the rice fields. Only after a household has achieved full independence (i.e., become a new domestic group) will its granary be filled with rice brought directly from the threshing floors in the fields.

[12] Two households in Bān Nōngtūen have young relatives living with them in the status of "servant" rather than that of "foster- child." Although it is difficult in some circumstances to differentiate between servants and foster children, in these two cases the heads of household are quite explicit in stating that the young people have no rights whatsoever to inherit land from the senior couple in the household in which they were living.

when the foster parents have no other children,[13] their rights within their family will probably be less than that of a true child. The actual inheritance of a female lūklīang who opts to stay with her foster parents after marriage will depend upon their magnanimity and relative wealth.

Since cases do occur when a couple has only boys, Bān Nǫngtūēn villagers recognize an alternative pattern of residence in which one son remains in his parents' household after marriage. The son who remains is usually the last one to marry. In such a case, however, all sons will probably get a part of the parental lands.

Thus far I have been discussing the ideal patterns of growth and fissioning of domestic groups in Bān Nǫngtūēn. By making reference to Table 2 which shows the composition of households in Bān Nǫngtūēn in mid-1963, and to Table 3, which shows, in less detail, the composition of domestic groups, it is possible to obtain some idea of how the ideal compares with the real. With only two exceptions (those in the "other" category in Table 2), all households in Bān Nǫngtūēn fit, once demographic considerations are taken into account, into the expected mold. Vestigial nuclear families represent cases where both parents have left the domestic group through death or remarriage prior to the marriage of all their children. In these instances the family is supposed to continue to follow the developmental cycle as if the parents were still alive. That is to say, the imminent marriage of a girl in the family should lead her married sister and brother-in-law to move out and establish a new household (and, in this case, a new domestic group). In the two instances I observed where this expectation was put to a test, the already married couple did move out. The presence of two married

---

[13] Villagers claimed that if a couple had no children at all, they would be more likely to adopt a son than a daughter because a son could not only be an heir but he could also make merit for them through being ordained. In the only one case in Bān Nǫngtūēn where a childless couple adopted a child, they did, in fact, adopt a son.

Table 2. Household composition in Bān Nǫngtūēn, 1963

Type of household	Households with "adopted" children	Households without "adopted" children	Total
Nuclear	12	78	90
Simple nuclear*	(11)	(69)	(80)
Vestigial nuclear†	(1)	(9)	(10)
Uxori-parentilocal stem‡	6	16	22
Broken sororal joint§	0	3	3
Viri-parentilocal stem‖	1	1	2
Other#	1	1	2
Total	20	99	119

* Married couple or broken nuclear family plus children and stepchildren, if any.

† Simple nuclear family plus one or more unmarried siblings of Mo/Wi also present.

‡ Household in which a son-in-law is, or has been, present in the second generation. Some cases where marriage in first generation is broken. May be other unmarried children in second generation and grandchildren in third generation.

§ Simple nuclear family plus broken nuclear family in which the surviving spouse is a woman and a sister of the wife in the first family.

‖ One case where one daughter-in-law is married to a true son of the couple in the first generation and the other where the daughter-in-law is married to an "adopted" son of the couple in the first generation.

One household comprises a nuclear family and a broken nuclear family in which the surviving husband is a second cousin of the wife of the first family. The other comprises two unrelated broken nuclear families (one with the wife remaining, the other with the husband).

couples under the same roof is thought to breed friction whether or not the parents of the wives are still living.

On the other hand, it is thought that for a woman to live in a household where there are no adult males is not good. When a young woman has lost her husband through death or divorce, she will either move back into her parental household, if she does not already live there, or will move in with or be joined by another married sister. This explains the three broken-sororal-joint families in Bān Nǫngtūēn.

The two viri-parentilocal stem families were both brought into existence as a consequence of a couple having no daughters. It should be noted that there are no cases of viri-parentilocal extended families. Only one son remains with his parents in cases where there are no daughters.

The thirty-six households included within sixteen uxori-parentilocal extended families (Table 3) again fit the expected pattern. However, among the eighty-three independent households are two, both nuclear families, which do not, since one or both of the wives' parents are still alive. Secession of daughter households who establish independent domestic groups occurs usually, as is true in both of these cases, as a consequence of inadequate land resources on the part of the wife's parents. In the two cases in question the households had combined small amounts of land and capital (cash) obtained from both sets of parents before setting up a neolocal residence. These families, however, are exceptional; the more usual pattern is for young couples from poorly endowed domestic groups to leave the village altogether in order to homestead on previously uncultivated lands in other parts of Northeast Thailand.[14]

Although they did not appear as aberrations at the time I conducted my survey, there were two other domestic groups which had been spawned from the husband's parental group rather than the wife's despite the fact that the husband had sisters. In both instances the landholdings of the man's parents were greater, even when divided among daughters and *sons*,

---

[14] Cases of secession in which the couple leaves the village to homestead elsewhere are very common. Between 1935 and 1963 the school records show that 131 school-aged children migrated away from the village with their parents. Allowing for the fact that some of these children were of the same parents and that others returned to the village at a later date, there were still at least 75 families which the school records indicated had left the village permanently. My genealogical survey also indicates that a number of families migrated out before they had school-aged children.

than those of the wife's parents. Villagers commented that these occurrences were contrary to custom, but they recognize the right of the men to remain in their parental domestic groups after marriage in order to obtain sufficient landholdings.

Table 3. Domestic kin groups in Bān Nǫngtūen, 1963

Type of domestic kin group	Number of kin groups	Number of households
Independent households	83	83
Uxori-Parentilocal extended families*	16	36
Parental household an uxori-parentilocal stem family	(6)	(14)
Parental household a nuclear family	(10)	(22)
Total	99	119

* Consists of a parental household and one or more daughter households.

This last observation points to one critical function of domestic groups in Bān Nǫngtūen: land control and use. It is because agricultural land belonging to the parents of a domestic group remains undivided until their departure from the group that the domestic group is kept economically interdependent even when it comprises more than one household. On the other hand, if the land is insufficient to support all members of a domestic group, early fissioning of the group is likely, or activation of land rights through a man rather than through a woman.

Rights to control all types of land (paddy, upland, and garden) in Bān Nǫngtūen are vested neither in individuals nor in domestic groups but in couples. Individuals who never marry have no rights to any type of land and must remain dependent upon some relative. In the normal course of events a man will marry and move into a domestic group whose land resources are controlled by his wife's parents. When he and his wife move out of the parental household to build a house of their own, the wife's parents usually give the couple some land on which to build a house. As the wife's parents grow older, daughters and sons-in-law will assume responsibility for cultivating a certain section of the parental land. Finally, when the last parent dies or remarries into another domestic group, the couple gains full control over land originally belonging to the wife's parents.

Divorce or death of one partner leads to modifications in the normal pattern of land control. When a divorce occurs, the man always relinquishes any rights which he obtained through marriage over the lands of his wife's parents. A women who has lost a husband through divorce or death prior to the final dissolution of the parental household is expected to remarry in order to fully justify her rights to parental lands. However, if she has had children and does not remarry, she will receive some land at the time of the division of the parental estate. A woman who has lost her husband through divorce or death after her parental lands have been fully divided continues to exercise control over land as if her husband were still alive provided that she does not, upon remarriage, move into her new husband's household. A man whose wife has died prior to the dissolution of her parental estate can remain within his wife's domestic group if he so wishes. If he does so and never remarries, he will also gain control over some of his wife's parents' lands when the estate is finally divided.[15] However, it is much more usual for the young widowed man to return to his own parents' home until he finds a new wife. If a man's wife dies after the couple has obtained clear right to landholdings, the man will continue to control the lands even if he remarries provided he continues to reside in the household which he shared with his first wife. If he moves into his new wife's household, his previous rights will be divided among his children. The same is true for a widow who remarries and moves into her new husband's household, a situation which

---

[15] The sororate, which might be expected to provide a mechanism for a man to remarry while maintaining rights to lands belonging to his first wife's parents, is not an approved form of marriage in Bān Nŏngtūēn.

is not unusual among middle-aged couples.[16] She cannot take her rights over her parental lands with her but must divide them among her children.

In the very rare case when a young man brings his first wife to live in his parental domestic group, the couple gains land rights from the husband's parents and not the wife's parents. Even in the usual instances where a man lives initially with his wife's family, he still retains the right to activate his claim to his own parental lands if he moves back into his parental domestic group. However, he loses this residual right on the death of both parents. In brief, each person, regardless of sex, has the potential right of control over a part of his or her parents' land. However, this claim can only be activated by marriage and continued residence in one's parental domestic group after marriage.[17]

Despite its importance in determining access to land rights, marriage is little regulated by domestic groups. At best they enforce the incest bans on marriage between siblings and between parents and children and strengthen the sentiments of disapproval against marriage between first cousins, uncles and nieces, and aunts and nephews. The contracting of marriages, however, belongs to the individual realm.

The right to participate in the making of decisions affecting the whole village is determined by one's status in a domestic

[16] Unless a widower would thereby come into control of considerably more land than he currently controls, he will probably bring his second wife to live with him rather than going to live with her. Even the possibility of more land would be unlikely to tempt a widower to live uxorilocally when marrying a woman from another village. If he married uxorilocally, he would give up his position in the politicojural realm of village society. His wife, on the other hand, has a much smaller role in the realm and stands to lose much less by marrying virilocally. All six cases mentioned in Table 1 where the wife has come from outside the village are ones in which a widower has taken a second wife.

[17] Adoption can lead to the acquisition of land rights in a domestic group other than the one into which one was born or into which one has married subject to the considerations discussed earlier.

group. If one is to play an active role in village affairs one should be male, own some paddy fields, and head an independent domestic group.[18] Strictly speaking, ownership of land and headship of domestic groups, insofar as these imply internal management, are shared between husband and wife. However, the criterion of sex restricts the application of the other criteria to men only. Ambiguous cases arise when a widow is the head of a domestic group that includes an adult son and/or a son-in-law. When participation of all domestic groups is required in some village affair, the widow, her son-in-law, or her adult son (sons-in-law take precedence over sons where both are present) could represent the domestic group. However, in the decision-making sessions of the "town meeting" of the village, which only men may attend, it is not uncommon for such households to be unrepresented.

Perhaps the most important functions of domestic groups are those relating to the care of the young, the elderly, and the spirits of the recently dead. Each domestic group is expected to produce offspring in order to provide for the perpetuation of the community. The responsibility for the young, at least until they enter school, lies almost exclusively with the domestic group. Villagers see in maternity and infant care a rationale for uxorilocal residence. To be surrounded by one's mother and sisters at the time of childbirth and during the period when one needs help with small children is far more assuring than living among strange women who are not bound to one by blood ties.

Women are also expected to fulfill their obligations to their parents by remaining close to them so that they can look after them in their old age. For the last daughter married this responsibility is greatest. Her sisters are preoccupied with their expanding families while she still has sufficient free time to help

---

[18] In addition, a man should also hold statuses, associated with titles, which indicate nonkinship achievement. The most important of these are ex-novice and ex-monk, specialist in curing and magical-animistic practices, and trader.

her aging parents. In return for her remaining in the parental household until the death or remarriage of the last parent, this daughter (and her husband) inherit the parental house.

Filial responsibility is not limited to daughters. Unmarried sons are expected to provide their labor for any endeavor which their parents' domestic group undertakes. They are expected to do the heavy chores which their sisters cannot do, although they will be assisted in these chores by sons-in-law if there are any. If a young unmarried man goes away to work in Bangkok or Vientiane,[19] he is expected to remit some of his earnings home to his parents. Even after a young man marries, he is supposed to take an important role in the funeral rites of his parents. However, marriage does lead to the transfer to his parents-in-law of many of the obligations which a man previously had to his own parents. Because the duties of a man to his parents are so considerably reduced after marriage, it is the ideal that prior to marriage all young men should undertake the supreme act of filial obedience which only men can make—namely, the entering of the monkhood for at least one lenten period to make merit for their parents.[20]

Filial piety of daughters is extended beyond the lifetime of the parents and even beyond the funerary rites, which are attended by both sons and daughters. Each Buddhist sabbath women set aside a small portion of the offerings taken to the wat to place on the reliquaries of their parents (and their siblings if they died before marriage). The concern expressed by daughters for the welfare of their parents' souls helps maintain ties among families that are no longer components of the same domestic groups. But these ties in practice weaken with time,

[19] In a 1963 survey I found that of the men in Bān Nǫngtūen between the ages of twenty and forty, 72 per cent had worked in Bangkok and/or Vientiane.

[20] This mode of expressing filial obedience is not universal among village men. My 1963 survey showed that 39 per cent of all Bān Nǫngtūen men twenty-one years of age and older (twenty-one being the earliest age at which a young man may be ordained) had not (yet) served as monks.

and in most instances each daughter makes a separate offering on behalf of her own family rather than acting in concert with her sisters.

There are a few occasions when kin relations between domestic groups are invoked to bring together a larger number of people than could be mustered by a single domestic group. In particular, moving threshed rice from the field to the granary, building a house, and other endeavors which require a fairly sizable work force may be occasions for instituting what is usually translated as "loan work" (*wān*). Domestic groups related by consanguineal or affinal ties to the group requiring the work will "lend" one or more members for the duration of the work. The group which has "borrowed" the labor, in addition to providing food and drink at the time of work, also has the responsibility to repay each group from which it borrowed by providing them with an equal number of laborers for an equivalent amount of work. Other than "loan work," forms of cooperation among kinsmen belonging to more than one domestic group are limited to the individual realm of social relations.

Ego-Based Descent Groups

Kinship ties are utilized by all individuals in Bān Nǭngtǖen as one basis for establishing dyadic relations on occasions when a person needs help or assistance. The connections utilized in this way vary from individual to individual and circumstance to circumstance. Within the local setting such relations are usually between individuals who are or were at one time members of the same domestic group, but in the town or city where many villagers go to work for temporary periods, more distant kin connections, as well as friendship bonds, may be utilized. More germane to our interest here is the fact that all villagers at specific times during their lives are also foci of kin-based action groups. Such groups may be activated on the occasion of the life-crisis ceremonies connected with marriage, death, ordination into the Buddhist clergy and, in some cases, the "soul-tying" (*sūkhuan*) ceremony for a person who is about to face some major personal undertaking (leaving for the army, leaving the village permanently, and so on).

The ego-based kin group that emerges at a person's ordination, wedding, funeral, and the like can usually be seen to consist of a core and a periphery. The core includes close kinsmen who have obligations to help provide the money, goods, and food necessary to the proper performance of the ceremony, while the periphery comprises those who attend to show their interest in the individual's welfare. The type of kin included within the core varies according to the individual involved. For weddings, the principals' parents and siblings are usually the ones to carry out the major obligations. For ordinations, parents alone (because they gain the merit made by the ordination of a son) have the responsibility for primary assistance. At funerals, the kinsmen with major duties consist of a person's parents, siblings, children, and spouse (and grandparents or grandchildren if they are living). In the absence of any of these principal kinsmen, others, such as parents' siblings, may be substituted.

The second, much larger peripheral group that emerges on these occasions is known in the village by the term *khāek*, 'guests'. To be a "guest" at a wedding, funeral, or ordination ceremony, one must be invited. Not everyone in the village expects automatically to attend every wedding, funeral, or ordination ceremony[21] The core of the "guest" group are those close relatives who were once part of one's own or one's parents' domestic group and who do not have more definite obligations of the type described above. These relatives are expected to attend whether or not they live in Bān Nǫngtūen. In addition, the group will include more distant relatives (both consanguineals and affinals) as well as "friends" who live in Bān Nǫngtūen.

[21] In actual fact, since all ordinations held in a year are carried out simultaneously, everyone in the village is usually invited.

Another type of kin group is brought into existence when a marriage is to be arranged. In the Thai-Lao village the initiative in contracting a marriage lies with the young couple themselves. However, once a couple has decided to marry, they are expected to confer with their respective parents and, with their help, choose one or more relatives to serve as *thaokāe* 'marriage brokers', who represent the couple. *Thaokāe*, who are always men, decide on the bride price in a long session during which the merits of the couple are discussed. Each side is represented by a chief negotiator, who is usually a father's brother or father's father in the case of the man and a mother's brother or mother's father in the case of the girl. As many as five or six other men may act as seconds on both sides. These men are usually brothers or first cousins of the couple's parents, but may also be more distant relatives or even "friends."

At "soul-tying" ceremonies for an individual who is about to undergo a major change in his life, the kin group activated is usually restricted to that inner core of kinsmen who would form the core at the person's wedding, ordination, or funeral. However, in one unusual case, that of a sūkhuan ceremony held for a high-ranking monk (the brother of the headman), who was about to go to Bangkok to take a major clerical examination, the whole village participated as part of the periphery. It was felt that his success would reflect well not only on his closest relatives but also on the entire village.

At a special rite held between six months and two years after a death, a group consisting of the deceased's siblings, spouse, and, if they are living, parents, children, grandparents, and/or grandchildren comes together. All are expected to contribute toward the offerings made to the monks in honor of the dead.

All of these ego-based kin groups are conceived by the villagers as being bilaterally constructed. In reality the "guest" group may show a slightly greater emphasis in matrilateral kinsmen because they are more often present in the village. At the funeral for a man who has married into the village, the "guest" group may also have a large percentage of "affines."

In short, the structure of the domestic realm of social relations results in some skewing of ego-based kin groups, but only in the larger, more amorphous group of "guests." In the groups composed of those who have very specific obligations toward a person in the various ceremonies, no emphasis is given either to the mother's or the father's side.

Conclusions

Descent in Bān Nǭngtūen, insofar as it is significant, is non-unilinear. However, this conclusion does not completely explain the presence of sons-in-law in domestic groups, the presence of more female descendants of phīpūtā than male in the village, or the presence of greater numbers of matrilateral kin than patrilateral kin in the "guest" group attending ego-centered ceremonies for some individuals. It is the rule of postmarital residence followed by most Bān Nǭngtūen villagers, not a rule of descent, which leads to the apparently matrilineal character of Bān Nǭngtūen kin groups.[22]

Marriage ties also provide an important basis for the structuring of kin groups. Some affinal kinsmen are included in the descent group and in some ego-based kin groups, but the greatest importance of marriage ties is to be found in the domestic realm. Although domestic groups in all societies must emphasize marriage or its functional equivalent to carry out their functions as units of social reproduction, Bān Nǭngtūen society has given even greater stress to this principle in recognizing couples rather than individuals as the components of domestic groups. Couples, not individuals, inherit land; and couples,

---

[22] Klausner (1972:57) suggests that "matrilineal clans" exist in Thai-Lao villages and speaks of the čhaokhot as the chief elder in such groups. His data, which come from from Ubon Province near the border where Cambodia, Laos, and Thailand come together, may indicate that kin groups which can properly be termed "matrilineal" do exist in some Thai-Lao villages. Turton (1972) also recognizes "matrilineal descent groups" as existing among the Yuan of Thailand, who are culturally not too different from the Thai-Lao. Davis (1973), however, presents an interpretation of Yuan kinship, based on data from Nān, which is closer to my own.

not individuals, succeed to the headship of domestic groups.

Both rules of residence and emphasis of marriage ties find their first expression in the domestic realm and then ramify to influence the structure of kin groups in the politicojural and individual realms. In turn, a nonunilinear rule of descent underlies not only the structure of the rather minimal descent group in Bān Nǫngtūen but also the bilateral emphasis of kin ties in the individual realm and the belief in the domestic realm that a person, regardless of sex, has *potential* rights to inherit land from his/her parents. It is not possible to ascribe any priority to the main principles upon which the structure of Bān Nǫngtūen kin groups is based, for the absence of any one would result in a different type of system.

In most of its features the Bān Nǫngtūen kinship system seems very similar to the Japanese, the Javanese, and the Iban,[23] and these societies in turn probably belong to a larger group of societies that are similar in structure. The Japanese, the Javanese, and the Iban, like the Thai-Lao, all have stem and/or extended families whose structure is predicated in large part on the rule of postmarital residence followed. Among the Japanese the rule is virilocal (or patrilocal); for at least some Javanese villages, it is uxorilocal; and for the Iban it is what J. D. Freeman calls "utrolocal"—i.e. either virilocal or uxorilocal. In each society the domestic groups fission into several "daughter" and/or "son" groups, with one couple left in possession of the parental household. Each society possesses some sort of weak descent group based on a nonunilinear principle of descent, although the actual structure of the group may reflect the residence rules. Finally, each society possesses ego-based kin groups which are predicated upon bilateral extensions of kin ties, but which also may reflect in their structure the type of residence rule which has been followed.

[23] My comparisons are based upon descriptions of the Japanese by Befu (1962, 1963) and L. Keith Brown (1966); of the Javanese by Koentjaraningrat (1957, 1960); and of the Iban by Freeman (1960, 1962).

This brief excursion into comparative ethnography may serve to show that the approach taken in this paper might lead one to look for similarities between social systems in a different way than one would if one started with the assumption that the descent principle is the most important conceptual tool for distinguishing between social systems. Such comparisons certainly would be the next step in the use of the approach to the study of kin groups which has been adopted in this paper. However, I can do no more than suggest the possibilities of such comparisons.

Like the researchers who worked among the Japanese, the Javanese, and the Iban, I found that many of the traditional models and terms used in the analysis of kin groups could not be applied to data from the Thai-Lao community of Bān Nŏngtūen without giving misleading impressions about the nature of kin groups in that society. Consequently, I have tried to assemble several recent ideas relevant to kin-group theory and to tie them together as a single approach which, when applied to a specific body of data, would result in a satisfactory analysis. For Bān Nŏngtūen this approach leads to seeing domestic groups of the extended-family type in their proper perspective as the most important kin groups in the society. The analysis also reveals that the structural principles upon which domestic groups are based—residence rules and marriage ties as well as consanguineal kinship bonds—have affected the structure of kin groups in the other domains. If it is possible to generalize from these conclusions in Bān Nŏngtūen, then it should follow that for any society the structural principles underlying the most important kin group will, for that society, be the most important principles upon which the whole kinship structure of that society is predicated. If this generalization can be confirmed, it would lead to a quite different comparative approach to the study of kin groups than that which classifies societies according to a single principle that is emphasized in some and not in others.

10. The Post-Peasant Village in Central Plain Thai Society

STEVEN PIKER

The characteristic sociological features of peasant society derive from the relationship of a rural, technologically unsophisticated agricultural hinterland to a state-organized polity, usually centered in one or more preindustrial cities and invariably possessed of a preindustrial technology and economy (Foster 1967b; Wolf 1966b). Accordingly, industrialization—or modernization, as some would prefer—with its attendant political and economic transformation everywhere heralds the end of the peasant era. What follows is not the dissolution of society but rather its metamorphosis. Successful socialist revolutions—in Russia, China, and North Vietnam, for example—provide dramatic instances of the transition to "post-peasant" society.[1] The immediate sequel to such revolutions has been the emergence of a government with a comprehensive master plan for a new society and the wherewithal to mount a serious effort to implement it. Elsewhere, at least to date, the transformation from traditional peasant institutions has been less abrupt, certainly less directed, and usually more ambiguous in its outcome. Nonetheless, there is no reason to suppose that those peasant societies following the various nonsocialist paths to modernization can preserve their traditional characteristics any more successfully than have those faced by the organized onslaughts of socialist governments.

[1] The term "post-peasant" is drawn from Foster (1967b).

298

Few students of peasant society would dispute this prognosis. Regretably, however, we have only fragmentary knowledge of the changes which collectively constitute the transformation of peasant society even though these changes are everywhere well under way. The lack of information is particularly acute as regards peasants themselves, the rural components of peasant societies, comprising 80 to 90 per cent of their population, whose communities and institutions have been the subject of numerous anthropological studies since Redfield's pioneering work in Tepoztlan. Although several studies of peasant migrants in cities and much statistical information describing demographic and economic trends in post-peasant societies do exist, surprisingly little has been reported of the transformations occurring within actual peasant communities or of the relationships of these rural institutional changes to the societal developments that have produced them.[2]

I propose here to present materials describing one segment of rural Thai society that address these aspects of modernization in peasant societies. Specifically, the following issues will be considered: first, a review of some of the major national trends underway in nineteenth- and twentieth-century Thailand which, in combination, have produced much of the impetus for modernization; and second, the consequences of these developments for peasant institutions in a typical Central Plain Thai peasant community.

An Outline of Modernization in Thailand

The institutions of peasant society are sometimes said to be stable and virtually timeless. However applicable this characterization might be elsewhere, it has certainly not been true of Thailand. Indeed, since the establishment of the Thai state of Sukhōthai toward the end of the thirteenth century Thai society has undergone a number of major institutional transforma-

[2] Notable exceptions include Bruner (1959), Foster (1967a), Halpern (1967), and Lopreato (1967).

tions.[3] Although it is difficult to specify precisely the starting points of historical trends, the beginnings of the Thai transformation to post-peasant society, a process still very much in progress, may be dated approximately to the mid-nineteenth-century reign of King Mongkut (1851–1868). During Mongkut's reign itself, perhaps the single most critical event was the signing of the Bowring Treaty with Britain in 1855. But before taking up the implications of this signal occurrence, let us look more closely at the immediate historical background.

The Chakkrī Dynasty, of which King Mongkut was the fourth ruler, arose amid the ruins of the kingdom of Ayutthayā, whose capital had been captured and sacked by invading Burmese armies in 1767. The reigns of the first three Chakkrī kings (1782–1851) produced two especially noteworthy accomplishments. First, the Burmese were driven out of the kingdom, and Siamese hegemony was re-established in virtually all regions where it had prevailed prior to the fall of Ayutthayā. Second, the authority of the central power over the nobility and particularly those segments of it that governed remote provinces, ostensibly in the king's name, was greatly enhanced. This trend continued throughout the nineteenth century and culminated in the administrative reforms of King Chulalongkorn (Rāmā V, 1868–1910) the son and successor to Mongkut.[4] Both developments were seen by their perpetrators as national imperatives, and both should be understood as a continuation of a series of policies originated by the Thai monarchs over a period of almost six centuries which established, strengthened, and perpetuated the Siamese state in the face of internal as well as external challenges.

---

[3] Among the most momentous of these changes prior to the nineteenth century were: the establishment of the Sukhōthai state by Rāmkhamhǣng in the thirteenth century; the subsequent re-establishment of the Thai state based on the capital city of Ayutthayā and the administrative reforms of King Trailok in the fifteenth century; and the restoration of Siamese nationhood by the first kings of the Chakkrī Dynasty following the fall of Ayutthayā to invading Burmese armies in 1767.

[4] See Wenk (1968), Vella (1957), Griswold (1961), and Riggs (1966).

The mid-nineteenth century brought with it another, and in many ways unprecedented, challenge to Siamese nationhood: the imperialistic presence of the militarily and technologically advanced European nations. And, in spite of the impressive accomplishments of the first three Čhakkrī kings, the kingdom was in many ways unprepared to meet this challenge. There is no need to relate here the manner in which the Thai polity, under the sure direction of King Mongkut and later King Chulalongkorn, fashioned both foreign and domestic policies which enabled the kingdom to weather this storm also, with only peripheral territorial loss. The policies themselves, and particularly their domestic institutional consequences, must, however, command our attention. We return, therefore, to the Bowring Treaty and its implications for the Thai state.

It was Mongkut's intention, not to resist the European powers, but rather to accommodate them insofar as this proved compatible with the perpetuation of the kingdom. However, since the European powers wished for trade and numerous economic concessions, effective accommodation entailed internal institutional adjustments perhaps even more than the alteration of foreign policies. In the interests of short-run security as well as the long-range well-being of the Thai people, Mongkut and his government were prepared to make such adjustments. The provisions of the Bowring Treaty show clearly what Britain wanted of Thailand; and the implementation of these provisions set in train a series of events which profoundly transformed Thai society, particularly its rural component.

Negotiated by Sir John Bowring, the treaty represented an unprecedented abridgment of Thai sovereignty. This was only temporary, however, and need not concern us here. On the other hand, the institutional consequences of the central economic provisions of this treaty have proven both profound and irreversible. To summarize: most importantly, Thailand's long-standing ban on rice exports was abolished; import duties were set for most commodities at the negligible level of 3 per cent (opium was to be imported duty-free); export taxes were both simplified and drastically reduced; and British subjects were granted the right of free trade in all ports. Between 1856 and 1899 fourteen other countries, all Western with the exception of Japan, concluded treaties with Siam modeled on the Bowring Treaty.[5] The immediate and anticipated consequence of these arrangements was that Thai economic institutions, which had previously been almost entirely insular, began to have access to international markets. As a result, the social and economic organization of the kingdom was systematically and fundamentally remade.

Thailand's increasing participation in international markets placed a premium on expansion of rice production and extensification of cultivation (Ingram 1971:36ff.). The court realized that the labor increment required to achieve these goals could only be achieved by relaxing the universal service obligation of the peasantry to the state and by abolishing slavery. Since the revenues of the kingdom were expected to increase dramatically as a result of burgeoning trade, it was anticipated that the state's labor requirements, previously met largely through corvée levies, could soon be met by hired labor, and that slaveowners might be able to find monetary compensation for the gradual abolition of bondage. Accordingly, slavery was gradually but systematically abolished during the last decades of the nineteenth century, and the corvée system was transformed into an arrangement in which categorical obligation took a back seat to wage payment.[6] This latter development was no doubt facilitated by the rapid influx of impoverished Chinese immigrants during this period, many of whom welcomed this opportunity for employment (Skinner 1957:91ff.).

The implications of these developments for rural society in

---

[5] The Burney Treaty of 1826 guided relations between England and Siam prior to the signing of the Bowring Treaty in 1855. The former stipulated that Siam could rigorously restrict British trade within its borders and did not grant extraterritoriality to British subjects.

[6] For a thorough and illuminating discussion of the hierarchical organization of Thai society in the early nineteenth century see Akin (1969).

the Central Plain were far-reaching. A peasantry both legally and actually free had now to adjust to an agricultural economy oriented increasingly to production for distant markets rather than for local consumption. Moreover, as a consequence of extensification of cultivation in response to favorable market conditions and a dramatic growth in population (a sixfold increase between 1850 and 1950), the availability of unused land came to an end. Until the first years of the twentieth century this had been one of the bulwarks of a relatively stable Central Plain rural society. At least as regards the Central Plain, all of these developments were well under way by the turn of the nineteenth century and had, by the mid-twentieth century, proceeded far enough to have remade much of the social and economic fabric of village life. To grasp the specifics of this transformation we must now examine the factors which historically contributed to the integration of rural Thai society in the Central Plain. This will require a consideration of characteristic village institutions.

The Traditional Rural Equilibrium in the Central Plain

We turn now to village case materials drawn largely from the Central Plain community of Bān Ǫi (see Map 3, p. 150, location 3) located in the province of Ayutthayā.[7] A perspective on the traditional integration of village society may best be developed by inspection of local kinship institutions, particularly the domestic cycle. The following summary will provide a reasonably accurate, if somewhat simplified, picture of this fundamental aspect of village life.[8]

[7] The village of Bān Ǫi, comprising two hamlets (*mūbān*), is located about five miles from the provincial capital of Ayutthayā. In the 1960's the village included about fifty households and approximately 225 people. Its history, social composition, and characteristic subsistence patterns are roughly typical of rice villages throughout much of the Central Plain province of Ayutthayā. Our research in Bān Ǫi was carried out during 1962–63 and 1967–68, both times under the full support of the National Institutes of Mental Health. This support is gratefully acknowledged.

[8] A detailed description of Bān Ǫi social organization including kinship is provided in Piker (n.d.).

Briefly, the kinship institutions of Bān Ǭi are, and have been traditionally, bilateral in structure. The minimal unit is the family/household, hereafter termed simply "family," defined as a group of kinsmen residing in one dwelling, eating from the same pot, and adjusting their finances mutually to a large extent. Throughout the twentieth century in Bān Ǭi and neighboring villages—that is, for a period of four generations—nuclear families and three-generational families (parent or parents, at least one in-marrying child, and child's children) have comprised in combination more than 80 per cent of all families, and nuclear families have outnumbered three-generational families by a ratio of more than two to one. These frequencies, which have remained stable throughout the twentieth century, are predictable from the norms which govern the domestic cycle (Piker n.d.). The largest kin unit of any social significance may be termed a kindred and is composed normally of two or three closely related families.[9] The manner in which kindred and family articulate may be seen by consideration of the typical domestic cycle. To summarize, marriage and residence arrangements generally involve the following: daughters of marriageable age attract in-marrying, bride-price-bearing husbands, while sons from the same family go armed with bride prices provided by their parents to marry, in parallel fashion, into other families.[10] It is understood that bride price purchases rights for the new couple in the landed estate of the bride's parents. Usually these rights involve immediate uses of some land, along with draft animals and farming equipment, and eventually ownership through inheritance. Sometimes, however, outright ownership of land is bequeathed to the new couple at the time of their marriage (Piker n.d.). The amount of bride price is proportional to the wealth, that is, the amount

[9] The term "kindred" has not been used consistently by students of Thai village society. The usage adopted here conforms to that proposed by Murdock (1960). See Piker (n.d.) for a discussion of this issue.

[10] Local custom frowns upon marriage between people of any known relation but strictly prohibits marriages only within the second cousin range.

of land owned, by the bride's family. Traditionally, these arrangements operated under conditions of almost universal landownership. Even today, with half of village families effectively landless, no legitimate marriage occurs without payment of a substantial bride price, measured in terms of family income. Normally, one of the married daughters, often the youngest, resides with her spouse and children in the parental home, caring for the parents in their retirement and old age. Some or all of the remainder of the in-marrying children, usually but not always daughters, reside at least initially in the parental compound or in the immediate neighborhood. Uxorilocal residence immediately following marriage is the widely accepted practice.[11]

In practice kindreds almost invariably arise among families thrown into close association through processes intrinsic to the domestic cycle. Typically, at least one of the families of in-marrying children will ally itself with the parental family in a hierarchical kindred, so termed because the parent family usually retains control of the bulk of the agricultural resources and, derivatively, of actual influence. Upon the death or retirement of the parents, at least some of the families of in-marrying children will come to constitute a sibling kindred. In fact, just over 90 per cent of all kindreds in Bān Ǫi during the 1960's were either hierarchical or sibling kindreds, or clear derivatives thereof, and had arisen from the workings of the domestic cycle in the manner just indicated. It should be added that kindreds are noncorporate, impermanent arrangements, seldom persisting for more than two generations; that for ego at least some kin of the requisite genealogical degree will not be kindred comembers (that is, there are no hard and fast criteria for kindred comembership, and frequently siblings are not kindred comembers); and that the *sine qua non* of kindred dura-

---

[11] In a sample of seventy-nine marriages in and around Bān Ǫi, sixty-two couples resided uxorilocally following the wedding ceremony. Of these, however, twenty subsequently shifted residence at least once.

bility, such as it may be, is the regular exchange of resources and services, particularly in association with the performance of rice agriculture. This last bears special emphasis, for it will shortly be shown how changes in the rice agriculture have, by disrupting the processes which have traditionally led to kindred alliances, produced fundamental changes in local social organization.

The combined importance for village life of family and kindred can hardly be overrated. Indeed, these two types of alliance—which, as we have seen, arise from the workings of the domestic cycle—are the very bases of the social existence of most villagers. Not only do they constitute virtually the only secular groups of any importance in village society; in addition, by virtue of membership in these groups villagers traditionally have been provided with the material wherewithal for subsistence, as well as with access to social relationships that ensure a measure of psychological security and also provide at least a partial hedge against economic misfortunes which can often be neither anticipated nor avoided. It is no exaggeration to state that the traditional integration of village society as well as the degree of well-being attained by most of its members depends in large measure upon the viability of precisely these two kin units.

However, even traditionally the system did not operate in a foolproof manner for everyone. It remains to examine strains intrinsic to it as well as the manner in which these strains were alleviated without producing disruption at the societal level (see Piker 1968). Briefly, the domestic cycle as described above conduced to a regular, if small, quota of local landlessness, primarily because inheritance practices involved the fragmenting of parental estates. In at least some families the combination of a relatively small amount of land with numerous children in two successive generations would yield one or more effectively disinherited offspring. As I have indicated, such occurrences were structurally determined. However, it should be clear that any factors which dissipate resources increase the likelihood of landlessness.

If, then, inheritance of land in the customary manner was unavailable for at least some villagers, or if they became dispossessed later in life for other reasons, what alternatives were available as a basis for subsistence and alliance? In general, villagers who found themselves in such straits could turn in one of two directions. On the one hand, they could place themselves in client status vis-à-vis others wealthier than themselves. On the other hand, alone, or in the company of others in similar circumstances, they could attempt to make a new beginning on unused land. The client alternative frequently involved voluntarily entering bondage, which was, contrary to the connotations of the term in the West, often a benign, secure, and sought-after status. Debts were frequently discharged by selling oneself or, not uncommonly at least, some of one's children into slavery.[12] The pioneer alternative involved moving off, often no further than a few miles, to unused and uncleared land and wresting a farm plot and shelter from the forest or the swamp. In this regard, it should be noted that even into the first decades of the twentieth century the population of Thailand was small in comparison to the amount of territory controlled by the kingdom, and extending areas of settlement—and, by implication, Thai control—was a primary desideratum from the point of view of the central government. Accordingly, traditional Siamese law encouraged pioneering ventures of this sort (Wales 1965). The slow but steady dissemination of Thai people throughout the central regions of modern-day Thailand was accomplished in large part in this manner.

The viability of the institutions of rural Central Plain Thai

---

[12] Selling one's children into slavery has a harsh ring to Western ears. Of the numerous Thai parents who did so, however, many or most doubtless felt that they thereby did their children a substantial favor, since the new master could usually provide greater security and better opportunities for the children than could the often impoverished parents.

society, therefore, was predicated in large measure upon the ready availability of career alternatives to the institutionalized domestic cycle. These alternatives consisted in practice of an acceptable client option or bondage as well as a pioneer option. The latter presupposed vast and accessible tracts of unused land, along with legal arrangements that opened it to the use of peasants.

For much of the Central Plain, these conditions persisted up to about the turn of the nineteenth century, but, as we have seen, they no longer do. Moreover, the abolition of slavery and the disappearance of readily available unused land occurred more or less simultaneously with a thorough commercialization of rice agriculture. It remains, however, to examine the institutional consequences of these national trends for peasant communities in the Central Plain. Toward this end, a résumé of twentieth-century events in a Central Plain rice-growing community, the village of Bān Ǫi, may now be undertaken.[13]

Bān Ǫi in the Twentieth Century

At the turn of the century, stability conditions—the status quo as described above—prevailed in and around Bān Ǫi. The oldest villagers living in the 1960's relate that in their childhoods vast tracts of unused land lay only two or three miles to the east of the village, an imprecisely bounded region stretching to the low range of mountains forty miles further east which separate the Central Plain from the Northeast of Thailand. This region is still termed *pā* or forest by villagers in memory of earlier days, although in fact the entire area has been cleared and under cultivation for decades. Tigers were hunted in this area into the twentieth century, and wild elephants were rounded up for a day's march, probably about ten miles, into the forest. Memories of older villagers agree with district rec-

---

[13] For a comprehensive review of economic changes in Thailand following the Bowring Treaty see Ingram (1971).

ords in recalling almost no landlessness at this time, although there is little doubt that substantial landlessness had developed by the 1930's. Older villagers also describe an occasional relation or acquaintance who pioneered in this area around the turn of the century, although this option had been effectively closed by the 1930's, at which time the most accessible regions of the forest were owned by large landholders, though often not yet cultivated. In those days villagers sometimes traveled to the provincial capital of Ayutthayā, and more rarely to Bangkok, but emigration of local populace to urban areas was virtually unheard of. In short, conditions into the first decades of the twentieth century made possible the traditional pattern of integration of village society.

The erosion of these same conditions was well under way by the quarter mark of the twentieth century. The prime movers of change on the local level were commercialization of rice agriculture and population growth. The two in combination had, by 1925, produced dramatic extensification of cultivation in the Central Plain (see Ingram 1971; Usher 1967) and effectively rendered unused or unowned land in most districts unavailable to peasants in need of new farming enterprises. As a result, population increased locally. The inevitable consequence was a rapid increase in landlessness, as population trends complemented traditional structural determinants of such occurrences.

Events in Bān Ǭi in the twentieth century closely conform to this general description. Local population increased steadily throughout the first decades, reaching a peak during the 1930's. During these years, many of the houses and compounds on the periphery of the village were erected to accommodate the burgeoning populace. The abbot of the local temple, who had been a young man in the 1930's, once remarked in recalling these years, "If a bird had flown over the village then, he could have found no place to land, it was so crowded." And landless families, although still a distinct minority, became a prominent and remembered part of village life.[14] Although many tried for awhile to subsist locally as farmers on rented land, this practice proved not to have long-range viability.[15] Of twenty-four families in Bān Ǫi and two neighboring hamlets who rented land in the 1960's, only seven were landless, and none of these had been engaged in exclusively rental farming for more than a generation. Finally, families who lost land, or who inherited none, normally could not hope to acquire new land subsequently through purchase. The rice lands in Ayutthayā Province are some of the kingdom's most productive, and this area is connected to national and international rice markets by excellent river and canal transportation. The price of rice lands has been driven to unprecedented levels as a result of greatly increased exports and rapidly growing urban populations.[16] Only the prosperous could contemplate buying land under these circumstances. Landless villagers turned elsewhere for subsistence.

[14] Zimmerman (1931) reports for 1930 an average landlessness rate of 36 per cent for his twelve sample Central Plain provinces and a landlessness rate of 42 per cent for the province of Ayutthayā.

[15] Renting in land usually requires paying either a fixed sum of cash or a fixed volume of rice regardless of the magnitude of the actual yield from the rented land. Therefore, profits, even under the best circumstances, will be marginal, and in-renting involves a definite risk since the tenant must pay a fixed amount regardless of the quality of his harvest. In practice it is primarily landed families with assured income from their own fields who can afford to attempt to augment their incomes by in-renting. For these reasons, families who lose their lands find it difficult to maintain a farming enterprise on rented land exclusively for more than a few years. Members of landless families, therefore, farm for the most part only as hired laborers on the lands of others. A similar situation prevails in an area near Lopburī (Hollis Mentzer, personal communication) where the landlessness rate is close to that of Ayutthayā province. Unfortunately, it is not entirely clear to what extent landless villagers elsewhere in the Central Plain subsist at least in part by maintaining a farming enterprise on rented land.

[16] In the mid-1960's one rai of the better rice lands around Bān Ǫi sold for 5,000 baht (or about $250 for .4 acre), which is more than the average yearly net income of village families in the same period. Poorer land sold for about 2,500 baht per rai. Villagers consider that a minimum of ten rai is required for a viable farming enterprise.

An immediate sequel was the diversification of subsistence practices. Whereas traditionally virtually everyone had subsisted by rice agriculture on family-owned land, today a slight majority of village families finds subsistence in other ways. The most important local alternative has proved to be agricultural wage labor. In addition, local crafts have sprung up, mainly hatmaking, in which members of landed as well as landless families engage, and a number of small-scale food selling operations. And at least some members of most landless families take whatever short-term nonagricultural wage labor they can find to supplement their incomes. Although nonlandowners on the average do not do as well as their landed neighbors, this combination of mainly local employment opportunities has made it possible for a number of village families to subsist as nonlandowners for two generations at a decent standard of living by village norms. Ironically, the viability, at least for many families, of subsistence as nonlandowners has been made possible by the same set of factors that produced a substantial increase in landlessness in the first instance. Briefly, substantial growth of rice exports and gross national product found reflection locally in the increased prosperity of landowners, particularly in an increase in the amount of fluid wealth of which they disposed. As a result, landowners became able to purchase services which previously they had either performed for themselves or left undone. Landless villagers have, therefore, been able to subsist in large numbers in and around Bān Q̇i, albeit not in the traditional manner. Just over half of the families in and around the village are landless, and more than two-thirds of their total income derives from labor or services performed for landed neighbors, including selling food to them. In other words, income from rice agriculture of less than half the village families is the major source of support, direct or indirect, for the nonfarming families as well.

Diversification of occupations was by no means the only local change in response to national developments of the twentieth century. For one thing, even a local economy thoroughly invigorated by a bullish national rice market could not support all of the increasing number of landless villagers. Often under the pressure of debt and with no prospects of acquiring land, many villagers, individuals and even entire families, left the locality to seek employment in Bangkok. Although population records are unreliable, villagers agree that local population peaked in the years immediately preceding World War II, and since has steadily declined. I would estimate that the local population declined by about 25 per cent between 1945 and the late 1960's. Consistent with this supposition, local temples, which keep meticulous records, have since the 1930's suffered a reduction of about one-third in their complement of "permanent" monks, that is, those that remain in the Sangha for more than one lenten period.

Second, and of more importance than simple population decline, out-migration in combination with increasing landlessness has brought about fundamental changes in the kinship institutions which traditionally comprised the mainstay of village life. Most immediately, emigration produces a quota of kindred ties normally depends upon comembers remaining in members. Although contact between erstwhile kindred comembers may be maintained, and on some occasions an emigrant from the village will receive help from a former kindred comember in getting a foothold in Bangkok, the persistence of active kindred ties normally depends upon comembers remaining in the same social orbit. However, even when, as is the rule, landless families do not leave the village, the active kindred ties they had previously maintained with other families normally atrophy. Why should this be so? Recall that in the summary of local kinship institutions presented earlier the regular exchange of services and resources, largely in association with the performance of rice agriculture, was identified as the *sine que non* of kindred persistence. Landless families, although often more in need of material support than are their landed counterparts, no longer possess the wherewithal—that is, a viable farming enterprise replete with draft animals, equipment, rice-filled granary, and substantial income—to undertake the kind of reciprocal arrangements with others which have been traditionally the major source of assistance in times of need. Furthermore, the income of landless families derives almost completely from individual wage labor or, less often, craft or commercial work. Cooperative or reciprocal labor arrangements are virtually meaningless under these circumstances.

If this interpretation of the social consequences of landlessness is correct, one expects to find, first, a substantial number of families not involved in kindreds, and, second, a definite correlation between landlessness, coupled with a comparatively low position on the village income scale, and kindred nonmembership. The following figures bear out these expectations. First, during the 1960's fully a third of village families (seventeen of fifty) were members of no kindred. Second, kindred nonmembership is definitely associated with both landlessness and low position on the village income scale. Of the seventeen families who belonged to no kindred, fourteen were nonlanded and only three were landed; thirteen fell in the lower half of the income scale and only four in the upper half. By contrast, of the thirty-three families who belonged to kindreds, twenty-one were landed and twenty-three fell in the upper half of the income scale. Finally, it may be noted that kindred nonmembership is viewed by villagers themselves as a definite liability. That is, they perceive no comparably reliable alternative for providing the material and security benefits that flow from kindred membership.

It has already been noted, however, that many landless villagers do manage to subsist adequately by agricultural wage labor supplemented by income from a number of other sources. Indeed, a complement of them have become a durable feature of village society. Therefore, it remains to explore the types of social relationships entailed by subsistence as nonlandowner and to compare these new patterns with the traditional ones.

As we have seen, the normal workings of the domestic cycle provided most villagers with reliable access to two types of alliance—family and kindred—upon which a secure existence depended. Indeed, traditionally, kin-group membership and the subsistence process were inseparable. Consequently, the social relationships undertaken by villagers in pursuit of subsistence were indelibly cast in the kinship idiom.[17] For village society the kinship idiom has involved most prominently the following four ingredients:

Reliability and durability. Although kin-group solidarity, family as well as kindred, is but one value in a complex balance for villagers—and it is by no means always the paramount value—kinship still provides the most stable alliances to which villagers have access.

Diffuseness. As a close corollary to durability, kin relationships are diffuse. That is, kin-group members normally interact with and support each other in a range of situations far broader than mere economic reciprocity would require, although perceived breakdown of the latter is a sufficient condition for kin-group dissolution.

Reciprocity. The *quid pro quo* attends virtually all active kin relationships. Among kindred comembers it often works itself out in a comparatively short time in the exchange patterns which effectively define kindred comembership. However, these patterns are not necessarily symmetrical at any one time. Among family members thoroughgoing reciprocity is ultimately tied to a role reversal which requires most of the life cycle for its accomplishment: offspring are to reciprocate the care and material support provided by their parents in child-

---

[17] Bondage, under terms of which many rural dwellers subsisted traditionally, constitutes only a partial exception to this generalization. Master-slave relations were often in practice much like informal patron-client relationships in which the client/slave, often with his entire family, received support from the master in much the same manner as did the master's own children.

hood by allowing the latter in old age to become dependent on them.

Hierarchy. The presence of several generations ensures that kinship will have a hierarchical dimension. Hierarchy need not on these grounds alone be quite as ubiquitous a feature of kin relations as it is in and around Bān Ǭi. Kin seldom interact with each other *qua* kin on an egalitarian basis. Within the family the major hierarchical gradient is that between parents and children, and the specifics of parent-child relationships revolve in large part around the disposition of family resources. Analogous conditions prevail within kindreds for at least a part of their duration. That is, the cycle in specific instances from kindred formation to kindred dissolution normally begins with the hierarchical kindred as defined above. In addition, in both kindred and family the client of the moment may confidently expect someday to be patron to his erstwhile benefactor, as occurs when grown children shelter their aged parents, or to junior members of the kindred of which eventually he (and his spouse ordinarily) will be the focus, or both. Traditionally, therefore, involvement in kinship institutions for most villagers provides experience with both components of a patron-client relationship.

For the landless, and usually kindredless, villager the social relations of subsistence are a different matter entirely. In most cases they revolve around employment rather than around kin-group membership, and this circumstance entails critical differences on each of the four dimensions enumerated above. (1) Employer-employee relationships, of which agricultural wage labor is both most important and characteristic, are highly impermanent and are usually undertaken on a year-by-year basis. Although landless villagers often work for the same landowner more than once, only seldom does this involve employment in consecutive years. More commonly, landless villagers hire out seriatim to a number of landowners. (2) Since agricultural wage laborers usually reside with their employers, sometimes for weeks, and are accepted almost as family members, albeit junior ones, the relationship during this period is diffuse. However, between periods of employment comparatively little in the way of mutual involvement is thought to obtain between erstwhile employer and employee. Significantly, such relationships are not normally undertaken between close or active kin. (3) Wage labor, of course, involves reciprocity: work in return for pay. However, it is not distinguished from the kinship *quid pro quo* simply by the asymmetry of the exchange but rather by the permanence of the asymmetry. The landowner does not turn in his old age, or under any other even remotely likely circumstances, to his former laborer for care and material support. (4) By the same token, although employer-employee relationships are definitely hierarchical, the landless villager has slight prospect of ever assuming a patron role vis-à-vis his onetime employer. Of more importance, his ability to adopt in full the patron stance toward his own children is seriously impaired. For although he certainly cares for them and provides for their material needs while they are young, he will not in all likelihood be able to provide them with access, via either inheritance or bride price, to subsistence in the traditional agricultural manner. Nor, because he is relatively poor as well as landless, will he be able to provide them with the urban education so useful for launching a nontraditional career. In his view, his inability to be full patron to his children jeopardizes the realization of the role reversal that results in dependence upon one's own children in one's old age.

Does this mean that the kindredless villagers are obliged to conduct their lives entirely without the kinds of material and psychological benefits that flow from kindred membership? Not entirely. Two partial fall-back positions may be available to them. First, in all likelihood they will be members of an active family, even if its membership has shrunk as a result of emigration. But family membership alone often does not entirely preclude personal hardship and insecurity. If the family is both landless and poor, its adult members will tend to fend for themselves financially even though they may continue to share one dwelling. And, as we have seen, this may prove to be a two-way street. Adult offspring who receive little or no help from parents in launching their own careers may subsequently be unable or disinclined to contribute much support to aging parents.

Landless villagers therefore frequently try to cultivate a second type of alliance, one which may promise more, at least by way of short-run material help, than can be expected from family members in the same straits as themselves. Specifically, they seek to become clients of well-to-do, usually landed, neighbors. Interestingly, patron-client relationships of this sort almost never arise between close or active kin. The benefits that flow from such clientship when established include opportunity for recurrent employment, an enhanced possibility of obtaining low-interest loans or, rarely, outright gifts of cash or rice in time of need, and sometimes informal permission to hang around and occasionally eat, drink, and take casual recreation with the patron family. In short, what is sought and sometimes attained is an increment of security. Of course, the patron family also perceives benefit in such relationships, for their clients perform numerous services, ostensibly without payment, and often provide congenial company. (Indeed, incompatibility prevents such relationships from forming, or ruptures them if it develops after their formation.) Consequently, well-to-do families may have a number of clients in this informal sense at any time, and because of their comparatively precarious position poorer villagers often attempt to cultivate more than one such patron. Indeed, to fail to do so would be foolhardy.

An essential qualification must be noted, however: both the substance and the duration of such patron-client relationships is enormously variable. This category of social relationships, like kin relations, verges upon an amorphous never-never land in which it cannot be said with certainty, by either the observer or the ostensible participants, that the relationship actually exists. Here we find the would-be client who thinks (or hopes) he has received a token of future patronship from a well-to-do neighbor, or thinks he deserves such on the basis of services rendered. Here we also find the sometime patron who expects loyalty from a poorer covillager on the basis of benefits conferred. Either may in fact be frustrated in their hopes. Nor are such patron-client relationships when established normally at all durable. For one to persist for more than a few years would be unusual, and for an entire adulthood almost unheard of. The security such relationships provide for landless, kindredless villagers derives primarily from the likelihood that a new one with another patron can be established later if an old one falls apart. Seen in this light, the importance of such relationships should not be minimized. Their widespread availability has doubtless helped to make possible the long-run maintenance of a substantial number of landless families in village society. In this regard, it should be noted that whereas the patron-client idiom has traditionally been ubiquitous at all levels of Thai society, its widespread embodiment in the type of relationship described here, linking villagers, non-kin-based and independent of bondage, is for the most part a recent development. In fact, it represents a part of the early and spontaneous strivings to adapt of a newly emerging social class, namely a rural proletariat.

Summary and Conclusions

Several important trends have been identified in this brief history of the emerging post-peasant village, some of which have implications for one most important aspect of rural Thai (or any) society, the socialization of children.

Nontraditional patterns of social differentiation. Rural Thai society, if viewed in its totality, has long been stratified into classes. For centuries peasants stood in relationships of varying directness and immediacy to the nobility who, in the name of the king, governed local areas. More recently, peasant life has come under the influence of government civil servant as well as the nonagricultural commercial strata of Thai society. But until recently no social class distinctions existed between villagers themselves, substantial wealth gradients notwithstanding. Indeed, even today landless as well as landed villagers continue to see themselves pretty much as rice farmers and affirm no class distinctions of any importance between themselves. Doubtless this is largely because most landless villagers today are children of landed families, and virtually all are grandchildren of landed families. As agricultural wage laborers many of them employ skills they acquired as adolescents working in the rice fields of their parents.

However, as memory of landownership with its distinctive way of life fades for these villagers, and especially for their children, they will begin to perceive social distinctions between themselves and their landed neighbors of a wholly unprecedented sort. And their perceptions will be accurate insofar as they derive from growing awareness of the new realities as outlined above. As we have seen, the critical emergent differential is not simply wealth or income level per se, but rather access to land and, more importantly, to kindred alliances. The twentieth century, particularly the period since World War II, has produced a substantial number of village families which are "marginal," not primarily because they are comparatively poor, but in the sense that they have effectively been denied access to the type of alliance arising from the domestic cycle which villagers recognize to be the most durable and reliable hedge against personal misfortune. This state of affairs has come about as the result most immediately of a sharp increase in landlessness. Kindred alliances depend largely upon the exchange of labor and services, particularly in performance of rice agriculture, and landless villagers no longer have access to the requisite resources. Further, over the long haul, security in old age depends upon a reciprocal relationship with one's own children, and this relationship is also jeopardized by landlessness. As a result, the marginal villager, denied landownership and excluded de facto from traditional kin alliances, subsists mainly by wage labor and turns for an added increment of security to non-kin-based patron-client relationships. To the extent that he is obliged to rely in times of personal difficulty upon such tenuous safeguards, he stands apart, and in a real sense beneath, his fortunate neighbors who own rice lands, participate in active kindreds, and bequeath substantial resources to their children. And this is so in spite of the fact that many landless villagers enjoy, by any objective reckoning, a higher standard of living than did their landed parents or grandparents.

This is not to suggest, however, that subsistence, and indeed, existence, as a landless villager is about to become impossible, or even that it need be terribly harsh or difficult. In fact, my expectation is just the opposite. Into the indefinite future village society will include a mix of landed and landless families. And most of the latter will subsist at a level far above the abject poverty which prevails in the rural areas of some other Asian societies. The comparatively high standard of living of the Thai nation makes this likely. But because the idiom of relationship surrounding the subsistence quest is changing so profoundly, newly emerging and as yet poorly recognized social class distinctions between villagers will crystallize. Whereas traditionally hierarchical distinctions between villagers were determined mainly by degree of seniority within kin units, they now depend upon ownership of the means of production. Whereas traditionally junior partners in economic enterprises were virtually assured a role of responsibility by the passage of time, this is today true mainly just for the children of landed families, not for their landless counterparts for whom participation in an economic enterprise depends upon contractual employment and not upon kinship. And finally, whereas traditionally the subsistence quest and kin-group membership were largely inseparable for most villagers, today adult members of about half of the village families seek income in large part on an individualistic basis, and in so doing receive little direct assistance from their socially active kin. In short, ownership of land and active membership in minimally extended kin groups have come to embody two fundamental and wholly unprecedented criteria for social distinction among villagers.

Changes in child-rearing practices. Space limitations restrict our attention to only the most general considerations.[18] Briefly, one of the most important features of village socialization patterns has been the marked contrast between the highly affectionate indulgence lavished upon youngest children up to about the time of weaning (two to three years), and the comparative neglect, though not mistreatment, experienced by the child, especially at the hands of the mother, as second-youngest sibling. Moreover, the sequel to second-youngest siblinghood varies significantly according to the sex of the child. Girls as young as five or six are initiated into a task-oriented mother's-helper role, whereas boys at the same age are provided with no positive or structured alternative to the drift of second-youngest-siblinghood. I believe the widely remarked greater ego strength of village women over village men is attributable largely to this differential. And many important features of the personalities of adult villagers of both sexes are the result, wholly or partially, of the sequence of events that dominates the first four or five years of their lives. These traits include withholding of affect, caution concerning personal involvement, and a tendency toward passivity sometimes allied with dependency, particularly in the face of new or challenging situations.

There is some evidence to suggest that a minority of village mothers are now self-consciously and deliberately modifying this child-rearing pattern, and that they are doing so in response to economic incentives which are part and parcel of the "new realities" alluded to above. Thoroughgoing commercialization of rice agriculture and occupational diversification in combination with a burgeoning economy have enormously multiplied

---

[18] Village socialization practices are described in detail in Piker (1964).

local opportunities for making money. Some villagers, particularly women (who, largely as a result of the sex differential just noted, are by and large more active economically than men anyway) are anxious to take advantage of these opportunities. Interestingly, wives in both landed and landless families are involved here, but, since the total is no more than a handful, no firm conclusions can be drawn. In any event, these same wives perceive that the time spent in high indulgence of youngest children is incompatible with their freedom to respond, even if only locally, to new economic incentives. Accordingly, in a few cases the wives report—and we observed it to be so—that the initial indulgence pattern is being diluted: by assigning a larger role in infant care to older children, by providing foods, such as bottle milk, which make it possible for a baby to go longer between feedings, and sometimes by simply letting a child cry unattended, the mother can be more fully and productively involved in income-producing activities.

The intended consequence of this innovation in child-rearing practices, of course, is to enable the mothers to make more money. At least one unintended consequence, however, will be to reduce substantially the contrast between what the child experiences when he is the youngest sibling and when he is the second-youngest sibling. For the children of these mothers something approaching gradual transition may come to replace the sudden demotion which has up to now been the rule. If this occurs then the socialization conditions that contribute to the adult's tendency toward passivity and sometimes dependency in the face of new and challenging situations will have given way to socialization conditions more favorable to the development of an active mastery orientation. Given the amount of information presently available to me this must remain conjectural, but the conjecture is nonetheless suggestive of the following extension: as adults, the children of these vanguard mothers ought to find more congenial than do most of their peers the lifestyles that conform to and take advantage of the realities of a class-stratified, highly commercialized, occupationally diversified, and no longer kinship-based rural society and economy. The innovative life trajectories we hypothesize for these individuals may, therefore, provide the point of crystallization for the inevitably new institutional patterns of tomorrow's rural Thai society.

11. The Culture of
Siamese Intellectuals[1]

HERBERT P. PHILLIPS

This essay is concerned with what has been correctly labeled
(Wilson 1959:68) a "tiny group" of Thai: those members of the
society who are seen by both the educated public and themselves as providing for Thailand the most articulate, persuasive,
precise, and perhaps accurate definitions of Thai society and
the Thai experience. Occupationally they are the kingdom's
major living novelists, poets, social commentators, folklorists,

[1] This paper was originally prepared in 1967, and with the passage of time
some of its details have inevitably become out of date. In the intervening
years, "P.A." has died, "W.D." has been promoted to general, and "P.U."
has served as a visiting professor in both the United States and the United
Kingdom. These years have also been marked by a dramatic increase in
expressions of political and cultural nationalism in the writings of many
intellectuals; some of these are presented in a forthcoming volume entitled
The Voice of the Domino: Thai Views on Development, Alliance, and Sovereignty,
edited by David L. Morell and Suchit Bunbongkarn. The student demonstrations of October 1973 that precipitated the sudden change from military to
civilian government in Thailand are much too recent to enable scholars to
evaluate their consequences to the work of Thai intellectuals, although in
the short term they seemed to have stimulated considerable ferment. I feel,
however, that our understanding of the history of Thai intellectual life can
best be served by publishing the text exactly as it was first written, rather
than to try to fit the numerous realities of 1967 to those of 1974.

I am indebted to the Rockefeller Foundation and the National Science
Foundation for grants which made possible the research for this paper.
Portions of the paper were originally presented at a University of California
Social Anthropologists Supper Meeting held at Berkeley, 31 May 1967. I
wish to thank my departmental colleagues and Daniel S. Lev and Michael
Moerman for their criticisms and comments.

and intellectual leaders of the Buddhist monkhood. Also included are some university educators, publishing technocrats, and judges, whose distinction is based in large part (although, as with all intellectuals, never exclusively) upon their intellectual contributions rather than upon their capacity to control and distribute power. The group under investigation is limited to intellectuals producing written materials of direct social relevance, and thus excludes artists, architects, and physical scientists.

The data for the study are based upon the following procedures. A somewhat complex method involving the administration of an open-ended questionnaire to seniors at Bangkok's two major universities was used to reduce an infinite universe to a list of "Thailand's 153 Leading Intellectuals." A number of expert judges, all of whom were on the original list, were then asked to order this list into three levels of "intellectual distinction." Several adjustments resulted in a final categorization of three echelons of intellectual distinction designated, in Thai, as:

Most distinguished	20
Important and famous, but not distinguished	26
Recognized by the educated public as contributing to Thailand's intellectual life	107

Detailed life-history materials (averaging twenty-six interview hours per informant) and a minimum of three major books or essays, selected by informants themselves, were obtained from eighteen of the twenty "most distingusihed" intellectuals, and somewhat more sketchy biographical materials were obtained from the twenty-eight additional persons in the top two categories.

A few words should be said about the nature of the sample. First, although these men and women represent many different, and sometimes conflicting, interests found in Thai society, it is in the nature of the selection process that they all are people who have achieved a considerable measure of success and respectability in the eyes of some segment of the educated public. Some represent the Thai establishment, or different facets of that establishment. Others are highly critical of aspects of the Thai social order, but they feel sufficient personal potency and identification with the fundamentals of the system to articulate their criticisms without fear of alienation—political, interpersonal, or intrapersonal. Indeed, of the eighteen persons I came to know well, only two could in any way be considered as experiencing the "identity crisis" that is supposed to be characteristic of many non-Western educated elite (Geertz 1963; Bellah 1965). The essential point about these people is that because they have been awarded and feel considerable social approval and because they are operating in a situation where there are explicit political constraints on their intellectual freedom (see below), they tend to be a somewhat conservative group. Those who are critical tend either to be indirect in their criticism, or to use traditionally sanctioned methods of challenge such as humor, or to link their ideas, or even their persons, to politically prestigeful groups in Thai society. Whether a viable, but hidden, group of radical intelligentsia that I have been unable to identify currently exists in Thailand, or whether such a group could emerge into the public arena in the immediate future, is rather problematic. The Thai cultural and political systems appear to be both too pragmatic and too authoritarian to permit a sympathetic audience for radical intellectual innovation. The professional history of the three leading leftist writers of the past two decades is instructive in this regard: one now manages a nightclub; one has a high position in the government's Department of Public Relations; and one lives in Peking. Even when they were writing, they owed their fame to their use of the Thai language and to the romantic interest of their plots, rather than to their political messages.

A second significant attribute of the sample is the fact that it is Bangkok-centered. Of the 153 persons, only two make their home in the North (Chīangmai), two in the Northeast (one in Khōrāt and one in Khǫnkaen), and one in the South (Chayā). Since Thailand is essentially a one-city kingdom (Bangkok has a population of approximately 3.1 million people; Chīangmai, the next largest city, has only about 85,000) and since institutionalized intellectual activity is essentially an urban phenomenon, this is perhaps not unusual. Too, examination of the data indicates that substantially more than half the persons in the sample were born and reared outside Bangkok and came to the capital either as adults or as adolescents, usually for further schooling. Discussions with informants indicate that they finally settled in Bangkok because it was the major center of intellectual excitement. There they found their friends, bookshops, publishers, and much of their readership. One result of this settlement pattern is to give the data, ostensibly descriptive of intellectual activity in the entire nation, something of a Bangkok provincial slant.

Finally, a few words should be said about the relevance of these men and women to the functioning of Thai society. On the one hand, their social significance is based upon their roles as codifiers and interpreters of the major values and ideas of their society, both traditional and emergent. Through their intellectual productions—writings, lectures, radio and television presentations, classroom performances—they award cognitive legitimacy and credibility to cultural events and in effect define, at least for the period during which they are working, what shall be admitted to or rejected from the history of Thai ideas. To the extent that their codifications are innovative, some are even creators of cultural values. On the other hand, the significance of the roles themselves should not be overestimated. In Thailand, as everywhere else on earth, a great many, perhaps most, cultural events take place without even the benefit of recognition, let alone examination, codification, and interpretation. However unusual the cognitive, ethical, or aesthetic gifts of the intellectual, he is always constrained by the traditions of his culture (Shils 1968), particularly those which define what are proper and improper subjects for intellectual discourse, what is or is not intellectual discourse, and what are the purposes of the discourse. Anthropologically viewed, intellectual activity is the process by which consciousness is institutionalized into specific culturally defined themes, forms, and goals, regardless of the "objective" events affecting the culture and the presumed significance of these events to the deliberations of its intellectuals. This last point is mentioned simply to underscore the fact that despite their talents, Thai intellectuals write about problems and issues that are culturally appropriate to write about, not necessarily those that are objectively important in their own experience or in the operation of their society. The intellectual's insight and sensitivity do not of themselves qualify him to exceed the limits of cultural understanding. He might do this if he were also required, by definition, to be an original thinker, a person who deals with problems that have never before been dealt with and who has the capacity to communicate his achievement to others. However, since these latter qualities are everywhere extremely rare they are not considered essential to the conception of "intellectuals" that is being presented here.

These abstract considerations provide some context for the selectivity that is evident in the work of Thai intellectuals. Many of the things they write about are, by any standard, major problems of their society. Thus, for example, they give repeated and elaborate attention in their writings to the necessity for public officials to be morally incorruptible and to have a sense of dedication and professional excellence. Although such exhortation is an old tradition in Thailand (it can be found in the thirteenth-century inscriptions of King Rāmkhamhāēng), it is especially germane to contemporary Thailand, which has very rapidly become a highly complex society, with a large proportion of the newer technical and

administrative jobs being assumed by government function-
aries (see Riggs 1966; Siffin 1966). Since in recent years some
government officials at the highest levels have been proved
corrupt, and since even the king of Thailand has publicly
remonstrated against widespread official corruption, the problem is real enough and clearly serious. The one element in the
intellectuals' plea that is somewhat new is the appeal for
bureaucrats to exhibit a sense of professional excellence. This
appeal is based on an emerging awareness that nowadays bureaucratic decisions tend to be extremely expensive and long-
lasting in their effects (the filling in of canals, the construction
of the National Theatre), and that if high standards are not
maintained, the results can be ruinous. Too, there is an awareness that since bureaucrats effectively control the future of
Thailand and since the interested public has almost no way of
amending official decisions, it is essential that bureaucrats take
seriously the *noblesse oblige* requirements of their positions. (That
Thai intellectuals should wish to provide such advice is also
not without its *noblesse oblige* elements.) Along these same lines,
intellectuals devote a considerable amount of attention in their
writings to the nature of education in Thailand. Education is
viewed as the fundamental prerequisite for operating a complex
modern society, and inordinate concern is given to the types
of education that are offered, how such education can be improved, and who in the population should receive what kind
of education.

On the other hand, various areas of Thai life are of obvious,
and even dramatic, importance to the society but tend for a
variety of reasons to be ignored by intellectuals. By way of
example, one of the most significant events to occur in Thailand
over the past decade has been the dramatic increase in the
number of foreigners, who, by their sheer physical presence,
have radically transformed the social and economic life of several provincial cities as well as of large sections of Bangkok.
With the exception of the famous anti-American broadside by

Thailand's most distinguished publisher (Khuekrit 1967) and occasional protests against the public sexual behavior of American soldiers and Thai girls, there has been no public discussion of the consequences of the foreign presence to Thai culture, particularly its economic and urban development. Some legal constraints do exist which prevent outright defamation of "friendly foreigners" (see below), but these are not sufficient to preclude discussion and analysis of the issue should writers feel the problem is important; also, as illustrated by Khuekrit's criticism of American influence, a writer can choose to ignore the constraints. Of a somewhat different order, but also illustrative of the selective silence of intellectuals, is their apparent indifference to the decline in the viability of Buddhist practice, at least as measured by the number of men entering the monkhood, the number of laymen participating in Buddhist sabbath, the increasing difficulty that urban monks experience in obtaining food on their begging rounds, and the like. As with the problem of the foreign presence in Thailand, individual Thai intellectuals talk in a free and animated way about these issues, but they do not raise them in their public presentations.

Finally, there are aspects of Thai life which on the surface seem prosaic or of minor importance but which appear so frequently, or are given such detailed exposition, in the writings of intellectuals that they are clearly of major significance in the thinking of author or audience. One of the most frequently occurring themes in contemporary Thai novels and short stories, for example, is intermarriage between a Thai man and an Occidental woman, and the resulting tension between the foreign wife and her Thai in-laws, particularly her mother-in-law. The fictional setting is almost always an upper-class or upper-middle-class home; the Thai husband is almost always caught in a conflict between loyalty to his wife and loyalty to his mother; and the mother is very often caught in a conflict between being hospitable and sympathetic and being jealous and resentful toward her earnest, kind, but alien daughter-in-law. The mother's hostility is usually represented as expressing one or more of the following elements: resentment of the daughter-in-law's foreign ways; resentment of her having stolen the son's affections; resentment of her as a symbol of modernism and a trigger for intergenerational conflict. It might further be noted that the sympathy and hospitality the mother exhibits tend to be viewed as expressing "old and true" Thai qualities, while the hostility is "modern," or an inevitable concomitant of modern situations. The question that an analyst raises about these themes is, of course, "Why a foreign daughter-in-law?" The number of Thai men who actually marry Occidental women is so small (there are probably no more than three hundred in the entire kingdom) that one would expect most Thai authors and audiences to have difficulty identifying with this type of situation or seeing its relevance to their lives. The use of a foreign daughter-in-law could be explained as an aesthetic device employed by the author for achieving psychological distance toward sentiments that are typically felt by *Thai* daughters-in-law in their dealings with their Thai mothers-in-law; the fictional use of a foreigner mitigates and makes more acceptable the painful, but very real, problems of Thai in-law relations. Since there are several novels which in fact describe Thai daughters-in-law getting into many of the same difficulties with their mothers-in-law, this explanation is not very persuasive. Perhaps the answer to the question is simply that, despite its atypicality and irrelevance to real life, Thai authors and audiences are fascinated by what they imagine to be the exotic quality of a Thai-European marriage. Moreover, since those few people who do intermarry generally come from extremely high-status, even royal, backgrounds, it is likely that readers gain vicarious pleasure from being made privy to the human, albeit fictionalized, problems of society's leaders.

This discussion of a few of the themes appearing in the writings of Thai intellectuals has been provided solely to illustrate the selectivity of Thai intellectual effort and how it is linked, or not linked, to some of the major problems of Thai society. Numerous other intellectual themes and forms could be cited: literature extolling the beauties of nature; Buddhist novels and short stories that attempt to illustrate the applicability of Buddhist teachings to daily life; a rich satirical literature that focuses on the postures and pretensions of the Thai status seeker; historical essays and novels describing the accomplishments of specific royal or noble personages or depicting life at the court in extremely human terms; a literature of "advice for living" and self-improvement (the best-selling trade book in the history of Thailand has been Dale Carnegie's *How To Win Friends and Influence People*, available in nine different translations); a scholarly-bureaucratic literature concerned with such social problems as delinquency, public administration, and economic development; a newly emergent "proletarian" literature that describes the joys and tragedies of both peasantry and the urban poor; the "Bangkapi" novel and short story, a fictional genre concerned with the tensions and emotional travil of Bangkok's *nouveaux riches*; the military-bureaucratic establishment literature produced by the government's Department of Public Relations and perhaps best illustrated by the 1965 collection entitled *Prachāthipatai baep Thai* (Democracy, Thai style); a modern erotic literature that emphasizes emotional conflicts and decisions as well as the pleasures of sex. (The last is linked historically to a classical erotic literature written at the court during the seventeenth-to-nineteenth centuries and claimed by one informant, well versed in Western literature, to be "Thailand's only original contribution to the great literature of the world.") Again, these are cited simply as illustrations of the rich and variegated nature of Thai intellectual activity. At the same time, it must be emphasized that even this richness does not reflect, at an ideational level, the rich and complex nature of Thai society as a whole. Thai intellectuals are obviously a very small number of people addressing relatively small audiences within a relatively small class of their total society, and their products inevitably reflect these limitations. A Bangkok novelist from a peasant background writing sensitively about peasants is read not by peasants (excepting perhaps his relatives and his village school-teacher) but by sophisticated urbanites like himself who wish to be informed or moved by his conception of villagers, a conception which is carefully designed for them, not villagers. In the same way, "Bangkapi" short stories are written by the *nouveaux riches* for the *nouvelle riche* woman suffering problems of the *nouveaux riches*. The point is that the work of Thai intellectuals is always characterized by a degree of cultural parochialism that is based upon their special, but restricted, status in society. They may be more "articulate, persuasive, and precise" than other Thai, but they are not necessarily more catholic or experienced. Since they are, by definition, an elite group, their work represents what the Thai leadership, rather than representative Thai, think is important in Thai thought.

The Context of Intellectual Activity

The intellectual's role and influence in Thai society is conditioned by several practical considerations. Following are the more important of these.

The Intellectuals' Readership

It is impossible to determine precisely who reads the writings of these intellectuals or knows about their ideas or persons. However, the following figures will provide some perspective on the composition of the educated public. The official literacy rate for Thailand in 1964, based upon the capacity to read and to write one's name, was 71 per cent (Thailand, Samnakngān sathiti hǣng chat 1965). Functional literacy represents approximately one-half to two-thirds of this figure, resulting in a potential reading public (those over ten years of age) of 7.5 to 10 million people. Of these, 130,000 have been graduated from high school or its equivalent, and an additional 58,000 (0.6 per cent of the total population) are college graduates. These 188,000 people represent the pool from which the intellectuals' readership is drawn. Of this number, I would estimate that a maximum of 35,000 adults read for intellectual or cultural stimulation. However, it must be emphasized that educational activities and pressures in Thailand are accelerating at an extraordinary rate—of the eight universities in Thailand, for example, three have been established only in the past three years—so that within the next decade the figure of 35,000 may swell to as high as a half million. Further, since some intellectuals write columns for the daily press and have regular programs on radio and television, they may on some occasions reach several hundred thousand people with their ideas.

Related to audience size and composition is the complex issue of Siamese reading habits and the nature and traditions of the publishing industry in Thailand. Two crucial considerations stand out here: (1) although writing and the temple school have existed in Thailand for more than 700 years, the printing press did not arrive in the country until 1835; (2) since that time probably no more than 150,000 titles have been printed in the Thai language. This figure includes *all* publications available to the public: novels, Buddhist sermons, astrological texts, histories, reference books, trade journals, textbooks, cremation gift books (currently representing an estimated 30 per cent of the total book publishing volume), newspapers, anticommunist pamphlets, and so on. The National Library of Thailand is, by law, supposed to receive a copy of every book published in the kingdom, and its holdings indicate that at least half the books published in Thailand since 1835 have been printed since World War II. There has in recent years been a clear acceleration in the number of books published: the most recent figures are 1,062 in 1962, 2,133 in 1963, and 4,198 in 1964. Given the basic differences in population and literacy rates, this last figure compares favorably with the 30,050 titles published in the United States in 1967.

Despite these increases it remains true that Thailand, in contrast, for example, to Indonesia or Japan, is not a "reading nation." Books are defined as costly luxuries and are not viewed as essential even to the learning process. Thus, in most Thai universities, students rely almost completely on the oral didactic tradition of the lecture; their normal lecture load is, in fact, twenty to twenty-nine hours per week. Students have graduated from Thailand's finest university having read no more than four books during their entire undergraduate career—and these books were in English and were necessary for passing the foreign-language requirement. One Thai university has no library. Indifference to books is further abetted by the conventions of the Thai publishing industry, which has no craft tradition and therefore also lacks the underlying sense of editorial and aesthetic excellence that we have known in the West since Gutenberg. Most Thai publishing houses lack editors for grammar and style, proofreaders, designers, indexers, and they use no manuscript referees. The results of such omissions can be horrendous: one of my informants, trained in the United States and familiar with the idea of an "errata sheet," insisted that a second printing of one of his books include a list of errors; the text ran to 207 pages, the errata list was 14 pages long.

Two recent developments suggest a possible change in the public's interest in books. First, books are increasingly becoming a status symbol as more students return from foreign study, assume important governmental positions, and decorate their offices with the textbooks they purchased abroad. Some high bureaucrats even vie with each other over the number of clean, brightly dust-jacketed volumes they have on their shelves. Although the motive is clearly one of status affirmation, sometimes the books get read. Further, this linkage between books and power (an extension of the traditional Thai linkage between knowledge and power; see Hanks 1958 and Mosel 1963) is not lost upon underlings and visitors. Second, there seems to be a noticeable change in the Siamese method of handling and storing books. Until approximately a decade ago it was impossible to find books in the home and library in anything but locked cabinets. The lock was to prevent theft and the total enclosure to prevent injury to the books from insects and dirt. While all this implied a sense of extreme care toward something valuable (prior to 1835 books were hand-written and therefore costly), it also meant denial of access to the books to anyone but the owner. In Thai homes children had to ask permission and obtain a key to read a book, thus creating a complicated social relationship out of simple intellectual curiosity; one informant, in fact, described his early childhood reading of books as requiring "stealing books from my father's book cabinet when he was not at home." In recent years this pattern has undergone a change: families are beginning to keep their books either on open shelves or in unlocked glass-walled cabinets; most of the books in the new National Library building and in university and school libraries are being stacked on open shelves. Librarians report a very marked increase in the number of books being read and, when permissible (most Thai libraries are still noncirculating), loaned out.

Political Constraints on Intellectual Activity

Of a totally different order in influencing the intellectual's role in society are the very real political, cultural, and inter-personal restrictions on his professional freedom and integrity. It must be emphasized that to most intellectuals these restrictions are annoying not because they are unjust or arbitrary but because they require the intellectual to devote an inordinate amount of time and energy to testing his limits and to worrying about how others will interpret his words. At the same time, some intellectuals, in a peculiarly Thai way, relish the restrictions for the opportunities they provide to play cat and mouse games with the authorities and thereby gain fame for their daring and imagination.

Of the three types of constraints, the political restrictions are probably the least burdensome if only because they are unambiguous and absolute. Thailand has been under continuous martial law since 1957. Originally prompted by the exigencies of a *coup d'état*, it has been maintained for purposes of political efficiency and stability.[2] Proclamation Number 17 of the "Proclamations of the Revolutionary Group," the basic documents of martial law, describes unabashedly the restrictions placed upon intellectual freedom:

. . . the authorities shall attach and destroy such papers and attach the machine on which such papers were printed for such period as they may think appropriate but not longer than six months . . . if any paper publishes matter of the following nature:

(1) any matter infringing upon His Majesty the King, or defamatory, libelous, or contemptuous of the Queen, royal heir, or regent;

(2) any matter defamatory or contemptuous of the nation or Thai people as a whole, or any matter capable of causing the respect and confidence of foreign countries in regard to Thailand, the Thai government, or Thai people in general, to diminish [this clause is the prohibition against criticism of the United States presence in Thailand];

(3) any matter ambiguously defamatory or contemptuous of the Thai government, or any ministry, public body, or department of the government without stating clearly the fault and

[2] Over the years the provisions and purposes of martial law have changed considerably as a consequence of changes in government. In the late 1960's, after the installation of a Representative Assembly, the provisions of martial law were greatly relaxed, leading to an increase in press freedom and to the expressions of nationalistic commitment noted above. After the abolition of the Assembly in 1970 by the National Executive Council, there was a widespread crackdown on all public commentary until October 1973. In fact, this crackdown precipitated the specific events leading to the student demonstrations and the eventual change to a civilian government.

matter [to most Thai writers this and the following clause are the most worrisome because the essence of effective public criticism in Thailand is teasing ambiguity];

(4) any matter ambiguously showing that the government or ministry, public body, or department of the government has deteriorated, is bad, or has committed a damaging offense without showing in what matter and particular;

(5) any matter promoting approval of Communism, or apparently [*sic*] a Communist plot to disturb or undermine national security;

(6) any false matter of a nature tending to panic, worry, or frighten the people or matter tending to incite, or arouse disorder, or conflict with public order or morality, or prophecies concerning the fate of the nation which might upset the people [although this last phrase is directed toward seers and shamans it is also used against the authors of such statements as "if the government continues policy X, it will have the following dreadful results . . ."];

(7) any matter using coarse language tending to lower national morals or culture;

(8) any official secrets . . . [Proclamations of the Revolutionary Group, n.d., No. 17].

Notwithstanding their imperious tone, these dicta have in fact produced relatively mild social and intellectual consequences. For one thing, police sanctions have rarely been applied, and on the few occasions that they have been, it has been either on the grounds of blatant defamation of character or because of the desire for personal revenge on the part of a particular military official. Ideological or political concerns have been largely irrelevant. Further, a comparison of the Thai press before the declaration of martial law in 1957 and eight years later in 1965–66 indicates that with two important exceptions—criticisms of the United States and attacks on named individual public figures, both of which have been markedly reduced—there are no major differences in the amount of political criticism being articulated. The reasons for this, of course, are terribly complex and have more to do with the presence and absence of certain political figures, and with the stability and changeability of public issues, than they have to do with the promulgation of Proclamation Number 17. At the same time, the power of this proclamation in inhibiting writers, particularly in developing in them an acute sense of self-censorship, should not be underestimated. Informants voicing antigovernment and antiestablishment remarks repeatedly indicated that they would never dare to publish these same remarks out of fear that either they or their publisher would be jailed; even more frequent was the explanation that they did not wish to place their publisher in the embarrassing position of having to reject their work because of his own fears. It should be noted that only two instances were encountered of manuscripts being rejected on the ostensible basis of a publisher's worries over the political acceptability of the work. The term "ostensible" must not be glossed over. The question of censorship—by government, publisher, or the author himself—was raised with almost all informants, and many pointed out that censorship had become so much a part of the cant of contemporary Thai intellectual life that some writers simply used it as an alibi for incompetence or laziness. They mentioned numerous ways to circumvent Proclamation Number 17—through humor, symbolism, hyperbole, understatement—and said that in some cases it had served as a stimulus for intellectual innovation and imaginativeness. Most important, they indicated that censorship was essentially a question of intellectual style rather than intellectual content, and that all serious writers knew how to avoid or invite it. In fact, some authors invited censorship precisely because it provided them with notoriety or with the opportunity to launch a crusade.

Cultural Constraints and Personal Motivations

Considerably more meaningful than these political considerations are the cultural and interpersonal restrictions on intellectual freedom. Here we are dealing not so much with the intellectual product as with the complex motivations people have in becoming intellectuals in the first instance. What is involved is the individual's sense of responsibility toward the truth and toward his traditions, his friends, his teachers and "students," and himself. It is in this area that Thai intellectual activity seems to become characteristically Thai rather than characteristically intellectual. By this is meant simply that intellectual activity becomes just one more arena within which to work out and achieve some of the standard social, political, and psychological goals of Thai life.

There are, of course, a multiplicity of motives for becoming a producing Thai intellectual, but the dominant one by far is the individual's desire for fame and a following. "Following" is used in two senses: (1) in terms of fans or readership, and (2) in terms of students or disciples, a clientele that the individual trains in the methods of his profession and to which he passes on his ideas and prejudices. In addition, he attends to the whole array of responsibilities incumbent upon any Siamese superordinate—helping his disciples find jobs, lending them money, sponsoring their weddings or ordinations, and publishing their writings. (This phrasing is not simply the result of an anthropological model; there is in fact an elaborate ritual which a disciple can choose to undergo in becoming part of his teacher's "following.") In addition to the desire for fame and following is the desire for power or—as is the case with most mandarin types—to be close to those in power, as adviser or counsellor. This motive is especially apparent among some of the young professors and technocrats who have studied abroad and who serve on government committees where they obtain prestige, honoraria, and the possibility of serving as principal aides to the most powerful men in the kingdom. Another motive is the belief in one's own intellectual excellence, usually phrased in terms of the scope of one's knowledge or experience, and the desire to communicate this to others. (Again, this is not an observer's rephrasing of informants' comments; this is precisely what some of them say.) There is in this attitude a powerful sense of public service that derives directly from the *noblesse oblige* assumptions of Thai royalty, until 1932 the major model of intellectual activity. Finally, there is the conviction that one has something true, important, novel, or entertaining to say—the commitment is to the idea, not to its social or political consequences—and one attempts to say it in the most effective way possible. However, even here one finds many intellectuals sidetracked into a preoccupation with the style and manner by which they communicate their ideas, rather than the ideas themselves; form rather than content becomes the standard of excellence. In a minor effort to confirm my judgments about the significance of stylistic considerations in their thinking, I asked a selected group of informants to rank "ten qualities that might characterize any piece of writing." Following, in descending order of importance, are what these intellectuals consider to be, in terms of the alternatives provided, the most significant attributes of writing. The writing should be: (1) clear and precise; (2) persuasive; (3) practical or useful; (4) true; (5) aesthetically attractive; (6) entertaining; (7) stimulating or provocative; (8) critical; (9) original; (10) profound.

The relevance of these various comments to constraints on intellectual freedom is that the major criterion of the legitimacy of an idea is not what is intrinsic to the idea itself, but rather audience response, utility, and the favor of significant others—followers on the one hand, or the respected and powerful on the other. On the behavioral level the life of ideas becomes a series of social and psychological, rather than intellectual, decisions and compromises. Examples are legion: almost every biography in the Thai language is either a paean or a condemnation, rather than a disinterested analysis, of the person being described; a brilliant young Ph.D. hesitates to publish his dissertation because a high prince has indicated his disfavor over a brief description in the text of a few of his own deceased relatives; a passionate young intellectual strikes from his manuscript his two most important and meaningful paragraphs because two friends indicated that *their* teacher would be offended by the passages; an American professor is attacked in a panel discussion, in the press, and on the air, for making a pejorative (and, in fact, incorrect) interpretation of Buddhism, but not a single one of at least fourteen critics bothered to read what he had actually written, including the writer who first brought the matter to the attention of the public: he had simply quoted a friend's completely inadequate report of what the professor had allegedly said. More than a year later, when he was passing through the United States, the writer asked to see for the first time the original text of the statement that had caused so much controversy.

None of the above of course should be especially surprising. The people in this study are not scholars. Their purpose and role in life is not merely to understand public events, but rather to affect them and perhaps even *be* them. And if their ideas are to have any credibility in society, they must express themselves in terms of what is socially meaningful and permissible, but not necessarily true.

Economics of Intellectual Activity

Finally, a few words should be said about the economics of intellectual activity. The data on this point are unmistakably clear. Of the eighteen members of the major sample, only five make their living primarily from their writing and related activities (lecturing, television appearances, and the like). For the balance, intellectual productivity has one of three economic characteristics: (1) it is a pleasant and easy way to make some extra income; (2) it is a natural and enjoyable, but not an essential, adjunct to one's regular job (teacher, foreign affairs official, and the like); (3) it is a social responsibility of the independently wealthy. The five persons who depend solely upon their writing are highly productive, popular, or have foreign organizations as their employers or patrons.

The reasons for these economic facts are obvious: until now there simply have not been enough customers in the intellectual marketplace of Thailand to provide a more substantial economic base for the life of ideas. Further, although there is a tradition of artistic patronage in Thailand—which conceivably might compensate for a more broadly based clientele—this patronage has been confined to painters, musicians, dancers, and those working on problems of history and antiquity, all literati-type activities. Several intellectuals have at various times hired themselves out at inordinately high salaries as public-relations men for powerful political figures, a position that is not without personal and public ambivalence. In this position the intellectual is seen as lending the patron not only his powers to persuade the public but also his own lofty idealism; the public is supposed to reason that "if writer X is willing to join politician Y's following, then politician Y must be a decent political figure." Excepting such special personages as the late Luang Vichitr Vichit-Vadakan—philosopher, essayist, and songwriter of Thai nationalism for several different regimes over three decades—most intellectuals who accept the patronage of politicians do so for brief periods of time. The usual justification, if any, of the acceptance of such patronage is that it gives the individual the financial freedom "to pursue his more serious writing."

Of the three types of books published in Thailand—cremation gift books, government and government-sponsored books (including textbooks), and trade books—only the last provides a consistent outlet for the intellectual's creative efforts. Most trade books are published in printings of 2,000 to 4,000 copies and typically sell for $.75 to $2.00 per copy; paperbacks have recently become very popular and sell for $.25 to $.50 per copy. The contract between author and publisher is almost always limited to a single edition and involves the payment of a flat, initial sum instead of royalties. If the book is successful and gives every appearance of selling more than the first edition, the author usually takes his rights to a second publisher, with whom he bargains for a higher payment. A few best sellers have been printed by as many as nine different publishers. The highest sum ever paid for the first edition of a book was 13,000 baht ($650) for a novel by Thailand's most distinguished intellectual; the story, a Thai Buddhist equivalent of the Don Camillo situation, was first serialized in the author's own newspaper. The best selling novel in the history of Thailand, a story of nationalistic and moral fervor, brought its author more than 120,000 baht ($6,000) over a period of twelve years. The most recent translation of *How To Win Friends and Influence People* has been the most successful, selling 27,000 copies, and has brought its translator slightly more than 20,000 baht ($1,000) over a period of three years.

These examples represent the very highest sums that Thai intellectuals can expect from their books. A beginning writer, on the other hand, can rarely expect more than 3,000–4,000 baht ($150–$200) for the first printing of one of his manuscripts. Even a well-established writer can rarely hope to obtain more than 10,000 baht ($500) per printing.

There is one important mitigating factor. Most trade books are first serialized in the daily press, and the author is paid for each installment. Minimum payment is usally 80–100 baht ($4–$5) per story; famous intellectuals sometimes receive as much as 500 baht ($25) per installment. Thus, if a novel or a collection of critical essays or short stories runs as long as twenty installments, the author can make an additional $80–$500 for his creative effort.

These low figures reflect not only the difficult economic condition of many Thai writers, but, more importantly, one of the fundamental substantive problems of Thai intellectual activity. That is, most authors require either an extraordinary degree of motivation or an independent income to work for months on a manuscript that may bring them only $250. Many Thai writers lack both, and instead of working for months they work only days or weeks. The results often are unresearched stories, superficial interpretations, and ungrammatical texts. Several authors are keenly aware of these problems and spend time training younger writers and colleagues in proper literary and research techniques. It is precisely from such training that teacher-student relationships and professional loyalties and prejudices develop; some aspiring writers even live at the homes of established authors, a few in semiservant status. Equally important, in recent years there has been considerable support among those authors whose major income derives from their writings for the idea of organizing their own publishing house to rectify the inequitable payment structure under which they they have been operating.

Some Individual Intellectuals

Following are brief sketches of a few of Thailand's major intellectuals. They are presented principally to suggest some of the rich variation in the backgrounds, activities, and interests of the people who determine the nature and quality of Thai intellectual life.

"*The Prince with the Scissors Tongue*" M.R.K.P. stands alone as Thailand's most distinguished intellectual. A descendant of the second king of the present Thai dynasty and the son of the superintendent of the Thai National Police during the reign of King Chulalongkorn, he is a publisher, editor, classical dancer, photographer, horticulturist, one-time Member of Parliament, banker, business executive, Hollywood actor, and the author of twenty-one books. His older brother is Thailand's most distinguished lawyer. In his early fifties, he is known to millions of people through his "Your Bedtime Friend" radio broadcasts, where he comments and advises on life's problems. He is also a friend, important unofficial adviser, and deeply loyal servant to the king of Thailand. He was educated at an English public school and at one of the finest universities in the Western world. Although his public distinction is based principally upon his personality—he is witty, knowledgeable, unpredictable, and cutting in his criticisms (hence his nickname)—his intellectual contributions are of considerable substance. One is a two-volume, fictionalized account of life at the court from the reign of King Chulalongkorn to the reign of King Ananda, covering approximately the first fifty years of this century. He describes the intrigues, loves, food habits, vanities, and sensitivities of the nobility during the final period of "pre-modern Thailand." Although he researched the novel by spending scores of hours over lunch with elderly ladies of the court, he wrote it all in unedited installments approximately one hour before the daily typesetting deadline of his own newspaper. Many other informants consider this book to be Thailand's greatest novel. Another significant contribution is his famous debate over the essence of Buddhism with Thailand's most distinguished scholarly Buddhist monk. M.R.K.P. argued that the central element of Buddhism was its moral teachings; his opponent took the position that the essence of Buddhism was the life of the Lord Buddha, which all living Buddhists should, in an existential sense, attempt to emulate. What was striking about this debate to most Thai was not what M.R.K.P. said but rather their discovery that behind his characteristic wit and entertaining sarcasm was a powerful sense of logic and extensive factual knowledge.

"*The Complex Cop*" At thirty-eight years of age, W.D. is the youngest colonel in the Thai National Police force. He is Thailand's most brilliant satirist, editor of the *Police Journal*, and teacher and lecturer to hundreds of junior-grade police officers and NCO's whose respect and loyalty to him is noticeably greater than that which typically attends a student-teacher relationship. Some informants suggest that because of his amiability, self-confidence, profound moral sense, and cutting but not insulting sense of humor, he may become one of the most powerful political figures in Thailand. The son of a provincial education officer, he came to Bangkok as a youngster, did well at his studies, and entered Chulalongkorn University where he has become famous as a humorist and essayist. He later attended a university in the United States, where he received an M.A. in police administration. He also worked for M.R.K.P., whom he considers one of the most influential people in his life. He has published scores of articles, some of which have recently appeared as an anthology. Like most satirists, his interests are wide-ranging, although he is particularly effective at puncturing the pretensions of status seekers, playboys, and lazy or incompetent public servants. Also, like most satirists, he has a powerful strain of utopian idealism in his writings. He currently has a high, policy-making position in the government's anti-insurgency program in Thailand's Northeast, and is writing a book on communism in fulfillment of a promise to the queen of Thailand.

"*The Indecisive Artist*" The son of a peasant, S.S. came to Bangkok as a youngster to further his education. He did better than satisfactory work and later entered Thammasāt University, where he became very interested in Marxism. Quite by chance he obtained a position as private secretary to a high government official, and he has since been in government service, mainly in the Ministry of Foreign Affairs. This position has permitted him to travel extensively. Now in his late forties, he is the secretary-general of a major department in this ministry. S.S. is a loyal public servant who works at and enjoys his job because of the security and prestige it represents. He says he writes novels because he enjoys writing and values the extra income it brings. One of the most respected, but not necessarily popular, authors in the kingdom, he writes sensitively and dispassionately about the moral and interpersonal difficulties in which people find themselves. However, unlike all other Thai authors, he does not suggest ways for resolving these difficulties or even promise that the problems will be solved. In our interviews he admitted that "deciding the right thing to do is the most difficult of all human problems and in my novels I would never make this decision for my characters or readers." One of

S.S.'s novels is the most sensitive and comprehensive account in Thai literature of the social and psychological meaning of the 1932 Revolution, the event marking Thailand's change from an absolute to a constitutional monarchy. Because of the momentous nature of the event and the scope and subtlety of S.S.'s conception, it would not be inappropriate to consider the book the Thai equivalent of *War and Peace*. The title of the novel, *Phīsad* (Ghosts, meaning the ghosts of Thailand's past), is suggestive of the author's conception.

"*The Walking Encyclopedia*" At eighty years of age, P.A. is the doyen of the Thai scholarly world. Philologist, ethnographer, literary critic, and lexicographer, he is the author of more than 200 articles and almost a score of books. Son of a Chinese pawn-broker and a Thai mother, he graduated from a missionary high school in Bangkok and became a clerk in the Customs Department, where he met a British adviser who stimulated him into learning English. He read widely in Victorian literature and in European mythology and folklore. An encounter with Prince Damrong, the most influential scholar-bureaucrat in Thailand in the early years of this century, led to his employment in the government's Department of Fine Arts. He later became director of this department, a position that he held for many years. He is the very model of the wise, gently humorous, not overly demanding teacher. While few younger intellectuals wish to model themselves after him—they see him as an accumulator of memorabilia rather than as a creator or user of knowledge directly relevant to their lives—they do consider him a major symbolic link to their own cultural past. Unlike many men of knowledge, he is unpretentious and relaxed in his personal contacts. P.A. is not a profound thinker, but this fades into unimportance when measured against the inordinate scope of his learning. Equally important, many Thai feel that because he initiated and for many years worked alone in the collection of factual ethnographic materials on Thai culture, he is one of the major innovators of Thai intellectual history.

"*The Artist as a Young Man*" The son of a peasant, thirty-five-year-old R.W. is the most popular and influential young writer in Thailand. His style, themes, and language are imitated by university students and by numerous journalists and short-story writers. He came to Bangkok as a child to further his education, and at the age of seventeen eloped with the daughter of a wealthy Bangkok merchant who called the police down upon him. He got his start in the intellectual world by working as a $25-per-month photographer and caption writer on M.R.K.P.'s newspaper and later became a reporter and columnist. He lived in the United States for four years as the "first foreign correspondent in the history of Thailand," but most of his writings from America focused on his memories of Thai life and culture. R.W. writes about sex and aggression, but, unlike previous Thai writers, he concerns himself with the feelings, conflicts, and decisions—rather than the display or exhibition—of sexuality and aggression. It is his sensitive introspection about what most Thai are explicitly not supposed to think about, but all do, that has made him famous. His writings are deeply rooted in his own personal experiences: as a child he was something of a delinquent, and as a young adult he became known as one of Thailand's most distinguished philanderers. In fact, he got his first job as a writer at the age of fourteen, when, serving as a scribe, he wrote for 25¢ a piece the love letters that neighborhood prostitutes sent to their paramours.

"*The Aggressive Editor*" At the age of thirty-five, Su. Si. is the editor of the only "intellectual magazine" in Thailand. Sponsored by a Western organization and modeled on *Encounter*, the magazine has in four years under his tutelage grown in circulation from 500 to over 4,500 copies. In addition to editing, as well as writing large portions of the magazine, he travels throughout the provinces lecturing and attempting to stir up apolitical intellectual controversy. Also, he recently opened what is essentially the first university bookstore in Thailand. The son of a chief clerk in a Western import-export firm, he won a scholarship to study law in England. A disciple of P.A., he is closely linked with a group of young university professors, although his aggressive personal qualities prevent him from assuming a leadership role in this group. Among the educated public he is famous for his highly combative, badgering, and idealistic personal style. In recent months he has become even more famous for a cutting personal attack on M.R.K.P.; it was written in the manner of a nineteenth-century British literary figure attacking a colleague. Su. Si. has two principal messages which he feels are inextricably linked: (1) that the current problems of Thailand are due mainly to the absence of a sense of excellence and of concern with the public welfare; and (2) that to develop these attitudes Thailand must return to the standards expressed by Prince Damrong and Prince Naris in the early years of this century. These two princes represent the models of the dedicated, knowledgeable, and, in the case of Prince Damrong, shrewd, scholar-bureaucrat.

"The Honest Technocrat" In his early fifties, P.U. is the chief executive officer of the most important banking institution in Thailand. He is also dean of the college of economics of one of Thailand's major universities. The son of a Chinese fishmonger and a Thai mother, he went to a missionary school, attended Thammasat University, and received a Ph.D. in economics at a British university. During World War II he played an important role in organizing the "Free Thai Movement" in England. P.U.'s high position is due to his thoughtful, carefully planned, but not overly daring economic policies; he is the first to make such an assessment of his success. His fame, however, is based upon other considerations. He has no personal or professional retinue, and he lives and works modestly, which to most Thai is prima facie evidence of his honesty. He is the only high government official who in his public speeches and writings *consistently* attacks corruption and inefficiency in the highest places; a recent speech before the Bankers Association of Thailand, written in poetic form, was an unveiled criticism

of one of Thailand's best-known—but generally believed to be most corrupt—officials. In recent years he has become the unofficial leader of a group of university education reformists and a group that wishes to publish Thai children's books. He is the author of a widely used economics textbook, which includes a lengthy chapter on "The Application of Buddhist Principles to Economics."

"The Passionate Monk" In his late sixties, B.P. is the most scholarly and influential Buddhist monk in Thailand. Some Thai consider him the most important figure in Thai Buddhism since King Mongkut. A large, outgoing, and energetic person, he is a voluminous writer, television personality, religious entrepreneur, and teacher to thousands of Thai laymen and hundreds of monks, foreign as well as Thai, whom he has reached with his message. Son of a small-town Chinese shopkeeper and a Thai mother, he and his younger brother, a schoolteacher, used the inheritance from their parents to establish a small monastery in a village near the provincial town where they were born in the mid-peninsula area of Southern Thailand. The act occurred upon the death of their mother and was merit-making in its intent. At the time, he already was a monk and had even spent two years alone in the forest meditating and "talking with my companions, the stones and birds." Since that time, the monastery, of which he is abbot, in association with a religious foundation and publishing house, of which his brother is chairman, has turned into a religious phenomenon. The monastery is essentially a retreat for monks and laymen (who come either individually or with their families) who wish to emulate the life of Buddha through action. Although they may spend some of their time in meditation, they must also act in a moral or creative way, either toward other people or through some creative performance: sculpting, painting, carpentry, translating Pali canon into a vernacular language, and the like. B.P.'s writings and television and radio messages contain the same theme: the essence of Buddhism is

living one's life like Lord Buddha. Moral intentions are not adequate expressions of a Buddhist existence: one must live one's Buddhism, not think it or believe it, and occasional ritual acts or ceremonials are poor substitutes for continuous commitment. One major element of B.P.'s message is that Buddhist living is a joyous experience, that if moral action is not experienced as fun it ultimately is not authentic. One visible consequence of these themes is to give B.P.'s monastery the appearance of being part traditional Thai temple, part summer camp, and part modern Buddhist museum. There are in fact special dormitories where children are given training in Buddhist living, and the central structure of the monastery is an immense concrete "Spiritual Theater," next to which is an equally large concrete boat, a symbol of the boat that carries one to Nirvana. As might be expected of such a movement, it has not been enthusiastically received by some elements of the Buddhist hierarchy in Bangkok. However, B.P. has been sufficiently successful to spawn three potentially similar monasteries elsewhere in the country; the abbots of these monasteries consider themselves B.P.'s disciples and are attempting to replicate his practices. Although B.P. reads English and has some knowledge of Christianity—which he explicitly rejects because of its concern with God rather than with man—he has no apparent familiarity with Western existential thought. Finally, it should be noted that B.P. has a disproportionate number of wealthy and upper-class followers and, because of both the nature of his teachings and his own concerted efforts, he has not developed the qualities of a charismatic figure.

Types of Intellectuals

A few words should be said about the way Thai intellectuals pattern into functionally specific groups. It is within these groups that teacher-student and patron-client relationships are developed and maintained, although there is considerable variation in the degree of social organization from group to group. Some groups (such as the "Royal Traditionalists") maintain a sharp sense of group identity and group sanctions, while others (like the "Journalists-Editors-Novelists") are characterized by a high degree of internal fission. Membership in the groups is not mutually exclusive, and some intellectuals (M.R.K.P. and B.P. for example) are almost institutions unto themselves and cannot be readily assigned to a specific category. More important, from a subjective point of view, the majority of intellectuals feel that they operate as individuals and do not identify with specific groups. The groups are important solely from the point of view of representing different intellectual traditions or fulfilling socially necessary ideational functions. Although the groups could be rank-ordered into a stratified system—if only because they are Thai groups—they do such different things, and there is such little contact between some of them, that such ordering would have little analytic utility.

"*Royal Traditionalists*" Heirs to the historically deepest and most prestigeful intellectual tradition, the members of this group are perfect literati. They are concerned with the glorification and maintenance of traditional Thai art forms, literary styles, history, poetry, manners, and even grammatical forms. Despite his royal title and wide-ranging interests, including Thai classical dancing and his appreciation of court life, M.R.K.P. is not a member of this group; his tastes are too cosmopolitan and his personality too abrasive to allow admission to the group. On the other hand, P.A., despite his birth as a commoner, is a central figure of the group; in fact, the "P." in his name refers to the title that was conferred upon him by a Thai king. Su. Si. is not yet old enough and is still too bumptious to be offered full admission, while B.P. is more interested in living Buddhism than in promulgating traditional Thai culture to participate actively in the group. Members of this group play a significant role in the functioning of the Siam Society, the Buddhist Association of Thailand, and the Thai Royal Academy (an official, select organization charged with issuing, among other things, official dictionaries and encyclopedias). The group has close ties with that segment of the Western, particularly British, intellectual world that is interested in Thailand. In the mind of the public, the leaders of the group are the president of the king's privy council and Prince Damrong's daughter (who has also been president of the World Federation of Buddhists). Despite its very special interests and lofty tone, the group is viable and powerful, playing an important role in national educational policy, in setting artistic standards, and in presenting a classical image of Thailand to the non-Thai world.

"*Social Technicians*" In the view of most Thai citizens, this is the most important group in the kingdom—intellectually, socially, economically, and technologically. Its membership is the bureaucratic leadership of Thailand, of which P.U. is one of the finest representatives. Most of its membership are consumers rather than creators of knowledge and policy. However, various members of the group are introducing into Thai society a rational-legal approach to bureaucratic organization, the concept of "public planning," and new academic disciplines such as public administration, sociology, and business administration. Members of the group play a crucial role in the educational and economic systems of Thailand through their affiliation with such government agencies as the National Economic Development Board, National Educational Council, National Research Council, Bank of Thailand, and the new National Institute of Development Administration. The publications of these organizations are concerned almost exclusively with applied bureaucratic and technical problems. Related to the group is a small number of military intellectuals who write for the Command and General Staff College journal *Raphtaa Pirad*, focusing on technical problems of modern military organization and planning.

"*Professional Debaters and Panel Discussants*" This is a group of approximately ten to twenty persons comprising a pool from which is drawn almost all the participants in public debates and television and radio discussions held in Thailand. M.R.K.P. is an unofficial charter member of the group and W.D., R.W., and Su. Si. are sometime members. They are people who are selected in part for the scope of their knowledge and in part for their quick wit and entertainment value. Topics of public debate in Thailand cover a broad range, but the following titles are representative: "What Is the Difference between Art and Pornography?"; "What Is Meant by 'A Good Man'?"; "Who Should Enter the University?"

"Dedicated Young Professors" This is a group of recent M.A.'s and Ph.D's from Western universities who now teach at Thailand's two major universities and have organized themselves into a bimonthly discussion group. The seriousness of their purpose and the high level of their discussion distinguishes them sharply from other Thai university instructors. Some of their seminars, such as one on "Problems of Higher Education in Thailand," have resulted in publications that have directly affected public policy. The seminar group itself is expressive of a potentially significant movement in Thai higher education: it represents, for the first time in Thailand, an attempt on the part of recent returnees from abroad to maintain as a central part of their professional experience at home some of the intellectual excitement and scholarly creativity that they encountered at foreign universities. In recent months they have established a student version of their seminar and plan to institute a program for translating Western scholarly material into Thai.

"Journalists-Editors-Novelists" Comprised of people of many different backgrounds, competencies, and intellectual persuasions, this group is in most direct contact with the educated public. Since most (but not all) of the novelists and short-story writers of Thailand have had some prior experience in journalism, the three occupations are usually linked together in the thinking of the public. The group is marked by a high degree of

professional competition and fractionalization into small, impermanent groups. There are now, for example, three different, but functionally identical, journalists' organizations in Thailand, the number due principally to personal disagreements between members of the parent organizations. Since most training for the profession is done on the job, the group tends to be highly democratic and recruits people from all levels of Thai society. Many young people are brought into journalism in the expectation of leading an exciting life and encountering important people. Those who stay with the profession usually turn to social or political commentary. The very best, or vain, then try their hand at fiction, usually starting on a soap opera level. A few outstanding people reach the level of persons such as R.W. or S.S.

Conclusion

I have attempted to describe some of the major features of Thai intellectual culture. Perhaps the most important characteristic of this culture is that it tends to be more Thai than intellectual in the sense that its participants are generally more concerned with the familiar and culturally acceptable issues of Thai society, or with how the discussion of such issues might contribute to their own social roles, than they are with facing the abstract, difficult, or unknown cognitive challenges that are typically associated with the intellectual endeavor. They are people who prefer to be "clear, precise, and persuasive," rather than "critical, orginal, and profound." In short, most Thai intellectuals tend to be literati rather intelligentsia. They are, to paraphrase Redfield's and Singer's cogent application (1954) of this famous distinction, specialists who reflect upon traditional cultural materials and create out of them new arrangements and developments that are felt by their readers to be outgrowths of the old; they elaborate what has already been said and accepted. They are not heretics, dissenters, or marginal men who bring forth new intellectual orientations by interrupting or challenging cultural traditions.

The literati emphasis is clearly not applicable to all Thai intellectual activity. The teachings of the monk B.P. are a fundamental departure from traditional Thai Buddhist practice. The activities and motivations of the young university professors differ radically from the customary bureaucratic behavior of most Thai university personnel. R.W.'s concern with sex as a means by which people reach each other emotionally is something new in a culture which has tended to view sexual behavior in the simplest hedonistic, but also manipulative, terms. Even P.A.'s literati-type interests are a major departure from what went before in the sense that he was the first scholar to want to study Thai peasants in factual, empirical terms.

However, as has been indicated by the thrust of the discussion, most Thai intellectual activity tends toward the elaboration of what is already admitted. None of this should be surprising. Whatever the field of human experience—politics, technology, administration, religion—Thai culture has almost always dealt with the new or alien through a process of adaptation and a sense of relevance to traditional values and modes of thought. The same is true of its intellectual concerns.

References Cited

Akin Rabibhadana
1969 The organization of Thai society in the Early Bangkok period, 1782–1873. Ithaca: Cornell University, Southeast Asia Program (Data papers, 74).

Amyot, Jacques
1964 Intensive village study project, April–May 1964: Ban Nonlan, Amphur Uthumphonphisai, Sisaket: Preliminary report. Bangkok: Chulalongkorn University, Faculty of Political Science.

Anderson, John
1890 English intercourse with Siam in the seventeenth century. London: Kegan Paul, Trench, Trübner.

Anuman Rajadhon, *Phya* (Anumān Rātchathon, *Phrayā*)
1954 The "phi." Journal of the Siam Society 41, 2:153–178.
1961 Thet mahachat. *In* Fiftieth anniversary publications, No. 1: Some of the papers read . . . Rangoon: Burma Research Society, 1960, 1–8.
1967a Chīwit chāo Thai samai kǫn [Thai life in times past]. Bangkok: Rātchabandit Sathan.
1967b Fūen khwāmlang [Later recovery]. Bangkok: Sueksit Sayām.
1967c Notes on the thread-square in Thailand. Journal of the Siam Society 55, 2:161–182.

Archaimbault, Charles
1956a Le sacrifice du buffle à Vat Ph'u (Sud-Laos). *In* Présence du royaume lao, edited by René de Berval. Saigon: France-Asie, 841–845 (France-Asie, 10. année 118/119).
1956b Une cérémonie en l'honneur des génies de la mine de sel de Ban Bo (Moyen Laos). Bulletin de l'Ecole française d'Extrême-Orient 48, 1:221–231.
1959a La naissance du monde selon les traditions lao: Le mythe de Khun Bulom. *In* La naissance du monde. Paris: Editions du Seuil, 385–416 (Sources Orientales, 1).

1959b Les rites agraires dans le moyen-Laos. France-Asie 160/161:1185–1194; 162/163:1274–1283.
1961 La fête du t'at à S'ieng Khwang (Laos): Contribution à l'étude du Ti K'i. Artibus Asiae 24, 3/4 (felicitation volume presented to Professor Coedès):187–200.
1963 Contribution à l'étude du rituel funéraire lao. Journal of the Siam Society 51, 1:1–57.
1966 La fête du t'at à Luong P'răbang. *In* Essays offered to G. H. Luce . . . , edited by Ba Shin et al. Ascona, Switzerland: Artibus Asiae, vol. 1, 5–47 (Artibus Asiae supplementa, 23).
1967 Les annales de l'ancien royaume de S'ieng Khwang. Bulletin de l'Ecole française d'Extrême-Orient 53, 2:557–673.

Archer, W. J.
1892 Report on a journey in the Me-Kong valley. Parliamentary papers, vol. 79, paper 337. London: H.M.S.O.

Ayal, Eliezer B.
1963 Value systems and economic development in Japan and Thailand. Journal of social issues 19, 1:35–51.
1966 Private enterprise and economic progress in Thailand, Journal of Asian studies 26, 1:5–14.

Backus, Mary (ed.)
1884 Siam and Laos as seen by our American missionaries. Philadelphia: Presbyterian Board of Publications.

Bangkok Times
1887–1941 Daily newspaper. Bangkok.

Befu, Harumi
1962 Corporate emphasis and patterns of descent in the Japanese family. *In* Japanese culture: Its development and characteristics, edited by Robert J. Smith and Richard K. Beardsley. New York: Wenner-Gren Foundation, 34–41 (Viking Fund publications in anthropology, 34).
1963 Patrilineal descent and personal kindred in Japan. American anthropologist 65, 6:1328–1341.

Bellah, Robert N. (ed.)
1965 Religion and progress in modern Asia. New York: Free Press.

Benedict, Ruth
1952 Thai culture and behavior. Ithaca: Cornell University, Southeast Asia Program (Data papers, 4).

Berval, René de (ed.)
1956 Présence du royaume lao. Saigon: France-Asie (France-Asie, 10. année 118/119).

Blakeslee, D. J., L. W. Huff, and R. W. Kickert
1965   Village security pilot study, Northeast Thailand. Bangkok:
        Joint Thai-U.S. Military Research and Development Center.
Bourne, Frederick S. A.
1888   Report by Mr. F. S. A. Bourne on a journey in South
        Western China . . . Parliamentary papers, vol. 98, paper 121.
        London: H.M.S.O.
Bowring, John
1857   The kingdom and people of Siam; with a narrative of the
        mission to that country in 1855, 2 vols. London: John W. Parker.
Briggs, Lawrence Palmer
1951   The ancient Khmer empire. Philadelphia: American Philo-
        sophical Society.
Brown, Donald M.
1953   The white umbrella: Indian political thought from Manu
        to Gandhi. Berkeley: University of California Press.
Brown, L. Keith
1966   Dōzoku and the ideology of descent in rural Japan. Amer-
        ican anthropologist 68, 5:1129–1151.
Bruner, Edward M.
1959   Kinship organization among the urban Batak of Sumatra.
        Transactions of the New York Academy of Science 22, 2:118–
        125.
Burtt, E. A.
1955   The teaching of the compassionate Buddha. New York:
        New American Library.
Cadière, Léopold M.
1944–1957   Croyances et pratiques religieuses des Viêtnamiens,
        3 vols. Paris: Ecole française d'Extrême-Orient.
Čhakpānī Sīsīnwisut, Lūang
1956   Rūeang khǭng Čhaophrayā Mahithǭn [Biography of
        Čhaophrayā Mahithǭn]. Bangkok: Tīranasān.
Chavannes, Edouard
1910   Le T'ai Chan: Essai de monographie d'un culte chinois.
        Paris: Ernest Leroux (Annales du Musée Guimet, Bibliothèque
        d'études, 21).
Chou Ta-kuan
1967   Notes on the customs of Cambodia. Transl. from the French
        version of Paul Pelliot by J. G. D. Paul. Bangkok: Social Science
        Association Press.
Chulalongkorn (Čhulālongkǭn), King of Thailand
1887   Phrabǭrommarāchāthibāi wā dūai yot khunnāng [Royal

explanation on the ranks of the nobles]. *Repr. in* Ton trakūn khunnāng Thai [The origins of Thai noble families], by Prayut Sitthipan. Bangkok: Khlangwitthaya, 1962, 1–5.

1915   Phrarātchadamrat nai phrabātsomdet phrachunlachǫm-klao chaoyūhūa (tangtae Ph.S. 2417 thueng Ph.S. 2453) [Speeches of His Majesty King Chulalongkorn, 1874–1910]. Bangkok: Sōphon Phiphatthanākǫn.

1927   Phrarātchadamrat nai phrabātsomdet phrachunlachǫm-klao chaoyūhūa songthalāeng phrabǫrommarāchathibāi kāe-khai kānpokkhrǫng phāendin [Speeches of this Majesty King Chulalongkorn giving the royal explanation on improving the government of the Kingdom]. Bangkok: Sōphon Phiphat-thanākǫn.

Coedès, George
1913   Etudes cambodgiennes. Bulletin de l'Ecole française d'Extrême-Orient 13, 6:11–17.

1924   Recueil des inscriptions du Siam, première partie: Inscriptions de Sukhodaya. Bangkok: Bangkok Times Press.

1925   Documents sur l'histoire politique et religieuse du Laos occidental. Bulletin de l'Ecole française d'Extrême-Orient 25, 1/2:1–202.

1947a   L'année du lièvre 1219 A.D. *In* India antiqua. Leyden: E. J. Brill, 83–88.

1947b   Pour mieux comprendre Angkor. Paris: A. Maisonneuve.

1957   The Traibhūmikathā: Buddhist cosmology and treaty on ethics. East and west 7, 4:349–352.

1962   Les peuples de la péninsule indochinoise: Histoire-civilisations. Paris: Dunod.

1964   Les Etats hindouisés d'Indochine et d'Indonésie. Paris: E. de Boccard.

Coedès, George, and Charles Archaimbault
1973   Les trois mondes (Traibhūmi Braḥ Rvaṅ). Paris: Ecole française d'Extrême-Orient (Publications de l'Ecole française d'Extrême-Orient, 89).

Colquhoun, Archibald
1885   Amongst the Shans. London: Field and Tuer.

Condominas, Georges
1959   Etude sociologique. *In* La plaine de Vientiane, rapport d'étude, edited by C. Gaudillot and G. Condominas. Mimeo. Paris: Bureau pour le developpement et la production agricoles, vol. 1, 42–111 (Royaume du Laos, Commissariat au Plan).

1962   Essai sur la société rurale lao de la région de Vientiane. Vientiane: Commissariat aux affaires rurales.

1968   Notes sur le Bouddhisme populaire en milieu rural lao. Archives de sociologie des religions 13, 25:81–110; 13, 26:111–150.

1970   The Lao. *In* Laos: War and revolution, edited by Nina Adams and Alfred McCorey. New York: Harper and Row, 9–28.

Crawfurd, John
1915   The Crawfurd papers: A collection of official records relating to the mission of Dr. Crawfurd sent to Siam by the government of India in the year 1821. Bangkok: National Library.

Curtis, Lillian
1903   The Laos of North Siam. Philadelphia: Westminister Press.

Damrong Rajanubhab, *Prince* (Damrong Rāchānuphāp, *Kromphrayā*)
1922   Rūeang prawat khǭng Čhaophrayā Phātsakǭrawong [On the life of Čhaophrayā Phātsakǭrawong]. *In* Khamklǭnā khǭng Čhaophrayā Phātsakǭrawong [The verse of Čhaophrayā Phātsakǭrawong]. Bangkok: Privately published, ii–xii.

1929   Rūeang chalōem phrayot čhaonāi [In honor of the appointment of princes], 2 vols. Bangkok: Rātchabandit Saphā.

1956   Rūeang rōngrīan mahātlek lūang [Concerning the Royal Pages School]. *In* Nithān bōrānkhadī (bāng rūeang) [Tales of the past (selections)]. Bangkok: Privately printed, 88–100.

1959   Laksana kānpokkhrǭng prathēt Sayām tae bōrān [Ancient administration of Siam]. Bangkok: Mahātthai.

1960   Thēsāphibān [Provincial government (of the type initiated by Rāma V)]. Bangkok: Phrungrūeangtham.

1962   Phrarātchaphongsāwadān chabap phrarātchahatthalēkhā [Annals, the royal autograph edition], 2 vols. Bangkok: Odeon Store.

1963a   Tamnān wangnā [History of the Front Palace]. *In* Prachum phongsāwadān [Collected chronicles], National Library edition, part 13. Bangkok: Kaonā, vol. 5, 88–207.

1963b   Tamnān kānkēn thahān Thai [History of Thai mobilization]. *In* Prachum phongsāwadān [Collected chronicles], National Library edition, part 23. Bangkok: Kaonā, vol. 6, 260–332.

1963c   Tamnān rōngrīan sūankulāp [History of Sūankulāp school]. Bangkok: Privately published.

1964   Athibāi rūeang rātchathūt Thai pai Yurōp [Explanation concerning the sending of Thai embassies to Europe]. *In* Prachum phongsāwadān [Collected chronicles], National Library edition, part 29. Bangkok: Kaonā, vol. 7, 310–345.

Davenport, William H.
1959   Nonunilinear descent and descent groups. American anthropologist 61, 4:557–572.

Davis, Richard
1973   Muang matrifocality. Journal of the Siam Society 61, 2:53–62.

deYoung, John E.
1955   Village life in modern Thailand. Berkeley: University of California Press.

Dodd, William Clifton
1923   The Tai race: Elder brother of the Chinese. Cedar Rapids, Ia.: Torch Press.

Dupont, Pierre
1959   L'archéologie mône de Dvāravatī. Paris: Ecole française d'Extrême-Orient (Publications de l'Ecole française d'Extrême-Orient, 41).

Filliozat, Jean
1965   Kailāsaparaṃparā. *In* Felicitation volumes of Southeast-Asian studies presented to His Highness Prince Dhaninivat. Bangkok: Siam Society, vol. 2, 241–247.

Fortes, Meyer
1953   The structure of unilineal descent groups. American anthropologist 55, 1:17–41.
1962   Introduction. *In* The developmental cycle in domestic groups, edited by Jack Goody. Cambridge: Cambridge University Press, 1–14 (Cambridge papers in social anthropology, 1).

Foster, George M.
1967a   Tzintzuntzan: Mexican peasants in a changing world: Boston: Little, Brown.
1967b   What is a peasant? *In* Peasant society: A reader, edited by J. M. Potter, M. N. Diaz and G. M. Foster: Boston: Little, Brown, 2–14.

Freeman, J. D.
1960   The Iban of western Borneo. *In* Social structure in Southeast Asia, edited by George Peter Murdock. New York: Wenner-Gren Foundation, 65–87 (Viking Fund publications in anthropology, 29).
1961   On the concept of kindred. Journal of the Royal Anthropological Institute 91, 2:192–220.

1962   The family system of the Iban of Borneo. *In* The developmental cycle in domestic groups, edited by Jack Goody. Cambridge: Cambridge University Press, 15–52 (Cambridge papers in social anthropology, 1).

Fung Ritthākhanī
1959   Prawat trakūn sām trakūn [History of three families]. Bangkok: Photthahānākāt.

Geertz, Clifford
1960   The religion of Java. Glencoe, Ill.: Free Press.
1963   The integrative revolution: Primordial sentiments and civil politics in new states. *In* Old societies and new states: The quest for modernity in Asia and Africa, edited by C. Geertz. New York: Free Press, 105–157.
1966   Religion as a cultural system. *In* Anthropological approaches to the study of religion, edited by Michael Banton. London: Tavistock, 1–46 (A.S.A. monographs, 3).

Gervaise, Nicolas
1690   Histoire naturelle et politique du royaume de Siam. Paris: L. Lucas. (English translation by H. S. O'Neill—Bangkok: Siam Observer Press, 1928.)

Giles, Francis H.
1959   A critical analysis of Van Vliet's historical account of Siam in the 17th century. *In* Selected articles from the Siam Society Journal. Bangkok: Siam Society, vol. 7, 91–176.

Goodenough, Ward H.
1955   A problem in Malayo-Polynesian social organization. American anthropologist 57, 1:71–83.
1961   Review of "Social structure in Southeast Asia," edited by G. P. Murdock. American anthropologist 63, 6:1341–1347.

Goody, Jack
1961   The classification of double descent groups. Current anthropology 2, 1:3–24.
1962   (ed.) The developmental cycle in domestic groups. Cambridge: Cambridge University Press (Cambridge papers in social anthropology, 1).

Graham, Walter A.
1924   Siam: A handbook of practical, commercial and political information, 2 vols. London: A. Moring.

Griswold, A. B.
1957   Dated Buddha images of northern Siam. Ascona, Switzerland: Arbitus Asiae (Artibus Asiae supplementa, 16).
1961   King Mongkut of Siam. New York: Asia Society.

1963a   A glass Buddha image and its associations. Journal of glass studies 5:75–104.

1963b   Notes on the art of Siam, no. 6: Prince Yudhiṣṭhira. Artibus Asiae 26, 3/4:215–229.

1964   Review of "Literary evidence for early Buddhist art in China," by A. C. Soper. Journal of the Siam Society 52, 1: 117–120.

1967   Towards a history of Sukhodaya art, 2d enl. ed. Bangkok: [Thailand, Ministry of Education] Fine Arts Department [B.E. 2511].

Griswold, A. B., and Prasert ṇa Nagara

1968   A declaration of independence and its consequences: Epigraphic and historical studies, no. 1. Journal of the Siam Society 56, 2:207–249.

1969a   The Asokārāma inscription of 1399 A.D.: Epigraphic and historical studies, no. 2. Journal of the Siam Society 57, 1:29–56.

1969b   The pact between Sukhodaya and Nān: Epigraphic and historical studies, no. 3. Journal of the Siam Society 57, 1: 57–107.

1970   A pact between uncle and nephew: Epigraphic and historical studies, no. 5. Journal of the Siam Society 58, 1:89–113.

1971a   An inscription in old Mòn from Wieng Manó in Chieng Mai province: Epigraphic and historical studies, no. 6. Journal of the Siam Society 59, 1:153–156.

1971b   The inscription of Văt Trabăṅ Jāṅ Phöak: Epigraphic and historical studies, no. 7. Journal of the Siam Society 59, 1: 157–188.

1971c   The inscription of Văt Jāṅ Lòm (1384 A.D.): Epigraphic and historical studies, no. 8. Journal of the Siam Society 59, 1:189–208.

1971d   The inscription of King Rāma Gaṃhèṅ of Sukhodaya (1292 A.D.): Epigraphic and historical studies, no. 9. Journal of the Siam Society 59, 2:179–228.

1972   King Lödaiya of Sukhodaya and his contemporaries: Epigraphical and historical studies, no. 10. Journal of the Siam Society 60, 1:21–152.

1973a   The epigraphy of Mahādharmarājā I of Sukhodaya: Epigraphic and historical studies, no. 11, part I. Journal of the Siam Society 61, 1:71–181.

1973b   The epigraphy of Mahādharmarājā I of Sukhodaya: Epigraphic and historical studies, no. 11, part II. Journal of the Siam Society 61, 2:91–128.

Hall, D. G. E.
1955   A history of South-East Asia. New York: St. Martin's Press.
Halpern, Joel M.
1961   The role of the Chinese in Lao society. Journal of the Siam Society 49, 1:21–46.
1967   The changing village community. Englewood Cliffs, N.J.: Prentice-Hall.
Hanks, Lucien M. [Jr.]
1958   Indifference to modern education in a Thai farming community. Human organization 17, 2:9–14.
1962   Merit and power in the Thai social order. American anthropologist 64, 6:1247–1261.
1966   The corporation and the entourage: A comparison of Thai and American social organization. Catalyst 2 (summer): 55–63.
Heine-Geldern, Robert
1956   Conceptions of state and kingship in Southeast Asia. Ithaca: Cornell University, Southeast Asia Program (Data papers, 18).
Ingersoll, Jasper
1966   Fatalism in village Thailand. Anthropological quarterly 39, 3:200–225.
Ingram, James C.
1971   Economic change in Thailand, 1850–1970. Stanford: Stanford University Press.
International Bank for Reconstruction and Development (IBRD)
1959   A public development program for Thailand: Report of a mission organized by the International Bank for Reconstruction and Development. Baltimore: Johns Hopkins University Press.
Iwata, Keiji
1962   Ritual symbols in the northern part of Southeast Asia, mainly in the case of the Thai peoples. Nature and life in Southeast Asia 4:395–402.
Katay D. Sasouth
1955   Au pays du million d'éléphants: Le "Kh'lam." France-Asie 107:553–556.
Kaufman, Howard Keva
1960   Bangkhuad: A community study in Thailand. Locust Valley, N.Y.: J. J. Augustin (Association for Asian Studies monographs, 10).
Keyes, Charles F.
1967   Peasant and nation: A Thai-Lao village in a Thai state. Unpublished doctoral dissertation in Anthropology, Cornell University.

Khachǭn Sukkhaphānit
    1962   Thānandǭn phrai [The status of phrai]. Bangkok: Khasem.
Khemo, *Bhikkhu*
    1957   What is Buddhism? Bangkok: Prachandra Press.
Khuekrit Prāmōt
    1967   Panhā prachamwan. Sayāmrat [Siam Rath], 26 Dec.
Kickert, Robert
    1960   A pilot study of Northeast Thailand. Bangkok: United
        States Information Service (Reports, 3).
King, Winston
    1962   Buddhism and Christianity: Some bridges of understanding.
        Philadelphia: Westminister Press.
Kirsch, A. Thomas
    1967   Phu Thai religious syncretism: A case study of religion and
        society in Thailand. Unpublished doctoral dissertation in Social
        Anthropology, Harvard University.
    1969   Loose structure: Theory or description? *In* Loosely struc-
        tured social systems: Thailand in comparative perspective,
        edited by Hans-Dieter Evers. New Haven: Yale University,
        Southeast Asia Studies, 39–60 (Cultural reports, 17).
    1973   The Thai Buddhist quest for merit. *In* Southeast Asia: The
        politics of national integration, edited by John McAlister. New
        York: Random House, 188–201.
Klausner, William J.
    1956   Progress report (on work in Nong Khon village, Ubon pro-
        vince). Mimeo., n.p.
    1966   The "cool heart": Social relationships in a northeastern
        Thai village. Wārasān sangkhomsāt [Journal of social sciences]
        4:117–124.
    1972   Reflections in a log pond: Collected writings. Bangkok:
        Suksit Siam.
Koentjaraningrat, R. M.
    1957   Preliminary description of the Javanese kinship system. New
        Haven: Yale University, Southeast Asia Studies (Cultural re-
        ports, 4).
    1960   The Javanese of south central Java. *In* Social structure in
        Southeast Asia, edited by George Peter Murdock. New York:
        Wenner-Gren Foundation, 88–115 (Viking Fund publications
        in anthropology, 29).
Kraisri Nimmanhaeminda
    1967   The Lawa guardian spirits of Chiengmai. Journal of the
        Siam Society 55, 2:185–225.

Lafont, Pierre-Bernard
1955   Notes sur les familles patronymiques thai noires de So'n-la et de Nghái-lô. Anthropos 50:797–809.
La Loubère, Simon de
1693   A new historical relation of the kingdom of Siam, 2 vols. Transl. from the French. London: T. Horne.
Leach, Edmund R.
1954   Political systems of highland Burma: A study of Kachin social structure. London: London School of Economics and Political Science.
Lebar, Frank M., and Adrienne Suddard (eds.)
1960   Laos: Its people, its society, its culture. New Haven: Human Relations Area Files Press.
Le Boulanger, Paul
1931   Histoire du Laos français, essai d'une étude chronologique des principautés laotiennes. Paris: Plon.
Lehman, Fredrick
1965   Report of a preliminary survey of the position of the Kayah (Red Karen) of Thailand. Unpublished manuscript.
leMay, Reginald S.
1926   An Asian Arcady: The land and peoples of northern Siam. Cambridge, England: W. Heffer.
Lévy, Paul
1940   Les traces de l'introduction du Bouddhisme à Luang Prabang. Bulletin de l'Ecole française d'Extrême-Orient 40, 2: 411–424.
1943   Le sacrifice du buffle et la prédiction du temps à Vientiane (avec étude sur le sacrifice du buffle en Indochine). Bulletin de l'Institut indochinois pour l'étude de l'homme 6:301–331.
1953   Ti-Khi, un jeu de mail rituel au Laos. Annuaire de l'Ecole pratique des hautes études, Sciences religieuses 1952–1953:3–15.
Lingat, Robert
1931   L'esclavage privé dans le vieux droit siamois. Paris: Domat-Montchrestien.
1938a   *Note sur la révision des lois siamoises en 1805. Journal of the Siam Society 23, 1:19–28.
1938b   (ed.) Pramūan kotmāi ratchakān thī nueng [Legal code of King Rāma I], 3 vols. Bangkok: Thammasāt University.
1939   Le culte du Bouddha d'émeraude. Journal of the Siam Society 27, 1:9–38.
1950a   Les origines du prêt à intérêt au Siam. Revue historique de droit français et étranger 28:213–235.

1950b   Evolution of the conception of law in Burma and Siam. Journal of the Siam Society 38, 1:9–31.
1951   La conception du droit dans l'Indochine hînayâniste. Bulletin de l'Ecole française d'Extrême-Orient 44:163–187.

Lopreato, Joseph
1967   Peasants no more: Social class and social change in an underdeveloped society. San Francisco: Chandler.

Luce, Gordon H.
1959   The early Syām in Burma's history: A supplement. Journal of the Siam Society 47, 1:59–101.

Lux, Thomas
1962   Mango village: Northeastern Thai social organization, ethos, and factionalism. Unpublished master's thesis in Anthropology, University of Chicago.
1969   The Thai-Lao family system and domestic cycle of northeastern Thailand. Wārasān saphāwichāi haeng chāt [Journal of the National Research Council] 5:1–17.

Madge, Charles
1957   Survey before development in Thai villages. New York: U.N. Secretariat (United Nations series on community organization and development, D/25).

Maspero, Henri
1950   La société et la religion des Chinois anciens et celles des Tai modernes. In Mélanges posthumes sur les religions et l'histoire de la Chine, by Henri Maspero. Paris: Civilisations du Sud, S.A.E.P., vol. 57, 167–177 (Publications du Musée Guimet, Bibliothèque de diffusion, 57).

Mayer, Adrian C.
1966   The significance of quasi-groups in the study of complex societies. In The social anthropology of complex societies, edited by Michael Banton. London: Tavistock, 97–121 (A.S.A. monographs, 4).

Mintz, Sidney W.
1961   Pratik: Haitian personal economic relationships. In Proceedings of the 1961 annual spring meeting of the American Ethnological Society. Seattle: American Ethnological Society, 54–63.

Mitchell, William E.
1963   Theoretical problems in the concept of kindred. American anthropologist 65, 2:343–354.

Mizuno, Koichi
1968   Multihousehold compounds in northeastern Thailand. Asian survey 8, 10:842–852.

1971   Social system of Don Daeng village: A community study in Northeast Thailand. Kyoto: Kyoto University, Center for Southeast Asian Studies (Discussion papers, 12–22).

Moerman, Michael
1965   Ethnic identification in a complex civilization: Who are the Lue? American anthropologist 67, 5:1215–1230.
1966   Ban Ping's temple: The center of a "loosely structured" society. *In* Anthropological studies in Theravada Buddhism, edited by Manning Nash. New Haven: Yale University, Southeast Asian Studies, 137–174 (Cultural reports, 13).
1967   A minority and its government: The Thai-Lue of northern Thailand. *In* Southeast Asian tribes, minorities and nations, edited by Peter Kunstadter. Princeton: Princeton University Press, vol. 1, 401–424.
1968   Agricultural change and peasant choice in a Thai village. Berkeley: University of California Press.

Mongkut, *King of Thailand*
1960–1961   Prachum prakāt ratchakān thī sī [Collected proclamations of the fourth reign], 4 vols. Bangkok: Khurusaphā.
1963   Phrarātchahatthalēkhā phrabātsomdet phrachǭmklao chaoyūhūa [Royal correspondence of King Mongkut], 3 vols. Bangkok: Khurusaphā.

Mosel, James N.
1957   Thai administrative behavior. *In* Toward the comparative study of public administration, edited by William J. Siffin. Bloomington: Indiana University Press, 278–331.
1963   Communications patterns and political socialization in transitional Thailand. *In* Communication and political development, edited by Lucien W. Pye. Princeton: Princeton University Press, 184–228.
1966   Fatalism in Thai bureaucratic decision-making. Anthropological quarterly 39, 3:191–199.

Mote, Frederick W.
1964   Problems of Thai prehistory. Sangkhomsāt parithat [Social science review] 2, 2:100–109.
1966   Symposium on the prehistory of the Thai people. Sangkhomsāt parithat [Social science review], special volume 3: 24–31.
1967   The rural "Haw" (Yunnanese Chinese) of northern Thailand. *In* Southeast Asian tribes, minorities and nations, edited by Peter Kunstadter. Princeton. Princeton University Press, vol. 2, 487–524.

Mouhot, Henri
1966   Diary: Travels in the central parts of Siam, Cambodia and
       Laos during the years 1858–1861. Abridged and edited by
       Christopher Pym. New York: Oxford University Press.
Murdock, George Peter
1949   Social structure. New York: Macmillan.
1960   (ed.) Social structure in Southeast Asia. New York: Wenner-
       Gren Foundation (Viking Fund publications in anthropology,
       29).
Mus, Paul
1934   Cultes indiens et indigènes au Champa. Bulletin de l'Ecole
       française d'Extrême-Orient 33, 1:367–410.
Nash, Manning (ed.)
1966   Anthropological studies in Theravada Buddhism. New
       Haven: Yale University, Southeast Asia Studies (Cultural re-
       ports, 13).
Nginn, Pierre
1961   Les fêtes profanes et religieuses au Laos. Mimeo. Vientiane:
       Centre culturel français.
Nhouy Abhay, *Thao*
1956   Les fêtes du That Luang (Pleine lune du 12ᵉ mois). *In*
       Présence du royaume lao, edited by René de Berval. Saigon:
       France-Asie, 962–967 (France-Asie, 10. année 118/119).
Notton, Camille (ed. and transl.)
1926–1932   Annales du Siam, 3 vols. Paris: Charles Lavauzelle.
Obeyesekere, Gananath
1968   Theodicy, sin and salvation in a sociology of Buddhism. *In*
       Dialectic in practical religion, edited by Edmund R. Leach.
       Cambridge: Cambridge University Press, 7–40 (Cambridge pa-
       pers in social anthropology, 5).
Pallegoix, Jean Baptiste
1854   Description du royaume thai ou Siam, 2 vols. Paris: La
       Mission de Siam.
Phillips, Herbert P.
1965   Thai peasant personality: The patterning of interpersonal
       behavior in the village of Bang Chan. Berkeley: University of
       California Press.
Phraphutthaloētla Naphālai, *King of Thailand*
1958   Bot lakhǫn nǫk rūam hok rūeang [Narration of six dance
       dramas in lakhǫn nǫk style], National Library edition. Bangkok:
       Samnakphim Sinlapā Bannākhān.

1973   Sang Thong; a dance-drama from Thailand. Written by King Rama II and the poets of his court. Transl. by Fern S. Ingersoll. Rutland, Vt.: Tuttle.

Phrasadet Surēntharāthibǫdī, *Chaophrayā*
1961   Phrarātchahatthalēkhā lae nangsūē krāp bangkhom thūn khǭng Čhaophrayā Phrasadet [Official correspondence between the King and Čhaophrayā Phrasadet]. Bangkok: Privately published.

Piker, Steven
1964   An examination of character and socialization in a Thai peasant community. Unpublished doctoral dissertation in Anthropology, University of Washington.
1968   Sources of stability and instability in rural Thai society. Journal of Asian studies 27, 4:777–790.
n.d.   A peasant community in changing Thailand. Unpublished manuscript.

Poon Diskul, *Princess*
1931   Buddhism for the young. Transl. by Phra Rajadharm Nides. Bangkok: Bangkok Times Press.

Prachāthipatai bǣp Thai
1965   [Democracy, Thai style]. Bangkok: Chokkai Thevet Press.

Prachum phongsāwadān [Collected chronicles]
1963   Rūēang tang Čhaophrayā Nakhǭn Sīthammarāt [On the appointment of the Governor of Nakhǭn Sīthammarāt]. *In* Prachum phongsāwadān [Collected chronicles], National Library edition, part 2. Bangkok: Kaonā, vol. 1, 433–495.

Prajuab Thirabutana
1971   Little things. Sydney: Collins.

Prayut Sitthipan
1962   Ton trakūn khunnāng Thai [The origins of Thai noble families]. Bangkok: Khlang Witthayā.

Proclamations of the Revolutionary Group
n.d.   Nos. 1–57. Transl. from the Thai. Bangkok: International Translations.

Raquez, A.
1902   Pages laotiennes: Le Haut-Laos, le Moyen-Laos, le Bas-Laos. Hanoi: F. H. Schneider.

Rātchakitchānubēksā [Royal Thai government gazette]
1858–59, 1874–79, 1888–. Weekly. Bangkok.

Rātchawǫrin, *pseud.*
1963   Nakrian Thai nai tāng prathēt khon rǣk [The first Thai students abroad]. Chāokrung [Bangkokian] 12, 4:35–39.

Redfield, Robert, and Milton Singer
1954   The cultural role of cities. Economic development and cultural change 3, 1:53–73.
Riggs, Fred W.
1966   Thailand: The modernization of a bureaucratic polity. Honolulu: East-West Center Press.
Robert, Romain
1941   Notes sur les Tay Dèng de Lang Chánh (Thanh-hóa, Annam). Hanoi: Imprimerie d'Extrême-Orient (Institut indochinois pour l'étude de l'homme, mémoires, 1).
Satčhāphirom Udomrātchaphakdī, Phrayā
1959   Lāo hāi lūk fang [Telling the children]. Bangkok: Mahātthāi.
Sathīan Lāiyalak et al. (eds.)
1935–1953   Prachum kotmāi prachām sok [Collected laws arranged chronologically], 69 vols. Bangkok: Various publishers.
Sathīankōsēt, pseud. [Phya Anuman Rajadhon (Phrayā Anumān Rātchathon)]
1967   Krasāethān thī mī nam tem [The stream of culture]. Sangkhomsāt parithat [Social science review] 8, 2:5–8.
Saund, Dalip
1969   Ban Khua Kaj: A case study of responses to development in a Northeast Thai village. Ann Arbor: University Microfilms Publ. 69–19, 507), 1969. (Doctoral dissertation in Anthropology, University of California, Los Angeles)
Seni Pramoj
1959   King Mongkut as a legislator. In Selected articles from the Siam Society Journal. Bangkok: Siam Society, vol. 4, 203–237.
Sharp, Lauriston
1962   Cultural continuities and discontinuities in Southeast Asia. Journal of Asian studies 22, 1:3–11.
1968   Cultural differences and Southeast Asian research. In American research on Southeast Asian development: Asian and American views. New York: Asia Society, 65–79.
Sharp, Lauriston, Hazel M. Hauck, Kamol Janlekha, and Robert B. Textor
1953   Siamese rice village: A preliminary study of Bang Chan, 1948–1949. Bangkok: Cornell Research Center.
Shils, Edward A.
1968   Intellectuals. In International encyclopedia of the social sciences, edited by David L. Sills. New York: Macmillan and Free Press, vol. 7, 399–415.

Shorto, H. L.
1963   The 32 *myos* in the medieval Mon kingdom. Bulletin of the
       School of Oriental and African Studies 26, 3:572–591.
Siam Weekly Advertiser
1869–1886   Weekly newspaper. Bangkok.
Siffin, William J.
1966   The Thai bureaucracy: Institutional change and develop-
       ment. Honolulu: East-West Center Press.
Sīwǭrawat, *Lūang*
1963   Withī pokkhrǭng bānmūeang borān [Ancient methods of
       field administration]. *In* Prachum phongsāwadān [Collected
       chronicles], National Library edition, part 15. Bangkok: Kaonā,
       vol. 5, 369–377.
Skinner, G. William
1957   Chinese society in Thailand: An analytical history. Ithaca:
       Cornell University Press.
1960   Change and persistence in Chinese culture overseas: A
       comparison of Thailand and Java. Journal of the South Seas
       Society 16:86–100.
Soper, Alexander Coburn
1959   Literary evidence for early Buddhist art in China. Ascona,
       Switzerland: Artibus Asiae (Artibus Asiae supplementa, 19).
Spinks, Charles Nelson
1965   The ceramic wares of Siam. Bangkok: Siam Society.
Suthēp Sunthǭnphesat
1968a   (ed. and transl.) Sangkhomwitthayā khǭng mūbān phāk
       tawanǭkkhīangnūea [Sociology of villages in the Northeast].
       Bangkok: Chulalongkorn University, Faculty of Political
       Science.
1968b   Khwamchūea rūeang "phīpūtā" nai mūbān phāk tawan-
       ǭkchīangnūea [Belief in "phīpūtā" in villages in the Northeast].
       In Sangkhomwitthayā khǭng mūbān phāk tawanǭkchīangnūea,
       edited by Suthēp Sunthǭnphesat. Bangkok: Chulalongkorn
       University, Faculty of Political Science, 139–165.
Tambiah, Stanley J.
1968   The ideology of merit and the social correlates of Buddhism
       in a Thai village. *In* Dialectic in practical religion, edited by
       Edmund R. Leach. Cambridge: Cambridge University Press,
       77–87 (Cambridge papers in social anthropology, 5).
1969   Animals are good to think and good to prohibit. Ethnology
       8, 4:423–459.

1970   Buddhism and the spirit cults in North-east Thailand. Cambridge: Cambridge University Press (Cambridge studies in social anthropology, 2).

Tarling, Nicholas
1960   Siam and Sir James Brooke. Journal of the Siam Society 48, 2:43–72.

Tej Bunnag
1968   The provincial administration of Siam, 1892–1915. Unpublished doctoral dissertation in History, Oxford University.

Textor, Robert B.
1960   An inventory of non-Buddhist supernatural objects in a central Thai village. Unpublished doctoral dissertation in Anthropology, Cornell University.

Thailand, Krasūang khommanākhom (Ministry of Communications)
1954   Anusǭn krasūang khommanākhom, B.E. 2497 [Commemorative volume of the Ministry of Communications, 1954]. Bangkok: Krasūang khommanākhom.

Thailand, Krom sinlapākǭn (Dept. of Fine Arts)
1942   Čhindāmanī [Thought gems], 2 vols. in 1. Bangkok: Sinlapā Bannākhān.
1961   (ed.) Phrarātchaphongsāwadān krung Sayām [Annals of Siam], British Museum recension. Bangkok: Kaonā.

Thailand, Samnakngān sathiti hǣng chāt (Central Statistical Office)
1962   Thailand population census, 1960: Whole kingdom. Bangkok: National Economic Development Board, Central Statistical Office.
1965   Statistical year book of Thailand, no. 26. Bangkok: Office of the Prime Minister, National Statistical Office.

Thiphākǭrawong, Čhaophrayā (ed.)
1961   Phrarātchaphongsāwadān krung Rattanakōsin ratchakān thī sī [Annals of Bangkok, the fourth reign], 2 vols. Bangkok: Khurusaphā.

Thompson, Virginia
1941   Thailand: The new Siam. New York: Macmillan.

Time
1965   Thailand: Behind every successful woman. 17 December: 91–92.

Transportation Consultants, Inc.
1959   A comprehensive evaluation of Thailand's transportation system requirements. Washington, D.C.

Turton, Andrew
1972   Matrilineal descent groups and spirit cults of the Thai-

Yuan in northern Thailand. Journal of the Siam Society 60, 2:217–256.

Udom Sombat, *Lūang*
1962   Čhotmāi Lūang Udom Sombat [Letters written by Lūang Udom Sombat (to Phra Sīphiphat)]. Bangkok: Privately published.

Usher, Don
1967   The Thai rice trade. *In* Thailand: Social and economic studies in development, edited by T. H. Silcock. Canberra: Australian National University Press, 206–230.

Van Roy, Edward
1967   An interpretation of northern Thai peasant economy. Journal of Asian studies 26, 3:421–432.

Velder, Christian
1963   Chao luang muak kham (The royal master with the golden crown): Report on the forest-spirit of Ban Saliem. Journal of the Siam Society 51, 1:85–92.

Vella, Walter F.
1957   Siam under Rama III, 1824–1851. Locust Valley, N.Y.: J. J. Augustin (Association for Asian Studies monographs, 4).

Wales, H. G. Quaritch
1934   Ancient Siamese government and administration: London: Quaritch.

Walker, George Benjamin
1968   The Hindu world: An encyclopedic survey of Hinduism. London: Allen and Unwin.

Weber, Max
1958   The religion of India: The sociology of Hinduism and Buddhism. Transl. and edited by Hans Gerth and Don Martindale. Glencoe, Ill.: Free Press.

Wenk, Klaus
1968   The restoration of Thailand under Rama I, 1782–1809. Transl. from the German by Greeley Stahl. Tucson: University of Arizona Press (Association for Asian Studies monographs, 24).

Wichīan Khīrī, *Phrayā*
1962   Phongsāwadān Mūeang Songkhlā lae Phatthalung [Annals of Songkhlā and Phatthalung]. Bangkok: Charōenphon.

Wilson, David A.
1959   Thailand and Marxism. *In* Marxism in Southeast Asia: A study of four countries, edited by Frank Trager. Stanford: Stanford University Press, 58–101.
1962   Politics in Thailand. Ithaca: Cornell University Press.

Wolf, Eric R.
1966a   Kinship, friendship and patron-client relations in complex
societies. *In* The social anthropology of complex societies,
edited by Michael Banton. London: Tavistock, 1–22 (A.S.A.
monographs, 4).
1966b   Peasants. Englewood Cliffs, N.J.: Prentice-Hall.
Wolters, Oliver W.
1960   Chên-li-fu: A state on the Gulf of Siam at the beginning of
the 13th century. Journal of the Siam Society 48, 2:1–35.
1966   A western teacher and the history of early Ayudhya.
Sangkhomsāt parithat [Social science review], special volume
3:88–97.
Wood, W. A. R.
1926   A history of Siam from the earliest times to the year A.D. 1781,
with a supplement dealing with more recent events. London:
Fisher Unwin.
Wyatt, David K.
1965a   The Buddhist monkhood as an avenue of social mobility
in traditional Thai society. Sinlapākǫn [Fine Arts] 10, 1:50–53.
1965b   Samuel McFarland and early educational modernization
in Thailand, 1877–1895. *In* Felicitation volumes of Southeast-
Asian studies presented to his Highness Prince Dhaninivat.
Bangkok: Siam Society, vol. 1, 1–16.
1966a   The beginnings of modern education in Thailand, 1868–
1910. Unpublished doctoral dissertation in History, Cornell
University.
1966b   (ed.) The Nan chronicle. Transl. by Prasǒēt Chūrat.
Ithaca: Cornell University, Southeast Asia Program (Data
papers, 59).
1968   Family politics in nineteenth century Thailand. Journal of
Southeast Asian history 9, 2:208–228.
1969   The politics of reform in Thailand: Education in the reign
of King Chulalongkorn. New Haven: Yale University Press.
1970   Almost forgotten: Ban Phraya Nana School. *In* In memo-
riam: Phya Anuman Rajadhon, edited by Tej Bunnag and
Michael Smithies. Bangkok: Siam Society, 1–8.
Yatsushiro, Toshio
1966   Village organization and leadership in Northeast Thailand:
A study of the villagers' approach to their problems and needs.
Bangkok: U.S. Operations Mission to Thailand, Research
division.
1967   (et al.) Village attitudes and conditions in relation to rural

security in Northeast Thailand. Bangkok: U.S. Operations Mission to Thailand.

Young, Ernest
1898   The kingdom of the yellow robe; being sketches of the domestic and religious rites and ceremonies of the Siamese. Westminister: A. Constable.

Zimmerman, Carle C.
1931   Siam rural economic survey, 1930–1931. Bangkok: Bangkok Times Press.

Contributors

Akin Rabibhadana is Lecturer, Faculty of Liberal Arts, and Assistant Project Director, Mae Klong Integrated Rural Development Project, Thammasāt University, Bangkok.

Georges Condominas is Directeur d'études at the Ecole Pratique des Hautes Etudes, VIᵉ Section, and Chairman of the Centre de Documentation et de Recherches sur l'Asie du Sud-Est et le Monde Insulindien, Paris.

A. B. Griswold is President of the Breezewood Foundation, Monkton, Maryland, and Visiting Professor of Southeast Asian Art, Cornell University.

Lucien M. Hanks, formerly a member of the Social Science Faculty at Bennington College, is Senior Research Associate of the Southeast Asia Program, Cornell University.

Jasper Ingersoll is Professor of Anthropology, Department of Anthropology, Catholic University of America.

Charles F. Keyes is Associate Professor of Anthropology and Asian Studies, Department of Anthropology, University of Washington.

A. Thomas Kirsch is Associate Professor of Anthropology, Department of Anthropology, Cornell University.

Michael Moerman is Professor of Anthropology, Department of Anthropology, University of California at Los Angeles.

Herbert P. Phillips is Professor of Anthropology, Department of Anthropology, University of California at Berkeley.

Steven Piker is Associate Professor of Anthropology, Department of Sociology and Anthropology, Swarthmore College.

Prasert ṇa Nagara is Under-Secretary of State for State Universities, Office of State Universities, Bangkok.

G. William Skinner is Professor of Anthropology, Department of Anthropology, Stanford University.

David K. Wyatt is Professor of Southeast Asian History, Department of History, Cornell University.

Index

adoption: and kin groups, 282, 283–284, 289

Akin Rabhibhadana, 19, 93f., 127

Ananda, *King*, 346

anattā, 244–249 passim

Anuman Rajadhon, *Phya*, 126, 219, 254n5

Australian aborigines, 10, 12

Ayudhyā, *see* Ayutthayā

Ayutthayā: compared with Sukhōthai, 18, 19, 29–92; education in, 126–127; founding of, 29, 51, 53; justice in, 72–73, 76–80, 80–81; Khmer influence on, 19, 29, 67–68, 69; social order of, 18, 19, 30, 67–69, 70–73, 76–77, 83, 99, 104, 115n20

Bāng Chan (village), 15, 151, 198, 210, 215, 216, 221, 222

Bangkok period, early: Chinese in, 116, 117–118; class in, 104–107, 113, 115; clientship and class in, 19, 93–124; formal clientship in, 108–115, 118, 120–121; informal clientship in, 114–123; justice in, 111–112, 115, 116, 118–119; king's role in, 96, 98, 103, 107, 110, 112–113, 114, 122–123; manpower in, 94–100, 101, 103, 104, 105, 107, 118, 119, 121; rank in, 101–107, 122; slaves in, 106

Berbers, 11

Bowring, Sir John, 95, 106n14, 301

Bowring treaty, 129, 172–173, 300, 301–302, 308n13

Brahmanism: at Angkor, 34; at Ayutthayā, 67, 69, 73; and Buddhism, 44, 181–182, 223; at Dvāravatī, 34; at Sukhōthai, 44–45, 48–49, 56–57, 59

Buddhism: at Angkor, 34; at Ayutthayā, 29, 67, 69; and Brahmanism compared, 44, 181–182, 223; and education, 126,

382

134, 149; and individualism, 21, 182, 186, 219–251; and intellectuals, 346, 351–352; in Laos, 22, 252–254, 257–258, 259, 263, 265, 270–273; and Mons, 34; and occupational specialization, 20, 177, 186–191, 198; reform in, 128, 146, 196; and Sayām, 32; and spirits, 22, 181, 227, 241, 252–254, 257–258, 259, 263, 265, 270–273; at Sukhōthai, 29, 41–42, 44, 47, 48–49, 50, 56, 57, 58, 59–61, 62, 63, 64, 65, 66–67, and world view; 179–186, 187, 189

Bun Bangfai, *see* Rocket Festival

Bun Phavēt, 253, 263; *see also* Vessantara

Bunnāk: family, 119, 130–131, 142, Chūang Bunnāk, 128, 132, 137, Dit Bunnāk, 128

bureaucracy: at Angkor, 35; at Ayutthayā, 18, 69, 77, 83; and Buddhist values, 176, 178–179, 186, 188–191; diffuseness of, 99, 208, 211; in Early Bangkok period, 18, 95–101; and education, 19, 135–136, 137–139, 141, 144–145; at Sukhōthai, 45

Burney treaty, 302n9

Čhakkrī dynasty, 19, 203, 207, 300, 301; *see also* Ananda, Chulalongkorn, Mongkut, Prachāthipok, Rāma I, Rāma II, Rāma III, *and* Wachirawut

Chandler, J. H., *Dr.*, 131

Chinese: and assimilation, 20, 114, 116, 145, 174, 191–195, 302–303; and clientship, 116–117; and economic roles, 20, 50, 116, 117, 118, 131, 147, 151–152, 153, 154, 165–166, 170, 173–174, 178, 191–195, 302; and education, 135, 139–140, 141, 145, 147

Chou Ta-kuan, 35

Change and Persistence
in Thai Society

Designed by R. E. Rosenbaum.
Composed by Syntax International Pte. Ltd.,
in 11 point Monophoto Baskerville, 2 points leaded,
with display lines in Monophoto Baskerville.
Printed offset by LithoCrafters, Inc.,
on Warren's No. 66 Text, 50 pound basis.